For Dicco
with love

1985

Menotti by the curtain of the old Metropolitan Opera House, 1964.

THE STAGES OF MENOTTI

JOHN ARDOIN

Photographs edited by Gerald Fitzgerald
Designed by Gregory Downer

DOUBLEDAY & COMPANY, INC., GARDEN CITY, NEW YORK 1985

For Ivan Davis—
together, we discovered the
music of Menotti—

and

with gratitude to
Robert L. B. Tobin

THE STAGES OF MENOTTI

ISBN: 0-385-14938-7

Library of Congress Catalog Number 82-45316

Copyright © 1985 by John Ardoin

PRINTED IN THE UNITED STATES OF AMERICA

ALL RIGHTS RESERVED

FIRST EDITION

Library of Congress Cataloging in Publication Data

Ardoin, John.
  The Stages of Menotti.

  Bibliography: p.
  Discography: p.
  1. Menotti, Gian Carlo, 1911–   Works.
I. Title.
ML410.M52A85   1985   782.1′092′4

Contents

Acknowledgments

It would have been impossible to complete this book without the close cooperation of Menotti's publishers—G. Schirmer, G. Ricordi and Belwin-Mills. Both Mario di Bonaventura and Howard Scott at Schirmer's and Robert Holton at Ricordi and Belwin-Mills went beyond generosity in providing scores, answering questions and lending their support. This was but one of many manifestations of the respect Menotti engenders.

Through the four years it took to listen to, to study and react to this immense amount of music, my editor, Louise Gault, and my agent, Helen Merrill, were equally encouraging and understanding. A great debt is owed to Mark Tiedtke, who provided the Discography, and who proofread the manuscript in its various stages. I also deeply value the time devoted to this project by Joel Honig. His suggestions were many and pertinent, and he supplied the Chronology of Menotti's music—an impressive labor of research. Two other good friends who helped with proofing are: Walter Schmucker and Robert Hay.

A very special obligation is acknowledged to Robert L. B. Tobin, not only for his tangible financial support to make this a beautiful book, but also for his welcome ideas on visual content and layout. His contributions, like the important ones of picture editor Gerald Fitzgerald, were the result of years of association with Menotti and an abiding affection for both the man and the composer.

Finally, there is Menotti himself. I pursued him from San Diego to Charleston, from New York to Philadelphia, from Spoleto to Scotland with endless questions and reams of manuscript. He was kind, ever patient and eager to contribute as much of himself as I required for this book. But even his good nature was occasionally taxed, and at one point in our work he described me as his "angelic tormentor." I appreciated his including that endearing modifier, and I hope he will now feel the torment was worthwhile.

John Ardoin
Dallas, 1984

Scharf—
1937

Chapter One

A PERSPECTIVE

*"Music history will place me somewhere,
but that is no concern of mine."*
GIAN CARLO MENOTTI

Somewhere in the world, virtually every day of the year, music by Gian Carlo Menotti is performed. It could be on the stage of the Hamburg or Vienna Opera, in a hall in Johannesburg, in a high school auditorium in Texas or on a television screen. In this century, Puccini is the only operatic composer to rival him in number of performances.

Menotti has enough firsts to his credit to start a mini-*Guinness Book of World Records* all his own. His first work for the lyric theater, *Amelia al ballo,* made so successful a debut it was taken into the repertory of the Metropolitan Opera a year after its premiere. *The Old Maid and the Thief,* which followed *Amelia,* was the first opera written for performance on radio, while *The Medium* was the first contemporary opera to have a long run on Broadway, to be recorded and filmed.

Amahl and the Night Visitors was the first opera created expressly for television, and Menotti is the only individual to have won both the New York Drama Critics and Music Critics Circle Awards, in addition to two Pulitzer Prizes. Finally, his comedy *The Last Savage* was the first work commissioned by the Paris Opéra from a non-Frenchman since Verdi's *Don Carlos.*

By the time of his seventieth birthday in July 1981, there would seem to be no question of his importance or of his standing. Yet, apart from the early critical success of *The Medium* and *The Consul,* Menotti's music has been as often damned as praised. He has been taken to task as "facile," "careless" and "superficial," and his immense popularity has long been viewed suspiciously by the establishment, as if succeeding too well and

too easily was not playing the game according to the rules. More than any other composer, Menotti must have come to appreciate a *bon mot* of Voltaire's: "My works are like chestnuts; the more they are roasted, the better they taste."

If it is true, as many have maintained, that Menotti has broken no new ground—as if this were a criterion for validity—he seems to have been equally mistrusted because of his conscientious desire to make contact with his audience. It is as if his fellow composers and the press have resented that his music has created a public and held it because, as stage director Henry Butler has observed, "he intended that it should."

It has been written of choreographer Martha Graham, with whom Menotti has collaborated, that her dance works are "a fever chart of the heart." The same observation on his own terms holds true for Menotti and is as sound an explanation as any for the special appeal of his music and its unmistakable emotional accessibility. Individual aspects of his work—his texts (for he has always served as his own librettist), his melodic style, his harmonic conservatism, his attempt to deal in his operas with such large issues as race and religion—may be decried or condemned. But the fact remains that he is a man born to the theater who rarely fails to drive home his dramatic premises however faulty his methods.

"It is not necessary," opera historian Donald Grout has written, "to make extravagant claims for Menotti's originality in order to recognize that he is one of the very few serious opera composers on the contemporary American scene who thoroughly understand the requirements of the

Portrait by Victor Scharf, commissioned in 1937 by Mary Louise Curtis Bok Zimbalist, the composer's mentor.

theater and are making a consistent, sincere attempt to reach the large opera-loving public; his success is a testimonial to the continuing validity of a long and respected operatic tradition."

In the case of Menotti, this tradition is reflected in the overriding prominence he gives the human voice. For it, he has shaped melodies that not only sing themselves with utter naturalness and explore the continuing challenge of *parlar cantando* that has faced composers from Claudio Monteverdi forward, but that encapsulate an emotion and vividly create character through music. Anything serves him—melodrama, polyphony, dissonance, popular strains—to conjure a mood or breathe life into a figure.

Noël Coward once remarked, "The trouble with opera is not that opera isn't what it used to be, but that it is." To Menotti, it isn't even that. "There is a certain indolence," he has noted, "toward the use of the voice today, a tendency to treat the voice instrumentally, as if composers feared that its texture is too expressive, too *human*. Also, in destroying tonality, we have destroyed one of the most useful dramatic elements; tonality may not be necessary, but its dramatic role has not as yet been replaced with an equivalent device. For these reasons, I prefer to write in a simple, recognizable language. Like today's writers and poets, I prefer to continue using the spoken language. I do not feel the need for Esperanto, nor do I find obscurity or complexity a virtue. I have run the risk of sounding

unfashionable [in the hope my music] will appeal to open minds and untutored hearts."

Even at less than his best, Menotti remains a master of musical atmosphere, and a composer who has doggedly pursued his own destiny with scant regard for fads. He appears to have been born with the realization that originality is not a matter of being different but of being oneself as honestly and candidly as is humanly possible.

To Menotti, "what people consider originality is nothing but a tiresome mannerism that enslaves the artist to the point of sterility. Potentially, we are all original if we are sincere, as no two people are born with the same face. But unfortunately, some faces are more interesting than others. By wearing a false nose or painting our hair green, we may be able to startle for a brief time, but not fool anyone as to our real identity. I believe that originality can only be achieved through a relentless process of self-discovery. If, after baring yourself, you discover that what you have to say is banal and unimportant, at least you have done all that an artist can possibly do."

Every page of Menotti's music, whatever its influences or antecedents, testifies to the profile of its maker and is indelibly marked by his artistic fingerprints. No doubt some have been put off by what to them appear as contradictions in his style, but in effect these amount to a refusal to let the success of any one work bind him to a predictable formula.

"He is," the late Robert Sabin has written, "a diverse musical personality—a skillful and witty comedian who nonetheless writes grim and horrible tragedies; an heir to the past who does not hesitate to satirize his beloved masters; a realistic social commentator who bursts out into the most fantastic impossibilities; a musical traditionalist who commits hair-raising heresies without the flicker of an eyelash."

To this catalog of contrasts, critic Winthrop Sargeant has pointed out in *The New Yorker* that Menotti has stood apart from all the systems and fashions of modern music. "He has also stood apart from the academicians, and from the conventions of the popular musical show. He has stood apart from the ponderous traditions of opera as performed at the Metropolitan Opera

Menotti with his brother Tullio at play, costumed as Pulcinella.

House and at other institutions dedicated to the masterpieces of the past. Many of his operas have been produced on Broadway, but he stands apart from Broadway, regarding it as a sink of mediocrity and commercialism. He has worked in Hollywood and for radio and television, but he stands apart from them, too. . . ."

While these contradictions fuel the fascination Menotti's music exerts, they are not enough to explain how he has succeeded so conspicuously in the face of repeated hostility. Part of the answer lies in the way he has found to harness the power of words and their imagery to the force of sound and its ability to suggest time, place and human feelings. An audience may not be precisely aware that this is what is happening, or even how it is happening, but it senses that something compels its attention. When this union works and produces something theatrically sound, Menotti feels strongly that credit for the results has to go equally to his music.

"Let anyone read one of my texts divorced from its musical setting to discover the truth of what I say. My operas are either good or bad; but if their librettos seem alive or powerful in performance, then the music must share this distinction. Nothing in the theater can be as exciting as the amazing quickness with which music can express a situation or describe a mood. Whereas in the prose theater it often requires many words to establish a single effect, in an opera one note will illuminate the audience.

"It is this very power of music to express feelings so much more quickly than words that makes *libretti*, when read out of musical context, appear rather brutal and unconvincing. In all civilizations, people sang their dramas before they spoke them. I am convinced that the prose theater is an offspring of these early musico-dramatic forms and not vice versa. Opera is the very basis of theater."

It has always struck me as prodigious that Menotti's chief means of expression apart from music has been the English language. Although

The house at Cadegliano, in the north of Italy, where Menotti lived during his youth.

he speaks it with an accent the years have been unable to shake, he writes it without one, and with extraordinary poise, insight and frequently poetic images of an impressive order. To him, English remains an exotic sound. What to another born to the language would be ordinary—the phrase "a pane of glass" or the word "papers"—has been able to trigger in Menotti powerful musical responses.

Yet in the partnership between Menotti the poet and Menotti the composer, it is the latter who has always kept the upper hand. It is not a whim that he has resisted his publishers' efforts to publish his librettos separately from his music, a struggle he has not always won. However much Menotti has responded to the lure of words and been satisfied by his command of them, he will ruthlessly cut his texts to save an operatic scene from prolixity, or excise poetry when it threatens to become self-sufficient or when it refuses to yield to music. Wagner's short suit, he feels, is that he would not sacrifice his words. To Menotti, a composer who is also a librettist must never hesitate to be a surgeon and operate on the text if the life of his music depends upon it.

"Just as a drop of water is created by an exact proportion of hydrogen and oxygen," he has observed, "so in creating a lyrical phrase you must have an equally exact proportion between words and music. As water is not merely hydrogen and oxygen, so must the composer of opera strive to create something which is neither a play with added music nor a symphony with words, but a new indissoluble organism."

Despite the often potent fusion he has forged between words and notes, it is Menotti's musical manner that has been the greatest thorn in the side of the music community, which persists in concerning itself more with what Menotti is not than with what he is, as though an apple tree could reasonably be expected suddenly to burst forth with oranges. Menotti is an instinctive musician rather than an intellectual one, and can be appreciated and understood only on his own terms. These terms have been defined by one writer as "the ability (the compulsion, really) to give vent to what he feels with scant premeditation and no apologies." This is an echo of the composer's own dictum: "As long as you do things out of passion, you should be forgiven."

But Menotti is rarely forgiven, perhaps because of his lack of remorse for his "sins" and his charming unwillingness to change. Not only has his style not altered through the years, Menotti has declared he does not want it to change. "I think a man must be his own measure," he has repeatedly asserted, "and my personality is that. By getting older, if anything, I'm trying to make what I have to say as clear and as perfect as I know how to. I'm not about to speak anyone else's language. If they didn't like [what I had to say] before, they won't like it now."

Yet the criticism that most often bubbles to the surface when Menotti's compositions are discussed is that they are derivative. He has been dismissed as "The Puccini of the Poor" ("better that than 'The Boulez of the Rich,'" he has countered), when in actuality he owes a good deal less to his noted countryman than most perceive. Between Menotti and Puccini there are only occasional parallels. Their greatest bond is melody. Puccini would doubtless have understood Menotti's reasoning that "when prose cannot say a thing, you turn to poetry. . . . When poetry can't say it, you must sing it out. The aim is to reach deep into the human heart. Melody does that. I am convinced that every great melody is buried deep in the memory of all men. When a composer brings it forth, we all respond to it as though we had always known it."

The ordering of melody by Puccini and Menotti is often pointedly different, with Puccini leaning more on the note, Menotti concerned more with the word. What they have in common is the ability to set recitatives so skillfully they are virtually unnoticed within a dramatic fabric, and to provide lengthy solo passages that are not arias in the accepted sense but narratives that continue rather than stop the action.

Still, it would be blind not to acknowledge the presence of influences and derivations within Menotti's music, as is the case with any lively person who has made a mark in the arts. "I would say that one composer who had a great deal of influence on me," Menotti has confided, "was Schubert. I adore his simplicity, and I love the way he can communicate, can create something inevitable out of the most simple means. ... He can write a song where one single dissonance is more dramatic than all the banging and screaming of a big symphonic work."

Menotti has also professed debts to Monteverdi, Mussorgsky, Debussy and, closer in time, Stravinsky. This is no mere lip service, as the close examination of Menotti's music bears out. There is ample proof, for example, of Menotti's long-held conviction that "Stravinsky is an indispensable item in a composer's workshop. He is like electricity: whether you approve of it or not,

you can no longer do without it."

While the Triplo Concerto a tre and *The Unicorn, the Gorgon and the Manticore* demonstrate how effectively Menotti plugged into the Stravinskian power source, this in no way devalues these works any more than *Pulcinella* is less of an achievement because of what it owes to Pergolesi. "It is the duty of every artist to steal what is good," Sarah Caldwell has remarked; Stravinsky knew this as well as does Menotti.

What is telling about both men is how they took what was of use to them and discarded the rest, remaining entirely themselves in the process. Menotti, however, unlike Stravinsky, was less able to reject the pull of the world into which he was born on July 7, 1911, in the town of Cadegliano on the shore of Lake Lugano. He was the sixth of eight surviving children, but the only one who displayed special gifts. There were piano lessons at four, and by the age of six he had produced his first songs ("erotic verses of D'Annunzio set to angelic little tunes," he recalls).

The influence of those years persists not

merely because Menotti was a musician growing up in Italy, with all this implies, and one trapped in the shadow of the nineteenth century, but because he was a part of a venerable culture and society uprooted by a world war. The gentility in which Menotti was cradled was forever rent but still very much a part of his sensitivities.

Beyond the sociopolitical upheavals about him, the music world he entered as a student at the Milan Conservatory was also in a state of flux. The year Menotti was born, for example, Mahler—the major revolutionary between Wagner and Schönberg—completed *Das Lied von der Erde*

and died in Vienna, and Ravel wrote *Daphnis et Chloë* for Serge Diaghilev; the next year brought Stravinsky's *Petrushka* and the premiere of Schönberg's *Pierrot Lunaire*.

Prior to these musical fissions, Marcel Duchamp had exhibited his *Nude Descending a Staircase*, cellophane and stainless steel were invented and four hundred movie houses flourished in London. Old values were being forced to coexist with new advances in the arts, science and technology. The old and the new were the joint heritage to which Menotti was heir, and the ambivalence arising from these forces would have its effect in his writing and his thinking. Part of his dilemma, conscious or not, would be attempting to reconcile these poles in his work.

It is a dilemma acute to a European. Across the Atlantic in America (where the sixteen-year-old Menotti was sent for more serious study and where he would build a new life) there was a lack of older values and thus a willingness to embrace what was new and daring. Because of Menotti's background and his sensibilities, the

Rosario Scalero, Menotti's composition teacher (left), Mrs. Zimbalist (middle), and the Curtis Institute of Music, where Menotti studied and where he has taught (right).

idea of the new *per se* was anathema.

For example, to him the label "modern music" is an "unnecessary chronological separation which implies that there is something fashionable about art, making the work of the past ridiculous and old-fashioned. On the same grounds, I have rejected the term 'music of the future' with its implication that art is a kind of industry which produces bigger and better works with the progress of civilization. It is impossible for me to imagine any artist consciously writing for something so inexplicit as 'the future.'

"We have no guarantee that we understand Sophocles better than his contemporaries did, nor that critics of the future will not be guilty of incorrectly evaluating works of art today. Any terminology which confines a work of art to a historical period is suspect because it proposes a system of snobbery which may eliminate artists of real merit who did not chance to harmonize with the fads of their day."

The conflicts that divided Europe were part of the baggage the young musician brought with him to the United States. But also in his backpack were musical gifts as natural as they were fluent. These quickly set him apart from his contemporaries (Menotti was only twenty-six when *Amelia* reached the stage of the Metropolitan). They also impeded him, for the facility with which he produced music (and Menotti rarely makes music out of his own compositional past) led at times to works that were not always as consistent or self-critical as they might have been. "His greatest enemy is time; his greatest sin is haste," Henry Butler has commented. Menotti has taken this a step further: "Hell begins on the day when God grants us a clear vision of all that we might have achieved, of all the gifts which we have wasted, of all that we might have done which we did not do.

"The poet shall forever scream the poems which he never wrote; the painter will be forever obsessed by visions of the pictures which he did not paint; the musician will strive in vain to remember the sounds which he failed to set on paper. There are few artists whom I can imagine resting in heavenly peace: Leonardo, Michelangelo, Goethe . . . but for the weak, the lazy,

the damned—their torture shall be the more horrible in proportion to the greatness of the genius they wasted. For me the conception of hell lies in two words: Too late."

For all of Menotti's activity, influence and fame, and despite time spent as a teacher at the Curtis Institute of Music, he has established no school or created any disciples. He did change opera in our time by being so successful at this improbable craft, and by writing *The Medium*, which spawned hundreds of imitative works.

He also created what can legitimately be called the "Menotti singer." This breed, however transitory or rare, consists of an artist, preferably unknown, who is equal parts singer, actor and presence, and who commands sung English to a remarkably communicative degree. The voice need not be beautiful in the normal operatic sense (and usually is not), but it must be individual, affecting and intensely expressive.

Menotti is not a performing composer, but has built an enviable second career as a stage director, and it has long been his dream, as yet unrealized, to found his own company. "I've always wanted to create a style of production that would prove to the musical world that opera could be given in an entirely new and different way," he has said. "I would have loved to teach students how to stage an opera. I would have loved to work with exciting new singers. I would have loved to prepare one opera at a time and prepare it perfectly; this is impossible to do within the current system of repertory opera companies. But I'm apparently destined never to do any of these things."

"For the dreamer I once was," Menotti confessed in the New York *Times*, "disillusionment is almost unavoidable. For the fighter I still am, the bitter taste of defeat, especially when defeat is considered unjust or treacherous, is apt to poison one's heart and sour one's smile.

"Fortunately, at the age when the gentle shadow of death becomes your constant companion, and when every dawn is welcomed as a gift, the merciful hand of indifference begins to erase both old and new scars. My friends may be surprised to hear me speak of disillusionment and bitterness. To them, I am a lucky, successful composer who has every reason to feel happy. But no artist worthy of the name can escape the compulsive search for Platonic perfection, the elusiveness of which is its very essence, and therefore avoid the bitterness of frustration.

"At best, an artist can find a certain kind of serenity in resigning himself to the curse of imperfection. Even the artist who like myself has often been accused of superficiality simply because, to use Jorge Luis Borges's happy phrase, 'they scatter their gifts with indifferent glee,' should not be so easily dismissed by suspicious critics simply as 'facile.' The seemingly happy-go-lucky attitude (Rossini, Cocteau or Bernini) is often but a screen for a deeper search. It is as if these artists scatter too heavy a load in order to run faster with their most precious possessions.

"But run where? Perhaps one should not have run so fast or been so negligent in scattering those gifts others then picked up, vulgarized or misused. Whether or not an aesthetic 'truth' exists, no serious artist can avoid, at least in his youth, the secret hope of being its discoverer. . . . When one finally realizes how pale a glimpse of it, if any, the jealous gods allow, the artist has to become a drunkard, a madman, or a sage.

"The word 'success' applied to my career becomes ambiguous or even ironic, and I am the first one not to take it seriously. I hardly know of another artist who has been more consistently damned by the critics. As for prizes, degrees and titles, how could one possibly ever take them seriously? What is one to think when a critic who declares you 'a man without talent' receives the Pulitzer Prize, the same prize which was conferred on you twice, supposedly for talent?"

Once, in a moment of what he termed "candid immodesty," Menotti offered this appraisal of himself: "I would say my talent is a tortuous mountain stream which runs deeper than people think, too impetuous at times, too easy-flowing at others, but never swerves from its single-minded and constant search for the wider sea."

It has been said that in the arts, survival is everything. Menotti has survived brilliantly. That stream and its irresistible swift currents have carried him far, whatever shoals have been encountered along the way. Neither critical blows, artistic failures nor personal disappointments have been able to strike him down or stem his basically affirmative outlook. There are still more commissions than he has time to accept, and he remains essentially the childlike optimist, ready to gamble, willing to believe in the goodwill and talent of others and with his hands outstretched to those younger who need someone to have faith in them. Though he would protest it, with the years he has become more than a composer; he has become if not an ideal, an idea.

Friends for life: Samuel Barber and Menotti, not long after they first met at Curtis.

Chapter Two

THE EARLY STAGE

Amelia al ballo

(Amelia Goes to the Ball)
Opera buffa in one act,
libretto in Italian by the composer

Amelia	Soprano
Il marito (the husband)	Baritone
L'amante (the lover)	Tenor
L'amica (the friend)	Contralto
Il commissario di polizia (the chief of police)	Bass
Prima cameriera (first maid)	Mezzo-soprano
Seconda cameriera (second maid)	Mezzo-soprano
Passanti e inquilini (Passersby and boarders)	Chorus
Poliziotti (policemen)	Chorus

World premiere in the Academy of Music, Philadelphia, April 1, 1937. First performance in Italian,, San Remo, April 4, 1938. Dedicated to Mary Curtis Bok. Published by G. Ricordi in Italian with English translation by George Mead. Scored for three flutes, two oboes, two clarinets, two bassoons, four trumpets, three horns, three trombones, tuba, timpani, percussion, celeste, xylophone, harp, strings.

When I was a young student," Menotti has written, "it was universally fashionable among musicians to disdain opera as an inferior form of art, and I am afraid I followed the fashion. Steeped in Palestrina masses, Schubert lieder and Stravinsky ballets, I scorned any suggestion that one day I might write an opera. How, suddenly, at the age of twenty-three I found myself writing *Amelia* is a mystery that I still cannot explain. But one thing is certain: After that, all the plans for my musical future had to be drastically revised."

Despite this disclaimer, Menotti had written two small operas by the time he was fourteen. The first was entitled *The Death of Pierrot* and the second was *The Little Mermaid*, based on the Hans Christian Andersen fairy tale. Only parts of *Pierrot* exist today; it was one of the works auditioned by Umberto Giordano, the composer of *Andrea Chénier,* who encouraged the youthful Menotti.

It seems safe to assume Menotti's "disdain" for opera did not set in during the five years he was a student at the Milan Conservatory, the school that also trained Puccini. It probably dates from his first years in America, where, in 1927, he was sent on the advice of Arturo Toscanini for study at the newly opened Curtis Institute of Music in Philadelphia. Menotti's teacher there was a fellow Italian, Rosario Scalero, and his output at first were contrapuntal pieces—motets, madrigals, canons—classical devices that Menotti would

Menotti's 1984 staging of his comedy for the Dallas Opera, with Malcolm Arnold as the suspicious Husband, Elizabeth Hynes as his determined wife, Amelia, and opulent décor by Zack Brown.

turn to his own advantage in time.

Prior to *Amelia* he had fashioned the piano pieces for children entitled *Poemetti, Pastorale* and *Dance* for Piano and Strings (the only pre-*Amelia* score that persists in his official canon of works) as well as six compositions for carillon and two pieces for string quartet. He would later describe *Amelia* as "the beginning of my end!" The roots of this comic work reach back to a visit to Vienna in 1935, when he and Samuel Barber (then a fellow student at Curtis) took up residence in an apartment house that belonged to a Czechoslovakian baroness. She often invited the

two composers to dine with her while she recounted stories of her youth and the great balls given then in Vienna.

"I was so amused to see this huge, fat woman gorging herself, and talking about the beautiful girl she must have been," Menotti told his biographer, John Gruen. "In one corner of her bedroom there was the most incredible dressing table made of porcelain and full of little cupids and ribbons and flowers. It was the dominant object in the room—the most coquettish thing I'd ever seen. It was this dressing table which gave me the idea for *Amelia al ballo,* and in my libretto, that dressing table plays a prominent part."

The opera was nearly finished when Menotti returned to America early in 1937. Excerpts were performed for Mary Curtis Bok, who founded the Curtis Institute. She was delighted by what she heard and determined the work should be produced. The school was planning a benefit

performance that April of Darius Milhaud's one-act opera *Le pauvre matelot,* and conductor Fritz Reiner, then a member of the Curtis faculty, approached Mrs. Bok to finance the production. She agreed to do so if Reiner would make the evening a double bill and include Menotti's opera.

The conductor resisted, but Mrs. Bok's ultimate triumph is reflected in Menotti's dedication to her of *Amelia.* Despite Reiner's misgivings about coupling the work of an unknown student to that of an established composer, it was *Amelia* that conquered. The production was repeated in Baltimore and New York City, and within a year *Amelia* was added to the Metropolitan Opera's repertory. It was premiered there in English on March 3, 1938, under the baton of Ettore Panizza, on a double bill with Strauss's *Elektra.*

Seventeen years later, *Amelia* was heard in its original Italian at La Scala. At that time, Menotti compared the writing of a first opera to a first love. "In afteryears, a 'first love' to some remains the 'one and only'; to others, a vague incident to be dismissed with a mixture of amusement and embarrassment . . . in most cases, it is remembered with nostalgia and a certain affection as a somewhat nerve-wracking experience.

"Some of my friends, to pique me I suspect (and hope), maintain *Amelia* is still the best opera I have written. I can hardly agree with them. But in re-listening to it, I was astonished to find in the libretto a phrase which, although somewhat incongruous in an *opera buffa,* seems to sum up the very essence of every libretto I have written since: '*Solo in una valle d'ombre meta non vedo. O mio cuore, nel tuo volo guida tu il mio errare. In te io credo.*' ('Alone among the shadows I see no goal. O my heart, in your flight be the one to guide my wanderings. In you I believe.')"

The overture to *Amelia* was an irresistible calling card from a young composer even in 1937, and it marked Menotti, as did the balance of *Amelia,* as a musician steeped in tradition. To some, this was the mark of Cain, but not to the Metropolitan's public or to the New York press. He was hailed for the spontaneity of his writing and his assured use of the orchestra. There were

Fritz Reiner, conductor for the world premiere of *Amelia al ballo,* discussing the score with the fledgling composer, Philadelphia, 1937.

also comments on the influences of others. In particular, Menotti's name was linked with that of Ermanno Wolf-Ferrari, a countryman who was then sixty-one, and whom Menotti first met during the composition of *Amelia.*

"To be honest about it," Menotti has recalled, "I didn't much admire his music. . . . I think he's a sort of fake Mozart. . . . He would have been a very good composer if he had had a true melodic gift. But I did admire his orchestration, and I learned one important lesson from him. 'I'll give you a little parting secret,' he told me. 'If you write an opera, especially an *opera buffa,* remember that the orchestra and the voice must be knitted together like cogs in two wheels. The accents of either must never come at the same time, so that the words will be understood.' . . . It was a small detail, but I've always remembered it, because it is very true."

What must have rung in the minds of those who heard echoes of Wolf-Ferrari in *Amelia* was the elder composer's famous one-act work, *Il segreto di Susanna,* written twenty-eight years before. In particular its overture has striking similarities of mood and thematic ideas. Both make bright, frantic beginnings, and the second theme of each is remarkably alike in spirit, though Wolf-Ferrari's *allegro* points downward while Menotti's soars upward:

Both works are alive with contrapuntal figures, and both abound in wit and *brio.* What the audiences of the 1930s could not have known, and what we only know with hindsight, is that Menotti's path as a composer would shortly and significantly turn to "emotional realism," as he terms his writing, just as Wolf-Ferrari turned to *verismo* in the years following *Susanna.* With Menotti, however, this reaching out would be expressed in more vivid, more original and tougher terms.

The tag *verismo,* as applied to Wolf-Ferrari and Puccini, is a label Menotti has long disclaimed. To him, *verismo* only produces "a photograph of life," while his operas have consistently aimed at a deeper involvement with their subjects and have sought to do more than tell a story, however theatrically effective that story might be. Virtually all Menotti operas, from the frivolous *Amelia* to the wrenching *Juana La Loca* forty-two years later, contain a moral or a theme bigger than their plot. They also invariably pose questions for the audience.

The Medium:	Did Toby actually touch Baba? Does he know more than he pretends?
The Saint of Bleecker Street:	Is the love of Annina and Michele more than they are willing to admit to themselves?
Maria Golovin:	Is Donato's love and jealousy focused on a real person or an imaginary phantom?
Juana La Loca:	Will someone—her father, her husband, her son, God—ever really love her?

The overture to *Amelia* (E minor, *allegro vivace*) is cast in sonata form with a coda that echoes Richard Strauss. It has other Straussian trademarks, as well, particularly the reharmonizing of the same tune in a wide variety of keys. The C section is only eight bars in length, and this brief interlude is heard midway before the form turns back on itself and retraces its steps. This deflection, however, is a seminal one—a broad expanse of *andante* in which are planted seeds that will later flower in *The Medium* and *The Consul.*

Apart from this, the overture is high-spirited and in the best comic-opera mold. It alone, of all the components in all the Menotti operas, has enjoyed an independent life in the concert hall. The curtain rises on three brass fanfares, which return during the work to punctuate salient points in the story. Although the score tells us the action is set "in a large European city just after the turn of the century," Menotti has said he has always considered Amelia to be a "very Milanese lady." This is one of the reasons he prefers the opera given in Italian. "Milanese ladies," he observes, "are notoriously uncosmopolitan."

The setting is Amelia's luxurious bedroom.

There is a wide window that opens onto a balcony and from which Milan may be seen bathed in moonlight. As the curtain rises, the shapely, red-haired Amelia is having her corset strings tightened by two maids. Her friend, all dressed and eager to leave for the smartest ball of the season, looks on with impatience. In a sprightly *duettino*, the two women anticipate the evening.

This *duettino* ("*La notte è troppo breve se donna deve andare al ballo*"—"The night is too brief when a woman must go dancing") is the first of seven set pieces that form the superstructure of the opera. In addition, each of the principals has a *romanza*, and there is another *duettino* for Amelia and her husband, a *terzetto* for these two plus

Amelia's lover and a full-scale finale. These traditional forms are folded into the flow of the music without orchestral introductions; the first two arias, however, are brought to a full close with breathing space afterward for applause. This practical consideration will continue to be of concern even for the mature Menotti, a further declaration, in effect, of his operatic loyalties.

Menotti's use of form in *Amelia* is easier to trace than it will be in later works, where lines between individual pieces are blurred in the name of continuity. Yet even here concise, closed forms are often set within and connected by freely wrought scenes that advance the action. The first *duettino*, for example, dissolves into a frantic

Setting for *Amelia al ballo* designed by Donald Oenslager for the original Curtis Institute of Music production . . .

ment. Over a melodramatic strain in F minor he informs Amelia he has found a note from her lover and demands she give him an explanation. She denies any knowledge of it or of the writer who signed the note "Bubi." The Husband insists on reading the letter, in one of the loveliest of lyric arias for baritone (E-flat major, *andante*). There is no trace of anger or hurt in the passionate strophes of his *romanza;* it is as if the Husband is as enraptured by the prose as his wife was.

This handsome piece not only is the hinge of the plot, but presents the baritone as hero or at least as protagonist in Menotti's operas. The Husband in *Amelia* will be followed by Bob in *The Old Maid and the Thief*, Ben in *The Telephone*, John Sorel in *The Consul*, Donato in *Maria Golovin*, Abdul in *The Last Savage*, the Groom in *The Labyrinth*, Toimé Ukamba in *The Most Important Man*, David Murphy in *The Hero* and the three roles for a single singer in *Juana La Loca*—Ferdinand, Felipe and Carlos.

Where the Husband in *Amelia al ballo* differs from the rest of Menotti's baritone heroes, or in some cases anti-heroes, is his lack of dimension and his cardboard-cutout status as a dramatic

search for Amelia's fichu, which has been misplaced. The music builds in brilliance, nervousness and volume until the resulting tension is released in the next appearance of the opening fanfare figure. This time it announces the arrival of Amelia's husband, who stands menacingly in the doorway as the two women are about to rush from the room.

"Non si va al ballo," the Husband declares—"We are not going to the ball." When the friend and the maids exit, Amelia demands to know what is wrong: "Has the coachman been drinking? Is this the wrong night? Have you got indigestion?" As the orchestra plays a self-important sequence of chords, the Husband savors his mo-

figure. Yet, it has been said with some justification that Menotti's theater, like that of Puccini, is, in the main, one more of heroines than heroes. "His principal male characters," as the critic Winthrop Sargeant has observed, "are as a rule damaged and groping figures—childlike, lame or mentally unbalanced. It is the women who

. . . and the opera onstage at the Philadelphia Academy of Music with Margaret Daum as the heroine, 1937.

carry the burden of dignity, strength, holiness or dominance."

It is undeniable that Menotti reserves his most expressive writing for the soprano voice. Basses usually serve in character parts, while tenors provide contrast or conflict, usually through an exacting aria such as that for the Magician in *The Consul* or Michele in *The Saint of Bleecker Street*. In only one instance, and a pivotal one, is a Menotti opera not built around a soprano, a baritone or both. That exception is Baba in *The Medium*, a contralto part.

As the Husband finishes the letter with its romantic sentiments of "moonlight, caresses, kisses," Amelia bursts into tears. Like a benign Canio, he repeats his demand for the lover's name as Amelia asks, "What of the ball? Shan't we go at all?" In the *duettino* that ensues (D minor, *allegro moderato*), two pages of vocal sparring are contrasted with a long soaring line for Amelia that rises defiantly above fussy, *parlando* figures for the Husband.

"I promise to tell you the name," Amelia replies, giving in, "if you will swear you'll take me to the ball." At first the Husband is outraged but he soon agrees. The orchestra trills in expectation along with Amelia's outcry of joy. To muted strains from the Husband's *romanza*, she confesses that Bubi is the gentleman in the apartment above.

The Husband puts on his hat and cloak and starts toward the door. When Amelia attempts to bar his way, he tells her there is time for the ball after a little chat with the man upstairs. He then takes out his pistol, loads it and stalks from the room, locking the door behind him. Amelia rushes to the balcony and calls to Bubi, telling him her husband is on the way up; he must climb down and hide in her apartment.

As she awaits him, Amelia gazes out onto the moonlit city. Belfries strike the hour as she muses on her situation in the *romanza* "While I Waste These Precious Hours" (D major, *andante espressivo*). Not only does the heart of the opera beat in this aria, but it presages many sentiments that will recur in the operas following *Amelia*, particularly a character's sense of helplessness in the face of fate or grave odds.

Men may pray for lands and oceans,
But woman holds more modest notions.
Not for glory I pray, nor power,
Just for a ball, an innocent ball.
You whose fingers move the stars,
Make them linger, stay the hours,
Hold back the moon, halt time's flight,
So that I may go to the ball tonight.

Musically, Amelia's aria (and to a lesser degree that of the Lover) is an anomaly in Menotti's writing, for the melodic line dominates the dramatic content of the words. Later the opposite would be true. There are, however, melodic twists and hints of what will shortly be a matter of style, particularly the phrase *"Tu hai disposto gli astri in ciel"* ("You whose finger moves the stars"), especially given its harmonic underpinning—the in-and-out-of-focus tonality. Incidentally, the Menotti-esque quality of the English words is a measure of how sympathetically George Mead executed his task as translator.

As Amelia finishes her aria, the Lover is seen sliding down a rope onto her balcony. He embraces her ardently to some delightfully exaggerated strains in the orchestra that parody all such clandestine encounters in opera. The orchestra continues in a *Tristan*-esque voice as the Lover demands melodramatically, "Did he beat you?" Pushing him away, the ever-practical Amelia, who is still determined to make the ball, puts the situation into perspective with a few

Frances Yeend as the corseted Amelia in Menotti's debut production for the New York City Opera, 1948, designed by H. A. Condell.

perky phrases: "Do not fear for me; you have to save your own skin."

Another *duettino* follows, in which Amelia begs the Lover to flee, and he demands she go with him. "I cannot go this evening," she replies. "We can elope next Sunday or better still on Monday. Tonight I must go to the ball." At this moment, the orchestra with heavy tread warns the pair that the Husband is on his way back to the apartment. The Lover rushes to the balcony only to find his rope has come loose. There is barely time for him to hide before the Husband bursts in. "I could not find the rascal," he snorts. "So," counters Amelia brightly, "we can go to the ball." Unable to put her off any longer, the Husband agrees, and the orchestra spins out a delicious *scherzando* derived from the overture. It is a classic example of Menotti's musical humor, with its parallel phrases and mocking sixteenth notes:

Allegro moderato

As it rattles merrily away, the Husband spies the rope on the balcony, immediately comprehends what has happened, and begins to search the room. As the music climaxes in a massive orchestral trill, the Husband pulls the Lover from his hiding place, points the pistol at him and pulls the trigger as Amelia screams. The gun, however, fails to fire, and the Lover now advances threateningly on the Husband, who suggests a quiet talk. The Lover agrees, and this sudden equanimity is more than Amelia can take.

On the verge of tears, and afraid the two men will talk all night, she cries out to her husband: "Did you say you'd take me to the ball, yes or no?" He tells her to be quiet, seconded by the Lover, and the two sit down to settle their differences. In his *romanza* (E minor, *adagio*) the Lover recounts his first meeting with Amelia. This is the most passionate moment of the opera and builds from a quiet, sustained triad to a full-scale outburst. It is in two halves separated by interjections from Amelia and the Husband.

The Lover provokes a thoughtful, envious look from the Husband with his confession, "I have lived in starlight beneath the sign of love, where in stately cadence move Venus and Virgo." Even Amelia, though obviously bored and impatient, is vaguely touched and sighs disconsolately. Her anger flares again, however, when the Lover and the Husband pick up their conversation. When she tugs at the Husband's sleeve, he shouts, "Be silent! You're a bore, you're stubborn, and you're dissonant as modern music." The orchestra breaks in with three strident chords.

This is not the only time Menotti used one of his operas to comment on contemporary music. In *The Last Savage*, the guests at Kitty's cocktail party are entertained by an atonal string quartet, and the premise behind *Help, Help, the Globolinks* is the power of consonant sounds to overwhelm electronic dissonances.

A *terzetto* follows that interrupts the action as Menotti meant it should; a note in the score instructs that it be sung, like the opening *duettino* between Amelia and her friend, to the public from the front of the stage. It begins lightly, even cynically, with the three voices in imitation.

The *terzetto* provides not the moral of Amelia (that will be intoned by the chorus in the final pages), but rather the *stato d'animo* of the principal characters:

What's right, what's wrong, is a very tricky question.
Can you offer any good suggestion?
Nobody knows whence he comes or where he goes,
Fearful lest the world be not what it seems,
But only be echoes, shadows and dreams.

The banter of the opening gives way to the searching line, "Alone among the shadows I see no goal." To emphasize its importance, Menotti sets the text to that arresting sweep of *andante* from the overture taken down a third lower. Marked *molto espressivo*, it is eight bars in length like its mirror image in the overture. The opening *scherzo* returns, and the *terzetto* ends resolutely in the voices as the orchestra adds exaltantly a short pastoral flourish.

The calm, however, is short-lived. Amelia demands once again that her husband take her to the ball, and when he refuses, she becomes blind with anger and smashes a vase on his head. At first amazed, then frightened by what she has done, Amelia becomes hysterical as the Lover attempts to revive the Husband. A fugal theme is then announced three times in the orchestra as Amelia screams for help. This is shortly followed by the fugue itself, a favorite device of Menotti's for first releasing and then rebuilding tension.

"I am a great believer in polyphony," he has written. "I wish I were less lazy in my counterpoint. I was brought up by a very severe teacher who believed as I believe that harmony must be the result of counterpoint. . . . That's why I am very suspicious of the twelve-tone system because it is a system that employs counterpoint very extensively, but it does not establish an harmonic system. . . . The greatness of Bach is that out of his incredible, intricate counterpoint, you have a marvelous harmonic system. I feel that any composer must be able to use counterpoint in a dynamic way, and that his harmonic system should be controlled by contrapuntal lines."

During the fugue, the maids rush in with bandages and a basin and apply compresses to the Husband's head. A crowd, attracted by the noise from the room, gathers in the street below, and soon neighbors hurry into the room as the fugue grows in momentum.

The orchestra is cut short by the arrival of the Chief of Police and his gendarmes. To a self-important, Offenbachian melody sung by the trombones, the Chief decides the matter is quite simple: "Here's a woman, a man and a corpse." But the chorus, like any gathering of Italians in a moment of stress, breaks in with its own analysis of the situation, insisting that the "corpse" is still breathing. When the Chief of Police inquires of Amelia who the Lover is, she claims she has no idea.

Gallantly, and to chorale-like figures in the orchestra, the Chief asks Amelia to recount what has taken place. As the orchestra limns the theme to which Amelia was corseted at the opening of the opera, she tells the Chief that while dressing for the ball, a man leaped in her window, pulled out a pistol and hissed, "Your money or your life." When the Lover attempts to defend himself, the chorus cuts him short. Amelia ends her tale by telling the Chief of Police that her hus-

band rushed to her rescue and was knocked out by the thief.

Despite the Lover's protestations, he is arrested, handcuffed and led off to jail. Meanwhile, an ambulance arrives, and the Husband is taken away to a hospital. When Amelia bursts into tears, the Chief assures her that her husband will soon recover. "I know," she wails, "but who will take me to the ball?" With a gallant bow, the Chief offers to escort Amelia. In an ecstatic phrase rising to high B and set in a waltz rhythm,

Artists for *Amelia al ballo*'s La Scala premiere, 1954: Margherita Carosio as the heroine, Rolando Panerai as the Husband and Giacinto Prandelli as the Lover . . .

Amelia demurely thanks him and asks if it will be proper. "My dear lady," the policeman answers, "how could anyone suspect me? For am I not the Chief of Police?"

In a great state of excitement, Amelia helped by her maids prepares for the ball as the chorus intones the moral: "If a woman sets her heart upon a ball, that's where she'll go." The orchestra swells triumphantly in C major as Amelia, magnificently dressed, gives her arm to the Chief and goes off amid cheers.

. . . in the production designed by Piero Fornasetti (above), and, after curtain calls, Prandelli, conductor Nino Sanzogno, Carosio, stage director Menotti and Panerai (top).

The Old Maid and the Thief

A grotesque opera in fourteen scenes,
libretto in English by the composer

Miss Todd	Contralto
Laetitia	Soprano
Miss Pinkerton	Soprano
Bob	Baritone

World premiere in New York, April 22, 1939. Commissioned by the National Broadcasting Company. First staged performance Philadelphia, February 11, 1941. Dedicated to the composer's mother. Published by Ricordi in English. Scored for two flutes, oboe, clarinet, bassoon, two trumpets, two horns, two trombones, percussion, piano, strings.

The success of *Amelia* led to Menotti's first operatic commission, the following year. It came from NBC and resulted in the first opera written expressly for radio: *The Old Maid and the Thief*. The opera was written to Menotti's first libretto in English. Though his knowledge of the language was, by his own admission, poor, he undertook it because of his fascination with English. "I thought," he has written, "that because of its greater sharpness and greater variety of sounds, English offered a musician much greater rhythmic possibilities than Italian. After studying Elizabethan madrigals, I became quite convinced of this. Only the arrogance of youth, however, could convince me that I was ready to supply myself with an English libretto. I thought, perhaps, that I could not do much worse for myself than some of Verdi's and Donizetti's librettists did for them."

As with *Amelia*, he found his material for *The Old Maid*'s plot firsthand. "I was in the habit of often visiting the family of Sam Barber in Westchester, Pennsylvania, which was then a very sleepy town of quiet oak-lined streets. Coming as I did from a noisy Italian family, the Barber household, with its quiet Presbyterian background and its subdued dignity, was quite a change for me. In fact, I was incredibly charmed by what seemed to me the exotic quaintness of that little American town.

"I soon found out, however, from the quiet gossip overheard during tea and bridge parties in Mrs. Barber's and her friends' parlors, that behind those innocent eighteenth-century wooden façades all sorts of secret dramas took place—some grim, some comic and all of them, of course, 'scandalous.' And so, it was the deceptive innocence of Westchester which inspired the subject for my second opera.

"Should I write such an opera today, I'd probably be much more sympathetic and charitable towards Miss Todd and more critical of Laetitia's happy-go-lucky cynicism. After *A Streetcar Named Desire*, it is difficult to contemplate sexual desires with anything but compassion. I, myself, an old bachelor, should know! But then, I was a devoted admirer of *commedia dell'arte:* Old unmarried people had to be grotesquely funny, the young *servette* had to be

Muriel Costa-Greenspon at Miss Todd, Sigmund Cowan as Bob and Karen Hunt as Laetitia in the production designed by Pasquale Grossi and directed by Pierluigi Samaritani for Spoleto's 1975 Festival dei due Mondi (left), and Alberto Erede, conductor of the world premiere, with Menotti at NBC, 1939 (above).

sparkling and witty, and the handsome hero had to get finally what he wanted.

"In spite of the cynical turn of the plot—a man cannot help becoming what people want him to be—and its gentle touch of misogyny, the opera is more or less stock *commedia dell'arte*. As for the music, what can I say? If, as I believe, the true artist is he who is able to reveal his inner self with both precision and spontaneity, I cannot but envy the young man who wrote *The Old Maid and the Thief*. It is now with gnawing self-doubt that I try to capture my real face beneath the layers of masks that little by little life imposes on me. What seemed so easy then has become unbearably difficult. If *The Old Maid* has any merits, the main one is that it faithfully reveals the young man I was."

Despite Menotti's hope that this short work might reveal the young man he was, it seems to reveal as much the young composer he was, and how well he had learned his lessons under Scalero. In fact, *The Old Maid* proclaims his mastery even more insistently than did *Amelia*. While there is no doubt the same hand is at work, it is accomplishing entirely different feats of legerdemain. *The Old Maid* is a score of the utmost transparency and lightness. Its sounds are clean, economical and highly contrapuntal, and solo flows into duet and through recitatives with an ease that does indeed tell us a good deal about the confidence and horizons of talented youth.

Menotti has said he wished to write an American opera, but he is wise enough to know that subject alone does not create a musical character; if it did, *Turandot* would be Chinese. Still, though this fast-paced comedy has no trace of the American vernacular (apart from some chorale-like harmonies when a character turns pious), it is not Italian in the unmistakable sense *Amelia* is. Menotti is moving ahead with remarkable individuality, invention and flair, and *The Old Maid* is filled with traits in the vocal lines and in the orchestra that will soon be more identifiably Menottian than any found in *Amelia*.

It is surprising that *The Old Maid*'s overture (the most Italianate part of the score) is not better known on its own. Perhaps its way to the concert hall has been blocked by the chamber-

music dimensions of its instrumentation, for *The Old Maid* is lightly scored, à la *Ariadne auf Naxos*, even down to the prominent presence of a piano, an instrument that will continue to play a major role in Menotti's orchestrations through *Juana La Loca*. But if the trim orchestration has kept the overture from symphonic programs, it has made the opera, and *The Medium* and *The Telephone*, which followed, accessible to amateur and student performers; this has helped to guarantee *The Old Maid* a long, prosperous life.

A dry, G-major chord, followed by a downward scale, plunges one into the breathless pace of the opera, a pace (*presto con brio*) that continues virtually without letup. Although loosely designed as sonata form, the overture's two main themes are not really contrasting enough. The first is sung by the cellos and is derived from a long line heard early on in the violins:

The second comes after the return of the opening chord and its attendant scale, and shares with the first a set of eight *staccato* notes:

This motive is developed through an elaborate series of imitations that lead back again to

Laetitia (Hunt) awakens Miss Todd's gentleman guest, Bob (Cowan), with breakfast in bed . . .

the G-major chord, in effect, the overture's recapitulation. There follows a fugal coda that gets no further than a three-voice exposition before it darts off as though impatient to conclude the prelude and get on with the story.

The opera opens in Miss Todd's parlor late in the afternoon. A ringing doorbell and a nervous, *allegro* figure in the orchestra announce a visitor; Miss Pinkerton has arrived for tea and talk. Their chat alternates between the weather *(adagio)* and gossip *(allegro)*. When these topics are exhausted, they reflect on themselves: "This is a lonely town, ours is a lonely life." In the *duettino* that follows (C minor, *andante)*, each recalls former loves.

For Miss Pinkerton, it was a sailor; for Miss Todd, a "learned man." The *duettino* has the character and simplicity of folk music, and during it, Menotti presents the first of a host of homilies hung throughout the libretto like samplers on the walls of Miss Todd's house: "Life is but a broken promise. And why should God keep his promise if men forget their own?" A sharp rap at the door brings the two back to reality.

Laetitia, the maid, informs her mistress a young man would like to speak with her—privately.

At this, Miss Pinkerton announces she must leave, the two exchange *staccato* good-byes, and Laetitia ushers in Bob. He is a wandering beggar, drenched by rain ("I've never been a host, I've never been a guest, a man with an ideal has no place to rest"). Because of the bad weather outside, Miss Todd invites Bob to stay overnight. She orders him to remove his shoes, socks, coat and shirt, and hands him a relative's bathrobe. This is the first instance in which a strong sexual pull is alluded to by Menotti. But as in the movies of the period, there was no room for the explicit here, nor is it needed in an *opera buffa*. Menotti left it to the imagination of his audience to come up with the reason Laetitia and Miss Todd are so willing during the course of the opera to lie, steal and plot to keep Bob under their roof.

Because *The Old Maid* was originally conceived for radio, where the imagination bridged scenes and supplied in the mind sets and action, when seen on the stage the opera conveys the impression of a series of separate, almost cinematic scenes. The second takes place in Miss Todd's kitchen the next morning. As Miss Todd enters, Laetitia is busy at the sink. In a gentle, swaying duet *(allegro molto mosso)* they exchange impressions of their guest ("charming, clever, bright, profound"). They begin scheming how to persuade him to remain awhile ("A hungry man is easily bent") and what to tell inquisitive neighbors. Laetitia (who is very Despina-like, and a prototype for Sardula in *The Last Savage)* announces she will take care of the matter.

The scene shifts to Bob's bedroom. Laetitia enters with his breakfast, and as she attempts to wake him, the orchestra sounds intervals of a second and third, a recurrent structural feature of the work. Their exchange is largely through recitative accompanied by rapid piano figures. Bob is surprised and delighted to be served breakfast in bed and readily agrees to stay a week longer. For the sake of the neighbors, Laetitia tells him, he must pose as Miss Todd's cousin Steve from Australia. "I'll be a cousin, nothing more," he says, "I hate women to the core." "Even when they're young?" Laetitia asks coyly. As Bob starts to answer, Miss Todd's voice from downstairs interrupts, aborting the scene.

A dozen years after *The Old Maid,* Menotti took the resolute theme (first sounded by the horns) that germinates the third scene and used it for the basis of a piece for pianist Ania Dorfmann; to her, his Ricercare and Toccata is dedicated. The statement of this vigorous motto:

... and the gossipy Miss Pinkerton (Margaret Baker) warns Miss Todd (Costa-Greenspon) of a thief.

(which also begins scene twelve) is repeated literally at the beginning of the Toccata, and so tightly made is this section that there are scarcely more than two dozen bars of music that do not reiterate the theme. The opening Ricercare also makes use of the same motto but transposed to C minor and given a quite different cast. The piece as a whole is more than a footnote to the opera; it provides further proof of Menotti's concern with form, tradition and compactness even at the distance of a decade.

In scene four, Miss Todd and Miss Pinkerton meet in the street amid insistent minor seconds in the orchestra as Miss Pinkerton tells her friend to be careful, for a thief has just escaped from the county jail. Over crisp chords in the orchestra she describes the wanted man: "Tall and burly, hair black and curly, light complexion, southern inflection, and altogether handsome." It is a description of Bob. As Miss Todd attempts to rush home, Miss Pinkerton tells her that everyone knows she has a male guest. "Oh yes," she admits nervously, "my cousin Steve . . . but he'll be going away, I believe, this very morning!"

The driving intervals of a second return for scene five as Miss Todd rushes into her parlor to tell Laetitia Miss Pinkerton's news. The maid urges her mistress to call the police. "How can we explain his presence here?" Miss Todd asks desperately. They realize they have no choice but to keep Bob for a while until it is safe for him to go. Philosophically, Laetitia comments, "To be killed by a man would really be much better than to live without one." She suggests Miss Todd give Bob a bit of money each day "to keep his interest alive." It can be "borrowed" from the funds of the New Mission Society and Women's Club of which Miss Todd is treasurer. Miss Todd protests feebly, but when Bob enters the room, the rich, expansive sound of the orchestra makes it obvious that she will gladly steal for him. "Oh, what beautiful eyes," the two women sigh, as the orchestra laughs at both in three stinging bars.

Scene six consists of a recitative and aria for

Laetitia, the best-known excerpt from *The Old Maid*. It is a week later, and she is discovered in the kitchen mending Bob's trousers. "What a curse for a woman is a timid man," she begins. "He has had plenty of chances, but he makes no advances." The aria itself (D major, *adagio ma non troppo*) is reminiscent of Amelia's *romanza*. The key is the same, the vocal line follows a similiar ebb and flow, there are many of the same rhythmic shifts (a basic factor of Menotti's style) and both are concerned with the passing of time. Though Menotti's music, especially his arias, invariably leaves the impression of a regular, steady flow of sound, a look beneath the surface of the music reveals that this is achieved, in fact, by very subtle shifts in phrase and bar lengths.

"Steal me sweet thief," Laetitia muses, "for time's flight is stealing my youth and the cares of life steal fleeting time." The aria is in two halves, and the whole adds up to the most sophisticated and harmonically complex moment of *The Old Maid*. Its rapturous mood is broken in scene seven by the return of those persistent intervals of a second as Miss Pinkerton rushes up to the porch of Miss Todd's house.

She is frightened because there have been a number of unexplained robberies in the past few days: "Miss Manning has missed lots of money, Miss Paxton has not seen her purse since that morning you came for a visit, the Sunday collection at church is missing." There is a long and awkward silence, then each of the women complains of the weather, Miss Pinkerton asks pointedly about the health of Miss Todd's cousin, and Miss Todd replies dryly, "I'm afraid that he will never be very well."

Bob has become restless, and in his room he describes his urge to roam, in an aria in F major *(andante calmo ma senza trascinare)*: "When the air sings of summer, I must wander again. Sweet landlord is the sky, rich house is the plain." Though the aria has metric irregularities, its character is that of a ballad, heartfelt and warm. Bob's reverie is interrupted by Laetitia's appearance with his breakfast tray. Seeing him packing, she begs him to reconsider. He tells her he is tired of being shut in and is not interested in money. However, things might be more bearable if he had a drink.

Laetitia runs downstairs, where, in scene nine, she tells Miss Todd Bob will leave unless he has liquor. To Miss Todd, who directs the Prohibition Committee, this is too much. The music shifts from the nervous bustling figures that accompany most of the exchanges between the women in *The Old Maid*, to a sustained passage that is an embryo of the droning music in the office scenes in *The Consul*. Against weighted chords, Laetitia convinces Miss Todd that Bob is only testing the two of them, and suggests they break into the liquor store at night as it would cause a scandal if either one were seen buying liquor during the day.

The daring and danger of the idea excites Miss Todd, and in scene ten they are seen approaching the liquor store at two in the morning; the orchestra plays a heavy and mock-sinister theme. The two women try to force a window, which under pressure breaks. Crawling in through the window they comment, "How many ways of committing the same sin! Virtue's mighty but sin has variety." Against a light *pizzicato* figure, they fill a basket with gin. In the dark, however, they topple a stack of bottles, which crashes to the floor awakening the owner. To a frantic *allegro* the two run through the streets back to Miss Todd's home.

The next morning in the parlor, scene eleven, Miss Pinkerton calls out for Miss Todd over the now familiar minor seconds in the orchestra. She brings word of the robbery the night before and the fact that a special detective has been hired to catch the thief. Suddenly the drunken sound of Bob in his room, singing to the strains of a raucous waltz, interrupts. "Your cousin sounds rather merry," answers Miss Pinkerton. "He's raving with fever," replies Miss Todd, ushering Miss Pinkerton out. Desperately, Miss Todd calls Laetitia and asks the maid what is to be done. They decide to warn Bob so that he can escape.

A solo horn sounding the G-major motto again opens scene twelve. As Miss Todd and Laetitia enter Bob's room, they find him sprawled on the floor. When they beg him to save himself, he replies he has done nothing wrong: "I'm a beggar and a dreamer and a lost wind-tossed leaf." The

women confess they have been stealing for his sake. "Would you see me in prison?" Miss Todd asks indignantly. "I don't see any reason for keeping you out of it," Bob answers callously.

Furious, Miss Todd replies she will condemn Bob to the police for larceny, robbery and rape. She, not he, will be believed: "My blood is the bluest in town; I direct all the social affairs; I'm chairman of every committee for hospitals, concerts and fairs." The orchestra, having calmed down following the hysteria of Miss Todd's outburst, suddenly breaks into Bob's drunken waltz once again. Miss Todd leaves Laetitia to guard Bob while she goes for the law.

The orchestra softly outlines Laetitia's "Steal Me Sweet Thief" at the outset of scene thirteen as Laetitia suggests to Bob they steal Miss Todd's car and run away together. He reluctantly agrees, pronouncing the opera's moral: "The devil couldn't do what a woman can, make a thief of an honest man."

As in *Amelia*, Menotti is again exploring questions of faith and belief, though admittedly on a superficial level. Amelia never lost faith that she would go to her ball, and because everyone believed Bob to be a thief, he became one. To a fugato *(presto)* in C major, Bob begins to ransack the house. He and Laetitia then run to the garage and drive away in Miss Todd's car. As the orchestra peaks, Miss Todd is heard calling Laetitia's name (scene fourteen). Discovering she has been robbed, Miss Todd drops fainting into a chair as the curtain falls.

Miss Todd (Costa-Greenspon), in the 1975 Spoleto staging, burglarizing the liquor store.

The Island God

Opera in one act and three scenes,
libretto in Italian by the composer
as *Ilo e Zeus*

Telea	Soprano
Luca	Tenor
Ilo	Baritone
Greek God	Bass
Voice of a Fisherman	Tenor

World premiere at the Metropolitan Opera, New York, February 20, 1942. Unpublished. English translation by Fleming McLiesh. Scored for three flutes (piccolo), three oboes, three clarinets, three bassoons, four trumpets, three horns, three trombones, tuba, timpani, percussion, xylophone, piano, harp, strings.

After the success of *Amelia,* the Metropolitan Opera asked Menotti to write a work expressly for the company, and he responded with the only major score to date he has suppressed—*The Island God.* It was a failure, as much to its composer as to anyone else. "Although my admirers kept saying I was a new Rossini," Menotti has remembered, "I was haunted by feelings of guilt, for I had not yet written a single one of those symphonies, *concerti,* motets and masses my teacher Scalero had trained me to write. Hopelessly trapped as I was by the theater, I thought I would at least try my hand at a heavy and tragic opera. What I wrote was a big bore. . . ."

The Island God is set on a small isle in the Mediterranean, a place deserted and barren of any sign of life except for the ruins of a Greek temple. Out of dense fog wander Ilo and Telea, who have fled their own country when it was invaded by enemy hordes. In his desperation, Ilo throws himself before the temple and invokes the help of the unknown god who was once worshiped there. The forgotten god is brought back to life by the faith of Ilo, but warns that a god requires great sacrifices from man. Ilo, exalted by this living evidence of his faith, promises to do all the god asks of him. To test Ilo, the god first demands his temple be rebuilt.

The second scene (bridged by the first of two orchestral interludes) takes place several years later. The temple is now partially reconstructed. Ilo, spurred by his devotion to the god, has accomplished the task single-handedly with almost superhuman strength. Yet while he is willing to disregard hunger and hardship, Telea is not. At this point, Luca, a young fisherman, lands on the island and tempts Telea with promises of a more sensuous existence. Because she cannot share Ilo's fanaticism and mystic devotion to the god, she succumbs to Luca.

In the third scene, Ilo discovers Luca and Telea together, and in desperation they flee in spite of a storm the god conjures up in response to Ilo's prayers. Left alone, Ilo rebels against the god for having let Telea leave him. He begins to destroy the temple, and as he starts to strike the altar, the god appears, warning Ilo that such a sacrilege must be punished by death. Yet the god knows he lives only because of Ilo's faith; should Ilo die, the god dies with him. Ilo now realizes he is less afraid of the god than the god is of him. At this ironic point, when the god must beg man to let him live, Ilo smashes the altar. The god is then forced to kill Ilo, and in doing so, must die with him.

One hour in length, *The Island God* was the antithesis of all Menotti had done up to this

Setting for *The Island God* designed by Eugene Berman for the Metropolitan Opera and, to Menotti's disappointment, rejected by the company as too surrealistic.

Set and costume designs by Zack Brown for Menotti's 1984 staging of *Amelia al ballo* at the Dallas Opera.

The Husband.

Amelia.

The Lover.

Designs by Lila de Nobili for *The Medium*.

Drawing by Stefano Cusamano, 1950, inspired by *The Consul*—the scene in which, hypnotized, the petitioners waltz.

THE TELEPHONE
or L'amour à trois
By
GIAN-CARLO MENOTTI

STEINBERG

Design by Saul Steinberg for the cover of the published score of *The Telephone*.

point. Robert Sabin has noted that "the heavy orchestration with resounding brass was influenced by late Puccini, as were the large-scale solos and duets. The musical dialogue at the opening of the opera and elsewhere showed that he had lost none of his flair for this type of writing, but *The Island God* was obviously a gesture toward grand opera, although a stylized and personalized one. The trouble was *The Island God* was neither fish nor fowl, and Menotti simply could not summon a sufficient intensity and grandeur of lyric expression to make a lasting impression in so ambitious a vein."

Menotti agrees: "I made a lot of noise with it, and I must admit the music was very uninventive. It's made up of very bad Italian music. I looked it over before destroying it and found no saving graces. While I think the idea of the libretto is a good one, musically the score is uninspired. The lesson I learned from it was that I should always be myself, that I should not try to impress anyone. And so I withdrew the opera. It's never been published, and I've tried to erase every trace of it. It is the only one of my children that I've willingly murdered."

Menotti is exaggerating, for the official catalog of his music represented by G. Schirmer's contains the two orchestral interludes from *The Island God* (these orchestral pieces made their

concert bow in performances by the Boston Symphony under Serge Koussevitzky shortly after the opera's performances at the Metropolitan). Nor has Menotti been entirely successful in obliterating the balance of the score. By chance, fifteen of its 114 manuscript pages were retained by the late Felix Wolfes, then a member of the Metropolitan's music staff and a rehearsal conductor for *The Island God.* These pages contain the opera's prelude, the first interlude, the duet for Luca and Telea in scene two, Luca's offstage song, the duet for Luca and Telea from scene three and the close of the opera.

Although the vocal extracts are not distinguished, there is strength to the interlude, whose material recurs at the end of the work. It is also clear that this is music much broader in range and more harmonically dense than that of either *Amelia al ballo* or *The Old Maid and the Thief.* To escape from this notable failure Menotti turned to the concert hall, producing his Piano Concerto, a piece as sunny and lean as *The Island God* was overcast and thick. But when he regained his operatic footing, it was to be with a work entirely different from anything that he had previously done or that had been previously achieved in the operatic theater. What until now had been exceptional promise was shortly to become extraordinary reality.

The Island God onstage at the Metropolitan Opera in 1942, with Raoul Jobin as Luca and Astrid Varnay as Telea in décor designed by Richard Rychtarik.

Dialogue I

JA: Was your family a musical one?

GCM: It depends on what you mean by musical. My father whistled after lunch and on his way to hunting, and that is as far as his musicality went. Two of my sisters played the piano up until their marriage, which confirms my belief that at that time girls used the piano as a sexual placebo. One of my brothers indulged for a short time in thinking himself a gifted violinist, and another, who later became a lawyer, played the cello with great determination, and up until his death, every Saturday night summoned to his apartment three of his business partners to form a quartet. The four submitted Haydn and Mozart to a passionate but unrequited courtship.

Only my mother seemed to practice her music seriously, and although she had to adjust the *allegros* and *prestos* to the limitations of her piano technique, hardly a day went by that she did not spend a few hours at the piano. It is from her that I first heard the music of Mozart, Schubert, Chopin and above all Beethoven, whom she adored. Later on, when I was old enough to be admitted to the concert hall, I was astonished to hear how much faster the first and last movements of the Beethoven sonatas were played. To get used to these new tempos, I had to cut my umbilical cord.

JA: Where did you hear your first opera?

GCM: It was early on, in Milan—not at La Scala but at the Teatro dal Verme, which was a sort of New York City Opera as opposed to the Met. The opera was *Rigoletto*, and I was terribly disappointed in it. I thought the shows I gave at home with my puppet theater were so much more exciting. Besides I thought everyone that evening sang badly, which they probably did. Also my oldest brother, who had heard a lot of opera in Milan, had described it to me as the most beautiful thing in the world—the wonderful scenery, horses onstage, palaces, fountains, gods and so forth—but all I could see at that performance was a lot of badly painted papier-mâché and canvas drops which billowed at the slightest touch. I thought, "If this is opera, I'm not interested."

JA: Can you describe your first compositions?

GCM: By the time I was six or seven years old, I already knew I wanted to be a composer and only a composer. Although I would torment the piano for hours, I was not at all interested in becoming a virtuoso; I practiced the piano just enough to satisfy my creative impulses. I must say I find it very mysterious how in a perfectly normal family, a little boy can be illogically marked for a particular and unrelated career. I was the only one of the children morbidly obsessed with theatrical fantasies. I am ashamed to confess it, but I read only fairy tales until the age of fourteen. These I adapted for performance in my marionette theater, the only toy I really enjoyed. I also improvised songs for these plays and had, so I'm told, a very pretty soprano voice until about the age of thirteen. A few of these songs were put on paper by my piano teacher and still exist. They are not much to listen to, but obviously it was through them I later started setting my dramatic texts.

JA: When did you write your childhood operas?

GCM: I must have been about nine or ten years old; only a little boy could have been so fiercely tragic. *The Little Mermaid* is the only opera for which I did not write my own libretto; the words were written by a priest, who was a friend of our family. But the opera had to be abandoned because he never completed the

Family trio: Menotti on Lake Garda with his brother Tullio (far left) and his mother, Ines.

text, although I remember setting to music the whole first act. Unfortunately, or fortunately, nothing remains of it. At the time, I was convinced it would be finished, orchestrated and performed at La Scala. I did finish *The Death of Pierrot* and even orchestrated it, but it is yet to be heard anywhere, much less at the Scala.

JA: Will you sum up your work at school?

GCM: I was a reasonably good composition student, and before getting my freedom, I accepted being an obedient prisoner. I had much to learn, and I knew that only by submitting myself to the tyranny of my teacher, who was quite a tyrant, I would widen my wings for a later flight. All that I composed between my childish pieces and *Amelia* were little more than exercises and the expression of struggle rather than inspired emotion.

JA: Then how do you explain the amazing leap from these learning pieces to a work as sophisticated as *Amelia?*

GCM: All I know is that my teacher always told me that if I wanted to learn I had to forget about being a free agent. I had to submit to what *he* wanted and accept the limitations he would impose upon me, so as to sharpen my ingenuity and imagination, and to restrain myself from undisciplined composing "on the side," so to speak. "The more you wait," he would say, "the stronger and higher your flight will be when you gain your freedom."

JA: Did you use any of this early material later?

GCM: Actually, yes. The beginning of *The Medium* came from part of a set of variations for string quartet on a theme of Caldara, and another bit I used for the peasants' dance in *Amahl*. But that's about it.

JA: What did you gain from Scalero?

GCM: I think it was a greater contrapuntal freedom within the musical texture and a more solid sense of form. However, except perhaps for the *fugato* which marks the entrance of the chorus in *Amelia*, I did not try to display academically my newly acquired technique. And

still now what I learned serves only as fertile ground in which to find my own sense of spontaneity. My music sounds easy but it flourishes in carefully cultivated fields.

JA: Do you like *Amelia* in English?

GCM: Mead's version of *Amelia* is ingenious, witty and musical and on the whole as faithful as one may wish. Only here and there, especially for rhyming's sake, a touch of musical-comedy lingo offends me a little. My original Italian text is more quaintly stylized, based as it is on Rossini and Donizetti's librettos. But as long as we are talking about translations, there are a few things I want to say about the problems involved in general. It is a very complex business. How much should one sacrifice of the meaning of the text to preserve intact the musical phrase, and how much can one modify the musical phrase to make the text more faithful to the original, or at least more intelligible? Most translators are loath to modify the musical line without the composer's permission, and who can blame them? But by being over-faithful to the music, one can change a charming libretto into outrageous nonsense. That in the end hurts the music just as much. If one didn't know the exquisite, original libretto by W. H. Auden for Stravinsky's *The Rake's Progress,* one would believe from the Italian translation of it the poet was drunk when he wrote the text, and Stravinsky insane for setting such gibberish to music.

JA: Can you discuss your first English libretto— *The Old Maid and the Thief?*

GCM: Since my school days I have never stopped writing poetry, essays, short stories and plays (at first in Italian of course). Most of them have ended in the wastepaper basket or at the back of my desk drawer where they will probably remain. However, the need to express myself with words as well as music led me naturally to the decision of writing my own librettos. The only reason why, after *The Old Maid and the Thief,* I reverted to Italian for the libretto of *The Island God* was simply because I thought my knowledge of the English language at that time was still much too primitive. The libretto of *The Old Maid* does show it, and it contains some very curious sentences! I remember Sam Barber reading it for the first time and making fun of my English. That convinced me that my venture into the English language was premature and presumptuous.

JA: Many people have heard different influences in your music. Do you?

GCM: I find it very natural that an artist should have ancestors and close relatives, but I have never been interested to inquire into how much Wagner owed Liszt, or Stravinsky owed Rimsky-Korsakov or Goya owed Tintoretto. Those musicologists who use tune detectors to look for sources and influences bore me. The most eclectic of artists has his own personality if he is any good. The question is, does his work move us? Does it command our attention? Was it Cocteau or Radiguet who said, "An artist never reveals himself more startlingly than when he tries to copy"?

JA: Does the frequent comparison of your music to Puccini's bother you?

GCM: The accusation of eclecticism thrown at me so often by critics, especially in reference to Puccini and Mussorgsky, seems to me exaggerated and unjust. No critic seems to mind, for example, in the exquisite *Dialogue of the Carmelites* of Poulenc, the undisguised use of *Pelléas*'s harmonic and melodic phraseology, or the quotations from the *Symphony of Psalms* of Stravinsky. Nor do critics mind, in contemporary twelve-tone music, the constant rehashing of Berg and Schöenberg. To trace the source of inspiration in a simple melodic style such as mine is of course an easier, therefore more tempting, musical exercise. But even in this pursuit, most critics fail to hit the mark, and the comparison constantly drawn between myself and Puccini is a shallow and undiscerning one. This charge, thrown at me again and again, clearly shows how critics judge new music without really analyzing it at all.

The influence of Puccini on my music has been a slight one, mostly on my dramatic technique rather than my musical style. What I studied in Puccini was his use of a melodic *recitativo* that does not impair the dramatic action, so that he is able to unfold the dramatic pace of the libretto without ever sacrificing the melodic flow of the music. I think that *Bohème* is a masterpiece in this respect; a miraculous achievement, an unsurpassed model of Italian *parlar cantando*. From beginning to end, it

is melodic action. It is the ideal of every opera composer to achieve this, and each one of us does it in his own way. In this respect, I do agree that Puccini has been for me a wonderful model; but for critics who specialize in musical genealogies, let me point out that my musical style owes little to Puccini. As any serious music student can see, if anything, my melodic source springs more from Schubert, whose deceptively simple melodies still mesmerize me, and the declamatory style of Mussorgsky. So you see, I don't disclaim having ancestors as long as the genealogy is correct. But if some stupid critic insists in linking my music to Puccini, God bless him.

Earliest surviving musical manuscript in Menotti's hand, probably written in his tenth year.

Chapter Three
THE BROADWAY STAGE

The Medium

Tragedy in two acts,
libretto in English by the composer

Madame Flora (Baba)	Contralto
Monica (her daughter)	Soprano
Toby (a mute)	Mime
Mr. Gobineau	Baritone
Mrs. Gobineau	Soprano
Mrs. Nolan	Mezzo-soprano

World premiere at Brander Matthews Theatre, Columbia University, New York, May 8, 1946. First performance on Broadway, the Ethel Barrymore Theatre, May 1, 1947. Commissioned by the Alice M. Ditson Fund. Dedicated to Edith Braun. Published by G. Schirmer in English with a French translation by Léon Kochnitzky. Scored for flute, oboe, clarinet, bassoon, trumpet, horn, percussion, piano, string quintet.

Menotti landed on Broadway through a chain of happenstances, triumphed there and exited ingloriously a decade later. The story of this stage of his career began deceptively with a letter from Columbia University wishing to commission a chamber opera from its Alice M. Ditson Fund. No one thought Menotti should accept. It seemed a comedown to write a chamber opera for a university after having been commissioned by NBC and the Metropolitan. In fact, Menotti broke with his publisher at the time, the house of Ricordi, over the matter. He knew himself better than those about him; he knew he had tried to go too far too quickly with *The Island God*. Before attempting to compose on so big a scale again, he had to return to a more concentrated form of theater.

Menotti was also convinced that one reason *The Island God* had not fared better was the poor staging it had received. He vowed he would stage his next opera rather than leave the task to another. Instinctively, he knew this would be more easily done initially in a limited and controlled situation. He accepted the Columbia commission on the condition he be permitted to stage his opera, and with this proviso, a second career was launched, one that would bring to him nearly as much success and recognition as the composition of music.

The roots of *The Medium*, the work that catapulted Menotti into world fame, reach back to the period when he was at work on *Amelia*. With Samuel Barber, Menotti had taken a cottage in the Austrian hamlet of St. Wolfgang, near Salzburg. Adjacent to their quarters was the estate of a Dutch baron and his English wife, who frequently entertained the two composers.

"The baron and baroness were most charming and hospitable," Menotti remembers, "but

The séance: Madame Flora (Marie Powers) summons a spirit for her clients—Mr. and Mrs. Gobineau (Frank Rogier and Beverly Dame) and Mrs. Nolan (Virginia Beeler)—in Menotti's Broadway staging, 1947

there was also something puzzling about them. After each dinner, the baroness would rise from the table and say, 'Excuse me, but I must go to chapel.' She would leave the room and not return until much later. Finally, I could not resist asking the baron about his wife's mysterious visits to an invisible chapel. He said, 'It isn't really a chapel. It's a room in which my wife holds séances. You see, we had a daughter named Doodly; that was her nickname. She died when she was fourteen of an infected tooth. My wife never got over her death. Of course, I don't believe in such things, but my wife met a medium in London who introduced her to the powers of séances. My wife retires into that room every evening because she thinks she sees our daughter and is able to speak with her.'

"Of course, I became instantly fascinated and asked the baroness whether she would allow me to come to one of her séances. The baroness said I could come any time. A few days later, when we again had supper at their house, the baroness asked me to come with her into the so-called chapel. We sat in the dark around a table. Suddenly she went into a trance and began speaking to her daughter. She kept saying, 'Doodly, Doodly, can you hear me?' It was a tremendously moving experience for me, so much so that I found myself with tears streaming down my cheeks. There was no doubt the baroness was actually seeing her daughter. I, on the other hand, saw nothing at all.

"It was I, not she, who felt cheated. The creative power of her faith and conviction made me examine my own cynicism and led me to wonder at the multiple texture of reality. It also made me wonder whether belief was a creative power and whether skepticism could destroy creative powers. Anyway, this episode was the beginning of *The Medium,* which despite its eerie setting and gruesome conclusion, is actually a play of ideas.

"It describes the tragedy of a woman caught between two worlds, a world of reality which she cannot wholly comprehend, and a supernatural world in which she cannot believe. Baba, the medium, has no scruples in cheating her clients, tricking them with fraudulent apparitions and contrived phenomena, until something happens which she herself has not prepared. This insignificant incident, which she is not able to explain, shatters her self-assurance and drives her almost insane with fear.

"From this moment on, she rages impotently against her still incredulous clients, who are serene in their naïve and unshakable faith, and against Toby, the enigmatic mute boy whom she has adopted, who seems to hide within his silence the answer to her unanswerable question. Baba's daughter Monica, in the simplicity of her love both for Toby and Baba, tries to mediate between them. But Baba, in her anxiety and insecurity, is finally driven to kill Toby, 'the ghost,' the symbol of her metaphysical anguish, who will always haunt her with the riddle of his immutable silence."

This was neither the first nor the last example of the occult and the supernatural in Menotti's stage works, nor of his fascination with them. In actuality, these dramatic facets are part of a larger question, to which Menotti would address himself most completely in another Broadway work, *The Saint of Bleecker Street.* The question is one of faith, real and abstract, or the lack of it. He once stated that "the intense and incandescent faith which nourished my childhood and my adolescence has seared my soul forever. I've lost my faith, but it is a loss that has left me uneasy. I often feel like a runaway who suddenly finds himself wondering if he has not left home too rashly or too soon. A certain nos-

Claramae Turner, the original Madame Flora, with conductor Otto Luening and Menotti during rehearsals for the world premiere, 1946.

talgia for my years of grace is, I believe, the knowledge that faith cannot be attained, but can only be given by God as an act of grace. But alas, or fortunately, depending on how you look at it, my mind is much too rational to abandon itself to faith. I am a would-be Voltaire yearning to be Tolstoy, and it is this very duality in my character, this inner conflict, which I have tried to express in some of my operas, first with *The Medium.*"

If the question of faith can be said to have both a secular and a sacred side to it, then *The Medium* is the shining example of Menotti's investigation into its secular nature. The personages in this work are as much symbols as they are characters. The drama is an emotional triangle between doubt (expressed by Baba), faith (her clients) and love (Monica). The catalyst is Toby. To Menotti, Toby represents "the unknown." Baba turns to him for reassurance that there is a natural explanation for the terrifying angst that grips her. But Toby has no answer; his muteness is in itself a symbol that tells Baba and the audience there is no way to allay her fears or calm her fevered anxiety.

Yet despite *The Medium*'s highly symbolic nature, in comparison to *The Old Maid* Menotti is moving from caricature to character, adding previously unsounded dramatic depth and dimension to his writing not only of music but of words. *The Medium* is extraordinary in its unchanging ability to charge our emotions and incite our imaginations; beyond this, it is an enviable work in that it contains not one excessive note. From first to last it is tense, lean and renewing theater. With it, Menotti in a single, swift, bold leap came into his own.

The opera opens with five stark chords (*molto lento*) which are repeated before the orchestra moves on to a murmuring figure that gradually builds in volume, speed and intensity. At its climax, the opening chords return. In these two

Oliver Smith's set design for the first production of *The Medium,* given at Brander Matthews Theater, Columbia University, 1946.

dozen bars of music, Menotti establishes the intensity of the tale to follow and sets up a frame within which the action will be contained, for the same series of chords opens the second act and returns with the greatest of force following Baba's shooting of Toby.

Menotti's emergence as a stage director is reflected in the score of *The Medium* by his greatly expanded dramatic instructions. With minute precision, he spells out the details of Madame Flora's squalid rooms and the action that is to take place within them. He leaves the time of day ambiguous throughout the opera and never reveals the country in which the story is set; there is little doubt, however, that it takes place somewhere in Europe.

As the curtain rises, Toby is seen kneeling near an open trunk from which he draws brightly colored pieces of silk, bead necklaces and bangles. With these, he improvises a fantastic costume. Across the room, Monica holds a mirror in one hand and combs her loose hair with the other. To a quiet, ripply accompaniment *(andante calmo)* in B major, the first solid feeling of key in the opera, she sings to herself a fairy-tale ballad of a queen who has lost her "new golden spindle and thread," and who will be struck dead unless they are found.

Noticing Toby in her mirror, Monica breaks off her song. She warns him that Baba will be home shortly and nothing has been prepared for the evening's séance. She resumes her song but again interrupts it when she sees Toby outfitted in the brilliant clothes and beads he has found in the trunk. Monica, with her vivid sense of imagination, proclaims him "the King of Babylon on his purple throne" *(andante con moto)*.

The line "I shall be your servant, I shall be your princess" reveals the imprint of one of Menotti's musical fingerprints—an ascending phrase immediately mirrored in the next phrase:

[musical notation]
I shall be your ser- vant. I shall be your prin- cess.

This figure slightly altered returns a few bars later ("How d'you do my master, how d'you do my King"), and foreshadows the Grandmother's

music in *The Consul* when she plays with her grandchild. But this brief outburst gets no further than did Monica's opening song. Menotti is not out to write set pieces in *The Medium*, but rather to tell his story as cogently as possible. Only once does he permit his audience the luxury of an aria (actually, an *arietta):* the "Black Swan" song at the end of Act I, a simple, folklike piece.

A slamming door announces Baba's return. Frightened, Toby with Monica's help, tries to free himself from the tangled silks and beads over a rapid, apprehensive figure in the orchestra. Both children stand frozen as Baba comes up the stairwell. With sinister calm, she begins to scold Toby. This is done in a form of dramatic recitative that is one of the principal features of the score. Menotti indicates that "all the recitatives throughout are to be sung very freely in regard to both rhythm and declamation."

A quick comparison of *The Medium*'s recita-

Monica (Evelyn Keller) with Toby (Leo Coleman) in the Broadway mounting.

tives with those in *Amelia al ballo* and *The Old Maid and the Thief* shows that these earlier works make less effective use of this bedrock operatic device. Those in *The Old Maid* are actually bits of accompanied conversation that lacked the electricity of the recitatives found in *The Medium*. Verdi once spoke of *Rigoletto* as a series of duets; in the same sense, *The Medium* might best be described as a chain of recitatives that are as personally constructed as they are compelling. One of the other characteristics and strengths of the score is the carefully planned silences that punctuate the vocal lines, allowing action and interaction to take place. Obviously Menotti kept in mind Verdi's advice that "to write good opera one must find the courage at times not to write music."

Madame Flora's mercurial nature is quickly defined by the manner in which she fluctuates from icy control to fiery flare-ups. From a dispassionate demand to know whether everything has been prepared for the séance, Baba suddenly becomes threatening and raises her arm as if to strike Toby: "If anything goes wrong tonight, I'll make you pay for it." As she removes her hat and coat, Monica asks where she has been. Against a churning, "walking" figure in the orchestra, Baba replies expansively, "Ah, money, my dear money," and throws a roll of bills on the table.

"I sat on Mrs. Campi's steps all night; she got so scared of seeing me there she paid every cent she still owed me." Waving aside Monica's concern for Mrs. Campi's poverty, Baba tells the two children to make ready for the séance. An animated canon begins in the woodwinds as Baba helps Monica in a white dress and covers her head with a veil. Toby goes to a primitive puppet theater, not unlike the one owned by Menotti as a child, and tests various levers and cables hidden within it; these levitate the table and lower the lamp above it. The instrumental canon has now turned to free counterpoint and builds to a peak of tension that is released by the ringing of the doorbell.

Monica and Toby hide while Baba takes out a deck of cards and pretends to be absorbed in a game of solitaire. Mr. and Mrs. Gobineau come

up the stairwell followed by Mrs. Nolan. Baba barely looks up from the cards as she greets them. This is Mrs. Nolan's first visit to Madame Flora, and she hopes to make contact with her daughter Doodly, who died at the age of sixteen the year before. As she chats with Mrs. Gobineau, Baba gets up abruptly and leaves the room. Mrs. Nolan leans over secretively to Mr. Gobineau and asks, "Have you known her a long time?" "Yes," he replies. "We have been coming here every week for almost two years. We come to communicate with our little son. He was only a baby when he died. But we hear him laugh; he sounds so happy."

With great simplicity, Mrs. Gobineau tells Mrs. Nolan the tragedy took place a long time ago, as the orchestra seesaws between D major and D minor: "We were still very young. We had a house in France with a garden full of lilacs and mimosa. The garden had a fountain, a silly little fountain, no more deep than that. . . ." In the fountain, the child drowned without making a sound. No longer able to hold her tears back, Mrs. Gobineau's voice breaks and she begins silently sobbing in her husband's arms.

"It is time to begin," Baba announces, as she returns wearing a bright-colored shawl. To a poignant stretch of music, Mrs. Gobineau leads Mrs. Nolan to the table as Mr. Gobineau helps Baba place chairs. The music underneath suddenly turns dry, heavy and uneasy as all sit and join hands. Here and indeed throughout *The Medium* one of the prime attractions of the score is the prodigious range of·colors and pliant sonorities Menotti is able to conjure from his small band of instruments (in a large theater, a string orchestra is allowed to replace the quintet). It is a further example of Menotti's making every instrument not only count, but give a full account of itself.

With a last look about her, Baba slowly and deliberately pulls the chain of the lamp overhead. Except for a candle in front of the statue of the Madonna, the room is in darkness. After a long pause, an eerie, expressive melody is outlined by the oboe, answered by the viola. Baba begins to moan lowly, simulating a trance. Her strange moans grow in frequency and intensity until she breaks into a prolonged and anguished scream. Monica is suddenly seen, bathed in a faint blue light, like a figure from beyond. Plaintively and *pianissimo* she chants, "Mother, mother, are you there?" repeating this telling matched set of phrases five times.

"Is it you, Doodly?" Mrs. Nolan asks timidly against a sustained note in the orchestra. The

those asides or commentaries that are part and parcel of his librettos: "What is death but a sweeter change? There's no parting, no end." Asking her mother to let her sleep in peace, Doodly's "voice" becomes driving and insistent: "Burn all my shoes, give away my bracelets, burn, burn, give away, give away." These are set in Menotti's by now familiar twin phrases, an ex-

bereaved woman then begins a gentle dialogue with her "daughter":

> *"Are you happy?"*
> *"Yes, mother, I'm happy."*
> *"Doodly, Doodly, are you near your father?"*
> *"Yes, mother, I can see him. . . ."*
> *"Why did you leave me?"*
> *"Are you so unhappy?"*
> *"I am very much alone."*

In an *arioso*-like passage, Monica sings a haunting strophe of great tenderness *(andante, senza trascinare)*, "Mummy, mummy dear, you must not cry for me," and for the first time Menotti relaxes his storytelling to permit one of

ample of this repetitive device pushed to its limits to create a sense of anguish.

The voice breaks off, begging, "Keep for yourself only the gold locket." Bewildered, Mrs. Nolan cries out, "What locket? I have no locket." As the voice recedes lamenting, "Mother, mother, are you there," Mrs. Nolan rushes hysterically toward the vanishing figure. Mrs. Gobineau restrains her and slowly leads her back to the table amid violent chords in the orchestra. Mrs. Nolan continues crying for a while as Baba again sighs deeply and moans. Then, very simply and almost mechanically, Mr. Gobineau says, "Send my son to me." These words are set as a sort of

As the beaten Toby (Coleman) is consoled by Monica (Keller), Madame Flora (Powers) sends away the Gobineaus (Dame and Rogier) and Mrs. Nolan (Beeler).

Sprechstimme, somewhere between the exact pitches of dramatic recitatives and free speech.

A gentle flourish shimmers in the orchestra and above it the voice of Monica simulating a peal of childish laughter. The Gobineaus, their faces animated with anticipation, ask, "Is that you, Mickey? You sound so near tonight." After they bid the child good-bye, there is a long silence. Suddenly, Baba clutches her throat, crying out, "Who's there?" The orchestra breaks in with a frantic, vaulting phrase as Baba throws her chair back and runs to the top of the stairwell and looks down. As the orchestra comes to a crushing halt, Baba demands, "Who touched me?"

In canon, each of the clients asks, "Why be afraid of our dead?" Over chilling trills and tremolos, Baba dismisses them. As they slowly file out, the orchestra subdues its anxiety in a dirge-like figure. When the door downstairs slams, Monica rushes out, still wrapped in her veils. Baba begs her for a drink, warning, "We must never do this again." She explains that during the séance she felt a cold hand on her throat. "Monica, I'm afraid," she sings in an upward phrase that will be repeated and extended in *The Consul* when Magda Sorel sings of her fears to her husband John.

Suddenly Baba cries out, "Where is Toby? He's the one." As Monica attempts to restrain her, Baba pulls the boy out of the puppet theater against driving figures in the instruments and a gibing trumpet solo. "Look at him," Baba rants, "the way he grins at me. He did it to frighten me. Just because he cannot speak, we take him for a half-wit. But he knows a great deal . . . he sees things we don't . . . beware of him."

Gradually the anger in the orchestra and in Baba is dissipated. Monica draws her away from Toby and cradles Baba's head in her lap. As the girl gently rocks Baba, she intones another balladlike song: "The sun has fallen and it lies in blood. The moon is weaving bandages of gold. O black swan, where has my lover gone?" As she chants this hypnotic melody in G minor (*allegretto con moto*), Toby picks up a tambourine and, lying on the floor, accompanies Monica's singing with soft taps on the instrument as he slowly rocks his body.

Soon Baba begins singing in imitation of Monica, but she stops when from the distance comes a voice that only Baba hears. It calls, "Mother, mother, are you there?" "We are not alone," she moans, as Monica attempts to calm her. Imploring the others to "pray to God to save our souls," she takes out her rosary as a talisman against her fear and begins mechanically mouthing "*Ave Maria, gratia plena, Dominus tecum.*" Menotti demands the words be clear and forward, not mumbled or garbled. Monica resumes the "Black Swan" song. As the curtain falls, the ghostly peal of laughter is heard one final time.

Act II is set a few days later in the same room and is prefaced by the same five chords that began the opera. They are followed by a pastoral, pavanelike variation in F major of Mrs. Gobineau's theme from the first act ("We had a house in France . . ."). After two dozen bars, this melody gives way to a fidgeting, scampering *allegro* in the woodwinds, trumpet and piano. Monica is seen watching a puppet show given by Toby. "Bravo," she cries, "and after the theater, supper and dance." She begins a delightful waltz (*allegretto*) to which are set nonsensical words: "Up in the sky someone is playing a trombone and a guitar. Red is your tie and in your velvetine coat you hide a star." Like the other ariettas for Monica, this one is a creation of fantasy, with neither an introduction nor an end but rather the character of an improvisation.

The song becomes more animated ("Follow me, moon and sun") until, without warning, Toby seizes Monica abruptly by the arm, and, trying through inarticulate noises to speak to her, he gently touches her face. Thinking it is a new game, Monica makes Toby kneel, and then she kneels beside him. Here begins the only love duet in opera sung by one person. With slightly exaggerated pathos, Monica starts it by speaking for Toby: "Monica, Monica can't you see that my heart is bleeding for you? I loved you Monica all my life, with all my breath, with all my blood."

She then jumps up and stands before Toby defiantly: "How dare you, scoundrel, talk to me like that! I'm the Queen of Aroundel! I'll have you put in chains." As Monica kneels again to resume Toby's voice, he falls in with the game, mimicking her words with gestures: "I love your laughter, I love your hair, I love your deep and nocturnal eyes, I love your soft hands so white and winged." At the height of this declaration, Toby turns away crying. Monica is at first bewildered, then lifting his tearstained face while the orchestra echoes her waltz melody, she tells him, "Toby, I want you to know that you have the most beautiful voice in the world."

This exquisite moment is shattered by the slamming of the downstairs door. Harsh, sharp chords overlay a long cello solo as Baba drunkenly drags herself up the stairs. Monica runs from the room and Toby crouches in a corner. She sits at the table for a moment before noticing the boy. Then, with strained affection, she calls to him, and Toby crawls toward her like a terrified animal. "What are you afraid of?" she asks, taking his head into her lap. With calculated tenderness she tells Toby she loves him as if he were her own (though dissonances subtly introduced into the orchestra contradict her).

She promises never to punish him again and to buy him a shirt of bright red silk if he will only tell her if he touched her throat during the séance. Insistent repeated notes in the piano and then in the trumpet betray the anxiety behind Baba's question. When he makes no answer, she makes a great effort to control her mounting anger. She tries to cajole him winningly by telling him, "I want to be your friend, Now tell me, my sweet, did you touch me that night?" This sinister attempt at friendship will be replayed shortly in *The Consul* between the Secret Police Agent and Magda Sorel.

After a long silence, Baba offers Toby the silks and beads from her trunk as if trying to enter his private world of fantasy. When this does not produce results, she tries yet another tack: "Perhaps it was not you after all . . . perhaps it was something I couldn't see. But you know, you saw it! I can read it in your eyes!" As the orchestra presses for an answer as well, Baba finally loses her self-control. When Toby tries to escape her rage, she grabs him by his shirt, ripping it off.

This moment is marked by Menotti as *declamato*, with the following note: "Whenever *declamato* appears in this score, the rhythm and pitch

"Was it you? Was it you?": Madame Flora (Powers) with the dead Toby (Coleman).

indicated are to be regarded as only approximate." As if to underline his words, Baba's vocal line disintegrates to loosely defined pitches as her mounting excitement gives way to uncontrolled fury. The orchestra becomes just as menacing and violent as Baba cries out, "You love Monica, don't you? How would you like to marry her? You could, but first you must tell me: Did you see anything that night?" Accusing the boy of trying to frighten her, she grabs a whip and to six heavy hammer blows in the orchestra, she lashes Toby. During the beating, the doorbell begins to ring repeatedly. Baba finally hears it and stands still for a moment, panting hoarsely as Monica rushes into the room and comforts Toby.

The alternating major-minor theme of Mrs. Gobineau is sounded as the Gobineaus and Mrs. Nolan come up the stairs. "I'm glad you came," Baba blurts out. "I've something to tell you." Informing them there will be no more séances, she brusquely throws a wad of money on the table. She insists they take it, adding that she has long cheated them and is nothing but a fraud. The orchestra repeats the five chords that opened the opera, and as they become stronger and more insistent, Baba goes to the puppet theater and exposes the cables that levitate the table and control the lamp. She makes Monica do the imitation of Doodly's voice and Mickey's laughter.

"Oh, no," the three exclaim, their faith unshaken. "That isn't the same voice." The one ensemble of the opera follows, begun by Mrs. Nolan followed by the Gobineaus. It is built on yet another favorite device of Menotti's—a declarative phrase:

Not to know my own daugh- ter's voice

answered by a pair of phrases:

Could that be?   Could that be?

Punctuating these sung passages are *declamato* ones for Baba. "It might well be you thought you were cheating all the while," Mr. Gobineau tells Baba almost fiercely, "but you were not." He and the two women beg in plodding phrases like automatons for the séances to continue. Unable to contain herself any longer, she orders them out, crying amid lashing orchestral chords, "You fools, you fools!"

Terrified, the clients disappear down the stairs, and turning on Toby, Baba orders him from the house as well. Hysterically, Monica begs Baba not to send the boy away, but she is adamant: Toby must leave alone, "before it is too late!" Monica runs to him, and they clasp each other in a brief but desperate embrace as the orchestra pours out the poignant music heard during the children's games earlier in the act. Toby frees himself and runs from the room. As Monica picks up his puppets lying on the floor, the orchestra pathetically plays a ghostly form of her waltz theme.

"Don't stand there like a fool," Baba orders Monica: "go to your room." The girl obeys, leaving her mother alone. After a moment a voice is heard calling softly, "Mother, mother, are you there?" Baba stands very still, terror-stricken. "Is it you, Monica?" she demands. She listens at Monica's door for an answer, and when there is none, she locks the door. But as she walks back to the table, the voice is heard again. "Stop it!" she screams. She pours a drink, and together with nervous, repeated notes, she begins an extended soliloquy: "Afraid! Am I afraid? . . . Can it be that I'm afraid? In my young days I've seen many terrible things! Women screaming as they were murdered, and men's hands dripping with blood, and men haunted by knives. And little grotesque children drained white by the voraciousness of filth; and loathsome old men insane with vice, and young men with cankers crawling on their flesh like hungry lizards. This I've seen and more and never been afraid. O God! forgive my sins, I'm sick and old. Forgive my sins and give me peace."

Drowsily and still drunk, she begins muttering part of the "Black Swan" song, breaking off at the end of phrases with a cry of fear, "Who's there?" Finally, accepting the fact that no one's in the room with her, she asks, "But if there is nothing to be afraid of, why am I afraid of this nothingness?" As the orchestra sets sail on waves of rising and falling chromatics, she reflects, "I must forget about it, laugh at it." She begins to chuckle slowly, and little by little her laughter becomes wilder until it reaches a hysterical pitch. It dies down to a whisper as Baba falls asleep.

Moments later, Toby is seen sneaking back into the room. He first scratches at Monica's door, whimpering like a wounded animal as the orchestra plays the phrases Monica sang earlier when pretending to be Toby's voice. Receiving no answer, he runs to the trunk and begins to rummage through its contents. When the lid falls sharply, Baba awakes with a start. Frightened, Toby hides in the puppet theater. "Who's there?" Baba rages. "Monica, is it you?" She takes a revolver from a drawer warning, "Speak out or I'll shoot." At that moment the curtain of the theater moves, and Baba fires. As if to ward off the bullets, Toby's hands appear above the curtain.

The orchestra intrudes with eight, massive sustained chords as Toby's hands clutch the curtain from inside and a spot of blood appears and soon runs the length of the white curtain. "I've killed the ghost," Baba screams triumphantly as the five original, germinating chords sing out *fortissimo* from the orchestra. The curtain rod breaks under Toby's weight, and wrapped in the cloth, he falls headlong into the room. As the orchestra continues to repeat the opening chords, Monica pounds violently on her door. When Baba finally unlocks it, the girl rushes in. Seeing Toby's body, she sways as if suddenly ill, then rushes outside. At first, she is hardly able to utter a sound. Then, in the distance, she can be heard screaming for help. The orchestra contracts to a slow, ominous tremolo, as Baba bends over the corpse. In a hoarse whisper, she kneels like a hunched spider beside Toby. "Was it you?" she asks, as she looks searchingly into his eyes, still for an answer to her metaphysical anguish. The curtain falls as the orchestra states *maestoso* the theme of Toby and Monica followed by three sets of brutal, slashing chords.

The first performance of *The Medium* took place at Columbia during its Annual Festival of Contemporary Music (a year later as *The Medium* was opening on Broadway, Brander Matthews Theatre was the scene of the premiere of

yet another major Ditson commission—Virgil Thomson's *The Mother of Us All*). Soon after the initial Columbia performances of *The Medium*, Menotti discovered that the Ballet Society, founded by Lincoln Kirstein to encourage productions of new works for the dance theater, was also planning a season of one-act operas.

He contacted Kirstein and asked him to include *The Medium*. Kirstein agreed provided Menotti would supply a curtain raiser, as *The Medium* was not a full evening's entertainment. Menotti complied with *The Telephone*, a happy leap backward to *opera buffa*. He also added a bit of additional music at the end of *The Medium*'s first act, creating the "revised version" of the score. The double bill premiered at the Heckscher Theatre on February 18, 1947. So pronounced was its success, it moved to Broadway two months later.

Broadway, however, was hardly clamoring for either opera or for Menotti. The double bill played the Barrymore Theatre only because of the faith of its two producers, Chandler Cowles and Efrem Zimbalist, Jr. (the stepson of Mary Curtis Bok, who had been *Amelia*'s midwife), and their willingness to invest $30,000 of their money. The notices were excellent, but the houses were largely empty. For a while it looked as if Menotti's Broadway career would end as unexpectedly as it had begun. Then a minor miracle happened. Menotti invited Arturo Toscanini to

Anna Maria Alberghetti as Monica and Marie Powers as Madame Flora in Menotti's 1951 film version of *The Medium*.

attend a performance, and so delighted was the conductor that he returned a second and a third time. This fact was picked up by several columnists and the resulting publicity created a sensation. The theater was sold out, *Life* magazine covered the production, and the run stretched to six months, with productions following in London and in Paris, establishing for all time Menotti's name and fame.

Three years later, he was asked to turn *The Medium* into a film at Scalera Studios in Rome, even though he had no prior experience in filmmaking. "It would be highly inaccurate to say that I enjoyed making my first film," Menotti has written. "I missed all along the spontaneity of the stage and its immediacy of expression. I felt all the time the defeating personality of the camera whose elaborate steel mask one must always wear, through whose glassy eyes one must look at the world—that devourer of time, that merciless Medusa which petrifies all freshness before it. Of one thing I soon became convinced: The director must be his own cameraman if his film is to be a real work of art, because to give personality to a film the poet-director's mind must live in the black room behind the lens; he must lend his human soul to the artificial limbs of the camera.

"That is the reason why so many films, exciting and convincing though they may be, never reach the level of a work of art. Too often they are nothing but photographed plays, while the camera is a hack reporter rather than a visionary re-creator. I even go so far as to believe that one shouldn't plan shots in advance, for in that way one cheats the camera of its creative power, as no one can really tell what its eye may unexpectedly discover. An accidental light, a seemingly unimportant detail, may suddenly be transfigured into all-important elements by the candor of the lens."

For the movie version, Menotti opened the opera up not only visually, taking us out and into the streets and parks in Baba's neighborhood, but by adding some twenty minutes of new music. A bit of this material would later find its way into *The Saint of Bleecker Street*, which Menotti was then composing, and even into the cantata *The Bishop of Brindisi*. These are two rare examples of Menotti recycling his music. This borrowing from himself would seem to confirm his skepticism about the permanence of film, an artistic medium he has never believed to be as important as a live performance.

At least two of the additional scenes in the film (that between Baba and Mrs. Nolan and the more extended carnival episode) date back to Menotti's original concept of the opera. The remarkable thing about the new material is how completely Menotti was able to reimmerse himself in the taut, sparse style he had left behind as he moved on to the more complex, elaborate world of *The Saint*. Of course the rethinking and extension of several of *The Medium*'s basic melodic ideas—chiefly Monica's waltz and the Monica-Toby music—helped. In fact, the brilliant carnival scene can almost be heard as a freewheeling fantasia on both these ideas. Of interest, too, is the fact that Menotti did not wish to have the important opening music serve as a sound track to the film's titles, so he presented the titles over neutral sounds.

"A great deal of the film of *The Medium*," he admits, "was improvised. My colleagues can bear witness that I never looked at my carefully prepared script, and that very soon everybody else stopped looking at it. To the orthodox, this may sound an extremely dangerous method of working, wasteful of time and money, but actually the improvised shots took less time than the carefully planned ones and were by far the most satisfactory. In spite of my brilliant collaborators [who included Leo Coleman as Toby, the only member of the cast from the Columbia premiere, and the powerful Madame Flora of Marie Powers, who played the role on Broadway and became identified with it], I often felt frustrated at having to depend so much on other people's skill.

"On looking at the rushes, I often felt like a young orchestrator who is surprised at the actual sound of what he has written. I am often asked whether I liked the filming of *The Medium*. I feel that that is like asking a surgeon whether or not he liked a certain operation. All I can say is that the patient is alive and even looks a little better than before."

The composer rehearsing his adopted son Chip, the actor Francis (Phelan) Menotti, as Toby in *The Medium,* a production created for French television.

The Telephone

or *L'amour à trois*
Opera buffa in one act,
libretto in English by the composer

Lucy   Soprano
Ben   Baritone

"That was Margaret," she says sheepishly to Ben over a big, rolling E-major chord from the piano. "You don't say," he answers. As he tries to get Lucy's attention again, the phone rings. This time it is a wrong number, which makes Lucy furious. Ben calms her down and begs her to listen to him. "The time is getting shorter," he pleads. "Would you like to know the exact time?" Lucy asks brightly, and then dials a number to six rolled chords in the piano. As she listens for the time, the orchestra repeats the pastoral theme from the overture. "It is four-fifteen and three-and-a-half seconds," she informs Ben. "Thank you," he moans, and starts in anew to propose to Lucy. But again the phone rings. To ominous tremolos and nervous, melodramatic figures in the orchestra Lucy answers. In a short but concentrated *scena* she speaks with a friend named George who is obviously enraged. "How dare you say such a thing," Lucy counters, "I never said that about you! If you don't believe me you can call up Phyllis!"

Realizing that George has hung up on her, Lucy bursts into tears. When Ben tries to comfort her, she runs from the room. In a brief soliloquy he reflects that he'd "rather contend with lover, husband or in-laws than this two-headed monster who comes unasked and devours my days. For this thing can't be challenged, can't be poisoned or drowned. It has hundreds of lives and miles of umbilical cord." Arming himself with a pair of scissors, Ben approaches the telephone menacingly over sinister music in the orchestra. As he starts to cut its cords, the instrument rings violently, like a child calling for help. Lucy rushes in and takes it protectively in her arms. Ben assures her he was only acting in self-defense, but Lucy refuses to listen.

Ben then attempts to change the subject, but Lucy says she must call up Pamela and tell her of the quarrel with George. As she relates with mock sadness her tale to Pamela, Ben pours out his feelings to the audience: "I've waited hour after hour, but she will never stop. I must tell her I love her, but that thing will not let me. Now I have to go, and she will never know." When Lucy hangs up, she is surprised to see that Ben has left and wonders what it was he seemed so anxious to tell her. As a lively figure invades the orchestra, a curtain to the side of the stage is drawn revealing Ben in a public phone booth. In a moment Lucy's phone rings as the orchestra erupts in a dazzling burst of C major. To a warm and loving accompaniment in E-flat major, Ben finally asks Lucy to marry him.

"But, of course, I'll marry you," she responds. As the duet swells to a climax, Lucy pledges to wait for Ben by the phone. "And while you're away," she adds coyly, "don't forget. . . ." "Your eyes?" Ben asks. "No . . ." "Your hands?" "No . . ." "Your lips?" "No . . ." "What, then?" "My number," Lucy answers to the infectious strains of an off-center waltz. "Please don't forget to call my number, my darling, remember to call it every day." This E-flat waltz is stopped dead in its tracks by a rolled C-major chord as Lucy instructs Ben to write it down: "Stevedore two, three, four, zero." The final number is sung on a high B-flat, and Ben joins in on the lower G as the orchestra breaks out into the little waltz one final time. It lasts barely a dozen bars before three final *fortissimo* chords.

Lucy (Marilyn Cotlow) finally connects with Ben (Frank Rogier), as staged for the world premiere by Menotti in décor by Saul Steinberg, 1947.

The Consul

Musical drama in three acts,
libretto in English by the composer

John Sorel	Baritone
Magda Sorel	Soprano
The Mother	Contralto
Secret Police Agent	Bass
The Secretary	Mezzo-soprano
Mr. Kofner	Bass-baritone
The Foreign Woman	Soprano
Anna Gomez	Soprano
Vera Boronel	Contralto
The Magician (Nika Magadoff)	Tenor
Assan	Baritone
Two Plainclothesmen	Non-singing

World premiere at the Shubert Theatre in Philadelphia, March 1, 1950. First performance on Broadway in the Ethel Barrymore Theatre, March 15, 1950. Dedicated to Emily Zimbalist. Published by G. Schirmer in English. Scored for flute, oboe, clarinet, bassoon, two trumpets, two horns, trombone, percussion, harp, piano, strings.

If Menotti's entry to Broadway was tenuous, his second venture there was triumphant from the first. *The Consul* was awarded the New York Drama Critics Award for the 1949–50 season and the Pulitzer Prize. Yet, ironically, there were those who did their best to dissuade Menotti from either writing or producing it. "I remember that my friends, including my publisher, said, 'You're out of your mind writing an opera about a consulate,'" Menotti has recalled with understandable satisfaction. "'Who'll want to hear that?' I went ahead anyway because the libretto inspired me. The wrong thing young composers often do is to think there is a formula for a good libretto, so they always try to find a subject that they think is operatic. No subject is operatic *per se*. A good libretto is what suits the composer. *Madama Butterfly* would have been a horrible libretto for Wagner, and imagine Puccini setting *Götterdämmerung!* It is up to the composer to find the subject that will make him burst into music."

Once again, Menotti knew himself better than anyone else, and with *The Consul* he took a giant step forward in terms of operatic craft, for it was his first full-length work and it stretched him both orchestrally and harmonically as a composer. For many, *The Consul* remains Menotti's most powerful and persuasive piece of musical theater. Not only is it timeless in its story and in Menotti's manner of storytelling, but it packs as hard a punch today as it did at the time of its premiere. An enormous part of this punch is its libretto, one of the finest of this century. This mighty linking of prose and poetry to music created a musically supercharged atmosphere of originality and strength.

Though Menotti was not the first to use aspects of contemporary life (in particular, post-World War II life) for a libretto, he was the first to do so with such impact and success. "Just as modern poets have been moved to examine and interpret the uniqueness of contemporary life," he has written, "there is no reason why the com-

"Papers! Papers!": Magda (Patricia Neway), driven to the brink, tears up documents in the consulate as Anna Gomez (Maria Andreassi) looks on—the original Broadway production, 1950.

poser should not do the same. That is not to say that modern opera must have a contemporary subject. As Lorca, Eliot or Dylan Thomas have found inspiration in sources as varied as folklore, remote historical events or newspaper headlines, so should the composer permit himself that same freedom."

It was, in fact, a newspaper story that led to the creation of *The Consul*. On February 12, 1947, the New York *Times* ran the following item: "Mrs. Sofia Feldy, a 38-year-old Polish immigrant, who was refused admission to the United States by a board of special inquiry at Ellis Island, committed suicide by hanging at the Ellis Island detention room. . . ." In Sofia Feldy, Menotti had not only the impetus for his new stage work but his heroine as well; renamed, she became Magda Sorel. To her were added several fragments of memory, for Menotti as we have seen has always been affected by circumstance and chance meetings, and many of these through the years have been woven into the fabric of his work. For example, his mind returned to an incident in childhood when he came to create the character of Anna Gomez. As a boy, Menotti was staying with his mother in a hotel in the town of Gardone, where they had gone to meet the renowned Italian poet Gabriele D'Annunzio.

One evening at supper, he observed a couple at a nearby table, apparently father and daughter. The woman was about thirty, and Menotti was struck by the fact she had a streak of white running through her hair. She and her father were conversing quietly when suddenly she ran her hand through her hair and cried out loudly, "No!" This recurred a number of times, and later that evening, Menotti had trouble going to sleep, thinking about the woman. That memory became one of the opera's most touching figures, a woman with no country whose life is a hindrance to everyone. We wonder if we will someday read about her in the morning paper as Menotti did about Sofia Feldy, or, as Menotti has mused, "encounter her again years from now in another consulate."

The touching part of the Foreign Woman grew out of a chance encounter between Menotti and an old Italian peasant who was traveling to New York on the same plane to join her daughter after a long separation. "Throughout the flight," Menotti has recalled, "she clutched an old bundle, her entire baggage, letting go of it only long enough to cling to my sleeve. She was tiny, like some shriveled child, and her wrinkled skin, the heritage of peasant ancestors, was the color of earth. . . .

"When we landed in New York, she trembled with fear, for her daughter was not there to meet her. Moreover, her papers were not in order and no one could understand her naïve explanations which she murmured in her strange accent. I did all I could to assist her but was finally obliged to leave her to the authorities. . . . I knew that I must write her simple story, for I could never forget it."

The other figures one encounters in *The Consul* are largely symbolic. To Menotti, the Mother "personifies the aging mother of everyone who carries the bitter taste of death in her dry mouth; she will live until she is no longer needed. . . . John Sorel's intense love of humanity renders him almost superhuman, and only for his wife and mother does he remain a man. . . . Mr. Kofner, probably an elderly schoolteacher, is the image of patience; one knows by looking at him that he will never get that which somehow represents the last hope in his life of privation and deception. . . .

"Of all the people waiting in the consulate, it was Vera Boronel who least needed a visa and who, naturally, got one. . . . And lastly, beware of Nika Magadoff, this mysterious conjurer who holds in his eyes the power to lull you to sleep. Beware of him, for the visions that he allows you to possess so clearly one moment, he will whisk away the next . . . he is Death." Mixed in with these character images is a sense of bureaucratic futility that is a residue of Menotti's screenplay *The Bridge*, also based on a story read in the New York *Times*, concerning a group of refugees stranded on a bridge between two countries, homeless and unwanted. Finally, as John Gruen has suggested, the tragic fate of Menotti's Jewish friends in Austria and Germany must have added fuel to the outrage he expresses so eloquently and so grimly in *The*

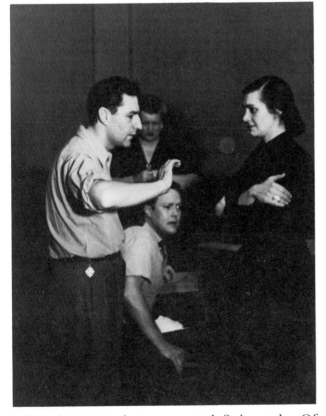

Consul for all those displaced and alone throughout the world—then and now.

"Of all my works," Menotti has said, "*The Consul* was written the quickest. I was very much inspired; the aria 'Papers, Papers' was written in one night. The orchestration of *The Consul* is very sparse. Every conductor who has ever done it has urged me to enrich the orchestration. They feel that for a large opera house, where it is generally given, it needs a richer sound. But I rather like the sparseness, which allows the text to be understood. I feel *The Consul* carries on in the tradition of *The Medium*. By that time my reci-

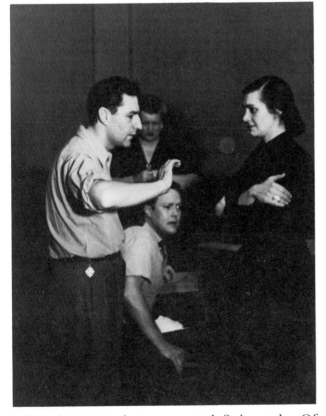

tatives began to have a very definite style. Of course, thematically and musically, *The Consul* is much stronger than *The Medium*. It's much richer melodically. I felt that in *The Consul* I was able to give instant life to my characters, which I think is very rare in opera."

Though one can agree with Menotti's appraisal, there is still a touch of irony in the fact that the title role of the opera is never more than a shadow thrown against a glass pane in the door to an office. He remains a disembodied spirit, the personification of fate, whose presence—menacing and real—dominates the opera and the hopes and dreams of those who people this macabre story.

As if to focus the audience's attention immediately on his characters and their plight, Menotti has written no prelude. The curtain rises immediately on a shabby apartment in a large European city—the Sorel home. A record being played in a café on the street below can be heard through an open window. The song is slow, bluesy and in French. Even here, while creating a purposeful cliché, Menotti cannot restrain himself from indulging his fondness for shifting metric patterns that create those uneven phrase lengths so basic to his style. (Most productions of *The Consul* use a recording of the song made by Mabel Mercer for the original Broadway production.)

After fifteen bars, the orchestra breaks in savagely with a series of crashing, violent chords. John Sorel, wounded, stumbles into the empty, dark room against these spurts of dissonance (the level of dissonance in *The Consul,* even in its highly lyrical moments, is not matched by any other of Menotti's operas). This opening blast dies away in a series of *staccato* bass notes in the piano (an instrument that plays an important role throughout the score), and John calls out his wife's name.

Magda rushes in from the alcove followed by the Mother. They help John into a chair and examine his wound. The Mother brings a basin of water and closes the window, shutting out the sound of the record. "Is this the only place?" Magda asks anxiously. As she bathes and cleans the wound, free sequential patterns ripple through the orchestra. When John admits he was shot by the police, the Mother begins a series of wailing recriminations soon taken up by Magda.

John explains he was given orders "to go to Nana's place for a secret meeting . . . I still don't know who could have betrayed us . . . Sudden in the night we heard the noise of cars and the screech of brakes. Out the garret window and down the slanting roofs we made our escape." As the orchestra expands on the Mother's recriminations, Magda laments, "Oh bitter love, this

Menotti rehearsing Marie Powers, Cornell MacNeil and Neway in Philadelphia shortly before the world premiere.

love of freedom, that locks the very air we breathe." Begging Magda not to fail him, John reminds her that "the seed [of freedom] needs darkness to spread its bitter roots. This we must do so that one day our son may see with innocent eyes the flower we nourish in bitter darkness."

The Mother interrupts with a warning that the police are downstairs, and for an instant all three are frozen with panic. Then Magda instinctively puts her arms protectively around John and helps him to a secret hiding place as the orchestra plays a dry, tight, chordal version of the music that will recur later in the scene during the searching and interrogation by the police. After disposing of all traces of John, Magda sits at a table with her sewing while the Mother rocks the baby's cradle.

To heavy orchestral chords, the door is flung open and the Secret Police Agent rushes in followed by two plainclothesmen. As the apartment is searched, the Mother laments the family's fate while Magda sits in stoic silence. When the Agent begins to question Magda with unctuous courtesy, the piano interjects a nervous theme that is one of the melodic building blocks of the work:

"Mrs. Sorel," the Agent begins, "your husband has many friends. We're interested in his friends. We would like to learn their names. . . . We could leave you alone if you proved to be of help. . . . You can help us crush the enemies of the state." When Magda does not answer, the Agent with sudden violence demands an answer. "I don't know, I don't know anything," Magda gasps. "Courage is often a lack of imagination," the Agent warns her. "We have strange ways to make people talk. Oh, not at all the way you may think. All we have to do is to quicken the beat of your heart. . . . Think it over Mrs. Sorel."

The Agent and his henchmen withdraw against a stark, marchlike theme. The Mother runs to the window as the desperate cries of a woman are heard below. "They're taking Michael the shoemaker away," she reports. As the cries gradually cease, the Mother turns to Magda asking, "Oh! God, how long must women cry over man's destiny? Have pity on Man, this bit of clay wet with women's tears." One of the extraordinary measures of the individuality of *The Consul* is how Menotti manages to interject such musical asides or more traditional set pieces without diluting the force and flow of his drama.

When it appears safe, Magda and the Mother help John back into the room, and the husband and wife embrace almost fiercely. "Go to the consulate tomorrow," John instructs her. "Tell him our story. Ask them for help. They will not bolt their doors to my wife and my mother and my little son." He will, he continues, send word of himself through Assan the glasscutter. "When a child on the street throws a stone and breaks this window, that will be a signal. Call Assan and ask for a new pane. He'll bring you news. . . ."

The music heard at the beginning of the act

Poster for one of the first Italian performances, at La Scala, Milan, 1951.

reappears in the orchestra, swells and then sub-sides as the three begin their farewell. This trio *(andante espressivo)* is founded on a deeply felt text that produces a compelling stream of music for which one has to reach back to the trio from Strauss's *Der Rosenkavalier* for an adequate comparison. Though the action momentarily stops, the emotional intensity of the work continues, tying together the raw feelings that have gone before and providing a needed release from the starkness of the drama.

In turn, each of the characters enters with the same melodic idea, beginning with Magda:

Now, O lips, say goodbye.
The word must be said, but the heart must not heed.
So, my lips say goodbye.
The rose holds the summer in her winter sleep,
The sea gathers moonlight where ships cannot plough.
And so will the heart retain endless hope,
Where time does not count, where words cannot reach.

The voices intertwine, mounting higher and higher before returning to earth and the coda:

So within the heart,
Let hope be the haven that words cannot reach,
Heart, do not listen, lest you surrender.
Parting turns time into tears,
Turns hearts into clocks.
Be like the dreamer who knows that
    his dream is a dream.

John embraces Magda and the Mother and leaves as the curtain falls and the orchestra begins the first of three interludes that connect the scenes between the Sorel home and the consulate. The first interlude is an unsettled, churning stretch of music that finds its release in a theme reminiscent of the police motif. This forceful idea is stated strongly and then quietly recedes into a reprise of the main theme of the trio. This lengthening of the interlude was added after the score was published.

The curtain rises on the Consul's cheerless, cold waiting room. A dry motif is heard that symbolizes the impersonal character of the Secretary and the impatience of those waiting:

"Next," the Secretary says in clipped tones, without looking up from her typing. Mr. Kofner gets up quickly and comes to the railing. "I believe we've seen you before," the Secretary comments. "Oh, yes," Mr. Kofner replies to a rocking figure, "yesterday and the day before, and the day before yesterday and every day for oh, so long!"

In droning, dispassionate phrases, the Secretary asks, "Did you bring your birth certificate, your health certificate, your vaccination, your affidavit, the statement from the bank, your passport, three photographs. . . ." Suddenly she turns on Mr. Kofner accusingly: "These are not the right size. I told you they must be three-by-three. Besides, this paper must be notarized." To a return of the rocking figure, she tells him there is a notary around the corner and the pictures can be brought tomorrow. "Oh, yes," he replies, like an automaton, "tomorrow and the day after tomorrow. . . ."

The Foreign Woman is next, but speaks only Italian. Mr. Kofner volunteers to translate. The extremely touching section that follows is an *omaggio a Puccini*, Menotti's only conscious attempt to compose in the style of his countryman, a style he felt fitted the character and qualities of the Foreign Woman. The music is in C minor *(andante con moto)* and wears its heart on its sleeve. As the Foreign Woman sings in Italian, Mr. Kofner provides a running précis in English: "It's something about her daughter. . . . It seems she ran away with one of your soldiers. . . . For almost three years she had no news of her and couldn't find out where she was. . . . This morning at last she received a letter from her daughter. It seems she's very ill and afraid to die. Her husband left her with a little boy. . . . She asks her mother to go there and help her out of trouble."

The translation provided by Mr. Kofner is but one more impersonal layer added to the consulate. While accurate, it misses (as surely Menotti meant it to) the anguish of the original Italian, especially when the Foreign Woman says, "*È proprio così che mi scrive la mia povera bambina. Immagini la mia pena. . . .*" The Secretary brusquely asks what they can do for her, and in a lovely but short canon, the Foreign Woman and Mr. Kofner tell the Secretary she wants to go and nurse her daughter. The Secretary gives the woman an application form and says it will take a couple of months to be processed.

Stunned, the Foreign Woman cries that her daughter needs her now. Shaking her head, the Secretary says coldly, "Nothing I can do," as Mr. Kofner leads the Foreign Woman to a writing

desk, urging her to have patience. At this moment, the orchestra explodes in a series of muscular chords as Magda approaches the desk. She asks to speak to the Consul, but is told no one may speak to him, for he is busy. "Tell him my name," Magda insists. "Your name is a number," the Secretary replies. "Tell him my story . . . my life is in danger." "And how can we help you?" "Help me to escape." "You're not one of our people." "But you are our friends, the friends of the oppressed," insists Magda.

"I give you these papers," the Secretary finally tells her, "this is how to begin." In a dull, waltz rhythm, the Secretary explains, "Your name is a number, your story's a case, your need a request, your hopes will be filed, come back next week." Magda interrupts with a gravely weighted phrase of great dignity asking the Secretary to "Explain that John is a hero, that flowers bloom in the blood that was shed. . . . Explain that the web of my life has worn down to one single thread and that the hands of the clock glitter like knives. . . . Explain that the heart of one man cannot be multiplied nor his life be divided. . . . Explain to the Consul, explain."

The Secretary promises nothing, but repeats her incongruous waltz before the orchestra subdues it with a dissonant, yearning variation on the music that accompanied Magda's plea. When the music finally calms down, a quintet ensues. This sad and disquieting musical section carries within it the depression and lack of hope of Magda, Mr. Kofner, plus Anna Gomez, Vera Boronel and Nika Magadoff, who during the preceding scene, have entered the consulate and occupied the benches in the waiting room.

> *In endless waiting rooms the hours stand still.*
> *The light goes pale and thin, the heart is dead.*
> *What are we waiting for?*
> *The answer comes too late or death too soon.*
> *Oh give us back the earth and make us free.*
> *It is God's gift to me—this ever flowering earth.*

As the light dies in the room, the Foreign Woman, still puzzled by the form she has been given, exits as the curtain falls.

The second act begins like the first with the playing of the record in the café below the Sorel apartment. It is a month later. Closing the window, Magda goes to the cradle and desperately looks at the child, who has been ill. As Magda leaves the room, the Mother tries to elicit a response from the baby: "What is the matter, little lamb? Why are you so still?"

As she speaks, she tickles the child, making (as Menotti puts it) "those absurd noises meant to enchant children." It is the one sticky moment in the opera where truth fails to prevail. Menotti now feels this as well; in the revival of *The Consul* for the first Spoleto USA Festival in Charleston (which was televised by the Public Broadcasting System) this part of the scene was cut, making it stronger and less maudlin. The Mother begins rocking the cradle and singing a

John Sorel (MacNeil) bids his wife, Magda (Neway), an anguished farewell (above), and the Mother (Powers) and Magda are questioned about John's whereabouts by the Chief Police Agent (Leon Lishner) and his henchmen (Donald Blackey, Chester Watson).

tender lullaby in F major (andantino):

I shall find for you shells and stars.
I shall swim for you river and sea.
Sleep my love, sleep for me.
My sleep is old.
I shall feed for you lamb and dove.
I shall buy for you sugar and bread. . . .

. . . .

Let the old ones watch you sleep.
Only death shall watch the old.
Sleep, sleep, sleep.

This, one of the most sustained lyrical and diatonic moments in the opera, is in strong contrast to the song-speech and spoken lines employed by Menotti elsewhere in *The Consul.* The simplicity of the Grandmother's expression, the gentle bond between her and the child obviously prompted so highly tonal and melodic a stretch of music. It is typical of Menotti that he can move without awkwardness or self-consciousness from dissonance to consonance, from melody to dramatic recitative, from contrapuntal polyphony to block harmony to create what one writer has aptly characterized as "a dissoluble whole," one that "coalesces the varied styles and techniques into an indissoluble unity." Whatever his means, or however familiar is their echo, Menotti manages to strike that peculiar note that is Menotti and no other. In doing so, he makes diverse materials his own, whatever their origins.

During the lullaby, Magda returns to the room, sits at the table and soon falls asleep. When the Mother exits, the postlude of the lullaby is gradually distorted and overlaid with strains of the first-act trio. Magda stirs in her sleep as a nightmare begins. John enters the door, bloodstained and bandaged, followed by the Secretary, who has about her an aura of oppressive evil. Magda rises stiffly, her eyes staring and sightless, and slowly sets the table as if for guests.

To an insistent *andante,* Magda asks, "John, John, why did you bring me all these branches and stones?" "They are to build us a cross and a grave," he replies. "John, John, who is that woman that you brought back with you?" "She is my sister, my dear little sister; you must love

her for she's my own blood, you must give her the keys of our house." As if in a daze, Magda brings bread, wine and glasses to the table. As the Secretary breaks the bread and pours the wine, Magda cries out in terror: "The wine has turned black like the blood that is shed. The bread is white like the flesh of the dead. John I'm afraid. Send her away. Your sister is death. She covets my child for a grave."

As John and the Secretary slowly disappear, Menotti instructs in the score that Magda fling the curtain to the alcove aside, revealing "the monstrous fetus of a child" as the nightmare ends. This moment has given Menotti the stage director continual problems over the years, and he has tried a number of experiments to avoid the danger of this climactic moment's becoming too unconvincing or gruesome. The most recent solution, which Menotti admits is still a

compromise, was to have the Secret Police Agent suddenly appear in the nightmare, supplanting John as he, John, is about to bend over the cradle. Whatever the solution, it must provoke a scream from Magda signaling a return to reality. The Mother in response rushes into the room and Magda tells her she is afraid the child will die and that something has also happened to John. The buildup of tension onstage is shattered by a rock thrown through the window. For an instant, neither woman moves. Recognizing this as a signal from John, Magda runs to the phone and calls Assan to repair the glass.

"Waiting! Waiting!": the Secretary (Gloria Lane) with Magda (Neway), who wonders if she will ever see the Consul.

Their excitement is cut short by repeated raps on the door. Even before Magda opens it, the orchestra tells us it is the Secret Police Agent. "What is it you want?" Magda asks sharply— "More money?" To a jaunty tune in F minor (*allegretto*), the Agent replies ironically that the money Magda could give him would hardly pay for his silence. But, he adds, "Your husband has many friends. We would like to visit them, and we can make it possible for you to join your husband."

Savagely, Magda orders him out. At the same time, there is another knock and Assan enters with the new pane of glass. "A pane of glass," the Agent muses as he exits, "a very fragile thing. It is amazing how much one can see through a pane of glass." Once the Agent has left, Assan tells Magda that John is hiding in the mountains and will not cross the frontier until he knows his family can join him. "Tell him everything is ready," Magda instructs. "Is it the truth?" Assan asks. "Oh, no! He mustn't know the truth," Magda replies. She leaves the room and as the orchestra plays a lyrical version of Magda's previous lines, the Mother beckons Assan to her side. She points to the face of the child, who has died. Assan hastily crosses himself as Magda returns. He bids her farewell and quickly leaves. Magda, too, prepares to go out, when she senses something is wrong.

To the hushed strains of the lullaby, Magda, who realizes her child is dead, with supreme composure asks, "Shall I call the carpenter and the priest? Shall I unfold the white silk coverlet? Shall I go to market to buy white roses? I cannot look at him, Mother, but tell me that he smiles." At this point, the Mother bursts into tears: "I'm not crying for him, not for us, but for John who will never see his baby again. When a heart is as old and worn and patched as mine, lesser things can break it than the death sigh of a child. Old people live for simple things: to see a birth, to bury the dead; but they themselves are dead and live on borrowed breath. . . . Now let me fold my things and lock my doors. I leave behind me nothing but sorrow, but I believe that God receives with kindness the empty-handed traveler."

The last ray of light dies outside the window as Magda lights a candle and places it at the head of the cradle and the curtain falls. The orchestra begins the second interlude, which is based on two ideas—the first, played high and softly in the strings, is drawn from Magda's aria in the scene to follow. It is punctuated by a *staccatissimo* motif. This theme, which echoes the Secretary's motto, prepares the audience for the massive confrontation between these two women that shortly takes place. Little by little the Secretary's theme takes over until it finally dominates in its original *allegretto* shape as the curtain rises.

It is several days later, and the Secretary is at the file cabinet while Anna Gomez, exhausted and frantic, waits at the railing. "Here it is," says the Secretary, and begins reading from a folder: "Three years in concentration camp; husband, prisoner; whereabouts unknown; no documents. I don't see how we can help you." "I have to leave the country by the end of the month," Anna Gomez answers desperately. "My permit has expired. . . . There must be a place for me somewhere in this world." When the Secretary suggests she return to her own country, Anna Gomez recoils in terror: "Do you realize what that would mean for me?"

"Well, I'll see what I can do," the Secretary replies. "Fill in this paper and come back tomorrow. "Next," she calls, and the Magician rises and starts to the railing as Magda bursts into the room and rushes to the Secretary's desk. "Can I speak to the Consul?" she pleads, pushing aside the Magician, who was next in line. The Secretary tells her she must wait her turn, and dejected, Magda sits as the Magician begins a very free and brilliant scene (E-flat major, *allegro*). He introduces himself as Nika Magadoff: illusionist, telepathist, prestidigitator, hypnotist, ventriloquist, electro-levitator. During this, he performs a series of tricks, such as turning his gloves into white doves and materializing a bouquet of flowers and then the vase and water for them.

"What can I do for you?" the Secretary asks. "I need a visa," he replies, "a simple little visa." "A visa, my dear sir," comments the Secretary, "is not a simple thing." "And why should it be

difficult?" the Magician questions. "Your country should be glad to receive a great artist like me. After all, art is the artist's only passport. . . ." While Menotti has admitted that factually there is something of himself in Mr. Kofner through his relationship in real life with the Foreign Woman, it seems equally clear that he is putting many of his own beliefs into the mouth of the Magician, even if with tongue-in-cheek.

In order to impress the Secretary, the Magi-cian begins to hypnotize the others waiting in the Consulate: "Look into my eyes, look into my eyes. You feel tired, you want to sleep. Breathe deeply, breathe deeply. . . ." When all five—Anna Gomez, Vera Boronel, Magda, Mr. Kofner and the Foreign Woman—are asleep, the Magician asks the Secretary what he should make them do. "Oh, I don't know," she says in frustration. "This is most irregular." The Magician then tells the others they are in a beautiful ballroom whose floor shines with precious marble. They begin to move, smile and bow to each other. Then, in mechanical, ticktock fashion, they dance to a simple strain in F major.

In the midst of the dance, the Secretary loses her patience and demands the Magician's papers. As he searches desperately for them in his pockets, he produces a confusion of scarves, cards, folding flowers and other tricks, which fall in a hopeless litter at his feet. At her wits' end,

the Secretary demands he wake up the others, who are oblivious to the confusion about them. "You ought to be ashamed of yourself," the Secretary says sharply. "Don't you know how to behave in a consulate?" As the Magician gathers up his tricks and trails out of the room pathetically, he comments that "even a great, great artist, must find a way to make a living," a line Menotti often jokingly quotes in reference to himself.

Magda strides to the Secretary's desk asking if there is any news. "You're not the only one, Mrs. Sorel," the Secretary replies dispassionately. "There are thousands of cases like yours." "Must we all die," Magda asks, "because there are too many of us?" "We must have time to think," the Secretary reminds her. "Your case is a difficult one and most irregular." "Liar," shouts Magda, who seems almost startled by her own outburst. "If you behave like this," answers the Secretary, "I must ask you to leave." At this point, Magda begins her "Papers" aria, the opera's most renowned set piece and one of the most overwhelming scenes in contemporary opera. Beginning in sustained, stately terms in D major *(adagio ma non troppo)*, Magda reflects, "To this we've come: that men withhold the world from men. No ship nor shore for him who drowns at sea. No home or grave for him who dies on land."

Although at the outset of the aria she seems exhausted and resigned to the fate that holds her so tightly, as the aria progresses the fact she is able at last to give vent to her deepest feelings and frustrations seems to strengthen her and renew her sense of purpose; her voice rings out with exaltation by the conclusion of the aria. This metamorphosis begins with a question: "If to men, not to God, we now must pray, tell me, Secretary, tell me, who are these dark archangels? Is there one behind those doors to whom the heart can still be explained? Tell me Secretary—have you ever seen the Consul? Does he speak, does he breathe? Have you ever spoken to him?"

Disturbed by the desperation of Magda's

The magician Magadoff (Andrew McKinley) hypnotizes those outside the Consul's office—the Secretary (Lane), Anna Gomez (Andreassi), Vera Boronel (Lydia Summers), Magda (Neway), the Foreign Woman (Maria Marlo), Mr. Kofner (George Jongeyans).

questions and the touch of madness in her voice, the Secretary tells her that she can apply for an appointment with the Consul by filling out a form. She hands the paper to Magda, who snatches it from her screaming, "Papers, papers. But don't you understand? . . . My child is dead. John's mother is dying. My own life is in danger. I ask you for help and all you give me is papers." In an *allegro* figure that moves chromatically down, and that has been heard during the Secretary's interrogations but never quite so persistently, Magda begins quoting from the form and answering it: "What is your name? Magda Sorel. Age? Thirty-three. Color of eyes? Color of hair? Single or married? Religion and race? Place of birth? Father's name? Mother's name?"

Tearing the form up, she grabs a stack of papers from the desk and hurls them about the room crying, "Papers, papers, papers," amid slashing chords in the orchestra. "What will your papers do?" she demands. "They cannot stop the clock. They are too thin an armor against a bullet. All that matters is that the time is late, that I'm afraid and I need your help." Then, with enormous reserves of simplicity and dignity, and against quietly rising and falling dissonances in the orchestra, Magda answers the questions: "My name is woman. Age, still young. Color of hair, gray. Color of eyes, the color of tears. Occupation, waiting." The *agitato*, chromatic figure returns and becomes more and more insistent as Magda repeats, "Waiting, waiting, waiting." She and the orchestra finally burst into the rhapsodic finale section *(largamente)*, an ecstatic statement of heroic proportions:

> Oh! the day will come I know,
> When our hearts aflame, will burn your paper
>   chains.
> Warn the Consul, Secretary, warn him.
> That day, neither ink nor seal, shall cage our
>   souls.
> That day will come!

This is one of several spots in Menotti's operas that have had detractors as well as admirers, those who feel such a ploy is too theatrical and out of context with the balance of the drama. To them Menotti has said: "To criticize a theater piece as too theatrical is as senseless as to criticize a piece of music for being too musical. There is only one kind of bad theater: when the author's imagination steps outside the very area of illusion he has created. But as long as the dramatist creates within that area, almost no action on the stage is too violent or implausible. As a matter of fact, the skill of the dramatist is almost measurable by his ability to make even the most daring and unpredictable [episode] seem inevitable. After all, what could be more theatrical than the last entrance of Oedipus or the death of Hamlet or the insanity of Oswald in *Ghosts?*

"The important thing is that behind these apparent excesses of action, the author is able to maintain that significant symbolism which is the very essence of dramatic illusion. In the words of Goethe: 'When all is said and done, nothing suits the theater except what also makes a symbolic appeal to the eyes. A significant action suggesting a more significant one.' Modern dramatists are much too timid about 'theater,' and such timidity is fatal to an opera composer, for music intensifies feeling so quickly that, unless a situation is symbolically strong enough to bear this intensity, it becomes ludicrous by contrast."

Magda's predicament and the outburst it prompts never fail to incite an audience's imagination and grip it tightly, whoever the singer. Like the public, the Secretary is visibly moved and profoundly disturbed as well. She tells Magda she will go at once to the Consul and ask him to spare a few minutes. Unable to believe what she has heard, Magda stands as though riveted to the stage. The Secretary returns with the news that the Consul has an important visitor with him, but as soon as he leaves Magda may go in.

As the orchestra plays a twisted, rising stretch of music, a light shows through the glass panel of the door to the Consul's office. Upon the glass fall the shadows of two men, bowing ceremoniously to each other. Great tension fills the room as all eyes focus on the door. As it opens, Magda rises and starts toward the railing. The departing visitor walks out of the Consul's office; it is the Secret Police Agent. Magda stares at him for an instant with terror and disbelief, then stum-

bles and faints as the orchestra cries out in anguish for her and the curtain falls.

The last act opens in the consulate several days later. After a short, morose prelude, the Secretary is seen at work while Magda sits woodenly on a bench in the deserted room. She remains motionless, staring straight ahead as the Secretary tells her the consulate will close in ten minutes. A moment later, Vera Boronel arrives to sign her papers, which have been approved. To crisp, *staccato* figures the Secretary leads Vera Boronel through the formalities: "Sign your name at the bottom of the page. Sign the original and all the duplicates. One must have one's papers."

To a purposefully inane tune, the Secretary turns each page as it is signed, stamping each with a seal in precise rhythm with the music. "Seas grow dry and suns grow cold, love may die and truth grow old, but one must have one's papers." While the signing is taking place, Assan hurries in, in search of Magda. The underground is in grave trouble, for John has learned of the death of his child and his mother and is determined to return for Magda. He begs her to find a way to stop John. The exchange between Assan and Magda intermingles with the prattle of Vera Boronel and the Secretary, welling up in a quartet of strong musical contrasts.

Then, to the weighted strains of the first-act trio, Magda rises dully and goes to the writing desk and scribbles a note. "I assure you, Assan,"

she begins, "that this note will convince John that there is no reason for him to come back." As Assan exits, the Secretary gives Vera Boronel her papers while Magda rises stiffly like an automaton and walks slowly out of the consulate. Vera Boronel notices that Magda has left her purse behind and calls out to her. "Oh, well," the Secretary says efficiently, "she'll be back tomorrow."

Left alone, the Secretary puts out the lights and prepares to leave. Suddenly she draws back as though she has seen a ghost. To a plodding *adagio*, she begins a dark soliloquy that reveals, at last, a human side to the character: "Oh, those faces. They hang from the ceiling and the walls. They wait for me all day long . . . boneless, pale in the dusty sun." At the conclusion of this lament, John Sorel appears in the doorway amid driving music in the orchestra. "Have you seen my wife?" he demands. "Who are you?" the Secretary counters. "John Sorel. . . . They've tracked me here. They're waiting outside." "But I have no authority to keep you here," the Secretary answers desperately. "Back there is a door leading to an alley. No one will see you go out from there."

To a throbbing restatement of the trio theme, the Secretary hands John Magda's purse and shows him the way out as voices are heard offstage barking sharp, urgent orders. John drops the purse and digs frantically for his gun as the Secret Police Agent, with two henchmen, overpowers him. "You cannot arrest him here," the Secretary says indignantly. "It is against all international rules." Releasing John, the Agent says calmly that Mr. Sorel will come of his own free will. "Yes," John repeats bitterly, staring at the drawn guns, "of my own free will."

As the orchestra mournfully intones the Mother's "How long must women weep?" John is led away over the protest of the Secretary: "Don't be afraid, Mr. Sorel. Something will be done about this. . . . I'll call your wife myself." She runs to the phone and begins dialing as the curtain falls and the final interlude begins. A series of rising, then descending block chords give way to a snare drum and an eerie march tune in 5/4 rhythm. The march begins

Magda (Neway) collapses in the Consul's antechamber upon seeing the Chief Police Agent—as performed at the Paris premiere.

slowly and softly, and gradually swells to a violent outcry before receding into nothingness as the curtain rises again, this time on the Sorel apartment.

The phone rings four times and after a moment's silence, the orchestra begins a series of quarter-note strokes as Magda enters. She seems dazed and moves like a sleepwalker, yet there is a terrible sureness and determination to her movements. "I never meant to do this," she intones. "Forgive me, John, I never meant to do this." She carries a chair to the stove and sits in front of the oven. After a moment of hesitation, she opens the gas jets. Then, covering her head with the Mother's shawl, she bends over open jets.

As the light fades from the room, leaving only a murky, strange glow around the stove, high sustained chords are sounded in the orchestra.

One of the walls dissolves revealing Vera Boronel, the Secretary, Anna Gomez, the Foreign Woman and Mr. Kofner (in recent productions, Menotti has also added Assan). With them stand the Mother and John. He is stiffly dressed in formal clothes, while the Mother wears an old-fashioned wedding gown.

To persistent quarter notes, like measured drumbeats, echoes are heard of the French song and the trio. The latter is cut short by an outburst in the orchestra during which the members of the ghost chorus cry out in turn, "Next!" They then begin singing the march theme from the last interlude: "Lo, death's frontiers are open. All aboard. Burn your papers, lock your bags. Bid farewell to benches and inkwells." Rising from in front of the stove Magda shouts in the direction of the voices, calling John's name. As she does, the Secret Agent's voice is heard demanding, "What is your name?" "Magda Sorel," she screams. "Age?" "Thirty-three."

The others then advance into the room singing, "Horizons! . . . There's no guard to bribe or beg. Death's frontiers are free." From behind the group, the Magician appears, and to the phrases that began the hypnotism scene, "Choose your partners, the dance is on." All begin a solemn, macabre waltz. "Magda, my dear," the Mother pleads, "don't stand alone. Why don't you come here and join our dance?" It is, of course, a dance of death, and it frightens Magda. "Why do their words weigh like stones on my heart?" she asks. "It's only a dream. God, let me dream it through quickly and wake." Yet as the Mother and John begin to say good-bye, Magda cries out for them to wait for her. She rushes to a chest of drawers and begins to pack a suitcase with papers.

Closing the bag, she tries to run after the receding figures of the Mother and John but can move only in agonizingly slow, dreamlike steps. Suddenly the bag falls open and all the papers spill to the floor. As she desperately tries to gather them up again, the Magician reappears chanting his lines from the hypnotism scene in Act II: "Look into my eyes. You feel tired, you want to sleep. Breathe deeply." As he sings, he leads Magda back to the stove. She sits, exhausted, and he draws the shawl over her head once again and then disappears.

For a moment, the only sounds are the gasps of Magda's heavy breathing. Then, the phone begins to ring. With each ring there is a crushing chord on the piano. Hearing the phone, Magda stretches out her hand in an effort to reach it, but she is already dazed by the gas fumes and unable to move. As the orchestra explodes in a *fortissimo* statement of the final sections of her "Papers" aria—a supremely theatrical gesture—her body slumps across the back of the chair. The phone continues to ring as the music finishes and the curtain falls.

The hallucination during Magda's death agony—John (MacNeil), Vera (Summers), the Secretary (Lane), the Mother as a bride (Powers), Magda herself (Neway), the Foreign Woman (Marlo), Anna (Andreassi), Mr. Kofner (Jongeyans), Magadoff (McKinley).

The Saint of Bleecker Street

Musical drama in three acts,
libretto in English by the composer

Annina	Soprano
Michele (her brother)	Tenor
Desideria	Mezzo-soprano
Don Marco (a priest)	Bass
Carmela	Soprano
Maria Corona (a newspaper vendor)	Soprano
Assunta	Mezzo-soprano
Salvatore	Baritone
Maria Corona's son	Non-singing
Concettina	Child's part
An Old Man	Bass
A Young Man	Tenor
An Old Woman	Soprano
Bartender	Baritone
First Guest	Tenor
Second Guest	Baritone
A Nun	Mezzo-soprano
A Young Priest	Non-singing

World premiere at the Broadway Theatre, New York, December 27, 1954. Published by G. Schirmer in English. Scored for three flutes, two oboes (English horn), two clarinets (bass clarinet), two bassoons (contra-bassoon), four trumpets, three horns, three trombones, tuba, timpani, percussion, harp, piano, strings.

Though only four years separated the premieres of *The Consul* and *The Saint of Bleecker Street*, it was a period of remarkable activity and growth for Menotti. It was as if he was exercising his imagination and flexing his compositional muscles to prepare for his most elaborate theatrical creation to date. He left the style and world of *The Consul* behind as he turned to the creation of the first opera for television (*Amahl and the Night Visitors*) and his first major scores for the concert hall—*Apocalypse* for Orchestra and the Concerto for Violin and Orchestra.

The Saint, which won for him a second Drama Critics Award and another Pulitzer Prize, is the only Menotti opera that comes close to bearing comfortably the label *verismo*, which is so frequently attached to Menotti's theater pieces. So

vivid are the loves and hates of the characters encountered in *The Saint*, and so void is the opera of supernatural elements and dreams (other than the castles in the air we all build to escape everyday reality), the feeling is unavoidable that we are at last up against real people as opposed to cartoons or symbols.

The grave humanity and dramatic dimension of *The Saint* grew entirely from within Menotti; no chance encounters, no random remembrances were recalled and adapted. In *The Saint*, he confronts two strong strains within his own being that run at times independent of each other yet have intertwined at other times. The first is his Italian heritage. This he parodied in *Amelia*, lovingly cameoed in *The Consul* and finally faced in depth in *The Saint*, principally through the figure of Michele. The other and

Act I finale, with Desideria (Gloria Lane) passionately holding the beaten Michele (David Poleri) as a San Gennaro reveler (John Reardon) passes— world premiere staging on Broadway, 1954.

dominant strain is the religious one, the wrestling within him of angel and devil, believer and doubter.

If we look for autobiographical elements in each of the Menotti operas, and the temptation to do so is irresistible, then where do they surface in *The Saint?* Or, as Menotti has posed the question, "On whose side am I? Michele the unbeliever or Annina the saint? But, of course, I cannot take sides because I am both." Still, Menotti seems more Michele than Annina because of the envy Michele feels for Annina's ability to believe. The opera thus symbolizes his own inner conflict, the split in his personality, the impossibility of being both.

This impossibility had been progressively tormenting to Menotti once the doctrines and dictates of his early youth were behind him. Despite spiraling doubts, the church remained anchored in his consciousness, and the element of faith in others has always struck a responsive note in Menotti and in turn in his operas, whether it was Amelia's simplistic faith that she would attend her ball, or Annina's blinding faith that she would become a bride of Christ. The difference between *The Saint* and the stage works that preceded it, however, is that religion and faith are no longer side issues or subplots but the main event—the opera's heart and soul.

"When I began writing *The Saint*," Menotti has revealed, "I felt emotionally disturbed. I felt a great impatience, a great need to find my faith again. I am definitely not a religious man. All the same I am haunted by religious problems, as most of my works show. Why? I can hardly explain it to myself. Can one be a secular mystic? Since the age of sixteen I had broken away from the Catholic Church, and I very much doubt, as some of my wishful religious friends predict, that at the last minute I shall ask for extreme unction and the holy sacraments."

Yet the need within him to publicly question faith and his lack of it led Menotti to undertake *The Saint.* With characteristic and almost childlike simplicity, Menotti decided that if he was to write about a saint, he should know one. His search for a living saint brought him to the late Father Pio de Pietralcina, an Italian Capuchin

monk, who suffered the stigmata of Christ's crucifixion just as Annina does in the opera. "He had a difficult personality," Menotti has recalled. "He was a rather rough and uncouth man. The Italian clergy tried to hide him in a little village in Apulia, at San Giovanni in Rotondo, where they thought people would forget him. Instead, thousands of people poured into the little village to see Padre Pio, who, like all true saints, never claimed to be a saint. He had always said he was a poor sinner and was rather embarrassed about the stigmata."

Menotti journeyed with a friend to meet Padre Pio and hear him say mass. "The church was crammed full; there was an awful smell of sick humanity. But what was extraordinary was that when Padre Pio came in from the sacristy, the smell suddenly changed. People talk about the odor of sanctity; well, it really exists. Suddenly there was a new odor, not a perfume, but a mixture of perfume and disinfectant which seemed to purify the air.

"When he came out, the people surged toward him. He wore gloves to hide his stigmata. They tried to touch him, but he would kick and push them away from him, protesting in rough peasant language that one could hardly call saintly. He recited the mass very slowly; it took

Annina (Gabrielle Ruggiero), comatose after her visions, is surrounded by neighbors who want to touch her stigmata wounds.

hours. Everyone stood. It was so hypnotizing, because in the middle of the mass, he would fall into a trance. He would stand for five or ten minutes without moving, as if he were seeing something. Of course, when he said mass, he would remove his gloves, and every time he would open his arms to say 'Dominus vobiscum,' you could see these huge bleeding scars on both sides of his hands. . . .

"When the mass was finished, I was so preoccupied and so assailed by so many conflicting emotions that I fell into a great unhappiness. I can't even tell you *why* I was so unhappy at that moment, but the whole scene was very disquieting. I remember it was in the middle of winter; it was very dark and the sun was just beginning to rise. Finally I had an audience with Padre Pio. He said to me, 'Do you believe in the Church?' And I said, 'No, i'm afraid I don't believe in the Church.' He asked, 'But who do you think gave you this great gift and talent that you have?' I replied, 'I did not say I don't believe in God, I only said I did not believe in the Church.' Padre Pio looked at me for a time, then said, 'Why do you come to see me, then? I believe in the Church, and if you don't believe in the Church, then you must think I am an idiot.'

"I didn't really know why I came to see him; that was the mystery. Somehow I wanted *him* to tell me why I came to him. At any rate, Padre Pio failed me. I think if he had simply taken me in his arms, I would immediately have gone back into the arms of the Church. Part of me had such a need for that. Still, it was quite an experience—one I never forgot. . . . I did have the feeling that I had met a saint."

Whether Menotti was possessed by the presence of Padre Pio or guided by his own inner doubts, the writing of *The Saint of Bleecker Street* in large part can only be described as inspired. Yet, it is one of Menotti's most derivative scores, perhaps because he meant it to be a questioning of his musical and ethnic heritage as well as his religious legacy. Of profound influence on Menotti as well was the death of a young painter and intimate friend, Milena Barilli, who had designed the costumes for his ballet *Sebastian* and who took her own life. Her self-portrait as a nun

receiving the stigmata is reproduced on the cover of the score of *The Saint.*

To Olin Downes (in his review of *The Saint* for the New York *Times*), those who inhabit this opera are "the lineal descendants of the Sicilians of *Cavalleria rusticana* and the players' troupe in *I pagliacci,* and the composer himself is in the lineage of the Mascagnis and Puccinis." The total effect of *The Saint,* however, is entirely individual and unmistakably Menottian not only in its musical stance but in the solidity and sureness of the writing. The first act, for example, moves with a swiftness of expression and cleanness of vision very few of Menotti's predecessors have commanded, characteristics he would still be able to summon twenty-five years later when writing *Juana La Loca* for Beverly Sills.

The devotional nature of the work is established from the outset by a dozen bars of hushed, sustained music *(andante mosso),* which pours from the orchestra like shafts of light breaking through a church window, cutting into the dark interior of a sanctuary. Softly there rises out of the orchestra an ascending, diatonic choral strain that symbolizes Annina and her faith, chords that bear a strong resemblance to the set of rising modal harmonies used by Puccini to characterize Suor Angelica.

The opening scene is set in a cold-water flat on Bleecker Street in New York's Greenwich Village, the heart of the Italian quarter in the city. It is shared by Annina and her brother Michele. As the curtain rises over rapid figurations in the orchestra (the largest instrumental ensemble Menotti has used since *The Island God*), a group of neighbors is seen—some standing, some kneeling—chanting the litany. In the midst of the prayers, a young man tiptoes to the open bedroom door and peeks in. "She moves, she weeps," he tells the others, describing the scene in Annina's room. "They hold her down, they wipe her cheeks. They have moved her to the chair. Her eyes are glassy like the dead. I believe her visions have begun." In the outer room, a shabbily dressed woman—Maria Corona—speaks out impatiently: "I'm tired of waiting . . . my knees hurt. Who can promise my child will be cured? One always hears about these miracles, then nothing happens."

Chiding Maria Corona for her lack of faith, Assunta and Carmela—Annina's closest friends—begin reciting past miracles attributed to Annina. A simple figure in the orchestra accompanies their testimonials, which sound at first like harmonized plain chant. "Once she saw St. Michael with two young archangels. Once she saw St. Peter with the keys of heaven. Once as she was praying the devil came and set her clothes on fire. She's a dove, she's burning flame, she's a lily, the cooling wave."

Their piety, however, makes little impression on Maria Corona, who demands, "If she can work these miracles . . . let's see them." With this, the orchestra begins its rapid figures anew as anticipation onstage builds into a full-scale choral ensemble. One of the recurrent features here and throughout *The Saint* is not only the range of the choral writing, but its variety. In none of his other operas does Menotti make the chorus so protagonistic, and only in concert pieces such as *The Death of the Bishop of Brindisi* and his setting of the mass does he manage again to weave so multicolored and magnificent a choral tapestry.

As the chorus peaks and breaks off, Don Marco appears on the threshold of the bedroom. He announces that Annina's visions have begun. "We will carry Annina out," he tells the

crowd to thin orchestral chords, "but I warn you, you must behave. She's very ill. If any one of you goes near her and tries to touch her bleeding wounds, I'll throw all of you out of here." The eerie, mystic ascending chords heard at the outset return as Don Marco and two neighbors carry the semiconscious Annina into the room. Her face is very pale and bears the marks of great suffering.

As the chorus chants in a highly polyphonic style a Latin hymn, Annina is gently placed in a chair. At first her eyes are closed in deathlike stillness as all kneel about her, the singing becoming more and more impassioned. As the chorus climaxes, Annina screams as though injured, and her body is convulsed by pain. Against heavy, sighing figurations in the orchestra, she begins an extended narrative that is more a scena than an aria. Though it is sectional like Magda Sorel's "To this we've come" in *The Consul*, it has far less of a sense of starting and stopping, of being a composite of phrases. This scene, however, is every bit as portentous for a singing actress and leaves the illusion of being more sustained and through-composed.

With a tormented expression as if fighting a fearful force, Annina begins: "Oh, sweet Jesus, spare me this agony. Too great a pain is this for one so weak. Ah, my aching heart, must you again withstand the trial?" The orchestra stops, and Annina opens her eyes, which have until now been tightly closed. "Where am I? Who are these people? When have I seen this road before, when this barren hill?" Against low-lying dissonant clusters of chords, whose density is pierced by the glare of distant trumpet fanfares, Annina rises as if in a trance and slowly moves through those kneeling about her. She flails her arms as if fighting her way through a crowd attempting to glimpse she knows not what, but something that draws her against her will.

As the polytonalities in the orchestra give way to an elongated statement of the "Annina" theme, she cries out in both agony and ecstasy: "I see now! O blinding sight! Oh, pain! Oh, love." The orchestra, stretching and yearning, breaks the tension with a resounding A-major chord. It is another of those splendid theatrical moments that

Menotti with the self-portrait of his close friend Milena Barilli, who painted herself as a nun—one of his inspirations during the composition of *The Saint of Bleecker Street.*

Menotti plots carefully and uses with such telling effect and, happily, with no self-consciousness.

The orchestra quickly contracts in range and dynamics as Annina's vision continues. It is, of course, a vision of the passion of Christ that is unfolding, and staring intensely ahead she describes the soldiers with their "golden armor" and "a purple cloak among them" as the figure of Jesus emerges. "Dust in His mouth and salt of bitter tears. His cheeks ribboned with blood shed by the sharp and cruel crown. But His eyes! Whoever saw in a man's eyes such patient love?"

A flutter in the woodwinds answered by thirds and seconds placed high in the strings suddenly intrudes as Annina's eyes search the imaginary crowd before alighting on Christ's mother. "Why Mary, why did you come?" she asks pathetically in a vivid phrase that hits with enormous impact after the musical ambiguities that have preceded it. In an impulsive and soaring phrase, Annina begs, "Oh, women, take her home. It is her very flesh that will be torn by spear and nail." Rising out of the orchestra are further martial strains—fanfare figures built on the intervals of a fifth and a fourth. Superimposed on these is Annina's motive, which returns again and again persistently until obliterated by a crushing anvillike blow in the orchestra. With an agonized cry on high C, Annina falls back into the chair. Like a reverberating echo from out of the orchestral din, the chorus in hushed awe sings, "How pale her cheeks . . . Christ has died."

Suddenly, Annina's limp hands slowly open revealing the bleeding stigmata as the running, nervous orchestra figures from the beginning of the act return. Little by little the neighbors crowd about her hysterically, trying to touch her wounds. At the height of the raging ensemble that ensues, Michele appears at the door screaming, "Stop it! Out of here, all of you!" Intimidated, the crowd falls back and Annina's motif is quietly outlined by the orchestra as Michele tenderly caresses his sister's hair and then carries her back into the bedroom.

The neighbors leave singing a dirgelike chorus in which some ask for forgiveness for Michele, and some bemoan, "He drowns our sun. He bars the light from Heaven's gates." Finding Don Marco still in the apartment, Michele orders him out as well: "Doctors she needs, rather than priests and candles. If we were rich this wouldn't happen. Rich people have no visions except in hospitals." The priest attempts to reason with Michele but he reminds Don Marco that Annina is "a sickly child who never grew, a simple mind in a pain-pierced body."

In descending phrases more reminiscent of the mood of *The Consul* than any other section of *The Saint*, Michele rants against "those people who create your saints. They worship God out of defeat. They look for wonders to forget their poverty, to redeem their failure." He demands to know if Don Marco believes Annina to be a saint. "A priest is not a judge but only a guide," he replies. "Then I must be her guide," Michele responds, "for I am her brother." "So are we all," Don Marco reminds him quietly. "It is not I who is your rival, but God himself. How can one fight what cannot be measured? Who can hold back the avalanche or quench the raging fire? What God decrees we can only witness. Who, by God's love is wounded and by its tide encircled, is then forever drawn into its tumultuous vortex."

As Don Marco leaves, Michele slams the door after him in frustration as the orchestra elaborates on musical ideas from Annina's vision. This postlude melts into the first of two orchestral interludes. It uses the impatient "waiting" music one further time, and to it, Menotti adds two different strains that will characterize the celebration of San Gennaro, a saint whose feast day is the occasion of a holiday and parade in New York's Little Italy. The first is the carefree noises of the festivity, while the second reflects the heavier, more measured processional music—in other words, the secular and sacred sides of the occasion. The orchestral scoring and textures here were heralded three years earlier in *Apocalypse*, particularly its last movement, "The Militant Angels." As these two thematic elements play themselves out, the curtain rises on an empty lot on Mulberry Street, flanked by tenements.

Annina and Carmela, armed with gold paper and thread, are sewing stars in a white dress worn by Concettina, who will be an angel in the San

Gennaro parade. From a nearby window, Assunta is heard rocking her child to sleep. She sings a lullaby in Italian *(andante calmo)* that is based on an actual *ninna nanna* from Friuli, a district northeast of Venice. It is filled with cross relations—major and minor chords sounded together—a device Menotti had just explored effectively in his Violin Concerto. They soothe and disturb at the same time, and the scene is an example of the affectionate way in which Menotti portrays the Italian-Americans in *The Saint*, an affection that will be intensified in the second act.

The lullaby's strains are lost in an explosion of sound as a group of children, also dressed as angels, rush in to get Concettina. She runs off after them, her angel wings limp and her gold crown askew. Left alone with Annina, Carmela tells her friend she has decided not to become a nun because Salvatore has asked her to marry him. "Will God be angry with me?" she asks through her tears of joy and fear. But Annina reminds her, "Your promise wasn't made to God, only to me, and I release you." Annina promises to come to Carmela's wedding if Carmela will come to hers as a bride of Christ.

Assunta joins them, and as she sits next to the two girls she muses, "Sometimes I wonder what heaven will be like. Shall I have a chance to sleep there? Tell me Annina, did you ever get a glimpse of heaven?" In a simple, quite naïve arietta *(andante affettuoso)* Annina tells her how St. Michael came to her and asked, "What is it you wish, my child?" Her wish was to see the golden gates of paradise. St. Michael took Annina on his back to heaven where St. Peter welcomed her saying, "You shall eat golden bread and wear sun-woven clothes." As Carmela and Assunta repeat the promise, Maria Corona runs in dragging her half-witted son behind her. She has heard that Michele refused to let Annina take part in the San Gennaro parade, and that the Sons of San Gennaro have vowed to take her by force.

In a nervous ensemble, the women exchange their fears and beg Annina not to go home. Maria Corona vows to defend Annina for, "since the day you touched my son, he—who hasn't spoken since he was born—has begun to speak.

Show Annina . . . *bello mio.* Say Mam-ma." In little more than a grunt, the boy manages to form the two syllables as Michele enters the lot. Ordering the others to leave him alone with his sister, Michele attempts to explain his wild feelings and actions.

This scene goes to the very heart of the conflict that generates the drama of *The Saint,* as does the scene between Michele and Desideria in the next act. Both underline Michele's possible incestuous feelings for his sister and his inability to admit them. Desperately, he asks Annina if she believes herself to be a saint. "Oh, no!" she responds. But, continues Michele, "Do you really believe it is Jesus who appears to you?" "Yes, that I know," she replies simply, as the theme of her saintliness rises in the orchestra. It returns with mounting fervor with each of her answers to Michele's questions, particularly when she tells her brother, "I do not ask to be believed, but I believe."

Frustrated, Michele demands to know why God

has chosen her of all people. "Perhaps because I love him," Annina answers ecstatically. "But you love God as if He were human," Michele counters. "How else can I love Him since I am human?" Annina replies. The quality of the two and their cross-purposes are summed up in a stormy duet *(allegro moderato, ma con agitazione)* which Michele begins with, "Sister I shall hide you and take you away." In a matched phrase, Annina responds, "Brother I shall lead you and show you the way."

The love of brother and sister: Annina (Virginia Copeland) with Michele (Davis Cunningham)—original Broadway production.

The intense passion of the duet is cut off abruptly by the sounds of the approaching procession. Annina tries to force Michele to go indoors and avoid the crowd but he stubbornly refuses. A row of women slowly pass by the vacant lot holding lighted candles, followed by men with holy banners. Both groups are singing a slow, sustained anthem tinged with measured, quiet fanaticism. A band behind the chorus then bursts into a vigorous march, and from the crowd a group of young men break off and enter the lot. While one of them holds Annina, the others leap upon Michele and subdue him.

In order to protect Michele, Annina promises to go with them if they do not harm her brother. Agreeing, the men tie Michele to a wire fence that separates the lot from the street and he is left hanging there as though crucified. In a moment of extraordinary theatricality, the men lift Annina on their shoulders and rejoin the procession. Michele's cries for help are soon drowned out by the chanting and the band mu-

sic, which grows more insistent as an elaborate effigy of San Gennaro rolls by.

As the procession moves out of sight, Desideria appears in a nearby doorway. She slowly approaches Michele and unties his wrists. He falls to the ground sobbing as Desideria kneels next to him, kissing him repeatedly. With a short abrasive outburst from the orchestra the curtain falls rapidly.

The second act is set in a typical Italian-American restaurant, festooned with multi-colored paper chains and lanterns. The curtain rises over a sustained, harmonically ambiguous chord over which the wedding party for Carmela and Salvatore stare at the audience in smiling stillness. They are having their photograph taken. With the snapping of the picture, the orchestra releases the held chord and launches into a bright, scampering bit of festive music. Wine is brought in and everyone cheers the bridal couple as a young man, glass in hand, jumps on a table for a toast to Carmela and Salvatore.

These toasts are an old Italian tradition that still survives in Tuscany, and Menotti remembers having heard them not only in his childhood but later at an Italian-American marriage in Philadelphia. These short poems, supposedly improvised by the singer, are known as *stornelli*. The crowd echoes the first two of these *stornelli*, and following the third (sung by Michele) a huge wedding cake is brought through the restaurant and into the adjacent banquet room.

As the guests follow the cake, Annina tells Salvatore in a tender *arioso*, "Be good to her, be kind. Of all my friends, I love her the most. . . . So gentle is her heart, so sweet and gay." Carmela embraces Annina lovingly and, with Salvatore, they join the other guests. As the sounds of merriment are heard offstage, Desideria enters against *secco, Consul*-like piano chords. She asks the barman to call Michele as the orchestra limns the theme first heard at her entry in Act I. Seeing Desideria, Michele freezes at the door leading to the banquet room. She has been turned out of her house, Desideria tells him accusingly that because of her affair with Michele, she was the only one not invited to the wedding.

"I never asked for your love," Michele says defensively. "You offered it to me and, at the time, no price was mentioned." This leads to a short *duettino* built of a series of parallel phrases— a question or accusation followed by a defense or denial. Finally, the two stare at each other helplessly as the offstage festivities peak and then subside. "Will you take me in there with you?" Desideria asks. Replying that he cannot, for Annina's sake, Desideria explodes: "Always Annina . . . You are bewitched by her . . . She

The wedding of Carmela (Maria Di Gerlando) and Salvatore (David Aiken) toasted by Michele (Poleri).

doesn't love you the way you think. She pities you."

Pianissimo trills overlaid with a jerking, rapid figure in the winds and then the strings invade the orchestra as Desideria describes Annina as "a blinded moth, beating her wings against a lighted window." As the orchestral figures consolidate into tense, tremolo chords, Desideria, in heavily weighted phrases, tells Michele, "I have but one love. My love blooms with the earth." Exasperated, Michele retorts that his sister is "a sick girl. She needs me." But, sneers Desideria, "she doesn't want to be your sister. She wants to be everybody's sister." With cruel persistence she continues to insist that Michele take her into the party, reminding him "that love can turn to hate at the sound of one word, if the word is said too late."

This scene, despite its vivid and poetic imagery and its attractive musical ideas, never quite comes off; it seems cut short before it can fulfill itself. It is the one moment in *The Saint* where Menotti's firm hand momentarily falters. His musical composure returns, however, a few minutes later in a large-scale aria for Michele. The aria is the consequence of Michele's agreeing to take Desideria into the party. As they try to enter the banquet room, Don Marco blocks their way. Michele threatens to strike the priest and the other guests rush to Don Marco's defense. Looking defiantly at the hostile crowd, Michele pours a glass of wine and begins *lento*.

In this extended *scena*, Michele deals forthrightly with the issue of immigrants' clinging to their old ways in a new land. He taunts his friends for living like strangers in America while, at the same time, being ashamed or apologetic for their heritage. He says he wants to "belong to this new world," and then is guilty of the same dichotomy by crying that if he might once see Italy, where "towns are built of stones older than sorrow," he might be proud to say "I am Italian." This is but another instance of the duality that tears at him—his Catholic upbringing and his lack of faith, his challenging of his heritage as he challenged Annina's faith.

The aria is the culmination of long pent-up rage, and it leads Michele in his confusion and questioning to hit out in any direction to wound those who have wounded him. It is the most Italianate and moving section of the score, and Menotti has couched it in intensely melancholy terms, particularly with a nostalgic vocal line that begins in C minor and then reappears, raised a half step to C-sharp minor. It ends with a ringing top C and with Michele throwing his wine in the faces of those about him as he collapses, burying his head in his arms (this section, incidentally, has been reworked and tightened by Menotti since its publication. It is only one of several sections of the score that have been reshaped and that will be reflected eventually in a new edition of the music.)

Annina apologizes for her brother to Carmela and Salvatore, and Don Marco leads the couple and the guests out of the restaurant. When Annina attempts to help her brother up, Desideria mockingly urges him to go with his sister. "It is all clear to me now," she taunts him, "the reason why you will not marry me. . . . It is not with me that you're in love, it is with her!" In the supercharged trio that follows, Michele advances menacingly toward Desideria as she continues to accuse him of desiring his sister, while Annina attempts to restrain Michele. Suddenly he grabs a knife from the bar and plunges it into Desideria, crying, "Bitch." Everyone freezes including the orchestra. After a long pause, Desideria's theme is hammered out *fortissimo*. She takes a few steps forward, her eyes wide open as if searching for something, then collapses. Annina rushes to her side as Michele bolts from the restaurant knocking over tables and chairs in his flight.

Annina attempts to comfort the dying Desideria, and together they pray in one of the opera's most compelling moments. When Desideria dies in Annina's arms, Annina sobs, "Oh, my God, I can wait no longer." The orchestra wells up and weeps along with her as the sound of sirens is heard in the distance and police are seen trying to make their way through the crowd outside the restaurant door.

The first scene of Act III is set in a dimly lit, underground subway stop where Maria Corona tends a newspaper kiosk. A bleak, running figure in the strings signals that Annina is nervously waiting for someone. As Maria Corona approaches Annina and speaks with her, it becomes apparent a meeting has been arranged between the girl and Michele. Maria Corona takes Annina into the kiosk to get warm and asks her if she has seen Michele's picture in the newspapers. "Oh, what a good-looking boy he is." She bemoans the fact that she has spent her life selling papers but has never been mentioned in one. "I guess I'll have to kill somebody to have my picture taken," she adds matter-of-factly.

The music from the opening returns as the rumble of a train is heard. The orchestra becomes bolder and bigger in its insistence as Don Marco appears followed by Michele. Intoning, "May God forgive us all," the priest leaves as an ominous motif is heard in the depths of the orchestra under a tremolo pattern. Obviously in great anguish and unable to control himself, Michele leans against the wall, covering his face with his hands. Annina rushes to him, and the two embrace warmly. "Where are my hopes and my dreams?" Michele asks. "Within a single hour, all was lost. In that one glass of bitter wine, my whole life was drowned." Their duet becomes more urgent as Annina tells her brother that her voices have told her she will soon die. As she solemnly assures him her voices never lie, the mounting theme of her sainthood is heard; it will return a number of times during the scene, often interrupted by intruding, impatient slashes of sound built on material associated with Michele.

When Annina tells Michele she will take the veil, he demands, "What good are you to the world if you can let down your own brother as he cries for help!" After a brief interruption by some passengers and a group of noisy children, their duet continues in a calmer, more lyrical mood. Annina tries to comfort Michele but can no longer reach him. She is already in the grip of a greater force and is slowly being lost to him. This section is the equivalent of what in another would be a love duet, and though it could be classified as such, it is not a duet for two people in love with each other. Instead it is an exchange dealing with two different kinds of love—Michele's implied, incestuous love for Annina and

her simple, unquestioning love for God.

Cursing his sister, Michele pushes her away and disappears up the subway steps. Annina collapses in tears as Maria Corona tries to quiet her. As the curtain falls, the orchestra is engulfed in wind-swept sounds derived from the opening prelude, which describes the noise of the subway. This in turn is resolved by a quietly triumphant tracing of the motif of Annina's

With Don Marco (Leon Lishner) and her friends in attendance, Annina (Ruggiero) takes the veil and dies.

sainthood, expanded gently and hauntingly through a hesitant rhythmic figure that is soon surmounted by Annina's prayer in the final scene played high in the strings.

As the curtain rises on the final scene, we are in Annina's tenement apartment. She is lying back in her armchair, wrapped in a shawl, her eyes closed, her face extremely pale. She is surrounded by her friends and a nun, and a small group of women recite the *"Agnus dei"* from the Ordinary of the Mass. Opening her eyes, Annina calls for Carmela. "My voices have told me that I would take the veil today," she confides to her friend. "What little strength I have, sweet, patient Death has kindly lent me." Over a brief quotation of the party music from the second act, she suddenly bolts forward saying, "If the permission comes today, I have no white dress to

wear." Lovingly, Carmela tells Annina she has brought her own wedding dress for the ceremony.

A young priest enters with a letter for Don Marco. Reading it, he tells Annina, "Prepare yourself for a great joy. The church has granted you your wish. In exaltation Annina cries, "Ah! I knew. My voices told me I would die tonight, but I shall die a bride." Underneath her joy, the orchestra restates the passionate melody that closed the first act after Don Marco had spoken of God's love for his chosen saints. Then in an aria briefly breached by recitative with Carmela, Annina attempts to check her anxieties and prepare herself for the ceremony to come. The second half of this aria contains a melody Menotti borrowed for use in the new music for the film of *The Medium;* he was at work on *The Saint* at the time. This melody bears a resemblance to Annina's saintly theme, and, to Menotti, it expresses blind faith. In the film it accompanied Monica's wistful looking at a white communion dress and in *The Saint* it finds a parallel with Annina's borrowed wedding dress.

As he often does in crucial dramatic moments, Menotti plays with a listener's susceptibility to harmonic suggestions by seesawing between minor and major tonalities, allowing the music to come to rest and into focus only when the doubts and fears in a character's mind have been alleviated. As Annina, with great intensity, finishes her final phrases—"Hold back, O Death, for still a little while, then come at last and make the night eternal for His eternal love"—the orchestra enters serenely into the key of G major.

As she rises from the chair and goes to don her wedding dress in the bedroom, Assunta enters with word that Michele has been seen in the neighborhood and that she is afraid he will try to stop Annina from taking the veil. Don Marco instructs Salvatore to guard the door to the apartment and then begins lighting candles on an impromptu altar. There is a sunburst of C major as the chorus intones a cappella *"Gloria tibi Domine"* and Annina appears in the doorway dressed as a bride. A sense of her anticipation suffuses the room. Don Marco begins the rites, and the chorus chants the *"Kyrie."* It is set in

elaborate polyphonic measures that are in strong contrast to Menotti's chantlike or homophonic settings of excerpts from the liturgy elsewhere in the score.

The chorus swells magnificently on extended melismas on *"Alleluia"* and then breaks off as Annina, now hidden behind a screen, knocks twice, beginning a condensed version of the investiture of a nun drawn from the Catholic liturgy. "What do you ask, my daughter?" says Don Marco. "The mercy of God and the holy habit of religion," responds Annina. A nun leads her to the center of the stage where she kneels as the chorus quietly sings, *"Veni, sposa Christi."* Annina then prostrates herself on the floor, with her hands extended to form a cross. She is covered by a black cloth.

"You are now dead unto the world," Don Marco proclaims. "Henceforth and forever you shall be called Sister Angela," an odd name choice for Menotti to have chosen considering his dislike of Puccini's *Suor Angelica.* As the nun approaches Annina and removes the black cloth, the chorus, having billowed from *pianissimo* to *forte,* intones, *"Ecce quam bonum et quam jucundum."*

At this moment, Michele bursts into the room but is restrained by Salvatore. Everyone turns to look at him but Annina who, completely transfixed, stares at the holy image on the altar. Michele cries out to her, but she hears nothing. "You are too late, Michele," Don Marco says quietly and continues the ceremony, next cutting Annina's hair and placing it on a tray. At this, Michele begins weeping, and then, controlling himself, he seems to accept the inevitable and for the remainder of the ceremony stares dumbly ahead as though incredulous.

As Don Marco holds out Annina's wedding ring, with a supreme effort she forces herself to take a step toward him but then falls to the floor. Carmela helps break her fall and then cradles Annina in her arms as Don Marco lifts her lifeless hand and places the gold ring on her finger. For the last time, the orchestra glows with Annina's ascending motif, pitted against the theme used in the *Medium* film, and on a shimmering *pianissimo* chord, the curtain slowly falls.

Maria Golovin

Opera in three acts,
libretto in English by the composer

Donato (a blind youth)	Bass-baritone
His Mother	Contralto
Agata (her maid)	Mezzo-soprano
Maria Golovin	Soprano
Trottolò (Maria's young son)	Boy soprano
Dr. Zuckertanz (his tutor)	Tenor
Prisoner-of-War	Baritone
Servant	Non-singing

World premiere at the American Theater of the United States Pavilion at the Brussels Universal and International Exposition, Belgium, August 20, 1958. First performance on Broadway at the Martin Beck Theatre, November 5, 1958. Published by Belwin-Mills in English and Italian. Scored for three flutes, three oboes, three clarinets, two bassoons, four trumpets, three horns, three trombones, tuba, timpani, percussion, harp, strings.

Menotti's last opera to be produced on Broadway was commissioned by the National Broadcasting Company, which later televised it, after its successful world premiere. *Maria Golovin* played only five performances in New York before closing, unfairly branding it a failure. But it is an important and special piece among Menotti's stage works. The problem on Broadway was not the score or the opera's effectiveness as musical theater or even the mixed reviews it received. Rather, it was the fact that Menotti entrusted the work to theatrical interests that were less than idealistic.

Producer David Merrick attended the premiere of *Maria Golovin* in Brussels and offered to bring it to Broadway the following fall. Though the producers of Menotti's previous Broadway pieces—Chandler Cowles and Efrem Zimbalist, Jr.—had promised to present *Maria Golovin* as well, NBC accepted Merrick's proposal instead. Merrick was subsequently offered the musical *La Plume de Ma Tante*, and believing it would be a hit, and needing a theater for it, he closed *Maria Golovin* prematurely. It was a crushing blow not only for Menotti but also for the pioneering of American opera outside of traditional opera houses. It was also a sad con-

clusion to a prodigious phase in Menotti's career.

Menotti has said he created *Maria Golovin* because he wanted to write "a conventional love story." In *Amelia* he made fun of love, and in *The Old Maid* he treated it cynically. While *The Con-*

Richard Cross and Franca Duval, the Donato and Maria of the Brussels world premiere, prepare their roles under Menotti's watchful eye, 1958.

sul and *The Medium* are not love stories, per se, the undertone of love in each is unmistakable, be it the irrational love of husband and wife that leads to the death of one, or the pathetic love of the mute Toby for Monica. Though *The Saint* is a love story of sorts, the spiritual love of the childlike Annina for Christ and the unacknowledged love of Michele for his sister are treated symbolically.

"In our century," Menotti has reflected, "love has been so thoroughly dissected that it no longer bears its former physiognomy. Neither the love of Petrarch nor that of Werther is possible or plausible among us. It is curious, nevertheless, that we are still deeply moved by them. May it not be that Plato is right after all and that only the idea of love is real—our dissected love being but a dead image?"

While *Maria Golovin* is a real love story, it is hardly "a conventional one." The story is warped and made complex by the potent intrusion of jealousy. Menotti subscribes to the definition of love advanced by Marcel Proust—"Love is space and time measured by the heart"—and like Proust, he has been unable to separate love from jealousy. "It is curious," he has said, "but the things I've been most ashamed of in my life were those I've done out of jealousy. People who have never felt the pangs of jealousy feel *Maria Golovin* much less than those who have. Not everyone understands that concept of love.

"I've done things in the name of love that are unworthy, even of the more unscrupulous side of my character—I mean steaming letters open, looking through keyholes. Like all jealous people, I follow the usual pattern. I hope to be betrayed so that I could feed that horrible monster, because jealousy is a hungry monster which, however, never dies of hunger. Fortunately, I think I've killed the monster in me. But for a long time it was a great shadow in my life and made me suffer a great deal."

Menotti has said that "love is born of faith, lives on hope and dies of charity," and in *Maria Golovin* (as in all his operas), he treats this primal emotion in an individual way. His imagination is never reduced to the ordinary boy-meets-girl, boy-loses-girl formula. Menotti probes beneath

the sexual surface of a relationship to search for reasons for mutual attraction and the development of a relationship. It could be jealousy as in *Maria Golovin*, pity or sympathy for the afflicted (*The Medium*), or concern for the dependent (*The Saint*) or the terrorized (*The Consul*). He responds to and treats compassionately love in all forms and guises without preaching or taking a moralistic stand.

What begins as a tender tale in *Maria Golovin* ends as an agonizing struggle between two people in the name of love. Complicating the plot is the fact Menotti made his hero blind. In Donato we have another of the physically handicapped whom he uses symbolically and who tellingly heighten the pathos of a story. Donato finds his counterparts in Toby, Anna Gomez, Maria Corona's son and, to a lesser extent, Amahl.

It is Donato's blindness that makes his jealousy and his possessiveness so infinitely poignant. Though Donato is a young man, it is not hard to believe he regards Maria as possibly his last hope of personal fulfillment and happiness. When this hope is threatened, Donato's desperation, his lack of logic and rationality in coping with the situation, is not only understandable but riveting.

Menotti did not conceive Donato as a blind man, however, simply to elicit pity for him nor because "love is blind," but "because jealousy is a form of blinding sickness." To Menotti, Donato was a prisoner of this sickness, and so he surrounds him in the libretto with symbols of captivity, such as birdcages and prisoners of war. The whole opera turns on Donato's fight against this double darkness in himself. "That is why the ending," Menotti feels, "is of the utmost importance to the plot. It shows Donato freeing himself, not by actually killing Maria, but by shooting the ghost of his jealousy, just as Baba shot the ghost of her fear in *The Medium*. In other words, he never really sees the real Maria Golovin, but only an obsessive image of her which he has created within himself. He has to kill the image in order to kill his love and regain his sanity."

As in *Amelia* and *The Consul*, a childhood incident was brought into play in the creation of

Maria (Duval) and the blind Donato (Cross) in the NBC Opera Theater telecast of *Maria Golovin*, staged by composer in early 1959.

Maria Golovin. An aunt of Menotti's owned a "huge and depressing villa" in the composer's hometown in Italy, and one summer she rented it to a countess, her young son and the boy's tutor. Menotti remembered the child as a very affectionate boy with red hair who looked frightened most of the time. On certain days, Menotti and one of his brothers were allowed to come and play with the boy, sometimes staying for lunch. "I remember sitting at the table and noticing the Contessa had brought with her a little whip," Menotti recalls. "Each time her son would deviate from good table manners, she would pick up the whip and strike his hands. The boy's name was Trottolò."

Many years later, following the premiere of *Maria Golovin,* at La Scala, Menotti met Count Lulling, the owner of the renowned Palladian masterpiece Villa Maser outside Vicenza. The count, who had heard the performance, questioned Menotti closely about the character of the little boy and why Menotti had chosen to call him Trottolò. Menotti recounted the story of the countess and her son. To his amazement, Count Lulling replied, "But I am that boy. I am Trottolò. But I never thought you were *that* Gian Carlo!"

To Menotti, the problems of writing a libretto about love were twofold: "To be able to keep the language as simple as possible without becoming prosaic, and to keep the action to the very essentials without losing motivating urgency." In other words, "A libretto is not a play."

In *Maria Golovin,* Menotti reaffirms the maturity so proudly proclaimed in *The Saint,* and he adds to it another quality that is part of the assured artist—repose. There are, of course, many traces of the younger Menotti, for whatever a man learns, or despite how he grows, he casts the same shadow and leaves the same fingerprints. But in *Maria Golovin* we find these traces largely in the details of the score. The overall work is an entity virtually unto itself, with page after page that owes nothing to any other piece.

A clue to this individuality is planted at the beginning of the score, for *Maria Golovin* has an unmistakable impressionistic cast to its music and the conversational vocal lines of its characters. There are few set pieces, and those we do find in the course of the opera have neither prelude nor postlude; they are woven into the fabric of the whole. This fact intimates that if *Maria Golovin* owes anything to anyone, the debt is more literary than musical. As others have pointed out, there is an atmosphere to the drama and the music that can be termed Proustian. This impression is heightened by Menotti's use of thematic material derived from a still unfinished dance work based on Proust's *À l'ombre des jeunes filles en fleurs.*

To Samuel Chotzinoff, the man behind the commissioning of *Maria Golovin* for NBC, the Proustian dramatic elements in the opera are two—"a disturbing, sometimes beneficent, sometimes painful awareness of time, of the ticking of the clock, which instantly relegates the present moment to the past, which in turn through the pathos of distance instantly becomes more treasurable than the present, and an unrelenting, an almost clinical examination of the progression of sexual jealousy."

Chotzinoff believes that Donato's need for unquestioning love harks back to Proust's tortured, more mature character Swann, and that the rapid advance and development of Donato's jealousy is akin to the agonizing progress of the disease in the soul of the generous and gentle Swann. Finally, Chotzinoff remarks that the music of *Maria Golovin* appears to have been dictated by the characters of the drama themselves.

"It is almost as if these fictional people had forced the composer to act as a medium between themselves and the public. And Menotti placed at their disposal a musical and literary equipment that had absorbed and digested all the technique of his craft, including his own former contributions, and was at last free to express the very modern delicate nuances of the story simply and directly, with not a note wasted, not a harmony or an orchestral color unmotivated. . . .

"With inspired prescience, Menotti makes use of a single leitmotif, a succession of the second, third, fourth and fifth notes of the scale, the

'How do you do?' with which Maria Golovin first greets Donato in the opening scene. These rungs of the scale are somehow touched with the wonder and pathos of new love; and throughout the opera the little theme flies aloft like a flag, now triumphant, waving, now drooping at half-mast, now fluttering in rags as in a bitter wind, but always in transformation, a palpable symbol of Donato's joy, helplessness or despair. In the whole of opera I know of no composer, Wagner excepted, who has poetically implied and conveyed so much with so little."

Twenty-five bars of *adagio* constitute the quietly tense prelude to *Maria Golovin*. The first ten are yearning, questioning phrases, whose rising patterns contradict an underlying B-flat pedal point. The effect is of *Pelléas et Mélisande* through a glass darkly. As the prelude switches from simple to compound time, the music turns affirmative and for the first time settles into the key it has intimated from the outset (the initial ambiguity will, however, assert itself once again before the curtain rises).

The first scene is the somewhat shabby living room of an old villa, perhaps in Italy or Switzerland, shortly after the Second World War. Strewn about the overcrowded room are empty birdcages of different shapes and sizes. The feeling is one of oppression, as though the people who inhabit the room are prisoners and this is their cell. Donato is sitting on a sofa finishing a small birdcage while Agata looks intently through the window out into the garden. As she counts the retinue arriving with Maria Golovin, who has rented the upstairs apartment for the summer, a busy, non-*legato* melody—like a bird pecking at seed—is piped over yet another pedal point.

Cataloging the arrivals for Donato—three maids, a cook, a tutor, a chauffeur—she adds gloomily, "Nothing for me. The tutor looks like a puppet and the chauffeur is old as an owl." Spotting Trottolò, she strikes a comic attitude and begins a mocking singsong farewell to the family china, certain "the young devil" will break it. She then describes Maria: "A fur coat large enough for both of us . . . blue scarf and a corsage of violets . . . so many people to help her

out of the car you might think she could not walk alone . . . your mother bowing and scraping before them as if they were movie stars." She breaks off her mimicry of the scene to open the door as the Mother and the others approach the house.

To the same sprightly *scherzo* tune that accompanies most of Agata's running narrative, the Mother enters the hall followed by Maria, Trottolò and Dr. Zuckertanz. Each in turn is introduced to Donato, together with a bit of music that will later be enlarged upon as a character portrait of each. With Dr. Zuckertanz it is a series of finicky, sharp chords and with Maria it is her quiet, questioning upward scale.

Not realizing Donato is blind, Maria extends her hand to him as the orchestra harmonically enriches her theme until it glows. A gesture from Zuckertanz makes Maria aware of the situation, and she walks to Donato and his extended hand. But Donato, unconscious of her movement, drops his hand and for an embarrassing few moments Maria is left standing awkwardly in front of him. She then leads Trottolò over to meet Donato as a bright but soft, almost shy tune accompanies the introduction. "I know that we shall all be good friends," Donato tells the boy. "I can be trusted with all kinds of secrets. A blind man never talks."

The Mother, who had been diverted by Agata to the kitchen, returns and offers to show Maria her apartment. The others join them and Donato is left alone until Agata enters with tea. "Tell me Agata," he asks, "is she beautiful?" Maria's theme returns tenderly in the orchestra. "There is something in her voice; it filled my darkness with a soft, golden glow." His reverie is shattered by Agata's answer: "Why shouldn't she be beautiful? Women like her spend their whole day patching up their faces. Buy me a hat just like this, and a scented scarf such as this, and I too shall be very beautiful." She dons both and parades in front of Donato, laughing. Annoyed, he snatches the scarf away when it brushes against his face.

To a sad strain, Agata—who obviously loves Donato and resents Maria—asks, "Don't I stand a chance, *signorino*? Not even with you who are blind?" (In the original version, Donato responds, "I was not always blind, and I still remember you," a line deleted from the printed score.) Crushed, she retreats to the kitchen, and Donato, left alone, rubs Maria's scarf against his cheek and then quickly drops it as he hears his mother returning. She enters with Trottolò, inspects the tea tray and then goes to the kitchen.

Again left alone, Donato runs his hand over a nearby chair until he locates once again Maria's scarf. Slowly, almost with guilt, he brings it to his nostrils and then to his lips as the orchestra enlarges on Maria's rising motive (this time, however, very slowly and in a brighter key). As his face contorts with frustration and despair, Maria is seen coming down the stairs. Catching sight of Donato, she stops, both embarrassed and obviously moved. Like an animal who senses danger, he throws the scarf back down on the chair, and Maria silently retraces her steps up the stairs. From the landing, she announces her presence with gentle coughing.

Donato asks who it is, as Maria descends into the room inquiring, "Am I too early?" Donato invites her in, adding that Trottolò has gone to the kitchen in search of cookies. "Has he been a bother?" Maria asks. "Oh, no," Donato replies, "this house needs the voice of children." Their talk then turns to the house and its gardens but is soon interrupted by the distant sound of shouting and the martial noise of drums and trumpets. Donato explains to Maria that nearby is a prisoner-of-war camp, and as Maria goes to the window and opens it, a chorus of prisoners can be heard singing a mournful melody to a marchlike accompaniment.

Closing the window, Maria confesses, "I would not have come here had I known. For over four years my husband has been a prisoner-of-war abroad. All winter I haven't heard from him. I fear he might be ill." Changing the subject, Donato inquires if Maria saw him kissing the scarf. When she answers yes, he asks her forgiveness. He tells her how lonely his life has been after losing his sight in the war three years earlier. "The worst of it," he continues, "is that I cannot think anymore. When I had my eyes, I could close them and find peace. Now I imagine things, I see things, things that are not always there."

In an effort to make light of Donato's affliction, Maria offers to read to him and play Chopin and Debussy on the piano. In a loving, flowing narrative, she tells him she also paints— "useless things women usually paint: bouquets of flowers on checkered tablecloths and flying sails on sunny seas." The accompanying melody and harmony for this section are firmly seated in G-flat major, and both are as unruffled and uncomplicated as Maria's pictures. "I must confess," she continues, "that at times I still enjoy reading horrible books where people die of broken hearts and love is always love at first sight." With this confession, the rising scale returns, suggesting that Maria's words are as applicable to her emotions as to her taste in books.

The aria quickly reverts to its original, simplistic mood following this diversion, as though Maria, suddenly embarrassed by her inner feelings, had retreated posthaste to a mask of pleasantries to hide her vulnerability. The second half of the aria was extensively reworked by Menotti after the premiere and the recording. In place of Maria's more innocuous desire to paint Trottolò and her husband, Menotti (in the printed score) has her poetically dreaming of painting "those subtle things that are beyond what people see. Oh, how I envy those hands that can arrest without blunders or doubts those visual longings of the heart which make us think there is an artist in us all."

Menotti has also recast Donato's reaction to these words. In place of the original platitude, "You are a great painter in my eyes," Donato now tells Maria, "You paint with your voice some wonderful pictures in my eyes." When she inquires about the architectural drawings and models that are stacked on a drawing table in the corner, half covered by a piece of oilcloth, Donato tells her, "I dreamed once of building houses for men. Now I build cages for birds. I build them to make shapes, not to hold a prisoner." Offering Maria one, he admonishes her to "be careful—the cage you take already holds a prisoner."

Maria's scale pattern surfaces deep in the orchestra in an uneasy, *staccato* form as Donato asks if he may touch her face. He then adds what the music has already asked before him: "Are you afraid?" "Perhaps a little," Maria responds before walking toward him with an outstretched hand. Delicately, as if his fingers were sensitive antennae, Donato slowly passes first one hand, then both over Maria's face and hair. She is at first intrigued and then tense and upset by his

chord is gone, the most rare, irreplaceable records by that great interpreter, Mademoiselle Felicia Fernanda La Fosse."

Here, Menotti indulges in a bit of private fun at Zuckertanz's expense, by having the orchestra play a transposed and "cracked" statement of the E-major Prelude from Book I of *The Well-Tempered Clavichord*, followed by the subject of the C-minor Fugue, also from Book I, which quickly

hypnotizing touch.

The music of the prelude accompanies this scene, to which Menotti has grafted elements of other musical ideas introduced thus far in the opera. As the music builds to a passionate climax, Maria gently pulls away, disturbed and almost frightened, leaving Donato standing in the center of the room with his arms outstretched. The intensity of the moment is allayed with the reappearance of the Mother and Trottolò, followed by Agata carrying a cake for the tea. A moment later, Zuckertanz appears in a state of great distress. "Broken," he cries, as the orchestra seconds him in angry, cascading arpeggios. "Split in two! The whole *Well-Tempered Clavi-*

breaks off, like Mademoiselle La Fosse's discs. Later in the opera, Menotti will draw the pretensions of the tutor in even sharper lines. It is Zuckertanz's artificiality and idiosyncrasies that contrast with and point up the warmer and truer feelings of those around him.

To calm Zuckertanz, the Mother offers him a cup of tea. The tutor asks about the birdcage Maria is holding, and awkwardly she tells him it is a gift for Trottolò. Hearing Maria's lie, Donato (who has been standing by the piano) steps forward with a pained expression on his face and suddenly throws a chair across the room. Everyone looks at him in amazement. "I'm sorry," he excuses himself, "but when you live in darkness,

Remembrance of things past: the Act II trio for Agata (Ruth Kobart), Donato's Mother (Patricia Neway) and Maria (Duval).

the most innocent lie becomes impossible to bear." "But who lied to you?" the Mother asks anxiously. "Somebody will, Mother," Donato replies calmly, and during a slow blackout onstage, the Mother looks meaningfully at Maria. Welling up from the orchestra is a running triplet pattern that inaugurates the first of four interludes in the opera. The triplets are cut abruptly short by the forceful return of the opening pedal-point figure which, in turn, is forced to give way to a heaving, rhapsodic melody derived from the triplet figure:

Once this idea has exhausted itself, the pedal-point figure returns, binding the end of the interlude into the second scene of Act I. It is late afternoon a month later. Agata, dressed to go out, is talking with Donato and it is soon evident that Donato and Maria have become intimately involved and that Agata is very unhappy about it. She makes one innuendo after another, planting the first seeds of distrust like a female Iago. She alludes to Maria's "past" and "the type of woman she is," all of this in fitful, darting vocal phrases. Finally, Donato cuts her short as his mother enters, dressed for church. To a motive cut from the fabric of *The Consul,* the two women exit. Making certain he is alone, Donato then runs to the back wall and knocks against it three times with his cane. The signal is repeated from upstairs.

With intense expectation, Donato waits for Maria. In a boyish way he smooths his hair, quickly arranges the room as best he can and places a braille writing tablet on the table in front of the sofa. During this, an expressive, long-lined theme develops in the orchestra and gradually accelerates and grows more and more intense. At its climax, Maria appears and rushes into Donato's arms. The orchestra then sings out rapturously before collecting itself and returning to a calmer mood.

After a kiss, Maria and Donato exchange pleasantries in easy conversational patterns. Donato has begun to instruct Maria in braille, and during her lesson the orchestra limns the expressive triplet melody from the first interlude, which creates a mood of the greatest intimacy, as though the world of Donato and Maria is no bigger than the room in which they are sitting. With the tablet, Donato writes "I love you" in braille, which Maria quickly repeats. "You do not read, you guess," Donato admonishes her, making her finish the sentence: "I love you too much; I am afraid."

"Why afraid?" she asks. "Can love make you afraid?" "Oh, yes," Donato explains: "Lost in vastness, you are crucified by noon. There is no direction, there is no escape." Then, in a passionate *arioso,* Donato tells Maria he wishes she might see "the shapes and colors of your voice. Like a dark, violet wave, it breaks over and drowns a deserted town by the sea" (here, the orchestra swells and ebbs in an almost impressionistic way). "It is bittersweet, like burnt sugar; it is fleeting like the dew on the spider's web. At times so near it cuts and burns the branch that grows within the flesh. At times so far the whole world stops to listen."

Donato's arioso flows on into Maria's response: "Listen then, listen. From the very first time you touched my face I felt that I belonged to you." Again they kiss and then fall into silence, with Maria holding Donato in a protective embrace. Without moving but in a quiet and tormented voice, Donato asks Maria if this is the first time she has been unfaithful to her husband. "Of course," she replies as an agitated, twisting motive snakes out of the orchestra—it signals Donato's incipient jealousy. "To tell the truth, I misbehaved a little last year." To rocking arpeggios, Maria recounts a summer by the sea and "some charming neighbors . . . they had a son. He was so young, barely nineteen. I believe it was his first love. We used to take long walks together by the sea. Next to me he would blush and tremble like a girl. . . . One day I let him kiss me."

"What happened then?" Donato demands. "Nothing," Maria replies lightly, "summer ended." "What was his name?" "Aldo . . ." "Does he love you? Did you ever see him again?" Donato's questions become more and more insistent until Maria cries out, "Stop it. I won't stand for this." Seeing Donato is in agony, she asks what has upset him so. Slowly he tells her, "You let him kiss you out of pity. Is that why you love me? Out of pity?" "Oh, my darling," Maria reassures him. "How can you say that? Can't you feel how much I love you, how wholly I belong to you?" To a desperate ecstasy in the orchestra, they embrace.

Almost imperceptibly comes the *a cappella* singing of the prisoners far in the distance and then Trottolò's voice calling his mother's name. Panic-stricken, Maria breaks away from Donato and throws herself against the back wall of the room in an effort to hide. Donato gropes his way to the window, opens it and tells the boy his mother must be upstairs. With a last suspicious glance, Trottolò runs away.

Frightened that they may have been seen, Maria dashes from the room leaving Donato alone. He suddenly realizes that in Trottolò, he has yet another rival, one even more dangerous than a lover, for he is a rival who cannot be fought and vanquished. "Why did I meet her," Donato cries out to the empty room. "It will mean suffering more than anything else. What can save me now? Oh, God, keep me from loving her. Help me!" Repeated strident chords seem to mock his cry as the act ends with the triplet that has come to symbolize the love of Donato and Maria. The printed ending to the act was added later by the composer and is more subdued, less painful and less stark than that of the first version.

The second act is also cast in two scenes, the first of which takes place on the terrace of the house. It is empty as the curtain rises. It is late afternoon, three months later, and from afar comes the sound of rifle fire, the wailing of a siren and the barking of dogs. After a few seconds, Agata runs out on the terrace followed by Donato. "Another prisoner has escaped," she concludes. As the shooting and sirens fade away, the two sit and Agata begins tying a piece of elastic into a black mask. Donato asks what she is doing, and she explains there is a children's party that evening next door and she is helping with Trottolò's costume. "They should have re-

turned from the picnic long ago," he says, rising nervously and turning his blind eyes toward the horizon as if he could will them to see. Not missing a chance to thrust the dagger of distrust once again into Donato, Agata says impatiently, "There you are fretting about her all the time . . . What will you do when her husband comes back?"

Agata ties the Pulcinella mask onto her face and with perfidious overtones tells Donato a letter arrived that morning for Maria. Again a pause. Donato asks where it came from. Triumphantly, Agata tears the mask off, crying, "You do want me to spy on her. I can read it in your eyes. . . . Let me be your eyes. I shall tell you everything she does." Donato struggles at first against Agata's entreaties and her willingness to take advantage of his first sign of weakness, but finally succumbs when she tells him there is a man's name on the envelope. "Her husband's?" Donata asks. "No, another name . . . Aldo something." "Aldo," cries Donato wildly, "are you sure?"

At that moment, the escaped Prisoner-of-War rushes onto the terrace with a drawn gun. As he points the weapon menacingly at Donato, Agata shouts, "Can't you see he's blind?" (In the first version of the opera, the Prisoner then commented, "So there are people in the world worse off than I," a line later cut.) The Prisoner then demands to be hidden until nightfall; Donato and Agata agree. As the maid takes the Prisoner-of-War inside the house, Maria's voice is heard in the distance, and a sprightly *allegro* breaks through the gloomy onstage mood. Donato drops Maria's letter on the table and runs toward the stairway leading down to the garden. Soon the Mother and Maria appear carrying a picnic basket, followed by Trottolò and Zuckertanz. All are exhausted from the outing, and Maria and Zuckertanz go inside at once to put Trottolò to bed for a nap. The Mother tells Donato she feels Maria spoils Trottolò. "Agata found another broken vase yesterday. I hope Madame Golovin is aware that she'll have to pay for damages."

Donato tells his mother to stop counting pennies, and she turns on him, surprised and wounded, commenting, "How you have changed

the stairs like a little ghost," Maria answers. To music of brooding apprehension, Donato asks if she knows what it is to wait all night, "when every second is like a piercing drop, when every noise is like a false signal for your heart to stop?"

As he cries out, "I wish I had never met you," the Mother appears in the doorway. She pretends to be unaware of what is happening. Donato, with studied casualness, tells Maria there is a letter for her. As she opens and reads it, Donato asks, "Is it from your husband?" "Oh! no," Maria says breezily, "it is from an old schoolmate of mine." At this Donato freezes as if Maria's lie has thrust a knife into his heart. Unaware of his anxiety, she joins the Mother on the other side of the terrace to help finish Trottolò's costume. The Mother calls to Agata for help, and as the setting sun turns the horizon red, the three women reminisce in a mood of melancholy, dwelling on remembrances of things past. This exquisite trio not only is among the most original and affecting by Menotti, it forms the heart of *Maria Golovin,* encapsulating the feelings of each woman within a framework of reflection.

Maria feels like a girl again, "sitting like this in the late afternoon, useless sewing in my hand, in my head useless thoughts." To the Mother, "it was a different world then, the gentle world in which we grew. We were told what was good, we were even told what was beautiful." Agata agrees, adding, "At that time the world wanted little from us. Oh how simple, how safe seemed the world of our youth." Midway in the trio, Maria and Agata become silent, leaving the Mother to recall the death of Donato's father and the blinding of her son. "I have been the one who waits, the one who counts, the one who weeps. . . . But a woman no." As the trio resumes, Donato, from a dark corner of the terrace where he has been licking the wounds inflicted by Maria's lie, comments, "There they sit, like the three fates, unwinding the thread of my life. One might think they loved each other, so gentle are their voices, but no two women love each other who hold the same thread."

The curtain falls briefly as the orchestra begins the second interlude, built on musical ele-

since that woman came into this house. At first I hoped that she might bring some happiness in your dark and lonely life. But now God is punishing me for kindling such a sinful love." Sadly, Donato tells her, "It is too late to weep or change, I am no longer free to want my freedom." Later he adds, "She's not bound to me the way I am to her. She loves too many things, too many people. One cannot love two people without lying to both of them, and I think she lies to all of us." Mother and son join in a short, unsettled duet in which she pities him and he gives into the doubts that tear at him.

At its conclusion, Maria's scale—lovingly and expressively warmed by B major—interrupts as she steps out onto the terrace. The three talk of the evening and the party to come as the scale figurations pervade every level of the orchestra. Soon the Mother goes indoors, and the affirmative tonality of Maria's entrance gives way to a doubting, almost sinister idea in the low strings. "You did not come to me last night," Donato begins accusingly. "I tried, but when I thought Trottolò was asleep, there he was at the top of

Maria (Duval) with Dr. Zuckertanz (Herbert Handt) and Donato's Mother (Neway)—opening scene of Act III, Brussels.

ments characterizing Donato's jealousy. Its unhappy strains soon give way, however, to a rapid figure as the curtain rises on the terrace bathed in moonlight. Trottolò, wearing his Pulcinella costume, stands on a little stool (a scene strongly recalling the outfitting of Concettina as an angel in *The Saint of Bleecker Street)*. The Mother and the Tutor admire the boy in exaggerated phrase, and Donato sits alone in a far corner. Pleased with himself, Trottolò runs toward Zuckertanz, waving his arms as if to frighten the tutor. The music here bears a striking resemblance to the episode in *Amelia* in which she is preparing for her ball. The Mother, Zuckertanz and Trottolò descend the stairs and disappear into the garden as Maria waves good-bye to them.

Walking toward Donato, who has barely moved during the previous scene, Maria asks if anything is wrong. To ominous, *secco* chords he replies, "On the contrary, at last I feel free. It is all over, Maria. I love you no longer. I am suddenly aware of loving a woman who does not exist. It was not you whom I loved, it was a voice that lightened the world for me. But the world I saw was false, the voice untrue, the mouth I kissed was full of lies."

He becomes more and more animated and violent, finally calling Maria a liar. Wounded and frightened, she tells him perhaps she loved him too much to understand him: "What am I accused of?" "What about the letter?" he snarls, "Aldo's letter." Realizing what has happened, Maria admits her lie, adding that she is guilty "if sparing useless pain can be called a sin." In a voice choked with anger, she goes toward the door calling Agata's name. "Evidently you believe her rather than me," Maria adds. Suddenly filled with guilt and feeling wretched, he begs her not to involve Agata. The maid appears and stands embarrassed before the couple as Maria demands she read Aldo's letter aloud.

"Dear Madame Golovin: All winter I waited in vain for a sign from you. Soon summer, too, will be gone and still my letters remain unanswered. I must now resign myself that I shall never hear from you, and that perhaps I shall never see you again. May I thank you for those few hours you spent with me. Goodbye, Aldo." Agata hands the letter back to Maria and reenters the house. As she leaves, Maria falls into a chair sobbing. Donato, shaken, rushes to her and kneels at her feet, embracing her tenderly.

To driving, highly charged music, he begs her forgiveness. "I cannot bear the thought of losing you. I love you too much. Don't forget, my love is blind." He rises and draws her to him during a powerful outburst from the orchestra over which can be heard the noise of fireworks from the party. As Donato tries to kiss Maria, she breaks away, frightened by his morbid passion, and and runs into the garden. As he searches for his cane, which he dropped, the Prisoner-of-War reappears. Hearing footsteps, Donato thinks Maria has returned and calls out her name. The Prisoner-of-War answers instead, admitting he has overheard the scene that just took place. In a striking aria (greatly rewritten for the published version of the opera), he tells Donato he cannot feel sorry for him. "I lost my wife, my child, my home. The land where I was born has changed its name under new masters. . . . This is the world around you, blind man, and here you are, choked with despair over a woman's lie." To this, Donato replies, "Who has ever been known to reason with the human heart? I, too, in my way am a prisoner like you, and, like you, I did not choose my prison."

A searchlight suddenly sweeps across the terrace and returns at intervals during the balance of the scene. The Prisoner-of-War throws his pistol on the table. The gun helped him to escape and he realizes Donato can only find a similar freedom through a similar act of violence. "If you truly hate your prison," he tells Donato, "find an escape the way I did." The character of the Prisoner-of-War is actually the *deus ex machina* of the drama. He has no direct connection with the tragedy that is unfolding in the story apart from bequeathing his weapon to Donato, but like Zuckertanz, neither is he an intrusion into the plot. The Prisoner-of-War puts Donato's irrational jealousy into perspective and acts as a grim reminder of the outer conflict ringing Donato's lonely and despairing world. His presence also sets Donato on the pathway toward the opera's denouement.

Without a word of farewell, the man jumps the balustrade and disappears into the black of the garden. Donato makes his way to the table and picks up the gun, holding it thoughtfully. To a stabbing motive with tremolo strings, he stares at the weapon as the searchlight illuminates him in its glare and the curtain falls.

The final act begins with a weeping, self-pitying figure in the orchestra out of which grows a melancholy strain in the strings, an elongation of material used earlier and associated with Donato's anguish. A harsh reappearance of Maria's scale interrupts, and then Donato's theme returns, singing itself expressively and quietly. The curtain rises on the same scene as Act I with Maria and Donato on the sofa sipping after-dinner coffee. The Mother and Dr. Zuckertanz are at the piano examining folios of music.

Zuckertanz dismisses the Mother's music as "romantic drivel," and in an elaborate aria, expounds his artistic preferences: "I only like what is archaic and pure, or very modern, very sparse and very dry; I like the sixteenth century, the seventeenth, too, but the nineteenth—jamais!" He goes on to catalog his favorites (Gesualdo, Caldara, Monteverdi, Stravinsky, Bartók, Piero della Francesca, Mondrian, Picasso) and to admit he finds Raphael "amusing" (but "only in the portraits, of course") and that he is at times "a little perverse" in his tastes.

In Zuckertanz's jaunty sequences, Menotti avoids the temptation of characterizing or evoking in the orchestra the styles and periods about which Zuckertanz is rhapsodizing. There is, however, a quasi-modal feeling as Zuckertanz talks of Gesualdo, a pecking rhythmic pattern as he praises Stravinsky and Picasso. In the main, however, Menotti restricts his comment to a series of banal, tonic arpeggios that tells us more of the character of Zuckertanz than of his predilections. Menotti surely was aware that the list of artists mentioned by Zuckertanz is in some cases anachronistic. Could Zuckertanz have been that familiar with Mondrian and Bartók at the time in which the opera is set? Menotti is probably using artistic license to make a point more bitingly to a contemporary audience.

If the others in the opera are prisoners of their emotions or their circumstances, then Zuckertanz is a prisoner of his aesthetic prejudices. He is the mannered connoisseur so often found among us, and his tastes and reactions are so far removed from the more vivid emotions of love, hate, pity and suspicion that his very presence in the story underlines the sensibilities of those about him, as the Prisoner-of-War's plight threw Donato's extremities into a different perspective.

Maria (Duval) is "killed" by Donato (Cross),
driven to desperation by jealousy.

Though inhibited by Zuckertanz, but hopeful she can persuade him to join her in a duet, the Mother hands him a piece of music. Disarmed by her insistence, he takes it and sits resignedly at the piano, asking Maria to join them. After a small flourish on the keys to limber up his fingers, he examines the music: "Italian barcarole, three sharps, oh dear!" Nervously, he hands the music to the Mother and motions her to play it instead. She begins the simple, arpeggiated accompaniment *(andante calmo)* followed by Zuckertanz singing the opening phrase. Maria follows canonically.

The duet is interrupted by Agata, who brings in a telegram for Maria. She is obviously shaken by its contents, and after an outburst in the orchestra, Maria gains control of herself. She tells the others her husband has been released and will be home in a few days. Donato rises, shattered by the news. Zuckertanz runs to tell Trottolò, and the Mother, aware of her son's anguish and realizing he wishes to be alone with Maria, leaves the room. Searchingly, Donato asks Maria what she will tell her husband. "I don't know," she answers in a voice lost and afraid, as the curtain falls on the first scene. The third interlude begins with a brisk, almost martial air. At its conclusion the chorus of prisoners is heard again, this time behind the curtain. Their voices now assume a greater significance than before; where originally they had been the constant reminder of war and suffering, now they are heard as the voice of Maria's husband, whose unseen presence has dominated the lives of Maria and Donato.

When the curtain next rises, the scene is the same, a week later. Donato is seen through the window sitting on the terrace as the Mother and Maria are unfolding a tablecloth Maria has borrowed for a party she plans for her husband's return. "I imagine you'll want to leave very soon," the Mother says pointedly to Maria. Taken aback, Maria replies her husband will need a long rest. "Then when are you planning to leave us?" the Mother demands harshly. When Maria replies she would like to keep the apartment until late fall, the Mother, barely bothering to disguise her hatred, asks, "Haven't you tortured my son long enough? Life in this house has become quite unbearable! I want you to leave us alone."

Maria reminds her, "You yourself at first smiled at our love, and now that we are all trapped in it, we must all bear the pain together. Don't forget Madame, I, too, have a son and must protect him. Much as I love Donato, I know that I should leave him for the sake of all of us. But who will tell him? Who can find the heart? I know I can bear my own sorrow, but not his. . . ." As Maria fights to hold back her tears, the Mother asks with sudden understanding and sympathy for forgiveness. "I am afraid," she adds, "his love is no longer within the bounds of reason. He can no longer find his way as he used to. Every day his darkness becomes deeper." Donato, from the terrace, calls out to his mother, who goes to help him into the room. He is pale and tense, his face a mask of obsession. After a

few steps, he stops, sensing Maria's presence. The Mother leaves them alone.

Donato asks Maria if she has told her husband about them. "Not yet," she answers, begging for more time. Donato says accusingly he has heard of her party that evening. "Hardly that," Maria tells him, "a few of my husband's relatives." Donato becomes increasingly angry and demands to know if there will be dancing. "Yes," says Maria, "It is my birthday." Straining to control his anger at not having been told of the party, Donato asks if she will come to him later. Feeling trapped, Maria will only say that she will try. Breaking down, Donato tells her he can bear waiting no longer. With pity, she finally agrees to come at midnight, and as she leads him to the couch, she places a rose in his hand. His features are suddenly suffused with tenderness, and as Maria sits on the sofa, he sits at her feet, burying his head in her lap.

As if lost in oblivion, Donato begins a duet (molto tranquillo e calmo) whose accompaniment has a sweet, apprehensive quality. "Oh, I wish that you would die right now," he tells her, "so that no one else could ever have you," a sentiment Menotti has admitted feeling: "It is never my enemies I wish to see dead, but often the people I love." With calmness, she rebukes Donato: "I do not know what kind of love destroys the life it cannot own. For me there is no love unless one dares to lose the very thing one loves."

Their conflicting thoughts and voices intertwine and quicken in tension before giving way to a touching E-major section, reflecting the desire of each for inner emotional security and peace. Donato alternately begs Maria to remain and to return to him at midnight after the party as the curtain falls and the orchestra launches into the turbulent, final interlude. As the music spins itself out and then dies away, the curtain rises and we hear the voices of Maria and Zuckertanz offstage singing the Italian barcarole. It is past midnight and the party is still going on upstairs. Donato is seen standing, waiting by the stairway as the curtain rises. His mother is sitting, knitting, on the sofa.

Donato goes to sit by his mother and asks her what time it is. She lies, saying it is not quite one

Stage design by Pierluigi Samaritani for Act II, Scene 1, of *Maria Golovin*, Marseilles.

Design by Pierluigi Samaritani for the ballet *Sebastian*, Trieste.

Painting by George Tooker for the settings of the world premiere of *The Saint of Bleecker Street*, 1954.

Act I, Scene 1; Act III, Scen

Act I, Scene 2.

Act II.

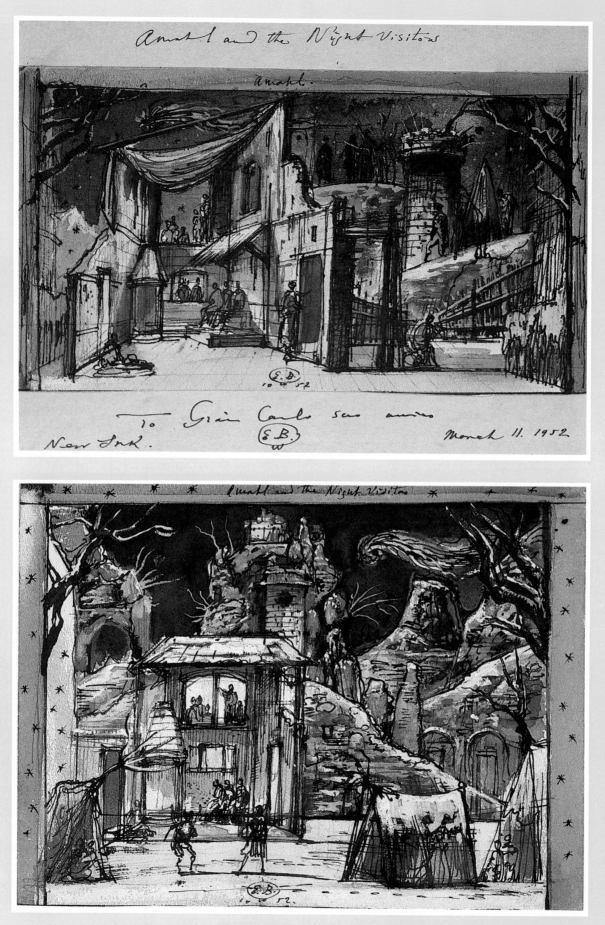

Set designs by Eugene Berman for the world premiere of *Amahl and the Night Visitors*, NBC-TV, 1951.

o'clock. A moment later, when Agata enters the room, she gives the Mother away by mentioning it is two o'clock in the morning. Angered by his mother's deception, Donato rises and begins pacing the room against menacing, sharp chords in the orchestra. From above comes the music of a small combo and the noise of people dancing and laughing (this is the main body of music transplanted from the Proust ballet). The players (described earlier by Maria as "the druggist at the piano, the schoolmaster at the violin, the midwife at the clarinet") are performing an off-center foxtrot in G major. Left alone by his mother, who has gone to bed, Donato listens awhile, then stumbles to the sofa, trying to gain control of his feelings. A few moments later, as if having made a decision, he goes to the piano, lifts the lid and searches inside. After a few seconds, he comes up with the Prisoner's gun and fingers it. As the orchestra builds to a fury to match Donato's, Maria bursts into the room. Donato hides the gun in a pocket and greets her stonily. "It meant nothing to you," he begins, "to know that I was suffering like a wounded beast." Maria tries to quiet him, afraid they will be overheard, but every explanation she attempts is thrown back into her face. Finally, Donato says they can no longer avoid the truth.

Desperate but relieved, Maria agrees with him; they cannot continue like this. "I promise to leave tomorrow," she says, "and you'll never see me again." As she tries to leave, Donato, brandishing the revolver, bars her way. When she realizes that he is pointing the gun in the direction of the sound of her footsteps, she freezes. "You are not going to leave me for another man," Donato threatens. "If I cannot have you, I will not lose you to anyone else." He cries out for his mother, who rushes in. After a few seconds of hesitation, she motions Maria out of the range of the gun. She then takes Donato's hand and guides his aim in a different direction. With a wild cry, she says "Yes, my son; kill her!"

Donato fires twice into empty space and then sinks to his knees completely drained. Like Baba, he has tried to kill his ghost. "She is yours forever now," the Mother says soothingly. "Now you'll have peace, my son. Here, cast this flower on her." The Mother hands him the rose which he has earlier dropped. Painfully rising to his feet, Donato extends his arm and lets the rose fall on the bare floor. The Mother then takes him in her arms, telling him they must hide until morning and then cross the frontier.

Not daring to move, Maria watches the Mother lead Donato out of the room. Then she slowly walks over to the rose, picks it up and brings it to her lips. As Zuckertanz calls her name, she bursts into uncontrolled weeping. Finally gaining control of herself, she turns and walks slowly toward the stairway as the light fades.

The period of *Maria Golovin* also brought the premiere at the Metropolitan Opera of Samuel Barber's first opera *Vanessa*, written to an original and supercharged libretto by Menotti. Apart from two other slight *librettini* (for Barber's *A Hand of Bridge* and Lukas Foss's *Introductions and Goodbyes*), *Vanessa* is the only instance of Menotti's providing words to be set by another composer. The late 1950s were also the time when Menotti produced his only incidental music for the theater—for Jean Cocteau's "mimodrame" *La poete et sa muse*. This, like *A Hand of Bridge* and *Introductions and Goodbyes*, was written for performance at the Spoleto Festival in Italy, which Menotti founded in 1958. All three were performed as part of an evening of skits and short music numbers entitled *Album Leaves*. The Cocteau piece, played entirely in mime, consisted of 100-plus bars of music scored for three strings, percussion and piano. Its six small bits of music were used to underline pivotal parts of the story. It deals with a young American poet who is unrecognized and desperate for fame. His muse appears to him and encourages him to attempt suicide as a way of attracting attention.

This he does, slightly wounding himself in the process, and he becomes the idol of the young as well as the very rich. He decides to celebrate his good fortune and opens a bottle of champagne. His friends, mistaking the pop of the cork for the sound of a gun, and thinking their hero has tried to kill himself again, rush into his room to find him quietly sipping champagne with his muse. Disillusioned, they attack him and disown him. Abandoned, he commits suicide for real.

Dialogue II

GCM: Let me begin this dialogue by pointing out that you are often describing my operas as you have seen them staged by me, but those who consult my printed scores may be puzzled by the variance at times between what you sometimes describe and what is printed. The practice of looking in the printed scores for the proper guidance and interpretation for certain of my operas is a dangerous one. Too often I leave important details to the imagination of the conductor or the stage director because these details seem to me too obvious to be spelled out. Besides, I hate correcting proofs of my works and often keep them for months before returning them more or less still uncorrected to my publisher. More than once, the publisher has given up in despair and printed a score without my final approval. But even those which have received my OK are not edited by me as carefully as they should have been. The result is that unless I am present, my operas now suffer in performance because of my slipshod editing; that, unfortunately applies to all my printed scores. Take *The Telephone*, for example. In Lucy's first aria, the high D followed by ad-lib semitones and the exclamation "Oh! dear," after the semitones, I should have added the words "She breaks freely into peals of laughter," which is the way I always have it performed. Why I was so stupid as to think that a singer would instinctively guess that was what I wanted, God only knows. In the piano score of *The Medium*, during the "Black Swan" song, I forgot to indicate when Toby's tambourine should be heard, with the result that in many performances Toby never accompanies this song the way he should. In the orchestral score, however, it is correctly marked, but I forgot to specify that the tambourine should be played onstage by Toby and not by a percussionist in the pit. I am still dissatisfied with all my printed scores. Although the omissions in many cases have been corrected or amended in subsequent editions, I only hope that God will give me the time and patience to revise some day all of my works. Some of these revisions will be very important. In *The Consul*, for example, there will be minor changes in the second act—very small changes indeed, but extremely important to the singers, both for acting and musical interpretation. I shall cut one of the magician tricks (the one in which a glove turns into a dove), which is difficult to perform and very dispensable, and shall shorten the mother's recitative before the lullaby, as it often becomes embarrassingly cute when performed by a not particularly gifted artist.

I shall also simplify the stage action which climaxes Magda's nightmare in the second act, as the appearance of the fetus called for is unnecessarily ghoulish; unless it is handled by a particularly imaginative stage director it is apt to become unconvincing, superfluous and dangerously close to cheap theatricality. I also need to lengthen the interlude between the first and second scenes of the first act to permit "more" time for the set change.

JA: What appeal did Broadway hold for you?

GCM: People have said that I wrote operas for Broadway, and that is untrue. I simply wanted to experiment and see if operas could be taken out of the opera house and run the way plays run—with consecutive performances—and be accepted by a so-called non-operatic audience. It so happened that I found two producers who were equally interested in this experiment and we found a theater on Broadway. But it had nothing to do with

The men behind *The Medium:* producers Chandler Cowles and Efrem Zimbalist, Jr., with Menotti at the time of the opera's first Paris production.

Broadway *per se*. It could have been done in any theater in any city.

At that time I hated the idea that opera could only be housed in those big mausoleums called "opera houses," where they had to fight to remain in the repertory and were given more or less perfunctory productions. I also rebelled against the repertory system because of its seemingly indestructible tradition of presenting a daily change of fare, which necessitates changes in cast, encourages inexactitudes in lighting and staging, and therefore is never able to preserve the image and sounds of the original production. I wanted to prove that opera, if presented with the care and love for details with which a play is presented, could find a new audience and even pay for itself, and no longer depend on subsidization. All of this I think I proved with *The Medium* and *The Consul*. But then I tried again the same experiment with a more ambitious opera, what one would call a "grand opera," *The Saint of Bleecker Street,* and although I won a Pulitzer Prize and it remains perhaps my favorite child, it was, as far as experiment goes, a failure, because it did not make money or even pay for itself, despite three months of consecutive performances and full houses. I eventually abandoned the experiment because I was not interested in becoming an impresario; it took too much time out of my work. But the experiment awakened much interest, not only in a public unfamiliar with opera, but also among composers who had not previously been particularly interested in opera, such as Martinu, Stravinsky and Poulenc, for example. Stravinsky, after seeing *The Consul,* seemed particularly interested to find out from me how I was able to organize the production and how financially successful it was; he loved money, as you know. When he wrote *The Rake's Progress,* I am pretty sure he hoped in the back of his mind it could someday be given on Broadway as *The Consul* was given.

JA: Speak of your role as stage director?

GCM: I could honestly say that it was only in self-defense that I became a stage director. There are plenty of competent conductors the world over in whose hands a musical score can be safely trusted. But that cannot be said about most stage directors, particularly those that "specialize" in opera. The spoken drama abounds in brilliant directors, but that does not mean they are equally qualified to handle an operatic production. Most of them limit themselves to the staging of the libretto, utterly insensitive to musical demands. And those directors who can read music and consider themselves musicians are, on the whole, sadly unimaginative in handling the dramatic implications of a libretto and seem unable to teach a singer how to move according to the music.

I can think of only four or five operatic directors in the whole world I do respect and admire. I particularly despise those directors who, instead of interpreting the intention of the author, use an opera to display their style of histrionics and think that opera, to be made palatable to a modern audience, must be "modernized," completely ignoring the musical style of the work and the background of the opera. To me it is a crime comparable to slimming down Rubens's women or pepping up Dickens's chaste humor. Worst of all are those directors who "discover" a symbolic meaning in a libretto and feel they must convey it to the audience with visual trappings, as if the audience were made up of idiots unable to see it for themselves. They do not respect the fact that often the author wants his symbolism discretely hidden within a realistic setting. I am horrified when I see *The Medium* staged as an abstract parable, and I cringe when I see my little, delicate *Telephone* portrayed with unrealistic props made of huge telephones or with a backdrop of telephone poles.

I was delighted when years ago we presented at the Spoleto Festival one of Eugène Ionesco's plays—I don't recall which—and I had the honor of having Ionesco there as my guest. The young stage director insisted in placing the action in a very surrealistic setting. Ionesco was outraged. "My text asks for a living room and I want to see a real living room," he said. He explained to the director that the absurdity of the text could only be heightened if contrasted with a very realistic set, not by repeating visually what was said in the text. Of course, I am a very different stage director when I stage my own works and those by others. When I stage the work of another composer I feel very nervous, and I try to discover as much as possible what the original intention of the composer and the librettist might have been, even if this forces me into stylistic boundaries not entirely of my choosing or taste. Of course the matter of cuts is a problem we all face when it comes to the staging of operas by composers of the late eighteenth century or early nineteenth. These cuts are often necessary, but we do know that at that time composers themselves allowed cuts and added music at the last minute according to the occasion or at a singer's demands. The whole operatic form was then more haphazard than it became later. So I don't feel guilty when I permit certain cuts in Rossini's operas, for example. However I do try to preserve as much as I can of the original, and do away only with the dispensable reprises and *da capo*s.

I find that in general by studying the libretto very carefully, by listening to the music, and by trying to discover the action hidden in the music itself without trying to impose my own personality on it, I can still produce something that can be quite astonishing, because few directors nowadays bother to look and to work with that kind of humility, and therefore most fail to discover what is hidden in it. They choose to be iconoclasts rather than interpreters. Most of them, being unmusical, are unable to be intuitive of the action described by the music, and they content themselves with reading the directions printed in the libretto. In my own operas, of course, I see the action as I write the music, so it is very easy for me to stage my own works, at least shortly after I have written them. It does become more difficult later on when I must try to remember what I imagined when I wrote a particular passage. I purposely keep no written rec-

ords of my stagings. As a stage director I have often been tempted to skirt my duty to myself as a composer, and say, "Oh well, I'll just cut this or change that to make the staging easier." But then I caution myself, "Don't do to yourself what you don't want other stage directors to do to you. Try to remember why you wrote three bars of music instead of two and why you asked for a long pause at that precise moment. What did you want to happen there?" Generally, I do finally remember and invariably I thank God for it, because of course the music and the pause *had* a reason to be there. This has encouraged me to approach other composers in the same way, to find a logical action behind the demands of the music, which at first may seem excessive for the action it indicates or too short to contain it.

Of course a composer must not expect each staging of a particular work to be exactly the same, because we must not entirely suffocate the personality of whoever interprets our work. A composer must leave a certain leeway to the interpreter. We would not have so many different singers, pianists and conductors were there only one valid way of performing a piece of music. But there must be a limit to how much of his own personality the interpreter can inject into the work he is handling—he must never betray the basic intention of the creator. We might say that interpreter and creator must become one being. When staging my own operas I seldom repeat myself. My view of my own works changes as *I* change; I am not the same person I was five or six years ago. However each interpretation, different as they may seem, is faithful to the original.

JA: What will be the fate of your operas without you to stage them?

GCM: This brings us back to your earlier question. It will all depend on the state of my scores at the time of my death. If I should die tomorrow, I shudder to think what would happen to my works, the later ones in particular, which are still unpublished. The manuscripts of these operas not only bear no stage directions to speak of but also contain countless errors, omissions and inexactitudes. It is imperative that I soon take time off to edit and reedit all of my scores, not only for musical corrections but also to indicate in my operas exactly what I expect to happen on the stage. Only then will future interpreters be able to capture the essence of what I intended. Of course, there is always room for misunderstanding, even in those scores I think sufficiently annotated. I am nearly always unhappy with stagings of my operas by others. I think, "My God, why didn't the director realize at this point that the character should be walking instead of sitting." The music says to me "walk," "run," "fall," "cry" and I am always surprised when it fails to say the same thing to others. Maybe I should follow Debussy's example. He was so pessimistic about interpreters that he spelled out everything: *"un peu plus lentement,"* *"doucement,"* *"très loin,"* etc. Practically every measure has some such indication. I probably should adopt this policy, for my music like his changes mood and meter continually, often from measure to measure. Of course all the directions in the world are not going to keep one from being betrayed. But then if I notate my scores well, at least the people who love my music will know I am being betrayed.

Menotti the mystic: rehearsing his Broadway cast for the séance in *The Medium,* 1947.

JA: What is your relationship in producing your operas with the set and costume designer?

GCM: I have often wished I had the gift of being a designer myself. What composer would not like to be the complete boss of every element in the production of his works? My relationship with designers has been both successful and unsuccessful. At the beginning of my career, I tried to obtain from a designer what I had visualized, then I came to realize that this was a mistake. Sometimes the designer can add certain visual elements the composer has not imagined, elements that can enrich the possibilities offered to the stage director, without distorting the original conception of the opera. In this sense a good designer can become an important collaborator. Therefore if you are lucky enough to find an intelligent designer you must not be too literal with him, nor should you expect him to be your slave; you must give him a certain freedom. The art of interpretation is a very mysterious and extraordinary process. You see yourself mirrored in other people's sensitivity and although the different mirrors may be equally limpid and clear, the image is never quite the same, even if you clearly recognize yourself in it. Just as a good pianist or conductor strives in his own way to be as faithful as possible to the score he is interpreting, so should the designer and stage director of an operatic production; for the miraculous thing is that the more the interpreter tries to be faithful to the original, the more his interpretation will differ from others who had the same aim. Alas, in the world of opera most mirrors, even the most expensive ones, do not reflect the image of the composer but more often than not a distorted unrecognizable caricature.

JA: What productions of your operas can stand as models?

GCM: Well, certainly Beni Montresor's designs for *The Last Savage;* that was a really charming production, and it was even better at Spoleto USA than at the Metropolitan Opera. I loved the sets of *The Medium* made for Spo-

leto by Pasquale Grossi and Zack Brown's for Washington. I quite like Horace Armistead's original designs for *The Consul*—they were very simple and made the action very stark. I didn't like, for example, Eugene Berman's concept of *Amahl.* I thought it too fussy and not magical enough. It was not Berman at his best and on television it all looked too much like painted cardboard; I don't think he understood the medium. As a matter of fact I have yet to see a production of *Amahl* that entirely satisfied me. Best of all were Luigi Samaritani's production of *Maria Golovin* for Trieste and the *Sebastian* he designed for Palermo. Both very poetic, and within the spirit of the music. And of course *The Medium* by the inimitable Lila de Nobili.

JA: How much do your librettos change once you begin composing the music for them?

GCM: Often a great deal; therefore I conceive my libretto as a very loosely constructed sketch that I eventually mold into a definite shape through the impetus of musical logic. I always sing my words as I write them even if they seldom retain this first spontaneous musical physiognomy. This helps me give to my scenes a dramatic rhythm which is musical rather than literary. I am not particularly proud of the literary quality of my librettos, which I consider a passive element of my musical structure. I can write much better than that and as a writer I would rather be judged by my plays or short stories.

JA: Are your librettos autobiographical?

GCM: Well, on a superficial level I often use the names of friends in the delineations of certain of my characters, as well as certain events in my own life. And sometimes I find myself mirrored in some of my characters, quite unconsciously however. I certainly think I am Donato in *Maria Golovin;* I am both Annina and Michele in *The Saint;* I guess I am a little bit of all my characters. I don't think any author can escape this. Perhaps I am even Madame Flora! Why not?

JA: So you feel that the best art is made out of life?

GCM: No, I think the artist must also learn by intuition what he has not felt himself; you must be attuned to the sufferings and emotions of others. More important than experience is intuition. Some artists are forced to write only about themselves, for they are not intuitive about other people. I question whether such an artist can be great, for to me a great artist, especially if he writes for the theater, must be aware of—what shall we call it?—the universal unconscious.

JA: Could you elaborate on the role you play in these translating your operas?

GCM: I cannot think of a more painful task for a composer than having to translate his librettos into another language. But it is less painful than having to accept other people's translations. The advantage of being your own translator is obvious: You can allow yourself all sorts of liberties which someone else would not dare to take. Only the composer can decide with impunity when and how vocal line can be modified without betraying the original. I have translated into Italian most of my librettos—*Amahl, Maria Golovin, The Saint of Bleecker Street, The Most Important Man, Tamu-Tamu, Martin's Lie, The Globolinks* and *Juana La Loca*. They are not particularly distinguished translations, but the phrases do flow naturally with the music and often make me forget the original.

Of course, I made my task easier by revising much of the vocal line, especially in the *recitativi*. In *Juana La Loca*, for example, there are whole pages of recitative which have been rewritten. I think it is wise for a composer to be responsible for at least one translation, or collaborate with one translator, thus offering to other translators two versions to work from. Most of my operas have been translated into many languages, but of course I cannot judge how good many of them are as I don't speak Polish, Turkish or Japanese, for example. The French translations of *The Saint of Bleecker Street* and *Maria Golovin* are serviceable, although

they do need some revision. The Italian versions of *The Medium* and *The Consul* by Fedele d'Amico are quite distinguished.

JA: What about the pairings of your one-act operas? Are there some you prefer to others?

GCM: It is extraordinary, that with all the one-act operas I've written—except for *The Telephone* and *The Medium*, and I'm very tired of that combination—I've never really worked out a plan to couple them successfully as I really ought. It is a problem, for example, how else to present *The Medium*, which is not quite long enough to be given by itself (although it was presented by itself at Spoleto without complaints). You cannot give it with *Amahl*, which is for children; you cannot give it with *Tamu-Tamu*, for both are too dramatic and both end with gunfire; and if you pair it with *The Old Maid* it makes the evening too long. On the other hand I hate to be paired off with the works of others. *The Medium* has been given successfully with *Gianni Schicchi*, but you are rarely that lucky with your bed companions.

JA: Did you ever regret that you did not save the libretto of *Vanessa* for yourself?

GCM: Oh, I would have loved to write the music for *Vanessa*, and in a sense I did. As I created the words for Sam Barber, I sang all of them—as is my custom—to my own melodies. So there is a Menotti *Vanessa* floating around somewhere! As a matter of fact, Sam would play sections of the opera for me as he finished them, and I would shout, "Oh no, it doesn't go like that." He would get very angry at me. The libretto, however, was tailored expressly for Sam, and now, in my mind, it is inseparable, from his beautiful music. It would, of course, have been different had I intended it for myself. It is filled with many references to things and people Sam loved—a menu of exquisite dishes and rare wines to begin with, a northern castle, an aristocratic background, winter weather, skating, the doctor (modeled after his father) and at the end a touch of *The Cherry Orchard*, his favorite play. I knew that would inspire him!

The composer behind a phrenological chart, part of the set for *The Medium* at Columbia University, 1946.

Chapter Four

THE DANCE STAGE

Sebastian

Ballet in one act,
scenario by the composer

The Courtesan
Sebastian (a Moorish slave)
The Prince
Fiora (his sister)
Maddelena (the other sister)
Townspeople and acrobats

World premiere at the International Theatre. New York, Commissioned by the Marquis de Cuevas's Ballet International, October 31, 1944. First performance of the suite at Lewisohn Stadium, New York, August 8, 1945. Study score of the suite published by G. Ricordi. Scored for flute (piccolo), oboe (English horn), two clarinets (bass clarinet), bassoon, two trumpets, two horns, two trombones, timpani, percussion, xylophone, bells, piano, strings.

With only a few exceptions, dance has not played a major role in Menotti's operas. There is a short dance episode in *Amahl and the Night Visitors*, as well as the choreographic dream sequences in *The Consul*. Even the role of Toby in *The Medium* has been considered by some to be as much choreography as mime, particularly since a dancer—Leo Coleman—created the part. (Menotti, however, has categorically stated that he prefers an actor to a dancer.) Yet music for the dance and dancelike music play an important part in his output, beginning before his Broadway period with perhaps his finest achievement in this form, *Sebastian*.

"Many are the dance works that I have *almost* written," Menotti has said, "and two of these I especially regret not having done. One was the ballet I had planned with Antony Tudor based on Marcel Proust's *À l'ombre des jeunes filles en fleurs*' parts of which were woven into *Maria Go-*

lovin. I wrote quite a bit of music for it, and we even obtained approval of Proust's niece for the project. Inexplicably, Tudor abandoned the ballet, and to this day I don't know why.

"Sometime later, I talked for hours with Martha Graham about doing a ballet based on the basic magic elements common to all fairy tales—a sort of surrealistic collage. But, again, it never came into being, although whenever I see Martha, we still talk about it, and I have not given up the hope of someday making it a reality, perhaps with another choreographer. More recently, I was commissioned by Rolf Liebermann to write a full evening's ballet score for the Paris Opéra, and I kept saying the score was on its way. Of course, we both knew I was lying!" (There was also a dance work commissioned by the Harkness Ballet in 1973, which remains unproduced.)

When speaking of *Sebastian*, it is necessary to stipulate which *Sebastian*, for though Menotti's

The Prince (Kari Karnakoski), the Courtesan (Viola Essen) and Sebastian (Francisco Moncion) in the original Marquis de Cuevas production of *Sebastian*, with sets designed by Oliver Smith, costumes by Milena.

score and scenario have remained constant, there have been at least six different productions of the piece in America alone involving three choreographers who have cast the work in differing lights. For many, *Sebastian* means John Butler's 1966 production for the Harkness Ballet (a refinement of an earlier staging for the Netherlands Dance Theater in 1963). The original choreography (with additions by Robert Horan) was by Edward Caton, a gifted dancer judged out of his depth. *Sebastian* was his choreographic debut, and though John Martin of the *Times* felt his work was "creditable," he reserved his full praise for the ballet's score and the "unblushing melodrama" of its story. In between the Caton and Butler versions, there was also a short-lived production in 1957 by Agnes de Mille of this tale set in seventeenth-century Venice.

Sebastian revolves about a prince who falls in love with a notorious courtesan—an alliance his two possessive sisters are determined to smash. They are well versed in black magic and know that if they obtain something belonging to the Courtesan, they will have her in their power. The sisters steal a veil of the Courtesan's and construct a wax fetish of her, which they cover with the veil. Rather than kill her at once by destroying the image, they plan to torture her by piercing the effigy with arrows, knowing that through their magic, the Courtesan will suffer the pain of each dart before dying. They begin piercing the image and to their delight, it shudders under each blow. What they do not know is that Sebastian, their Moorish slave, loves the Courtesan from afar, and learning of the sisters' plot, he has removed the wax figure and taken its place under the veil. Like his saintly namesake, it is Sebastian who is pierced by arrows, and who through his sacrifice breaks the power of Fiora's and Maddelena's witchcraft. His death enables the Prince and the Courtesan to be united.

Though the scenario is broken into three scenes, the score is cast in seven sections: "*Introduzione*" (adagio-allegro molto), "*Barcarola*" (andante con moto), "*Baruffa*" (allegro energico), "*Cortège*" (l'istesso tempo), "*Danza di Sebastian*" (tempo di valzer, moderato), "*Danza della cortigiana Ferita*" (molto moderato) and "*Pavana*" (andante calmo). This diatonic score calls for what is nominally a small orchestra, but one that is swelled beyond the norm for a dance accompaniment by a large percussion section.

Menotti justifies this added battery through many original instrumental effects. In fact, the brilliant orchestration of *Sebastian* is rife with uncommon colorations—bright piano-harp sonorities, piquant doublings of a melodic line (for example, English horn and violas) and the singing of a long melody by violins and cellos spaced two octaves apart. In general the score is highly sectional to accommodate the many shifts in the drama and the episodic nature of the piece. In the main the music is of an openness and transparency that would spill over into the Piano Concerto, which followed *Sebastian*.

From the opening strains, *Sebastian* is a harbinger of much to come, sounds that would shortly be recognized as Menottian. In the first flourishes are heard his penchant for dotted rhythms, for motives that turn back on themselves and revolve around or return to the same two or three notes and for Stravinskian, neoclassic motor rhythms that drive a score forward. The spareness and sharpness with which he makes use of woodwinds in particular heralds the scoring found in *The Medium*, as does the soft, quasi-waltz in the "*Barcarola*"—the loveliest idea in the work:

As *Sebastian* looks forward to what is to come, it also, Janus-like, turns to what has been with such sprightly *Amelia*-esque tunes as this one, found early on in the manic "*Introduzione*":

The complete ballet runs some thirty-seven minutes and contains about fourteen minutes more of music than the concert suite Menotti drew from it. The suite, in effect, eliminates transitional material.

Errand into the Maze

A duet for two dancers,
scenario by Martha Graham

World premiere at the Ziegfeld Theatre, New York, February 28, 1947. Scored for flute, oboe, clarinet, bassoon, trumpet, horn, percussion, piano, strings.

As *Sebastian* was a prelude to *The Medium,* so Menotti's next dance score was its postlude. *Errand into the Maze* was commissioned and choreographed by Martha Graham as a vehicle for herself and dancer Mark Ryder. This relatively short score was accompanied at its premiere by the following note from Miss Graham: "This is an errand journey into the maze of the heart's darkness in order to face and do battle with the Creature of Fear. There is the accomplishment of the errand, the instant of triumph and the emergence from the dark."

A description of the choreography is supplied by Don McDonagh in his 1973 Graham biography: "In *Errand,* she follows a tape lying tangled on the stage. This leads her into a maze and ultimately to a large bony V shape through which she can escape. Crossing a dangerous area, she is menaced by a man wearing a bull's head (later eliminated), whose hands are held in a yoke that lies across his shoulders. The yoke was an unusual device to harness the man's menacing energy. Though he could still rush around the area, he could not hold on to the woman. The idea was of a powerful but not overpowering presence. It came under control only when the woman exercised her own strength of character to dominate it."

Actually, the work as originally proposed to Menotti was a dance enactment of the story of Ariadne. But, as Menotti has recalled, "to work with Martha was both very exciting and very frustrating. As other composers will tell you, she begins by giving you a very detailed scenario of what the dance is going to be. She gives a vivid description of its general mood. Martha has the extraordinary gift of inspiring her composers by throwing them all sorts of visual images. Often she does this in a rather inarticulate way, but somehow through her great effort to express herself, the ideas become even more suggestive. . . ."

For *Errand into the Maze,* Menotti maintains he "followed Martha's instructions scrupulously, but during the very first rehearsals I realized that the dance she was weaving over my score had nothing or very little to do with what she had planned originally. This was unnerving because in my music I tried to keep in mind the visual images she had given me. Still, I soon found out that Martha had a magical gift for going to the more abstract core of the music—that she could enrich it with her own highly evocative personality. At first I thought she was turning my music into something other than it was intended to be. When she finished creating the ballet, it seemed quite appropriate, although I can't help thinking that if I had known in advance the sort of dance she finally conceived, I would have given her a different and perhaps better score."

It is clear from McDonagh's *précis* that *Errand* has little to do with Ariadne, and is little more than a suggestion of the Theseus myth—a person facing and conquering fear, symbolized by a Minotaur-like figure. The scoring of the work is more what one tends to expect of a dance piece than was *Sebastian.* The music begins in starkness with the solo piano hammering out a dry, fortissimo motto that for a moment threatens to evolve into a serial sequence. The mood throughout is tense and disjointed, and the music unfolds more as a sound track to action than as the independent piece that *Sebastian* was. Perhaps this is why *Errand* has never had a separate life outside the theater.

Errand is also more rigid music than the free-flowing *Sebastian* and has sharper edges than *The Medium*, despite that opera's exposed musical nerve ends. There is little letup in the driving stride of *Errand*, and it becomes nonabrasive only in its final pages. But even there, the structuring of the last chord is such that we are left dangling harmonically. *Errand* may not be one of Menotti's most individual pieces, but it is an ef-

fective bit of musical conjuring, and it serves its purpose well in heightening the impact and trauma of Graham's dance patterns.

Thirty years later, Graham revisited Menotti when she made a miniature dance piece she called *Shadows* out of his *Cantilena e scherzo* for Harp and String Quartet. Menotti, however, never intended this brief chamber music piece for choreography, and for this reason it will be discussed in "The Concert Stage" and not here.

The battle with the Creature of Fear: Elisa Monte and George White, Jr. of the Martha Graham Dance Company in *Errand into the Maze,* a score commissioned from Menotti by Miss Graham.

The Unicorn, the Gorgon and the Manticore

("*The Three Sundays of a Poet*")
A madrigal fable for chorus, ten dancers
and nine instruments,
text in English by the composer

The Man in the Castle	The Doctor
The Count	The Doctor's Wife
The Countess	The Unicorn
The Mayor	The Gorgon
The Mayor's Wife	The Manticore

World premiere in the Coolidge Auditorium of the Library of Congress, Washington, D.C., October 21, 1956. First New York performance at the City Center of Music and Drama, January 15, 1957. Commissioned by the Elizabeth Sprague Coolidge Foundation. Dedicated to Selma Farr. Published by Franco Colombo in English. Scored for flute, oboe, clarinet, bassoon, trombone, percussion, harp, cello, bass.

Although Menotti does not consider madrigal-fable a ballet, he admits it is difficult to classify. Some have even seen it as a madrigal or chamber opera. But as the work was choreographed at its premiere and soon entered the New York City Ballet's repertory, it would seem to be more dance than not. However one pigeonholes it, *The Unicorn, the Gorgon and the Manticore* is arresting and affecting theater. It was inspired by Orazio Vecchi's *Amfiparnaso, commedia harmonica* or madrigal comedy from 1597, an operatic prototype. Menotti also worked under the influence of madrigals of Monteverdi, an influence that reaches back to his days with Scalero.

Menotti's fable is allegorical—a musical three ages of man, or, in this case, the poet. These are symbolized by the Unicorn (youth), the Gorgon (manhood) and the Manticore (old age). It was Menotti's premise that the poet, or any creator, is always ahead of the crowd and his critics, and those who are destined to follow rather than to lead fall into line or adopt fashion as poets move on to new dreams. The piece is aimed at the dilettantes who lack the courage to feel or only mimic emotion and therefore they are unable to make their own judgments.

Quoting Samuel Barber's definition of a dilettante as "someone who loves art without humility," Menotti has noted that "an artist has to be judged in his entirety, not just on the basis of one work which might be popular or fashionable. Everything an artist does is equally important to him, even his failures. His quest for beauty and aesthetic truth is represented by everything he does, not only by the works which succeed."

In *The Unicorn*, Menotti was attempting to express his feelings about the life of an artist, the quality of the artistic life and the difference between real feeling and the mimicry of feeling. As the poet in *The Unicorn* (another unmistakable self-portrait) says so lovingly when dying, "Oh foolish people, who feign to feel what other men have suffered, you, not I, are the indifferent killers of the poet's dreams." It is moving to remember that in his will, Barber asked to have this closing madrigal performed at his funeral.

This fable in music consists of twelve madrigals plus an introduction, interludes and a march (twenty numbers in all). The introduction, first madrigal and first two interludes form a prologue to the following three sections, or three Sundays of the poet. The first two Sundays are made of three madrigals and an interlude each, while the final and longest section varies the scheme by interspersing madrigals and interludes. All of the madrigals but two are performed *a cappella;* the third and eighth madrigals are accompanied.

The *andante* introduction (straightforward in design and built of block chords) sets up not only the dramatic premise but a musical one as well. The writing is modal and makes a feature of the open intervals of a fourth and a fifth. The singers tell us, "There once lived a man in a castle and a strange man was he. He shunned the Countess' parties; he yawned at town meetings; he would not let the doctor take his pulse; he did not go to church on Sundays."

The first interlude *(allegretto con moto)* is the dance of the Man in the Castle, or the Poet, a jaunty piece in F-sharp minor that grew out of the world of *Amahl,* written five years earlier. It is transparent, uncomplicated music containing brief solos for most of the instruments, beginning with the oboe; it is as though Menotti were introducing them one by one to his audience.

The first madrigal sets the scene to take place

each Sunday afternoon in the town below the castle, when "all the respectable folk went out walking slowly on the pink promenade by the sea. Proud husbands velvety plump with embroidered silk-pale ladies." Their conversations are highly rhythmic but pitchless nonsense syllables. To the babbling of others, they respond, "How profound, how clever, how true! Only you could understand me," leaving us with little doubt of the extent of their depth and sincerity.

The second interlude, a promenade, is more gentle and playful, led off by the flute playing a busy, charming pattern in A major. With one exception, the interludes alternate between two and three sharps, usually in a major tonality. The madrigals wander much farther afield harmonically, and several are rooted in tonality for only brief stretches. For example, the second madrigal (which inaugurates the first Sunday of the Poet) begins staunchly in A major, but after nine bars shifts abruptly to the Dorian mode.

In the second madrigal, the Man in the Castle joins the Sunday promenade leading on a silver chain a unicorn. From T. H. White's translation of the twelfth-century *Book of Beasts,* quoted by Menotti in his score, the Unicorn is described in these terms: "No hunter can catch him but he can be trapped by the following stratagem: A virgin girl is led to where he lurks, and there she is sent off by herself into the wood. He soon leaps into her lap when he sees her and embraces her and hence gets caught."

On seeing the poet and his unicorn, the people first stare unbelievingly and then burst into laughter. "If one can stroke the cat and kick the dog; if one can pluck the peacock and flee the bee; if one can ride the horse and hook the hog; if one can tempt the mouse and swat the fly, why would a man rich and wellborn raise a unicorn?" Musically the madrigal alternates between fugal and canonic devices, and the questions asked are repeated in intensity until the music climaxes in a *maestoso* statement asking one last time, "Why would a man raise a unicorn?"

The third madrigal is both the Poet's song to his unicorn and the dance of the man and the beast. After a quasi-fanfare introduction, blown away by gentle, zephyr scale patterns, the mad-

New York City Ballet premiere of *The Unicorn, the Gorgon and the Manticore,* 1957: Arthur Mitchell, Eugene Tanner and Richard Thomas as the creatures, Nicholas Magallanes as the Poet.

rigal (one of the loveliest in the set) begins, "Unicorn, unicorn, my swift and leaping unicorn . . . Beware of the virgin sleeping under the lemon tree, her hair adrift among the clover." The fourth madrigal is a morose and chromatic dialogue between the Count and his Countess (symbols of fashionable snobbism) in which the lady rejects "velvets from Venice, fur from Tatary and dwarfs from Spain" in favor of a unicorn of her own.

To a delightful dance in D major *(allegro vivace ed energico)* she appears in the next section promenading her newly acquired unicorn. At first, the townsfolk stare at her and the Count with surprise, but soon everyone is imitating them and leading a unicorn about as well. In the fifth madrigal, the Poet enters with a gorgon, "a beast," according to White, "all set over with scales like a dragon, having no haire except on his head, great teeth like swine, having wings to fly and hands to handle, in stature betwixt a bull and a calfe." This martial madrigal *(allegro moderato)*—"Behold the Gorgon stately and proud"—soon puts its tongue in its cheek, commenting that the Gorgon "does not pause to acknowledge the racket of the critical cricket nor to confute the know-how of the sententious cow,"

the clatter of the cricket being drawn in repeated intervals of a second sung *staccato*. The madrigal evaporates in harmonic ambiguity as it describes the Gorgon as "he slowly sarabands down the street," fascinating the maiden and frightening the child.

Consternation spreads among the townspeople as they demand to know what the Poet has done with the Unicorn. "He only liked to gambol and tease, so I peppered and grilled him." The people explode in mock outrage in the midst of this sixth madrigal, deploring in darting vocal lines the killing of the pretty Unicorn and the replacing of it with the horrible Gorgon.

Once their anger is spent, the singers moralize in a slow, quasi-chorale in C minor: "Wicked is Man, Patient is God. All He gives Man to enjoy, Man will destroy. Muffle the horn and the lute, silence the Nightingale, banish all sleep, for the Unicorn slain by Man will not leap ever again." In the final measures of this lament, a solo tenor voice in its upper register wails mournfully and chromatically as the piece contracts to a single, sustained middle C.

The seventh madrigal is a dialogue between the Count and the Countess, which subtlely portrays the decadence of middle-age marital

The Countess (Janet Reed) and the Count (Roy Tobias) parade their prized unicorn for the townsfolk in the New York City Ballet production featuring costumes designed by Robert Fletcher.

relations. The vocal lines are free and the phrases episodic, almost like choral recitatives. The Countess has secretly poisoned her unicorn because "they have grown too commonplace," and she tries to persuade her husband to now buy her a gorgon. He roars at the idea, but when she breaks into tears (set chromatically for divided sopranos and altos in opposing cross rhythms), he gives in. "No! Not that I pray. Calm yourself, my dear. I shall find a gorgon this very day."

One of the most beguiling stretches in the piece follows, as the Count and the Countess appear at a picnic with their gorgon. Of course, it is only a matter of time until all the unicorns in town are slaughtered and every respectable couple is seen promenading a gorgon. The music for this interlude is a lulling, swaying pastoral (allegretto comodo) first sung by the oboe, then taken up with greater animation by the clarinet and later the flute and harp. Its gentle, airy mood is breached only at the end, as two stinging blasts of fanfare bring us out of this reverie and back to the story.

Menotti builds a bridge to the eighth madrigal by continuing the instruments of the interlude as accompaniment. Now the poet enters leading a manticore. This beast, White tells us, "has a threefold row of teeth, the face of a man with gleaming blood-red eyes, a tail like the sting of a scorpion and a shrill voice which is so sibilant that it resembles the notes of flutes." To the leggero lines of the madrigal, the Poet warns, "Do not caress the lonely Manticore unless your hand is gloved. Feeling betrayed, feeling unloved . . . he often bites the hand he really meant to kiss." The mood here is a grotesque one, an extension of the preceding interlude, and it is one of the more immediate and disarming of the madrigals. It's through-composed texture is in contrast to the improvised character of the others.

Menotti returns to this more spontaneous stance in the ninth madrigal, a dialogue between the townspeople and the Poet. When they ask what happened to the Gorgon, the poet tells them, "He was so proud and pompous and loud, I quickly grew tired of his ways." Convinced that the Gorgon has also been murdered, the people cry out, "He must be out of his mind. . . . Had he found something prettier at least, but this Manticore is a horrible beast."

During the fifth interlude, in which the Countess stabs her gorgon, tinges of L'histoire return, this time with an exotic, near-Eastern harmonic cast. The tenth madrigal begins in rocking patterns of triads and is, once again, an exchange between the Count and his lady, now a totally disenchanted couple. Predictably, she now wants a manticore. When her honeyed request is refused, she delivers a resounding slap (a clap of the hands from the singers), and the husband again gives in. "I knew we would finally see eye-to-eye," gloats the Countess. "Yes," moans the Count, "with the one eye I have left."

In the sixth interlude, the couple parade their manticore, which leads to the killing of the other gorgons in town and the acquisition of manticores by all. The ensuing interlude begins with fussy woodwind solos that playfully flit from measure to measure and quickly play themselves out. The eleventh madrigal is the voice of the townsfolk, and it opens with the same sort of canonic imitation used in madrigals two, four and six when the text dictates an exchange between two or more people. In this case it is the men and the women of the town wondering what has become of the Man in the Castle, for "he is seen no more, walking on Sundays his manticore." Curious as to whether or not he had done away with his manticore as he did with the other two beasts, they decide to go to the castle and find out for themselves.

Next we hear the snapping, brash phrases of the highly chromatic March to the Castle. As the music slackens, the singers take over to a solemn, almost death march: "Slow, much too slow is the judgment of God. But God's law works in time and time has one flaw: it is unfashionably slow." The music gains in power and drive until it leads us to the inevitable Menotti moral, in this case almost an indictment: "We detest all except what by fashion is blest. And forever and ever we shall respect what seems clever," words that Dr. Zuckertanz in Maria Golovin would have been comfortable mouthing.

Having spent their rage, the vocal and instrumental parts gradually wind down to nothingness—to a single spoken "Oh!" as they enter the

castle and find the Poet dying, in the loving arms of the three creatures. In the final madrigal, the Poet bids farewell to his beloved animals. He has not, of course, murdered them as he said. "How could I destroy the pain-wrought children of my fancy? What would my life have been without their faithful and harmonious company?" This simple but moving finale is not unlike the quieter *a cappella* choral writing found in *The Saint of Bleecker Street*. As the Poet bids each beast farewell, the harmony becomes more complex, rising from fourths and fifths during his fare-well to the Unicorn to lusher tonalities as he takes his leave of the Gorgon ("behind whose splendors I hid the doubts of my midday") then to the chromatic textures of his good-bye to the Manticore ("who gracefully leads me to my grave").

The music peaks one final time before the Poet's life is spent. With his final breath, he tells the creatures mourning him, "Equally well I loved you all. Although the world may not suspect it, all remain intact within the Poet's heart. Farewell, farewell. . . ."

Menotti with choreographer John Butler and the beasts of the first staging of the madrigal-fable, Washington, 1956.

Chapter Five
THE CONCERT STAGE

Pastorale and Dance for Strings and Piano

First performance in Vienna, 1934. Unpublished.

This short work is the only composition by Menotti prior to *Amelia al Ballo* to survive in his official catalog of works; it was also his first composition to be performed publicly. It is a slight but graceful effort, not unlike those disarming salon pieces by Sir Edward Elgar—the handiwork of a professional on his day off. The mood of the piece is ingratiating and rarely swerves from a gentle course during its eight-minute duration.

Concerto in F for Piano and Orchestra

First performance at Symphony Hall, Boston, November 2, 1945. Dedicated to Robert Horan. Published by Ricordi in a two-piano score. Scored for two flutes, two oboes, two clarinets, two bassoons, four trumpets, three horns, three trombones, tuba, timpani, percussion, xylophone, strings.

Until the twentieth century, composers renowned for operas usually wrote little else of consequence. Who today knows Verdi's String Quartet or Wagner's Symphony? The exception to this rule—as he was the exception to everything—was Mozart. The situation has been different in our century, however. Apart from Puccini (in effect, a nineteenth-century composer), virtually no composers have made their mark solely with opera. The trend began in the last decades of the previous century with such Slavic composers as Tchaikovsky, Dvořák and later Janáček.

But despite the ability of contemporary composers to balance their operatic output with symphonies and chamber music, and the disposition of the public to see nothing unusual in this juggling act, it still comes as a surprise to many to realize that Menotti has produced four concertos plus the *Fantasia* for Cello and Orchestra, a symphony and other large-scale works. These concert pieces have never received the acclaim that has been heaped on his theater pieces, or achieved the same frequency of performance. The loss is music's, for the best of his concert music is beautifully made—rich in imagination and solid in invention. The concertos, in particular, speak of the thoroughness of Menotti's technique on every page, and the depth of the training he received at the Curtis Institute under Scalero.

If Menotti truly felt he had been sidetracked from his real calling as a composer and seduced by *Amelia* and *The Old Maid*, then he demonstrated with his Piano Concerto how resiliently he was able to refocus his sights and reframe his musical outlook. There are those who argue that many of his concert pieces and particularly this concerto are little more than operas for instruments; indeed, the Concerto's first movement

Menotti working in his studio at Capricorn, mid-1960s.

could easily have been conceived as the prelude for an *opera buffa,* given its light, classical scoring and the pronounced vocal quality of its entrancing melodies.

If this is truly the case, then Menotti is in handsome company, for it has been said of Mozart that he wrote only vocal music whether for soprano or bassoon, just as there are those who feel that Stravinsky wrote only for the dance, whether he labeled a given score a ballet or a concerto. George Balanchine has amply proved this point about Stravinsky; Mozart and Menotti have needed no such advocate. The character of their melodic lines and the theatricality of their phrases speak for themselves.

The Piano Concerto was composed in traditional forms, with three movements: *allegro-lento-allegro.* The solo writing is extremely linear with nearly half of it restricted to two-voice writing. The resulting transparency of approach and the exuberance of the phrases harks back to the spirit of the keyboard sonatas of Domenico Scarlatti, while in the same instance recalling the wit and propulsion of Dmitri Shostakovich's First Piano Concerto, written a decade before Menotti's.

The first movement is generated by a pair of mottos sounded in the first four bars. The first of these is a martial statement of five punctuating chords:

The second theme is a quasi-bugle call played by the pianist. It plunges into a scampering fugal exposition that soon is exhausted but leaves a residue (the rhythmic idea (♪♪♪ ♪♪) that continues without letup and dominates the movement:

The movement proceeds along a classic *sonata-allegro* pathway, with many metric shifts and with an elaborate cadenza that comes as the climax of the recapitulation. This recapitulation,

in which Menotti introduces a new second theme, thrusts us into a short, brilliant coda that brings the movement to an end.

The elegiac slow movement is one of Menotti's signal achievements as a craftsman, not only a section of great melodic beauty and balance, but a touching evocation. Here he moves from the attractive but exterior values of the opening movement to graver, more interior ones, reflecting his ability in the theater to turn with conviction and ease from the charms of *The Old Maid and the Thief* to the terrors of *The Medium,* or to range from the simplicities of *Amahl and the Night Visitors* to the complexities of *The Saint of Bleecker Street.*

While the musical character of the opening theme of the last movement is martial, the movement itself is a five-part rondo with a lively second theme. The fourth section is the least convincing stretch in the movement and seems more to constrict the flow of the music than to serve as a contrast. Taken as a whole, however, this neoclassic composition, to quote Arthur Cohn, "enriches the formality of old Italian music with contemporaneously colored content. It is not a virtuosic concerto, notwithstanding the difficulty of the solo part; Menotti has understood the birth-sense of the word 'concerto' from its Latin meaning of *concertare,* 'to compete side-by-side.' "

Victor de Sabata, conductor for the first performances of *Apocalisse,* with Menotti in Pittsburgh, 1951.

Apocalisse for Orchestra

(Apocalypse)
Symphonic Poem for Orchestra

Premiere of first two movements, Pittsburgh, October 19, 1951. First performance of complete score, at the Academy of Music, Philadelphia, January 18, 1952. Commissioned by Victor de Sabata. Unpublished. Scored for three flutes (piccolo), three oboes, three clarinets (bass clarinet), three bassoons (contra-bassoon), six horns, four trumpets, three trombones, tuba, timpani, percussion, celeste, piano, two harps, strings.

Menotti's first major orchestral score is a full-scale work of theatrical dimensions. But it is not necessarily as apocalyptic as its name and opening fanfares suggest. "Most people know only the apocalypse of St. John the Divine in the last book of the New Testament," Menotti has observed. "I have read many different accounts of the apocalypse, most of which are in the form of poetry. This composition is a sort of synthesis or general impression of all the literature on the subject, the best known of which, aside from St. John, are those of Baruch and Enoch. Whereas most of us think of the apocalypse as a description of a future catastrophe, I found inspiration in the more lyrical, ecstatic and mystical pages of the writings."

Apocalypse is in three sections: *"Improperia"* (adagio solenne), *"La città celeste"* (andante sereno) and *"Gli angeli militanti"* (allegro ma non troppo). The *"Improperia"* section is named after the liturgical chants sung on Good Friday morning during the adoration of the cross. Menotti's "Reproaches" (a traditional literal translation of *"Improperia"*) is constructed on a series of contrasting slow-fast sections that suggest the contrasts found in the texts themselves. There are some ten of these sections, the first three of which form an introduction to the main body of the movement, an extended *allegro*. This introduction opens with two prophetic trumpet calls supported by the violins, which quickly evolve into fanfares built on a chantlike theme centering on E, which returns frequently:

After an outburst from the full orchestra (like a great cry of pain), the fanfare figures, heralding a renting of the sky, return to begin the principal *allegro*. This turbulent section finds Menotti leaving behind the world of *The Consul* (which preceded *Apocalypse)* and rushing headlong toward the broader sonorities and grander design of *The Saint of Bleecker Street. The Saint* is presaged not only in the use of the orchestra (especially in the high, yearning writing for the violins), but in the power of *Apocalypse* to evoke an aura of ritual and religious zeal.

The Messiah of Menotti's *Apocalypse* is an aggressive one who brings about his kingdom with a fiery sword in hand. This is suggested by Menotti partly through his musical means (a use of modality and of harmonizing with the open "church" intervals of the fourth and fifth) and partly through the enormous emotional intensity he brings to bear on the score. The second movement, "The Celestial City," is a musical description of the New Jerusalem, "built with sapphires and emeralds and precious stones, thy walls and towers and battlements with pure gold. And thy streets . . . paved with beryl and carbuncle and stones of Ophir." The quasi-Gregorian themes, which intermingle and intensify polyphonically, are developed as a *passacaglia*.

The shortest section of *Apocalypse*, "The Celestial City" is a static piece, as though the New Jerusalem were suspended in midair. The movement is one long, steadily mounting, incandescent crescendo built on three interwoven themes that are realized in tour-de-force fashion, involving at its climax the resources of the entire orchestra. In immediate contrast is the opening of the final movement, "The Militant Angels." It begins as a shimmering scherzo high in the violins and winds and races without letup until the orchestra has reached full sail.

So relentless and single-minded is the drive of the music that it peaks too soon and robs the fi-nal surge of its full dramatic effect. The score of *Apocalisse* is one of the few instances in Menotti's music where he seems to be repaying a conscious debt to a countryman, in this case Ottorino Respighi; there is no mistaking that Menotti's angels are marching militantly up the Appian Way.

Concerto for Violin and Orchestra

First performance at the Academy of Music, Philadelphia, December 5, 1952. Commissioned by Efrem Zimbalist. Published by G. Schirmer. Scored for two flutes (piccolo), two clarinets, two bassoons, two trumpets, two horns, timpani, percussion, harp, strings.

Of all of Menotti's concerted works, the Violin Concerto is the most poised, inventive and inspired. Though formally it follows the same patterns as the Piano Concerto, there is less of a sense of *concertare* and more one of a virtuoso instrument supported by a virtuoso orchestra. The soloist dominates throughout; the orchestra is left to propose ideas or second them, ideas that are nearly always coached in violinistic terms. They leave no doubt where Menotti's heart and interest lay while composing this piece for Efrem Zimbalist, the second husband of his longtime patroness, Mary Curtis Bok Zimbalist. His use of the orchestra, however, is of the greatest clarity and dexterity.

The first movement (*allegro moderato*) is in fairly orthodox *sonata-allegro* form and makes much of the cross relationship between C-sharp and C-natural. As the harmonic base of the movement is A, the music constantly rocks ambivalently between A major and A minor. The effect gives a near-Eastern flavor to the movement, one Menotti reinforces in contrasting sections of the third movement (like the Piano Concerto's finale, a rondo) in which he uses a timbal, or Indian drum, plus tambourine.

The harmonic contradictions of the first movement are introduced in the lower strings and immediately taken up by the soloist:

The entire movement is set in the shifting metric patterns so favored by Menotti (in this case they create intriguing and irregular phrase lengths in which units of six, nine and twelve in compound rhythms predominate). There is considerable development of the main theme through dazzling passagework for the soloist and by means of extension and fragmentation. Menotti departs from tradition by saving his cadenza for the second movement.

This *adagio* is an extended and lyrical three-part aria for violin and orchestra, which spins a mood of bittersweetness again amid ever-changing metric designs. The cadenza separates the two halves of the movement, and it is charged with the unrest and sadness that permeate the whole. Midway in the cadenza, Menotti introduces a change in attitude—a bouncing, jiglike figure based on repeated notes and used to propel the soloist back into the mainstream of the movement and toward its ecstatic conclusion.

The finale (*allegro vivace*) harks back to *Amelia* and the world of *opera buffa*. This rollicking rondo develops a highly accentuated *staccato* figure through a variety of moods and stances, with brilliant, imaginative touches and a sense of technical security that remains as individual as it is impressive.

The Death of the Bishop of Brindisi

Cantata for Chorus, Children's Chorus,
Bass and Mezzo-soprano soloists
and Orchestra,
text in English by the composer

The Bishop of Brindisi   Bass
The Nun   Mezzo-soprano
Townspeople and Children   Chorus

World premiere at the Cincinnati May Festival, May 18, 1963. Commissioned by the Cincinnati May Musical Festival Association. First performance as a stage piece, the University of New Mexico, Albuquerque, January 11, 1968. Published by G. Schirmer. Scored for three flutes (piccolo), two oboes, two clarinets, two bassoons, four trumpets, three horns, three trombones, tuba, timpani, percussion, piano, harp, strings.

This thirty-minute cantata is Menotti's first full-dress work for chorus and orchestra. It has been staged on several occasions, but not with the composer's encouragement; he sees *The Bishop* as exclusively a concert piece. The text was derived from a passage he found in Adolf Waas's book *History of the Crusades:*

Shortly before the Fifth Crusade (1218–1221), almost simultaneously from France and Germany, unarmed children set out to liberate the Holy Land. It is difficult . . . to understand that, after the death of so many men, children believed that God had chosen them to liberate Jerusalem without weapons; through the failure of the former Crusades, He seemed to have indicated that He disapproved of a struggle for the Holy City by force of arms. Even less can we understand . . . that grownups shared in this belief and assisted in the departure of the children. But if we take into consideration the almost trance-like enthusiasm of the Crusaders and their faith in the direct and miraculous help of God and His angels in the God-willed struggle, the Children's Crusades are more understandable. In 1212 . . . a ten-year-old boy named Nicholas began recruiting for such a Crusade in Germany. He was convinced that he was called by God, and that he would lead his band without being touched by the water straight through the sea to Jerusalem. Through the help of adults who were impressed by the enthusiastic faith of the children, they managed to cross the Alps and enter Italy, although with great difficulty and heavy losses. In Italy, the marchers began to disperse, as many could go no further. The rest reached Brindisi, where the Bishop tried to prevent their sailing. Those of the children who left onboard various ships were captured by pirates and sold as slaves in the Orient. The rest returned home. Quietly, depressed and singly, they returned who had left in singing and confident groups.

In addition to this account, Menotti made use of another (also described in Waas's book) that concerned a group of French children led by a shepherd boy named Stephen. Thirty thousand children joined him, also in 1212, to Marseilles where they embarked for the Holy Land in seven ships. Two of these were wrecked and went down with all their passengers. Five reached Alexandria, where the children were sold as slaves. Menotti tells their story through a succession of flashbacks as the Bishop on his deathbed relives this painful episode and, prodded by his conscience, questions his role in the affair. The cantata is yet another work exploring the quality of man's faith; in this instance, it is compounded and intensified by the added dilemma of guilt—real or imagined—with, once again, an autobiographical basis.

"Although I think that essentially I am a good

person," Menotti told John Gruen, "I also nurse a secret feeling of guilt about my life, and the Augustinian problem of Grace had intrigued me long before I wrote *The Bishop.* You see, I could never be a halfway Christian. T. S. Eliot's compromise, preached in *The Cocktail Party,* which was probably inspired by St. Basil's statement that 'a man's imitation of Christ can only go so far as his vocation allows,' would never satisfy me. Whatever I do, I like to do *all* the way. I am untouched by the Bible, but immensely moved by the teaching of the New Testament. One must, however, be a St. Francis to go all the way according to Jesus' teachings. So I have detached myself from the church, but I am still dangerously attracted to its history and to the lives of its saints. I never pray, nor go to church, except for purely sentimental reasons—like at Christmas or Easter—but I have a curious feeling of envy towards the lives of certain saints, like St. Teresa, St. Francis, St. John of the Cross, or even of St. Joseph of Cupertino, who often, upon hearing Mass, would fall into ecstasy and fly high above the congregation, throwing his little beretta into the air and uttering cries of joy!

"Of course, this kind of metaphysical anguish, as I like to call it, includes the problem of ethics—of how we must be held responsible for the good and evil we do. Is the Bishop responsible for the death of the children? Or is God only responsible for his mistakes? Surely the Bishop is not evil and acted in good faith. Why then does he bring disaster? Is the Bishop only a tool of God? Or must he alone bear his guilt?"

Though a far more complex and wide-ranging work than *Amahl, The Bishop* could well be said to be an extension of this world, the world of innocence, untrampled belief. The difference here is that where *Amahl* was concerned with the faith of a single child, *The Bishop* enlarges the theme to embrace thousands. The text is one of Menotti's most poignant and expressive achievements as a poet—words and images are ever clear-eyed, evocative and minus the cloying that at times invades and devalues his writing.

The cantata opens with a soft, rising theme in F minor *(adagio)* that we will identify with the voice of the child crusaders. It is harmonized in

open intervals that give it a medieval cast:

This almost stately motive suddenly accelerates with the entrance of the Bishop's voice. The writing here and throughout for the bass soloist is more than recitative and less than an aria; it is that middle ground of speech-song that Menotti finds so attractive for advancing the action of a story, and with which he is so pointedly proficient. It is used to remarkable effect in this cantata to express the agony and self-recrimination of the Bishop. It comes as no surprise that his outcries when he imagines the young crusaders returning to accuse him of their death are reminiscent of the hallucinations of Boris Godunov when he sees a vision of the child Dimitri, whom he had murdered. Not only has Menotti professed great admiration for Mussorgsky's music, and *Boris* in particular, but the Russian was also a master of the same sort of dramatic recitative Menotti finds so appealing.

"No longer can the deceptive sun eclipse the hovering ghosts," the Bishop sings; "the unraveled mind can no longer weave its reassuring patterns." He commands the Nun to lock the doors, and in quiet, measured phrases she attempts to reassure him: "Dark and voiceless is the palace . . . it is a cold and windy night." The voices he hears, she continues, are but the sea "pounding its green hooves over the marble terraces." The shadows he sees are but "swift, migrating clouds flowing along the moon's paths."

"Ah! save me, sister," the Bishop pleads, "save me from the children . . . the bloodless, glass-eyed children hung with weeds, crying for help." Little by little the Nun manages to calm his fears. Reminding him that death is near, she begs him to "rescue the heart from the wreckage of your past." To a plaintive flute solo, the Bishop relives this wrenching episode in his life: "Holding a glass of sweet Salernian wine, I saw the setting sun place a golden sword upon a sluggish sea . . . Suddenly I heard them along the beach, among the olive groves. . . ."

Very faintly, as if from afar, the voices of the children are heard limning the theme that opened the cantata, now recast in C minor: "Good men, let us pass. Conquer we shall Jerusalem guided by Gabriel's flaming flight, for we are God's own infantry. Give us your ships, give us the sea." Their martial song increases gradually in strength before it is broken off by a strain in the oboe playing a tune that is almost a continuance of Amahl's piping.

In time, the townspeople take up the children's song and bring it to a full-throated conclusion: "Behold the singing children, God's own little knights. Barefoot and ragged and consumed with loneliness they come toward us. What burning vision in their sunken eyes gave them such lasting strength?" The Bishop, crying out in agony, brings us back from memory to reality: "Give me an enemy to kill, O Lord, but not a child to help!"

The Nun interrupts saying, "It is not your fault if they all drowned. You tried to stop them, we all remember, but the people would not listen. . . ." The townspeople are heard in a vigorous chorus (*presto, con energia*) demanding the Bishop allow the children to proceed to Jerusalem: "Are not the innocents the very messengers of God? Let them depart. Give them your blessing!" "Oh, God," the Bishop cries out, "you gave me a ring, you gave me a staff and called me a shepherd. If I must guide your flock, why did you leave me unguided?" Relenting, he blesses the crusade, and as they set forth from the harbor of Brindisi, their voices chant: "I shall kiss our Lord's tomb, I shall free the Holy Land. Do not cry dear Mother; it is God's command."

But against the B-flat major cadence at this point Menotti sounds an F-sharp to tell us all will not be as the children believe. Fifteen measures later, a torrential storm breaks in the orchestra. This superb bit of descriptive music is couched in rising and falling chromatic passages in which one all but feels the sting of the wind and the force of the waves lashing at the ships. As the fury of the storm mounts, the frightened children call out to their parents and the Bishop again commands the Nun to lock the doors so that he can escape their voices. Singing "*Jesu Deus*

noster, miserere nobis," the children quietly, serenely drown as the storm abates.

"I blessed them to their doom," the Bishop moans. "Was it God's will or my own folly? I do not think I blessed them out of pride or vanity, but then our soul is deeper than we are, and who can trace and kill the Minotaur who haunts the labyrinth of our hearts?" His self-recrimination is interrupted by the violent chorus of towns-

people: "Cursed be the shepherd who leads his flock to death! Stone his palace, burn his books, break his staff, cast his ring into the sea. Let him walk naked among men." Their fury is soon spent, leaving the Bishop alone with his guilt.

For a final time, the Nun urges him not to ask vain questions but to prepare his soul for death by prayer. Over the Nun's chanting of "*Requiem aeternam,*" the moral of the work unfolds. In answer to the Bishop's question "why I, who loved so purely, was cursed with such destructive love," the chorus answers, "Nothing is purposeless. Why should God have given you in life a questioning mind, if not to hand to you in death the blinding answer?"—a belief that will be reaffirmed in *The Labyrinth.*

This absolution is intoned *a cappella* over the Bishop's lifeless body, first in unison and then in the simplest chorale setting. It is music at once moving and consoling, a piece Menotti has requested to be performed at his funeral: "Sleep, sleep in peace, o gentle pilgrim, sleep into the dawn." The final word, however, belongs to the orchestra—seven, crushing, *fortissimo* blows that bring the cantata to a riveting conclusion.

Curtain call following the premiere of *The Death of the Bishop of Brindisi,* Cincinnati: conductor Max Rudolf, Menotti, soloists Rosalind Elias and Richard Cross.

Triplo Concerto a tre

First performance at Carnegie Hall, New York City, October 6, 1970. Commissioned by the Samuel Rubin Foundation. Published by G. Schirmer. Scored for two flutes (piccolo), two oboes, two clarinets, two bassoons, two trumpets, two horns, three trombones, tuba, timpani, percussion, harp, strings.

Seventeen years were to pass before Menotti turned again to the concert stage. The task he set himself this time was an intricate one—a triple concerto in three movements for three groups of solo instruments and orchestra, each group composed of three instruments. The first solo group consists of piano, harp and percussion; the second of oboe, clarinet and bassoon; and the third of violin, viola and cello. At work here, of course, are the principles of the eighteenth-century *concerto grosso*—the interplay between a *concertino* group (which Menotti triples) and the main body of instruments, or *tutti*. It is yet a further reaffirmation on his part of traditional, formal strictures.

One can easily understand why he responded to this form, for Menotti thrives on self-imposed limitations. Music thus becomes a puzzle to be solved, an intellectual challenge to be met. In the process of establishing boundaries, he produced with this concerto the exciting interaction, resulting from contrasting sonorities and contrapuntal designs, that is the basic appeal of the *concerto grosso* form for composer and audience alike.

This piece was written in an effort to return to a greater simplicity in his writing, for Menotti feels "contemporary music has gone too far from what I call the inevitability of music. This inevitability is the only thing that really interests me in music: it is a kind of Platonic truth I feel. It is what I love in Schubert, Mozart and Beethoven—the inevitability of their themes. It is there, and you cannot change a note of it without disturbing the whole. Whenever I hear music where notes can be changed and it makes no difference, I am no longer interested.

"I believe very much what Michelangelo said: 'The statue is already in the marble. All a sculp-

tor must do is take away what is too much.' I want to discover that kind of melody, to find that kind of musical truth. That is why I returned to utter simplicity, just tonic and dominant chords. But not the way Virgil Thomson has gone back, with his sort of 'sick' tonic and 'sick' dominant. The problem of writing like this is, of course, how to wed this simplicity to contemporary theatrical needs. After *Wozzeck* and the operas of Strauss, it is very difficult to achieve great dramatic tension using very simple musical means. But this is what I am searching for. I am sure I will die before I find it."

If the *Concerto a tre* can truly be said to have been molded from simple harmonic clay, then it is a simplicity of the greatest sophistication. The first movement *(allegro)* is firmly anchored in C major, but Menotti works in, around and through this key to form the needed contrasts of tension and relief. A great virtuosity is required of the nine soloists here, but their parts seem conceived not so much for technical display as for creating attractive textures and perceptible layers of sound. This first movement owes a debt as well to classical sonata form, but the connection here is more tenuous than in the Concertos for Piano and for Violin, for the interplay between the orchestra and its soloists inevitably overrides purely structural considerations, creating in the process its own intricate designs.

The contrast in the Concerto's first-movement themes reflects a duality of design that wears differing melodic masks, but that never quite obscures Menotti's face underneath. The first theme is bright, bouncy and open:

The second is dutifully softer, and sighs rather than proclaims itself.

The writing throughout has an almost X-ray clarity, exemplified by the piano part, which like the Piano Concerto is predominantly structured as two voices. The work abounds in bracing, tingling sonorities, especially in the large solo percussion battery, which includes celesta, snare drums, cymbals, bass drum, tambourine and xylophone. Rather than overweighting the crystalline textures of the piece, these instruments are used sparingly and sharpen and define the contours of the music.

The Concerto is permeated with a jaunty, French quality—à la Poulenc and his *Concert champêtre*—a quality that has never made itself felt quite so persistently before in Menotti's writing. This Gallic sound occurs primarily in the first movement, for the second could not be more Menottian in its swaying, pastoral gait. It is built on a charming theme in G major *(lento molto)* that, like so many Menottian melodies, is embellished with a turning flourish:

After twenty bars of this, the piano, percussion and harp abruptly switch moods, chromatically increasing the tension in an almost intrusive way. When this *concertino* group tapers off, and the opening material returns, it, too, has an unsettled character and lacks the repose of its first appearance. This unrest spreads throughout the orchestra for a moment before the music regains its composure. Even a final, raucous outburst from the piano cannot alter the orchestra's now serene course, as it quietly outlines one final time the lyric opening material in its original form.

The third movement is cast in E-flat major *(allegro con brio)* and is *alla marcia*, though the beginning sounds more like a reel masquerading as a march rather than an all-out, double-time quickstep. The melodic material for this section, however, is thinner, less thoroughly worked out, and lacks the good-humored spontaneity of the first and the mesmerizing atmosphere of the second.

Leopold Stokowski, conductor for the premiere of Triplo Concerto a tre, leading the American Symphony Orchestra, 1970.

Suite for Two Cellos and Piano

First performance at Alice Tully Hall, New York City, May 20, 1973. Commissioned by the Chamber Music Society of Lincoln Center in honor of Gregor Piatigorsky. Published by G. Schirmer.

On the surface, it appears this four-movement suite was tailored not only to the lyrical style of Gregor Piatigorsky, but at moments to the Russian cellist's Slavic background and temperament. The piece begins with an introduction (originally labeled *"arioso"*), followed by a *scherzo, arioso* (originally a *romanza* and positioned initially as the second movement) and finale.

The introduction *(andante maestoso, ma con moto)* is unusual for Menotti in its harmonic density. Over thick, somber chords in the piano (usually appearing in inversion), the first cello sings out a brooding melody soon echoed by the second. As might be expected from a work for two like instruments plus piano, the grist for this mill is imitation, and in all but the finale, a mirroring of ideas and the overlapping of solo lines forms the basis of the two cello parts. There is also a distinctive elegiac character to the movement, as if the song being sung by the cellos is a lament.

The *scherzo (allegro)* second movement is more serious than playful, but here emerges an open, trim style of writing more easily recognizable as Menottian. Harmonically, however, there are only hints of the composer's favorite intervals and the particular twist he imparts to a melodic line. Though the *scherzo* ranges far, exploiting the extremes in registers of the instruments, the impression left is one of containment.

The third-movement *arioso (lento, rubato)* is in the vein of the *adagio* of the *Triplo Concerto,* and in it, Menotti seems to be reminding us of Piatigorsky's magisterial way with the Bach Solo Cello Suites by weaving a handsome, neo-Baroque musical tapestry. Like the previous movements, the *arioso* is predominantly in minor.

With the finale, we land securely on the *terra firma* of C major, proclaimed in a bright, unmistakably Menottian fanfare figure, one not that far removed from the opening of the Piano Concerto. Italian sunlight bursts through the darkness of the steppe, and for the first time, strong, homophonic blocks of sound fill the musical landscape. The movement bustles with humor, and pizzicato figures (encountered previously only in the *scherzo*) make a playful return. The energy level is extremely high, the parts are dazzlingly difficult and the work is brought to a rousing conclusion amid a barrage of double scales. Menotti has described this Suite as being among his favorite scores.

Fantasia for Cello and Orchestra

First performance RAI, Turin, Italy, January 16, 1976. Commissioned by the Ford Foundation. Unpublished. Scored for two flutes (piccolo), two oboes (English horn), two clarinets (bass clarinet), two bassoons, four trumpets, two horns, three trombones, tuba, timpani, percussion, harp, strings.

Though Menotti first labeled this single-movement work a *"capriccio,"* he must have realized on finishing it that the serious, probing quality of its main theme was more fantastic than capricious. Although the piece is cast freely, it conveys the impression of sonata form, and thus the first movement of a standard three-movement concerto rather than an independent work that stands on its own. This feeling is reinforced by the large orchestral forces required.

After a bar of restless, intricate figures in the orchestra *(andante con moto),* the soloist sweeps in with the primary theme—a long-lined melody couched in D minor (the predominant key of the Suite for Two Cellos as well) and built on the wide, ascending intervals of which Menotti is so fond:

Little more than a dozen bars and a brief cadenza later, the orchestra takes up the first idea, in effect creating a double exposition. The development begins with the return of the soloist, whose part is echoed at first by the orchestra and then urged on to a full-scale *allegro*. Here the solo part is more filigreed, adventurous and complex, and it builds steadily to a torrent of scales that leads to yet another orchestra *tutti*.

When the solo cello reenters, it is with a dotted, *scherzo*-like figure set within a much lighter orchestral texture. Gradually this secondary figure is exhausted, and the final section of the Fantasia is ushered in by the original theme softly recapitulated in the orchestra. The soloist then limns a mutated version of the theme and adds a second and more extended cadenza built on a diminution of the main idea. A final *allegro* (the *scherzo* figure now in full orchestral dress) amounts to an elaborate coda that carries the *Fantasia* and the solo cello to a brilliant, breathless conclusion.

Symphony No. 1 in A Minor ("The Halcyon")

First performance at the Saratoga Performing Arts Center, Saratoga, New York, August 4, 1976. Unpublished. Scored for two flutes (piccolo), two oboes (English horn), two clarinets (bass clarinet), two bassoons, four trumpets, three horns, three trombones, tuba, timpani, percussion, piano, harp, strings.

On the eve of his First Symphony, Menotti remarked, "I loathe to begin a new work. Like Tobias, I am always terrified by the prospect of my battle with the angel. Unconsciously, I keep postponing the day when I am to embark on a new project. Any excuse is good. I know that once I begin, I am trapped. When that happens, the day, often the night, no longer belongs to me. To begin or finish a work I have to be cornered. That is why I eagerly accept commissions or force myself into a position of having to accept commissions.

"I am just as loath to relinquish my works and declare them finished. As I said, I have to be cornered . . . and that is why I have so often been accused of 'last-minute writing,' and of doing unpolished, slipshod work. I must admit that this frenzied writing does affect the precision with which I convey my thoughts to the written page. But not the main conception and the core of my work, for if some of my works have been written hastily, they have all been planned slowly and carefully. They have all had a long period of incubation. When people marvel at the speed with which I compose . . . they don't realize that most of the music has been in my head for months, and my notebooks are full of music destined for future works."

This symphony, premeditatively labeled "No. 1," as Menotti hopes eventually to add to its number, is scored for large orchestra and was written with the virtuoso capacity of the Philadelphia Orchestra in mind. Its subtitle, "The Halcyon," is a name applied to the kingfisher. The ancients believed the bird bred at the winter solstice in a nest floating on the sea, and so charmed the wind and the waves that both remained at peace during this period. Thus, the symphony represents a stretch of calm weather, and in Menotti's stormy life that is exactly what moving into Yester House, his present home in Scotland, meant. It was here that the First Symphony was composed.

"This house is my last folly," he mused in 1979. "I bought it because I love cold weather, I love rain and I love silence. Silence is very expensive in most countries, especially in Italy where you have to be a millionaire to afford it. But in Scotland silence is very cheap." The joy Menotti felt at Yester is abundantly reflected on every page of this sunlit, effervescent score cast in three movements—*allegro moderato, adagio ma non troppo* and *andante mosso/allegro con brio*—and in a Haydnesque vein.

The first movement, though centering on A minor, begins deceptively on a bright, unison C, followed by a flourish that quickly corrects the first impression of a major key. This major feeling is not easily stilled, and it continues to bob within a sea of sound that is essentially minor. Here again is the sort of ambiguity felt so strongly in the opening movement of the Violin Concerto. Here it is blatant and less a structural unit; "playful" would be the better description.

Also, that indefinable yet unmistakable French quality that perfumed the *Triplo Concerto* resurfaces in the first movement. As with many Menotti orchestral *allegros*, the urge is strong to listen to this movement not so much as a piece of symphonic character (well-seated as it is in a solid sonata form) but as a three-part overture to a comedy. Theater is implicit in its phrases, and the drama on which the curtain never rises must have been a lighthearted, *Amelia*-esque one.

The slow movement (an harmonic *passacaglia*) is brief and songlike, whose principal D-minor theme is presented in harmony first by the winds and the strings rather than in a bass line (as would be the case in an orthodox *passacaglia*); later are added variations in the horns and a rather jazzy bit for the trumpets. The entire section has a mournful character that one can never take quite seriously, as though Menotti was in a mockish mood with his tongue firmly lodged in his cheek. This movement is one he has earmarked for revision, for he feels it needs lengthening to give the music a greater breadth.

This mock-serious quality spills over into the *andante* that prefaces the finale, but it is almost instantaneously brushed aside by a bustling figure high in the violins. This figure is continually interrupted by other choirs of the orchestra, which attempt to assert their supremacy over it but to little avail. This constant seesawing gives the movement a schizoid rather than *scherzo* cast, and until the very end the music seems unable or unwilling to settle on a single course and maintain it. The symphony ends with a manic dash to the home base of E major with nothing decided and no one element the victor.

Eugene Ormandy, conductor of the Philadelphia Orchestra, with Menotti at the time of the premiere of the Symphony No. 1.

Landscapes and Remembrances

Cantata for Soloists, Chorus and Orchestra,
text in English by the composer

First performance Milwaukee, May 14, 1976. Commissioned by the Bel Canto Chorus. Published by G. Schirmer. Scored for two flutes (piccolo), two oboes (English horn), two clarinets (bass clarinet), four trumpets, three horns, three trombones, tuba, timpani, percussion, piano, harp, strings.

Outside of his operas, Menotti's only choral composition prior to this cantata had been *The Death of the Bishop of Brindisi,* an odd fact given his special ability for writing for voices in combination. The nine-part *Landscapes and Remembrances* is a set of musical impressions drawn from the composer's life, ranging from his arrival in America as a teenager to his discovery of South Carolina, where he founded the Spoleto USA Festival in 1977. It ushered in (either by design or chance) a four-year period of extensive writing for both adult and children's choirs. It was a stretch of creativity broken only by the composition of his first historical opera, *Juana La Loca,* a work that curiously enough contains a minimum of choral writing.

The structure of *Landscapes* consists of alternating choruses and orchestral songs, although several of the choral sections make use of solo voices as well. The titles in general reflect the geography of remembrance at the root of each: "Arrival in New York by Sea," "The Abandoned Mansion," "Parade in Texas," "Nocturne," "A Subway Ride in Chicago," "Picnic by the Brandywine," "An Imaginary Trip Through Wisconsin," "Farewell at a Train Station in Vermont" and "The Sky of Departure."

One of the most striking aspects of these highly individual pieces is the wide-ranging imagery of Menotti's free-form poetry, and the telling way he mirrors these images in sound. The first chorus, for example, vividly evokes the apprehension and awe of an immigrant sighting New York City for the first time ("The huge profane cathedral of our earthly gods"). "I was sixteen," Menotti remembers, "when I first landed in New York. It was a cold winter morning, a few days before Christmas. My mother was with me."

It also captures the sound of screaming gulls and the slow, churning motion of the ship as it neared land and recalls through heavy, tonal chords the voices of the passengers as they wonder aloud whether "those towers bend to hear .my voice or shall I, too, be lost among those sunless lanes. . . ." Oddly enough for a man who is so intimately linked with singing, Menotti has written comparatively few songs outside of the four in this cantata. His first, "The Hero" (which owes nothing to the opera of the same name or vice versa) is also one of the few instances in which Menotti has set the words of another to music—in this case, his poet friend Robert Horan. Almost twenty years were to elapse before Menotti again turned to song. This time (as if to make up for his neglect of the genre) he wrote a cycle of seven moody and arresting works—*Canti della lontananza* ("Songs of Absence")—to Italian poetry of his own. They were premiered by soprano Elisabeth Schwarzkopf at Carnegie Hall on March 18, 1967, and they deal with passion in its various temperaments and guises. Then in 1981, there followed a more direct and lyrical set of four love songs for tenor and piano commissioned by Joseph Porrello, and premiered by him in New York City at Merkin Concert Hall of the Abraham Goodman House on October 21, 1981. (A fifth song was added to this set in 1983.)

The first song in *Landscapes*—"The Abandoned Mansion"—is for mezzo and is subtitled "South Carolina" and indicates in terms of time that we have taken a giant step forward to the mid-1970s. But displacement of time is as characteristic of this cantata as it is of memory itself. A brooding piece in E-flat minor *(andante con moto)*, it is a song infused with the past. Its constantly arcing melodic lines are supported by persistent tremolo figures that give way only briefly in the middle of the song to sustained chords—a section of quasi-recitative. The key to the song lies in these words: "A visitor to the South is an intruder into the reign of ghosts."

"Parade in Texas" *(allegro),* the second chorus, is like an old college pep song played by a brilliant but seemingly out-of-tune marching band. It is boisterous, stirring and almost Ivesian in its exploration of a martial idea through a half-dozen keys beginning with E-flat major. In the course of this chromatic kaleidoscope, Menotti first shouts, "Hurrah for the American parade," and then asks rather wistfully, "Youth of Texas, what dragon are you marching out to slay, what citadel to storm, what prisoner to free?" As the chorus melts away, it confides to us in a whisper, "The dragon is already wounded, and not far from Texas the citadel is crumbling and outside of Texas the prisoner is free." It reaffirms Menotti's belief that "no youth in the world is younger than American youth; it is both its weakness and its strength."

The second song is for baritone—"Nocturne," subtitled "Driving at Night Through the Desert." Though it ends resolutely in C major, it begins far afield in E major *(adagio ma non troppo).* Against lyrically intertwining lines in the orchestra and the repeated admonition in the singer's part of "I must not fall asleep," the singer-driver muses what a "strange gardener is God who plants nothing but a full moon on his barren ground. . . . The road unfolds in front of me, an endless empty scroll on which to inscribe my dreams . . . the black angels of death like mute sirens in a parched sea hum their hypnotic call." The song is a souvenir of Menotti's first drive West in the mid-1940s, where he spent a brief time as a Hollywood writer.

"A Subway Ride in Chicago" *(andante),* the third and longest chorus of the set, begins with the percussion battery suggesting the rhythm and monotony of the trains that follow the same un-

alterable paths day in and day out. Against this droning clickety-clack, one traveler tries to guess the secrets behind the faces of the others: "I wonder who you are? Italian? Armenian? Greek? What long *via crucis* has lined your face? You stare intently as if trying to recapture the sound of the distant sea." Sea-sounds sweep through the orchestra (like those heard in the first chorus) and are displaced by sharp chords as the chorus turns its attention to another passenger.

"And you black woman, so old and haggard, what treasures has your Baptist God put in your shopping bag for you to smile with such heroic contentment?" Before this thought can be explored, the orchestra breaks into a gentle, dancelike figure in compound time (a sort of *Sylphides* nocturne) diverting the chorus's attention to a young ballerina in a far corner of the train. "Will you ever find the dark swan prince of your heart," it queries, "or will you have to drown your sorrow in glorious mad scenes?" At this point the music segues from, so to speak, *Giselle* to *Lucia di Lammermoor,* as a solo soprano and mezzo-soprano embark on a florid cadenza.

The music turns homophonic once more as the chorus demands almost indignantly in *fortissimo* chords, "Why are you looking at me through your harlequine glasses, old maid? After so many years of faithful, faultless typing, will your boss at last bestow his cigar-flavored kisses on your pale, pursed lips?" On these last words, a sustained chorale is heard in the orchestra as the chorus comments, "Strange brothers we are, briefly staring at each other without a sign of recognition. . . . We shall all call for help and never help each other, we shall all search for love and never find each other, we shall all die in different beds and never be told of each other's death." To Menotti, one's dreams of brotherhood "are often buried in squalid subways."

With ripples of watery sound in the orchestra *(allegretto),* the third song—"Picnic by the Brandywine"—begins. It is for soprano and carries us back to a golden afternoon during Menotti's student days at Curtis when he discovered the bucolic side of America "so little known to foreigners." Frequently during weekends with Samuel Barber and his family, there were outings along the Brandywine, a river that flows near the Barber home. "Can one be happier than gathering stones and twigs to make a fire by the Brandywine?" the singer asks. The middle section of the song traces each member of the group during their picnic of "turkey, ham and roasted corn. Uncle Sidney [composer Sidney Homer] is lecturing Sam on Brahms, Sue [Barber's sister] is struggling with Marcel Proust in French, Daisy [his mother] is knitting and Roy [his father] is asleep."

The music bubbles quietly and gently along until the soloist (the voice of Menotti) suspends the motion of the song on a *pianissimo* high B-flat: "Stretched out on the warm, damp grass, I close my eyes, time floating over me like an aimless river." With these words, the song dissolves in a quietly sustained F-major chord with an added sixth. In a miniature sense, the piece might be termed Menotti's *Knoxville*.

The fourth chorus—"An Imaginary Trip Through Wisconsin"—is emotionally the biggest section of the cantata, and is essentially a love song that builds to an ecstatic climax. It is a song of renewal, one that begins with the premise that "Europe is the antique garage where all American bric-a-brac is gathered—neon in Spain, plastic chairs in Greece, blue jeans in Paris, tin food in London." Against a single, high, clean D in the orchestra, the chorus almost mystically contrasts Europe with America: "Here in Wisconsin, carefree and forgotten, I shall start my voyage at Calumet." Obviously the evocative names of towns in Wisconsin—Fond du Lac, Cornucopia, Boscobel, Eau Claire, Lac du Flambeau—triggered exotic ideas in Menotti's mind, and in the balance of the piece he undertakes a fantasy journey through the state as the music grows chromatically to great heights.

The final song is for tenor ("Farewell at a Train Station in Vermont") and is also concerned with love, but this time with the bitterness of parting. "In everyone's life," Menotti has commented, "there is a farewell never forgotten, the pain of which never heals," a sentiment he had previously expressed in his libretto for Barber's opera *Vanessa*. It is evident that this section of *Landscapes* is as rooted in actuality as the pre-

ceding one was a product of imagination. Over a solemn, *adagio* figure, the solo voice sets the stage for this short *scena:* "The train is late. It rains as it must when lovers part forever. Without a word we pace the empty platform, measuring our protracted agony with uncharted steps."

Against weeping, two-note phrases in the orchestra, the tenor asks, "Why must we part? Why must it end? All this could be changed by words not yet said. Please don't go." The pace tightens (now *allegretto)* and the accompaniment becomes turbulent and driving as the train pulls into the station. With its halting ("the iron bull to take my Europa away"), the orchestra bursts into one of those streams of yearning of which Menotti is such a master. Above it the tenor cries out, "I hardly heard your quick goodbye, nor could you have heard my silent cry." The original, stark punctuating figure returns as the singer walks away from the station, "repeating the senseless incantation against my unremitting pain—'Why must we part?' "

The last chorus, "The Sky of Departure," is thoughts on "Leaving America by plane at sunset." After having lived, loved and worked in America for over forty years," Menotti reflects, "could I ever leave it without feeling exiled?" This feeling will eventually cause Menotti to confide during the course of this section that "in the aging heart a gnawing doubt persists . . . Is it fear of having been rejected? Is it the bitterness of the defeated? Is it the shame of the deserter?" These questions are prefaced by an *a cappella* sweep to top A by the chorus (then echoed by the orchestra) proclaiming, "As a frustrated Zeus I ascend the fiery sky" taking one last look at the land's "unconquered body, its unsurrendered beauty."

After the contrasting, questioning section, Menotti casts his dark thoughts aside and with them the uneasy, chromatic chords that had underlined them. He returns triumphantly to the opening flourishes crying out in a paean of joy, "America, goodbye, oh love of my youth. If I return to you no longer as an impatient, eager lover, but as a wistful, undemanding friend, will you then open again your skies to me?"

Cantilena e scherzo

for Harp and String Quintet

First performance at Alice Tully Hall, New York, March 15, 1977. Commissioned by the Chamber Music Society of Lincoln Center. Dedicated to Alice Tully. Unpublished.

The opening section of this lovely twelve-minute piece *(andante calma)* is a moody, songful barcarole section. It is one of the few pieces by Menotti that echo the style of Samuel Barber through its opening, angular melodic idea. Still, there is no doubt who is the composer of the ensuing *scherzo (allegro ma non troppo)*. In its intervals and harmony, every bar bears Menotti's stamp. The *scherzo* climaxes in an extended cadenza for harp, followed by a return to the *andante* opening material. It is in this introspective frame of mind, capped by a broad coda that stretches from *lento* to *adagio,* that the work ends. It was choreographed by Martha Graham two months after its premiere under the title *Shadows.*

Miracles

for Boys' Choir and Orchestra,
texts from poetry by children

First performance at the Tarrant County Convention Center Theater, Fort Worth, Texas, April 22, 1979. Commissioned by the Texas Boys' Choir. Unpublished. Scored for two flutes (piccolo), two oboes, two clarinets, two bassoons, two horns, two trumpets, two trombones, timpani, percussion, harp, strings.

This set of eight musical miniatures was based on poetry by children ranging in age from five to twelve printed in an anthology compiled by UNESCO. Originally a dozen poems were to be set by Menotti, together with several instrumental interludes, but the four poems and the interludes were not ready for the premiere and remain to be added.

It is not difficult to imagine why Menotti was attracted to these brief, naïve and often touching poetic images, yet another example of his fashioning music to texts of others. The poems, some of which rhyme and some of which are abstract, presented the composer with not only a wide variety of moods, but disarming honesty and charming perceptions as well. It was Menotti, after all, who once observed that when the emperor was wearing no clothes, a child was the first to notice.

Miracles is not a major score but it is an affecting one. In the tall tale "Two Million, Two Hundred Thousand Fishes" there are *Amahl*-like qualities, and the lilt and life of a phrase such as "If you put a golden egg on them" from "I Love Animals and Dogs" is the purest Menotti. Several of the choruses flow together, and one section ("I Am a Nice Boy") is for solo voice. The musical settings, like the poetic thoughts, are free, fantastic, exuberant and childlike.

In every instance Menotti has captured not only the particular sense of a given poem, but its innocence as well. The problem with the score now is one of balance. Perhaps another large-scale piece on the order of the raging "A Thundery Day" would prevent this number from overshadowing the others, while orchestral interludes would provide breathing space between the poems and keep them from tumbling in one upon the other. It is yet another work earmarked by Menotti for revision.

Missa "O Pulchritudo"

for Four Soloists, Chorus and Orchestra,
text from the liturgy

First performance Milwaukee, May 11, 1979. Commissioned by the Bel Canto Chorus. Unpublished. Scored for two flutes (piccolo), two oboes, two clarinets (bass clarinet), two bassoons, four horns, three trumpets, three trombones, tuba, percussion, timpani, harp, strings.

In retrospect, it seems inevitable that Menotti would compose a setting of the Mass. Many operatic composers, whether they hold fervent religious convictions or not, have been attracted to the liturgy of the Catholic Church for the beauty of its Latin texts, the manner in which the open vowels of the language resound in the voice and the tremendous drama implicit in its words, with their vivid pleas for mercy and their rapt affirmations of faith.

In his forty-minute Mass—Menotti's only use of Latin apart from the choruses in *The Saint of Bleecker Street*, Baba's ravings in *The Medium*, brief moments in *The Death of the Bishop of Brindisi* and the chanting on Felipe's death in *Juana La Loca*—he makes one notable departure from the Ordinary of the liturgy. While the *"Kyrie," "Gloria," "Sanctus," "Benedictus"* and *"Agnus dei"* sections are in their accustomed places, the *"Credo"* (which follows the *"Gloria"*) has been replaced by a motet whose text is St. Augustine's self-recrimination *"O Pulchritudo,"* in which he berates himself for departing from the ways of beauty and for having looked for beauty outside of God. It is charged with a sense of guilt and self-questioning for a lapse from faith, which must have struck a painful chord within Menotti himself.

This frankly sensuous passage is substituted for the traditional affirmation of faith in "one God the Father Almighty, Maker of heaven and earth . . . in one Lord Jesus Christ, the only-begotten Son of God . . . and in the Holy Ghost, The Lord, and Giver of Life." Thus Menotti's Mass is more than a mass; it is a *mea culpa*, in which the character of St. Augustine, his fiery visions and his profound struggle with the Bible and orthodox religion, colors the entire spirituality of the work.

It is like a hostile force trying to fight against the praise of God. In so many ways, Menotti's need to believe and his inability to do so find an even more immediate outlet here than was the case in the more allegorical *Saint of Bleecker Street*. He has described it as having a dark quality—a mass for a troubled world.

This work is a dramatic answer to those who have lamented what they felt to be a waning of Menotti's gifts. Here he is creating at not only a highly expressive level, one in which rich melodic ideas pour forth with almost embarrassing generosity, but one as individual as at any stage of his career. The results are an expansive canvas of sounds, one harmonically fresh (with strong key centers and only quick brush strokes of dissonance) and one continually resourceful in its rich use of the contrapuntal arsenal.

This joyous, spontaneous piece belongs first to the chorus and a quartet of soloists; the orchestra supports, colors, underlines and provides relief through cannily positioned interludes but in the main fulfills a secondary function. The Mass begins *a cappella* with a vigorous statement *(andante)* of *"Kyrie eleison"* by the full chorus that is built on a stark, open interval of the fourth and fifth. After four statements, which form a sort of prologue to this first section, the orchestra is heard in a chorale prelude-like passage firmly lodged in A major. In this stately yet festive mood, the first part peaks and dies away unexpectedly in B-flat major.

The solo quartet initiates the *"Gloria" (allegro energico)* with the tenor leading off *a cappella*. This lively start leads to a fugal exposition at *"Et in terra pax,"* and for the return of the *"Gloria"* the chorus joins the quartet in a sunburst of sound.

This section is broken into several contrasting parts, each marked by a change in the textures and rhythms of the orchestra's music; indeed, here and elsewhere the orchestra seems the wellspring from which the chorus flows. The first such shift occurs at *"Qui tollis peccata mundi,"* a series of upward phrases, canonically stated. After a thundering climax on *"Miserere nobis,"* the next mood is pastoral with harp arpeggios and a garland of woodwinds wreathing *"Quoniam Tu solus sanctus,"* couched in a modal Gregorian style. A sense of jubilation crowns the movement with the final, *allegro* amens.

"O Pulchritudo," which follows, begins with an unadorned line for the sopranos and doubled quietly by the orchestra. But as happens throughout the work, this simplicity gives way to exuberance as Menotti responds to St. Augustine's call to recapture beauty. Once past the canonlike opening, the choral writing is more often structured in blocks of sound than not.

Menotti has chosen to combine the *"Sanctus"* and *"Benedictus"* into a single musical statement linked by a hushed but restless orchestral interlude. A feature of this section is the casting of the *"Benedictus"* for solo soprano and mezzo-soprano. It is only in the final third of this section that the chorus finally joins in, intertwining with the lines for the two soloists and reinforcing them for the concluding hosannas. If Menotti's concept of *"Hosanna"* is more restrained than one might have expected, his setting of the final *"Agnus dei"* is bigger and more fervent than is usually the case. It forms a response to the opening gloom, and is almost like a desperate cry for peace. It also contains a violent outburst from the orchestra midway, and the final *"Dona nobis pacem*s" are delivered like hammer blows through a series of high G's for the sopranos. With the last chord, Menotti raises doubt for the first time in the course of this affirmative work. The superimposition of an F-minor triad over a C-minor one leaves us at the end with a question instead of an answer—"Is peace possible?"

Menotti's *Missa "O Pulchritudo"* as performed at the Spoleto Festival U.S.A. in 1981 under conductor Joseph Flummerfelt with soloists Suzanne Hong, Diane Curry, Tonio DiPaolo, Boris Martinovich.

A Song of Hope

("An Old Man's Soliloquy")
for Baritone, Chorus and Orchestra,
text in English by the composer

First performance in Hill Auditorium, Ann Arbor, April 25, 1980. Commissioned by the University of Michigan Musical Society for its one hundredth anniversary. Unpublished. Scored for two flutes (piccolo), two clarinets, two oboes (English horn), two bassoons, timpani, percussion, xylophone, harp, piano, strings.

One could look upon *A Song of Hope* as the final third of an autobiographical choral trilogy that began with *Landscapes and Remembrances* and continued with the *Mass*. All three are highly personal statements—impressions that taken as a whole form a continuity in Menotti's life from the age of sixteen to virtually the eve of his seventieth birthday.

A Song of Hope is, of the three, the least localized and the most philosophical. It is a short work haunted by war and death, and, like the Cello Fantasia, seems part of a larger scheme rather than a self-contained entity. In this score, Menotti makes peace with the rage he expressed in *The Consul*, a work that arose from similar emotional impulses. But where his concern there was man's inhumanity to man, here his purpose is consolation.

Musically, *A Song of Hope* grew out of the world of *Juana La Loca*, which preceded it; indeed, its orchestral prelude seems but a slight variant on Juana's second-act aria "At last, my master lies unmasked." It is a sectional piece, and the many shifts in mood and tempo were dictated by the emotional about-faces of the text, which relives events of the Second World War—the marching of "barbarian hordes," the burning of books, the killing of neighbors. It is clearly music whose purpose is as much commemorative as it is occasional.

Moans, Groans, Cries, Sighs

("A Composer at Work")
for mixed voices *a cappella*,
text in English by the composer

First performance in Usher Hall, Edinburgh, Scotland, August 31, 1981. Commissioned by the King's Singers. Unpublished.

A year after *A Song of Hope*, Menotti added a witty postscript to his series of choral works in the form of a short madrigal for six unaccompanied voices. It continues in the same autobiographical frame of mind as the works that preceded it. Set in D minor, the text laments:

> *Blank paper, empty head*
> *And no text in sight.*
> *Why did I accept this commission?*
> *What made me think I could do it?*
> *Work, Gian Carlo, work.*
> *Whoever said that music is a pleasure!*

> *It's more like a sickness.*
> *It can drive one to drink.*
> *It never leaves you alone.*
> *It haunts your dreams,*
> *It digs your grave . . .*
> *Ah! to be young again!*
> *It's always too late . . .*
> *But thank God, this piece is finished.*
> *I hope someone will like it.*
> *Addio, adieu, Amen.*

The music is as manic as the words, by turns pulsing, dark, reflective and jubilant but always with a sense of fun to it.

Muero porque no muero

Cantata for Soprano, Chorus and Orchestra,
text from St. Teresa of Avila

First performance at the Cathedral of St. Matthew Apostle, Washington, D.C., October 15, 1982. Unpublished. Scored for two flutes, two oboes, two clarinets, two bassoons, four horns, two trumpets, trombone, tuba, percussion, harp, strings.

This haunting, brief cantata is one of the few Menotti scores that has a pointed ethnic profile to its phrases. It is predominantly modal, even to suggesting Gregorian melody, and this modality is of a Spanish cast, achieved through the interplay of parallel harmonies and sharp rhythm snaps in the vocal line. At the same time, Menottian trademarks are everywhere, from mystic chords, such as he conjured in *The Saint of Bleecker Street,* to the yearning melody that is the core of the opening *adagio* (the cantata is cast in a slow-fast design, with the chorus employed in the latter section):

The musical patterns underline the ecstasy and melancholy of St. Teresa's text, as well as her mercurial and secular personality, with a suggestion of dancing rhythms. The poem echoes the theme of his *Nocturne* premiered later the same month: a yearning for death and the release it offers.

I die because I cannot die . . .
I already live outside myself,
Since I am dying of love . . .
Oh! how long this life is,
This jail, these chains in which my soul is placed . . .
Come sweet death, come quickly, because
I die because I cannot die . . .

The work is couched in extraordinarily direct terms, yet the impact of words and music together is riveting. Like his mass, this cantata is a stirring instance of the rejuvenating, creative spring Menotti has been able to tap in his seventies.

Nocturne

for Soprano, String Quartet and Harp

First performance at Alice Tully Hall, New York City, October 24, 1982. Commissioned by the Chamber Music Society of Lincoln Center. Unpublished.

This short occasional piece was a second birthday salute to music patroness Alice Tully. Menotti's text was an elegiac poem of his own, on the theme of growing old and the regrets it brings, the promise of rebirth and, by implication, death. His principal image is the night, hence the title *Nocturne*, with its symbolism of the close of day (and life) and an innocent, childlike acceptance of this inevitability with serenity. The music flows evenly along with the text, with no untoward harmonic or melodic ripples to disturb the tranquil surface of the score. The vocal line mixes both song and recitative into an easy, homogeneous whole, a sort of *berceuse* for modern man:

At last,
I found the night again.
Again I trace my hopes
upon a starry sky,
and search the darkness,
for my fears . . .

Concerto for Double Bass and Orchestra

First performance at Avery Fisher Hall, New York, October 20, 1983. Commissioned by the Wenger Company (Minnesota). Unpublished. Scored for piccolo, two flutes, two oboes, two clarinets, bass clarinet, two bassoons, four horns, two trumpets, three trombones, tuba, timpani, percussion, harp, and strings.

In returning to the concerto form and writing for double bass, Menotti was "apprehensive and intimidated by the bulk of the instrument and its apparent unwieldiness. One is apt to think of the double bass as a lugubrious, threatening and unmanageable creature. Only on closer acquaintance does one discover its hidden charm and the many surprising facets of its personality. The double bass can be nimble and humorous, as it can be graceful and tender—and its melancholy lyricism has a pathos that is inimitable.

"Far be it from me to claim that in my Concerto I was able to explore all the different moods of this forbidding instrument. But I am happy to say that what . . . seemed to be an elusive and somewhat unfriendly acquaintance has now become . . . a most lovable friend. The Concerto is loosely constructed along the lines of classic sonata form. There is no proper cadenza in any of the movements, although the first and third movements are introduced by short soliloquies."

The Concerto speaks throughout of Menotti's undiminished ability to build with solid craftsmanship, and it is filled with brilliant wind, brass and percussion highlights. A brief introduction presages the principal material used in the first movement—a figure in compound rhythm stated first in the winds and then rekindled in the strings. This leads immediately into the entry of the solo bass in the first of the two extended, recitative-like, unaccompanied passages found in the piece.

The orchestra then returns with the principal theme, an extension of the first motif. It is a dark, brooding, shaped-edge idea in A minor of intense theatrical portent. A secondary idea is stated by the bass, a sort of malevolent *scherzo*, and the marchlike development harks back to the manner of the march idea sounded so strongly in the first interlude of *The Consul*. Both the march and the opening, vaulting theme alternate with lyrical sweeps and a reappearance of the *scherzo* motto in major that combine to keep the movement's atmosphere positive.

The slow movement (*adagio ma non troppo*) is a warm *cantilena*, a three-part song in E-flat major for the soloist and the orchestra; it is among the loveliest and most tranquil pages in all of Menotti's writing. Its two outer, sustained sections are balanced by the unrest of an *agitato* middle stretch, but this brief ruffling of the movement's mood only momentarily disquiets the calm that prevails and predominates.

The last-movement *allegro* (essentially a rondo construction) is launched by a free, downward cadenza that leads without pause into the finale. The theme is jaunty, playful and cast in a compound rhythm. In a style that is second nature by now to Menotti, he proceeds with what might be best described as a network of musical checks and balances. The busy, rolling character of the first theme is offset by a *grazioso* second idea and then by a *marcato* idea that pushes itself forward through strong, offbeat accents. But again, and typically, no one idea is allowed to dominate, so that there is always present a vivid element of contrast—once more the idea of *concertare*.

Dialogue III

JA: How satisfactory was it to create music for dance?

GCM: I have only written two works for the dance, so I can hardly call myself an expert in the field. *Sebastian* was written at the time when many choreographers—Antony Tudor, Agnes de Mille, Roland Petit, to name a few—still followed dramatic guidelines. It was still possible for composers like Stravinsky, Prokofiev, Copland etc. to write ballet scores linked to a definite dramatic action. Things have changed now. Choreographers no longer work within the tyranny of a dramatic-musical score. They want to be their own masters, therefore prefer impersonal electronic noises to underline their movements or take well-known symphonic or chamber-music works on which to superimpose what seems to me arbitrary movement. I find this latter trend very debatable and often comical if not offensive. Dancing to a Beethoven symphony is, to me, little short of blasphemy.

JA: Discuss your concept and approach to form in your concertos and the symphony. How far do you bend traditional forms and personalize them?

GCM: Symphonic and chamber music have attracted me mostly because they give me a chance of dealing with the architecture of a piece intellectually rather than emotionally. The struggle with form is ever present in my music, and the challenge is essential to my inspiration. I like to be limited within a given form; I feel that only by adopting and adhering to a blueprint can you build a musical scaffolding of any strength. Self-imposed restrictions such as the sonata form, the rondo, the fugue, the canon, etc., are nothing but challenges to spark off intelligence and inven-

tion. This is why many modern poets still accept the challenge of the sonnet, of rhyme and classic versification. Too much freedom is dangerous to art. It immediately opens the door to amateurishness. I often think of art as the highest intellectual game. Indeed, there is a great affinity between sports and art, an affinity that the statisticians have not bothered to explore. A game, to be interesting, must define its rules and must clarify its goals. The more difficult the challenge, the more satisfying the victory. You cannot cheat or change the rules of the game to make your task easier. Bach, of course knew all this, and he remains the greatest musical athlete of us all. But while in sports, the athlete must display physical grace in overcoming his hurdles, the artist's achievement must appear not only effortless and spontaneous, but also emotionally expressive, which, of course, makes our game more noble than pure sport.

JA: Why is it then that your output of chamber music has been so small compared to your operas and your music for the concert hall?

GCM: It is lack of time. I hardly finish one opera when I am propelled into a new one. Actually I love chamber music best and I think I could be rather good at it. I regret not having written more songs. Perhaps I am a little afraid of writing chamber music because I am quite certain that if I devoted more of myself to it, I would probably stop writing for the stage forever. In symphonic and chamber music you are less the victim of arbitrary interpretations than you are in the theater. In opera you must hope for a good conductor, good singers, good stage direction, good lighting; you have to put your work in the hands of so many people who feel that the

Samuel Barber and Menotti in the living room of Capricorn, their country house at Mt. Kisco, New York, 1950s.

stage allows them all sorts of liberties—and you know how easily a pudding can be spoilt by too many such cooks; while in pure music, not only are you in fewer and safer hands but you face your creative task on safer ground. The rules of the "game" are clear and you are a surer master of your material. What makes good musical theater is an elusive and unpredictable element no composer has yet mastered to the point of safeguarding himself from the possibility of sudden total failure . . . see the lives of Puccini, Wagner, Verdi etc. In opera your material can be too easily distorted

and ruined by too many inexpert cooks, while in symphonic or chamber music works a piece can be played too slow or too fast but still the boundaries imposed on interpretive freedom are more apt to preserve the original intention of the author.

JA: Why do you think that between Mozart and Tchaikovsky it was so rare to encounter composers equally at ease in both the opera house and the concert hall?

GCM: Not every composer is capable or willing to use music in a dramatic context, because it forces one to employ a very elusive quality of music that some musicians, not without some justification, find impure. Of course, I do not agree. Music has always been associated with human action as dance, worship, ceremony or drama. But music, indeed, is essentially ab-

stract and self-contained. It does not need to illustrate action or accompany it or be applied to a definite human feeling. However, it does also have the powerful, evocative power to illustrate a situation, describe a mood or express and intensify emotions. At the same time, it cannot escape its own independent logic. Here is the main problem that the composer has to face when writing an opera, a problem some composers refuse to face. The music must be made capable of following a dramatic action or illustrating a visual situation. At the same time, it must not be robbed of its own logical impulse; it must not be watered down to mere background music. Good music cannot be asked to be literal because its course is essentially independent. It is only with emotional or visual associations that it can become descriptive of passion and feelings. That is why we accept Schubert setting different verses of a poem to exactly the same tune.

We also accept the fact that composers, myself included, often take a theme destined for one work and use it successfully in a completely different context. In an opera, the same theme can underline different situations, as Verdi, Wagner and Puccini have shown us. In my case, for example, the theme I applied to Annina in *The Saint of Bleecker Street,* when she is preparing herself to receive the veil, I stole from the film of *The Medium.* It is the music that underlines a brief added sequence showing Mrs. Nolan opening the cupboard in her daughter's room to look at the girl's first communion dress. (The theme by the way is based on yet another theme, which underlines the dialogue between Mrs. Nolan and what she believes to be her daughter's ghost during the seance earlier in the opera). Of course the situations are not wholly dissimilar; in both instances there is a white bridal gown and the expectation of a communion with God. Still, they are two very different operas. Again, in *Apocalypse* I used the theme that first appeared in the dance score I wrote for Martha Graham's *Errand into the Maze.*

JA: Discuss your instrumentation, the use of the

Changing seasons at Capricorn . . .

piano. Have you preferred certain orchestral sounds for different moods and emotions?

GCM: I must confess that I have never been over interested in orchestration *per se*. I feel that good music must be able to adapt itself to the limitations of available instruments without being enslaved by them. No outrageous instrumental adaptation can kill the music of Bach, whether adapted for guitar, mandolin or accordion; it even survives inflated orchestral transcriptions by Stokowski or Schönberg. Besides, instruments change. The orchestra of today is really quite different from what I remember as a child. You can be sure that a hundred years from now, another kind of sea will be mirrored in Debussy's *La Mer*.

I do not consider myself a particularly brilliant or original orchestrator, nor do I spend too long over my orchestral scores. I make the orchestra serve my music as clearly and simply as possible, rather than tailor my music to exotic orchestral effects for the sake of them. I avoid as much as possible harmonics, flutter-tongues, *col legno* and all those effects so dear to most contemporary composers. I do not ignore their possible dramatic use, and I have employed them when I find them necessary to some theatrical effect. But I do find it extremely irritating in Bartók, for example, his excessive use of such superfluous noises.

My inclusion of the piano in my orchestrations is mainly dictated by the need I feel in my musical texture for a more agile and percussive bass than either the strings, the brass or the woodwinds can offer me. The piano also creates a very dramatic change of texture when you have the piano alone or only with a couple of other instruments. It can cut the thickness of the orchestra and give a dry sound that I find very effective. Every composer has certain favorite instruments; I have always had a predilection for the oboe, and I certainly do consider my instruments as sort of sweet animals or pets. One is my little dog, one is a lamb, another a vixen. To me they are living creatures. But I will not let them enchain me. They must always know who the master is.

JA: Do certain tonalities or sounds appeal to you for evoking certain moods or emotions?

GCM: If they do it is an unconscious preference. I do find that very often I lean to certain keys and avoid others, but it is never for any specific reason.

JA: Your scores are filled with metronome markings; how literally should these indications be taken?

GCM: None of those markings are really mine. I accepted them at the insistence of some con-

ductors. It is very difficult to pin my music down with metronome markings because its meter changes continually as it follows its melodic or dramatic impetus, often changing slightly its tempo from measure to measure. Those markings should be taken only as a vague indication of what the point of departure for the interpreter's intuition should be.

JA: A number of today's composers also conduct. Were you ever tempted to conduct your own music or the music of others?

GCM: Conducting never tempted me very much, perhaps because I know I would be a very poor conductor. Not only is my ear not infallible, but I lack a sense of rhythmic precision, and when I listen to music I am often so carried away that I forget where I am and what I'm doing. Need I say more?

. . . the composer's home, 1943–73.

Chapter Six

THE TELEVISION STAGE

Amahl and the Night Visitors

Opera in one act,
libretto in English by the composer

Amahl	Boy-soprano
His Mother	Soprano
King Kaspar	Tenor
King Melchior	Baritone
King Balthazar	Bass
The Page	Bass
Shepherds and Villagers	Chorus and Dancers

World premier New York, December 24, 1951. First professional stage performance by the New York City Opera, April 9, 1952. Commissioned by the NBC Television Opera Theater. Published by G. Schirmer. Scored for flute, two oboes, clarinet, bassoon, trumpet, horn, percussion, harp, piano, strings.

"This is an opera for children," Menotti has written, "because it tries to recapture my own childhood. In Italy . . . we had no Santa Claus. I suppose that Santa Claus was much too busy with American children to be able to handle Italian children as well. Our gifts were brought to us by the Three Kings instead," the Magi who followed the Star of the East to the Christ-child's crib.

"I actually never met the Three Kings—it didn't matter how hard my little brother and I tried to keep awake at night to catch a glimpse of the . . . Royal Visitors, we would always fall asleep just before they arrived. But I do remember hearing them. I remember the weird cadence of their song in the dark distance; I remember the brittle sound of the camel's hooves crushing the frozen snow; and I remember the mysterious tinkling of their silver bridles.

"My favorite King was King Melchior, because he was the oldest and had a long, white beard. My brother's favorite was King Kaspar. He insisted that this King was a little crazy and quite deaf. I don't know why he was so positive about his being deaf. I suspect it was because dear King Kaspar never brought him all the gifts he requested. He was also rather puzzled by the fact that King Kaspar carried the myrrh, which appeared to him as a rather eccentric gift, for he never quite understood what the word meant.

"To these Three Kings I mainly owe the happy Christmas seasons of my childhood, and I should have remained very grateful to them. Instead, I came to America and soon forgot all about them. . . . But in 1951 I found myself in serious difficulty. I had been commissioned by the National Broadcasting Company to write an opera for television with Christmas as a deadline, and I simply didn't have one idea in my head. One November afternoon as I was walking rather gloomily through the rooms of the Metropolitan Museum [of Art], I chanced to stop in front of *The Adoration of the Kings* by Hieronymus Bosch, and as I was looking at it, suddenly I

Christmas Eve, 1951—the birth of what was to become Menotti's most frequently performed opera, with Chet Allen as Amahl and Andrew McKinley, Leon Lishner and David Aiken as the Three Kings bearing gifts for the newborn child.

heard again, coming from the distant blue hills, the weird song of the Three Kings. I then realized they had come back to me and had brought me a gift."

The gift they brought was not only for Menotti, but through him, for the world. It was his one-act miracle play *Amahl and the Night Visitors.* Like the stage version of *The Medium, Amahl* has remained relatively free of changes and tampering through the years. Menotti seems to have known instinctively that it could not be bettered. *Amahl* poured from him in an amazing

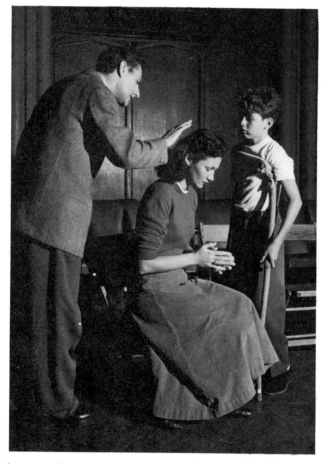

burst of creative energy, and it remains one of his most securely crafted, affecting and concentrated works. It is a masterful blend of naiveté and sophistication—the sort that never calls attention to itself—simplicity and artfulness. Once more, the roots of this opera are grounded in faith—the blazing faith of the Three Kings and their intrepid pursuit of the star and the Child. Amahl may be the focus of the story, but it is

the kings and their pilgrimage on which the story turns and which forever alters the lives of Amahl and his mother.

Amahl is Menotti's most popular opera and the most frequently performed opera in the United States. It has been translated into dozens of languages, and so great is its appeal, it has become one of the universal symbols of Christmas and the Christmas spirit. Though much has been made of *Amahl* as the first opera for television, ironically Menotti hardly thought of the medium *per se* during the writing of *Amahl.* "As a matter of fact," he has said, "all my operas are originally conceived for an ideal stage which has no equivalent in reality, and I believe that such is the case with most dramatic authors. For the creator, the moment of nightmare in a dramatic work occurs when he finally sees his idea frozen in the realistic frame of the theater. Something infinitely precious to the author is altered when the original poetic impulse has been translated into literal and visual terms, no matter how excellent they may be. When realized in the theater, the work becomes suddenly a disassociated and detached entity in front of which he finds himself almost a stranger. That mysterious moment of vision has been made wonderfully and fatally concrete.

"I'm sure that to very young people the stage must appear histrionically primitive compared to the cinema and television, but to me the stage still comes the closest to that 'ideal theater,' perhaps because its greater use of symbolism, imposed by its own limitations, demands of the audience a wider range of imagination and a deeper poetic sense. To me, cinema, television and radio seem rather pale substitutes for the magic of the stage. This is the reason why, in writing *Amahl and the Night Visitors,* I intentionally disregarded the mobility of the screen and limited myself to the symbolic simplicity of the stage.

"The spectator who takes no journey and has no appointed time or seat but, carelessly clad, sits casually on the first available chair in his living room, and who, knitting or perhaps playing with the kitten, turns on what he takes to be a theatrical performance, will never know the emotion of a real theatrical experience. The theater

Menotti coaching Rosemary Kuhlmann, the Mother, and Allen for the world premiere, presented on NBC-TV.

must be a choice—a carefully made appointment. Machiavelli, even after he retired to the country, used to don his most elaborate and richest clothes before setting to work on his books. Symbolically, at least, every artist does the same. He addresses you in utter dignity—whether his message be comic or tragic—and to partake in his experience you must share this seriousness and receive his message wearing your 'Sunday clothes.' "

The specific challenge of opera on television, Menotti feels, is the fact that "opera is not a theater of action. It is a theater of contemplation. What interests us in opera is not what happens—it is what people think about before something happens or after it happens. Action is dealt with very quickly . . . Only children are very startled when the swan comes in. But we are waiting for Lohengrin, to hear what he has to say to his swan. And that, again, is another hurdle for television, because what is important on television is the image and not what people think about the image."

Amahl was written, scored, rehearsed and premiered in only a matter of weeks. A messenger from New York would travel several times a day to Menotti's country home, Capricorn, in Mount Kisco, pick up a page or two of manuscript and take the next train back to have it copied and delivered to the performers. So pressed was Menotti for time that Samuel Barber pitched in and helped with the orchestration. The Morgan Library in New York owns the manuscript orchestral score of *Amahl*, and the pages of the score can be seen there in both Barber's and Menotti's script. Even for Menotti, infamous for working on a new score well beyond a reasonable deadline and even up to the day of a dress rehearsal, this was tempting fate. "People, they say, dig their own graves," he has reflected, "and I guess this is my way of killing myself. But . . . most of my successful operas were written like that.

"My publisher likes to remind me that Stravinsky once said, 'Inspiration is like a baby; you have to sit it on the pot every morning.' Well, I try to sit my inspiration on the pot each morning, but it doesn't always work. It seems I'm never

finished with a score. I had to sign a letter promising my publisher I would not put any more changes in my first opera . . . and I had to force myself to finally publish *Maria Golovin* so that I would stop making changes in it."

Though the action of *Amahl* should take place in what is now Israel, Menotti has always visualized the setting as a Neapolitan crèche scene or *presepio*, with the characters of the opera dressed anachronistically in the medieval clothes found in a *presepio*, a further evocation of his Christmases as a boy. The single scene takes place

on a stage divided between the interior of the shepherd's hut where Amahl lives with his mother, and the countryside around and beyond the hut. The room is virtually bare, with only a few pieces of crudely fashioned furniture, but outside the night sky is pierced by stars, dominated by the Star of the East, whose flaming tail floods the sky and landscape with a glowing radiance.

Costume sketch of Amahl and his mother by designer Eugene Berman.

The prelude to the opera, only a dozen bars, is in A major *(andante sostenuto)*, and in a few, quick brush strokes Menotti creates some of the most touching phrases in all of his operas. It is a picture in sound of the crystal-clear winter night and its star, music that is both chilling and warming at the same time. As the curtain rises, Amahl is seen outside the hut playing his shepherd's pipe, with a roughly hewn crutch lying on

It is the expressed wish of the composer that Amahl always be performed by a boy. To Menotti, "neither the musical nor dramatic concept of the opera permits the substitution of a woman costumed as a child . . . All the action, and even the characteristics of the adult figures, is dictated by his [Amahl's] point of view. The seeming severity of the Mother, the occasional colloquial conduct of the Three Kings, the visit of the

the ground beside him. The tune he pipes is a merry one built around scale patterns and the intervals of a fourth and fifth, which suggest a *corna musa* or bagpipe drone (despite the folk-like character of this and the other modal tunes in *Amahl*, Menotti's score is original):

Shepherds, the theft of the gold, and the miracle—all these must be interpreted simply and directly in terms of a child's imagination."

Menotti further feels that Amahl must be "a naughty little boy—a little devil. The character should be impish. He tells lies, he is disobedient." He is, in fact, one further composite of characteristics of Menotti himself with his tendency toward pranks and his Italianate love of exaggeration. There is also a real-life link between the two as well. During a brief time in his childhood, Menotti was slightly crippled. His leg

Amahl (Allen) tries to sleep on the straw pallet, his crutch by his side.

was blessed in front of an image of the Madonna in the sanctuary of Sacro Monte near his home and was healed shortly afterward.

Amahl's mother, working at household chores, pauses to listen to his playing and then calls to him to come indoors. A series of empty descending chords in the orchestra tells us before the Mother tells Amahl that it is too cold to be outdoors. Amahl answers but doesn't stir; after a moment's pause he begins playing again. When he ignores the Mother's second call she orders him sharply into the house. In a brief *duettino*, Amahl begs to stay outside. This lively exchange capsules in succinct form two of the basic qualities of Menotti's vocal writing—repetition and use of sequence. Because these appear here in their simplest state, they seem to dominate the writing more than is the case elsewhere. For example, each of Amahl's pleas and each reply by the Mother are virtually the same, varied only slightly in rhythm and pitch to accommodate the text and add urgency to the vocal lines. This embues the music with a ballad-like character, which is certainly what Menotti was striving for.

The Mother warns, "There will be a weeping child soon if he doesn't hurry up and obey his mother," and with this admonishment, Amahl reluctantly rises and hobbles into the house to a short, dirgelike passage that echoes his plea to remain outdoors. "Oh! Mother," he exclaims, "there has never been such a sky. Damp clouds have shined it and soft winds have swept it as if to make it ready for a king's ball . . . Hanging over our roof there is a star as large as a window and the star has a tail, and it moves across the sky like a chariot on fire." This passage and most of the vocal parts in *Amahl* are of a free sort of accompanied recitative, or, at the most, an *arietta*. This is in keeping not only with the intimate scale of the piece but with Menotti's desire that the story be experienced through Amahl's sensibilities. This is surely what prompts the melodramatic outburst of the Mother that follows: "Oh! Amahl, when will you stop telling lies? Here we have nothing to eat and all you do is to worry your mother with fairy tales."

Amahl tugs at her skirt, insisting that she look,

pleading that he is not lying, but she brushes him aside. "First it was a leopard with a woman's head, than a fish as big as a boat; now it is a star as large as a window . . . with a tail of fire." "But there is a star," Amahl insists, "and it has a tail this long." He measures the air as far as his arms can reach. His mother frowns, and he reduces the size by half. "Hunger has gone to your head," the Mother says sadly. "Unless we go begging,

how shall we live through tomorrow?"

As she sinks weeping, Amahl gently strokes her hair and attempts to console her in a touching *arietta* that later becomes another *duettino*. "Don't cry, Mother dear, don't worry for me. If we must go begging, a good beggar I'll be . . . We'll walk from village to town, you dressed as a gypsy, and I as a clown." The Mother kisses Amahl and puts him to bed as the light in the room dies except for a faint glow in the fireplace and the radiance of the sky as it pours through a window.

From the distance, a soft, measured tread is

The Mother (Kuhlmann), desperate because her son is hungry, is tempted to steal gold guarded by the Kings' sleeping page (Francis Monachino).

heard, and over it the solemn, weighted song of the Three Kings: "From far away we come and further we must go. How far? How far, my crystal star?" As their song becomes more audible, Amahl rises on one elbow and listens with astonishment to the singing. Soon, unable to control his curiosity, he throws back his cloak and, to a scampering single line of music played by flute and *pizzicato* strings, he hobbles to the window. As their song gains in intensity, the Three Kings appear on the road outside the house. First comes Melchior, bearing a coffer of gold; then Balthazar, with a chalice of myrrh; and finally Kaspar, with an urn of incense. They are preceded by a page bent beneath a heavy load and carrying a lighted lantern.

Reaching the hut, King Melchior knocks. The Mother instructs Amahl to see who is at the door. To the same *pizzicato allegro* as before, he goes to the door and opens it a crack. When he sees Melchior, he closes it quickly and runs to his mother. Breathlessly he tells her, "Mother, Mother, come with me. I want to be sure you see what I see." When she asks what all the fuss is about, Amahl tells her there is a king with a crown outside. The unbelieving Mother sends him back to the door; he opens it a second time and closes it just as quickly. "Mother, I didn't tell you the truth before. There is not a king outside; there are two kings!" "What shall I do with this boy," the Mother laments. When Amahl returns a third time and reports a third king ("And one of them is black!"), the Mother rises wearily and goes to the door herself. As it swings open to a shining, widely spaced E-major chord, the kings are bathed in radiant light. Amazed, the Mother bows to them, and they respond in close harmony with "Good evening!"

"What did I tell you," Amahl whispers triumphantly, as the Mother invites the Kings to enter. Preceded by the Page with his lantern and bundles, the Kings enter one by one to a jaunty march tune, one of several stretches of music that remind one *Amahl* followed on the heels of *The Consul*. King Melchior tells the Mother they can only rest a brief while so that they do not lose track of their star. "What did I tell you?" Amahl interjects with a grin. As the Mother goes to

gather some firewood, Amahl asks Balthazar if he is a real king. He patiently answers Amahl's questions and then asks the boy what he does. "I was a shepherd. I had a flock of sheep. But my mother sold them. Now there are no sheep left."

Amahl next goes to Kaspar and asks if he, too, is a real king. "Eh?" Kaspar replies, and Balthazar indicates to Amahl that Kaspar is deaf. Amahl then repeats his questions louder, in longer note values and on higher pitches. Finally, Amahl points to a jeweled box the king is holding, and Kaspar becomes very animated. Opening one drawer at a time, he tells Amahl in a lively *arietta*, "This is my box, this is my box, I never travel without my box." He explains that the first drawer contains magic gems to ward off evil, make one sleep, heal wounds, help one find water, soothe one's eyes and protect one from lightning. The second holds beads that Kaspar loves to play with, and the third contains black, sweet licorice. "Have some," Kaspar smiles.

Amahl seizes the candy and gobbles it down as his mother returns with a few sticks of wood for the fire. She sends Amahl to call the other shepherds nearby and have them bring whatever they can spare to make the Kings more comfortable. As the Mother crosses the room to tend the fire, she notices the rich gifts spread out on the floor before the Kings. They are for the Child, she is told, a child "the color of wheat, the color of dawn. His eyes are mild, his hands are those of a king, as King he was born." With these words, Melchior begins a stately quartet built on a descending vocal line, one of the few ensemble pieces in *Amahl*. The music has a swaying gait to it with an overlay of oriental harmonic tints. To each of the questions posed by the Kings ("Have you seen a child the color of earth, the color of thorn?"), the Mother replies, "Yes, I know a child the color of earth, the color of thorn. His eyes are sad, his hands are poor, as poor he was born. But no one will bring him incense or gold, though sick and hungry and cold. He's my child, my darling, my own and his name is Amahl."

As the quartet finishes quietly, the call of the neighboring shepherds falls sharp and clear on the night air, breaking the silence that has filled the room. The Mother opens the door, and singly and then in twos and threes the Shepherds appear over the hills caroling a joyous *a cappella* song and bringing baskets of fruits and vegetables. As they enter they are struck dumb by the sight of the Kings, but the Mother urges them, "Don't be bashful, silly boy, don't be bashful, silly girl. They won't eat you." As each group of Shepherds describes the gift they have brought, the Kings respond in rhythmic, matched phrases: "Thank you, thank you, thank you kindly."

The Mother then urges a young girl to dance for the Kings, but, embarrassed, she tries to flee. A young man, however, pulls her back, and as Amahl and another shepherd begin playing their pipes, the shepherds begin to dance (here, Menotti made use of part of a string quartet piece written while a student). The dance, which starts in E major, is a ceremony of welcome and hospitality, and combines qualities of primitive folk dancing and ritual. The movements at first are shy, faltering and hesitant, but as the music shifts from *lento, ma non troppo* to *allegro vivace*, the dancers gain in confidence and their dance takes on the character of a *tarantella*, growing in animation until it concludes in an exciting, swirling frenzy. The intertwining oboe lines that form the principal accompaniment for the dancer are ac-

Amahl (Allen) astounds his Mother (Kuhlmann) by offering his crutch to the Three Kings (Lishner, McKinley, Aiken) as a gift for the Child.

cented by a tambourine, and the music is modal in character (because of a D natural within a key center of E) until the *allegro,* when the tonality becomes solidly seated in A major.

At the end of the dance, Balthazar thanks the Shepherds and bids them good night: "We have little time for sleep and a long journey ahead." The Shepherds bow to the Kings as they leave, and even after they are out of sight, their voices continue to be heard in the distance on the winter air. Closing the door, the Mother and Amahl also bid the Kings good night, Amahl pausing to ask Kaspar if among his magic stones there is one to cure a crippled boy. But again Kaspar fails to understand him, and Amahl retires sadly to his straw pallet by the fireplace.

Once again the orchestra limns the lovely music that opened the opera as the Kings settle themselves on a bench, leaning against one another for support as they sleep, with the Page at their feet. The dim glow from the fireplace slowly melts into the first pale rays of the dawn. As the others quickly fall asleep, the Mother sits on her pallet staring at the treasures guarded by the Page. Slowly and haltingly she begins the one aria in the opera, a soliloquy in E-flat minor: "All that gold! I wonder if rich people know what to do with their gold!" The model for her aria in its obsessiveness, text and harmony is, of course, the last-act scene for the Secretary in *The Consul.* The Mother's anguish and her concern for Amahl grows in intensity and power as she slowly drags herself across the floor, determined to steal a piece of the gold. As she moves as if hypnotically drawn to the treasure, she whispers over and over, "For my child . . . for my child."

Reaching the gold, she touches it and the Page is instantly aroused. He seizes her arm and cries out for help. Amahl, seeing his mother in the Page's grasp, grabs his crutch and begins beating the Page hysterically in an effort to free her. "Don't you dare, don't you dare, ugly man, hurt my mother," he cries, and rushing to King Kaspar he pleads, "My mother is good, she can't do anything wrong. I'm the one who steals. I'm the one who lies." At a sign from Kaspar, the Mother is released and Amahl falls sobbing into her arms. Gently, to the music of the prelude now played

lento, King Melchior tells the Mother compassionately, "Oh, woman, you may keep the gold. The Child we seek doesn't need our gold. On love alone he will build His kingdom."

Throwing herself on her knees before the Kings, the Mother tells them, through her tears, "For such a King I've waited all my life, and if I weren't so poor, I would send a gift of my own to such a child." Amahl interrupts, begging, "Let me send him my crutch. Who knows, he may need one, and this I made myself." The Mother moves to stop him as he lifts his crutch and steps toward the Kings. There is a complete hush as Amahl realizes he is walking for the first time without the aid of the crutch. Step by step he moves toward the Kings, the crutch held out before him. "Look, Mother, I can walk," he first stammers, then shouts with joy. In awe, the Kings one by one exclaim "He walks!" Then they chant, "It is a sign from the Holy Child." With growing confidence, Amahl begins to hop, then leaps about the room: "Look, Mother, I can walk, I can dance, I can jump, I can run!" The Mother and the Kings follow the boy breathlessly, supported by a light *scherzando* in the orchestra.

One at a time, the Kings pass before Amahl and lay their hands on him: "Oh! blessed child may I touch you?" When the Page prostrates himself with the same request, Amahl (enjoying his first taste of self-importance) frowns: "I don't know if I'm going to let *you* touch me." But after a gentle reproof from the Mother, Amahl relents. He then begs his Mother to let him go with the Kings and take the crutch to the Child himself. The Kings join in the request, and the Mother gives her permission.

In a final *duettino,* mother and son bid each other farewell, with Amahl promising to wear his hat, and the Mother promising to mind the cat. Led by the Page, the procession departs, and again the song of the Shepherds is heard echoing from the hills. As Amahl begins piping the little tune heard at the outset of the opera, a few flakes of snow begin to fall. The Mother stands in the doorway of the hut and waves one final good-bye as Amahl and the Kings disappear out of sight and the curtain falls slowly over a quiet, sustained bar of C major.

The Labyrinth

An operatic riddle in one act,
libretto in English by the composer

The Groom	Baritone
The Bride	Soprano
The Spy	Mezzo-soprano
The Old Man	Tenor
The Executive Director	Mezzo-soprano
The Astronaut	Tenor
Death	Bass
Death's Assistant	Bass
The Italian Opera Singer	Baritone
The Bellboy	Non-singing

World premiere New York, March 3, 1963. Commissioned by the NBC Television Opera Theater. Unpublished. Scored for flute, oboe, bass clarinet, bassoon, two trumpets, horn, trombone, percussion, piano, strings.

The decade of the 1960s brought a cutback in Menotti's output following his launching of the Festival of Two Worlds in Spoleto, Italy, and his struggle against enormous odds to keep this child of his dreams from being stillborn. It is not melodramatic to see him during this period as a St. Sebastian figure, pierced by the arrows of worry and struggle. He has described Spoleto as his "cross," and there is no doubt the festival cost him in both time and money. Yet by the time it had weathered five summers of activity, the pressure (though never alleviated) had lessened enough to allow Menotti the composer to compete with Menotti the impresario, and the result was *The Labyrinth*.

This is Menotti's only opera to have had only one performance and his only theater piece never to have played before an audience inside a theater. For his second venture into television, Menotti decided to make full use of the medium's opportunities, and in the process he fashioned an opera that (unless extensively revised and rethought) could never be given on the stage. His surrender to television was so total (perhaps too

total) that the cinematic techniques he used tended to overpower his message, which echoed that of *The Bishop of Brindisi:* Death is the key that finally reveals to man the blinding answer to his metaphysical questions. *The Labyrinth*'s moral, however, is all but submerged in video trickery,

The Secretary (Bob Rickner), the short-tempered Executive Director (Beverly Wolff) and a transient guest, the Groom (John Reardon), who has lost the key to his room.

from a gravity-free sequence aboard a rocket ship to a railroad car that fills with water to become a swimming pool, then empties as the water gurgles down a drain to the accompaniment of electronic sounds.

The piece is highly symbolic ("a puzzling concoction," Menotti dubbed it at the time of its premiere), an operatic riddle that is perhaps more a riddle than an opera. It has been described as "surreal," but Menotti challenges this description. To him *The Labyrinth* is the opposite of surrealism because "beneath its apparent nonsense there is a logical meaning for almost everything that happens. It is more a morality play than anything else. Each character and every incident has a precise role to play. The opera describes the journey of man through life—his hopes, his loves, his relation to society, his faith and disappointments about religion and science and his disillusionment in marriage. In the end, alone and naked, he finds himself before death. It is, however, important to notice that he is not afraid of death, and that death comes away with an empty coffin while man is left holding the key to life with a serene smile on his lips."

Menotti presents his allegory through the character of a groom lost in a grand hotel with his bride on their wedding night and through their desperate search for the key to their room. The hotel is the world, and in its corridors the young couple encounter a strange assortment of people. There is a spy, who represents science, religion, philosophy and any other branch of learning that claims to have an explanation of the world or life. The traditional past is present in the guise of an old man, the self-centered present is a busy female executive, while the chimerical future appears in the form of an astronaut. The train with its passengers, who wait for the conductor to leave the carriage so that they may plunge into the sinful pleasures of a tepid pool of water, is, of course, a transparent symbol of a hypocritical attitude of society toward the code of conventional morality.

At the time of the premiere, Menotti urged the viewers not to look on the opera as "grim," because "I believe that death is not the end of life but its happy solution. . . . The more we search

in life, the more will be revealed to us in death." While the idea has theatrical potential, it is largely unrealized here. Whether it was the tailoring of his work to a specific forum or simply his expressed and rather perverse claim that he was to see "how unoperatic an opera could be," *The Labyrinth* is a weak score despite some undeniably attractive stretches. Its formal plan is a series of alternating arias and sequences, and the sequential scenes serve primarily as links between the adventures of the Groom.

To a volley of percussion and a series of woodwind flourishes, the work begins with the camera searching the hotel's corridors—the sort of heavy, paneled hallways one finds in older European resorts. It comes to rest on the Bride and Groom, and to a darting, *staccato* theme, the Groom turns his pockets inside and out searching for the key to their room. In the midst of the search, the Bellboy (religion) appears, stops in front of a door, knocks and slips an enigmatic message under it. The couple call out to him for help, but, winking at them, he quickly disappears out of sight.

To an angular, canonic section, the Groom peeks in the keyhole of the room where the note was left. His eyes follow a woman's leg up to a table where people are eating spaghetti. As he watches, a series of biting chords followed by arpeggios are heard as the Spy appears. She speaks in a polyglot—part German, part French, part Italian, part English. To her goes the first aria, a charming, Poulenc-esque, hobbling waltz (*andante languido*). She tells the newlyweds she is the "official spy of the Grand Hotel," and if they want her on their side, they had better hire her.

A moment later, the Old Man enters the corridor, pushed in a wheelchair by an attendant. When the couple explain their problem, he responds with an aria of many contrasting parts. It is filled with nonsense phrases that are delivered with great seriousness as though they were the answers the couple seek. In the midst of his ravings, the Old Man begins to fall asleep, but just as suddenly he bolts upright and continues to rattle on. Finally, he tells the Groom he will divulge all he knows if the Groom will join him in a game of chess. Leaving the Bride behind,

Consternation at the Grand Hotel: the Bride (Judith Raskin), the murdered Bellboy (Nikiforos Naneris), the Spy who killed him (Elaine Bonazzi) and the Groom (Reardon).

they enter a room that looks strangely like a jungle growing in a solarium. Amid the plants and leaves are several chess tables. All the players seated at them are very old and wear dated evening clothes—rich but tattered.

The Old Man is wheeled to a table opposite an old woman and motions the Groom to sit in her chair. As he sinks into her lap, she dissolves into dust. As the game begins, the scene dissolves back to the hallway where the Bride is sitting disconsolately on her suitcase. Once again the Bellboy rushes past her. She cries out to him but to no avail. Left alone she begins her aria *(lento ma non troppo)*, the loveliest and most substantial moment in the score. There is a disarming directness to it, and the simplicity of a folk song: "Oh how far, how far my evening hills, how far my burning path of secret dreams." The aria becomes more complex and turbulent during its middle section, but returns in the end to the calm of the opening phrases.

The scene dissolves back to the chess game, where the Groom realizes the Old Man has fallen fast asleep and will provide none of the answers the Groom is seeking. He makes his way through the junglelike growth in the room until he finds his way back to the corridor and his wife. No sooner are they reunited than the Spy returns. Once more she drops a folded piece of paper and vanishes. It contains a crudely drawn arrow pointing to nowhere. Continuing down the hall, the couple notice a door marked "Executive Director" and the Groom eagerly knocks on it. To fussy, strident music, he opens the door and finds himself in a cluttered office. Behind a huge desk sits a masculine-looking woman speaking impatiently on the phone (a revved-up version of the Secretary in *The Consul*). In between calls ("If you cannot buy it, sell it"—"Bury him and call me later"), she demands to know what the Groom wants. In the closest thing Menotti allows the Groom to an aria, he tells the Executive Director he has lost his key and does not remember his room number.

While he is recounting his problems, the Director shouts instructions to her assistant: "Wrap it," "Lick it," "Mail it." Her telephones also continue to ring and she answers one after the other,

each time crying out operatically, "Hello!" On the final "Hello!" the Groom is sucked into her throat and slides down it as if she were a chute, landing back in the corridor where his wife has been waiting. For a third time, the Bellboy brushes past them, but this time he winks in the direction of a nearby door. The Groom looks through the keyhole and sees a huge operatic chorus dressed in *Aida* costumes in front of heavy, elaborate scenery. A mustachioed baritone is crying out *"Abbiate pietade"* to a disheveled soprano clinging to his legs while the chorus responds with *"Maledizione, o traditor."*

Turning to his bride, the Groom laments, "The boy again lied. The room is occupied." The Bride, however, is certain that the Bellboy pointed to another door, and the Groom goes to it and puts his ear up against it. Hearing strange sounds, he enters, and to eerie, high-pitched chords begins to float. The room is the inside of a rocket ship and through a porthole a starry sky beyond can be seen. In floats an astronaut, and to ascending chromatic chords, he offers the Groom tea. The Groom replies he only wants his key. "But why look for key or door," the Astronaut comments, "with so many stars to explore?"

As he floats away from the Groom, the Astronaut sings of the wonders of space. In the midst of his aria, he suddenly breaks off crying, "The meteors, the meteors!" There is a blinding explosion, and the Groom is catapulted into space, landing once more in the hall beside his wife. Despondent, they huddle together, and in a plaintive duet each consoles the other. At its conclusion, the Bellboy appears for a final time, and the Groom manages to grab his coattail and then hold him fast by the nape of the neck. As the Bellboy opens his mouth to speak, the Spy creeps up behind him and plunges a dagger into his back.

"He had to die," she explains nonchalantly, "he was a counterspy." Frightened, the Bride runs screaming down the hall to a cascade of chromatic scales, followed by the Groom. In his effort to catch up with his wife, the Groom is seen charging blindly through rivers, over mountains, amid forests. He finally finds himself out-

Hopelessly lost in the labyrinth, the Groom (Reardon) tries to read in a train compartment, but it is flooded and he nearly drowns in a stormy sea.

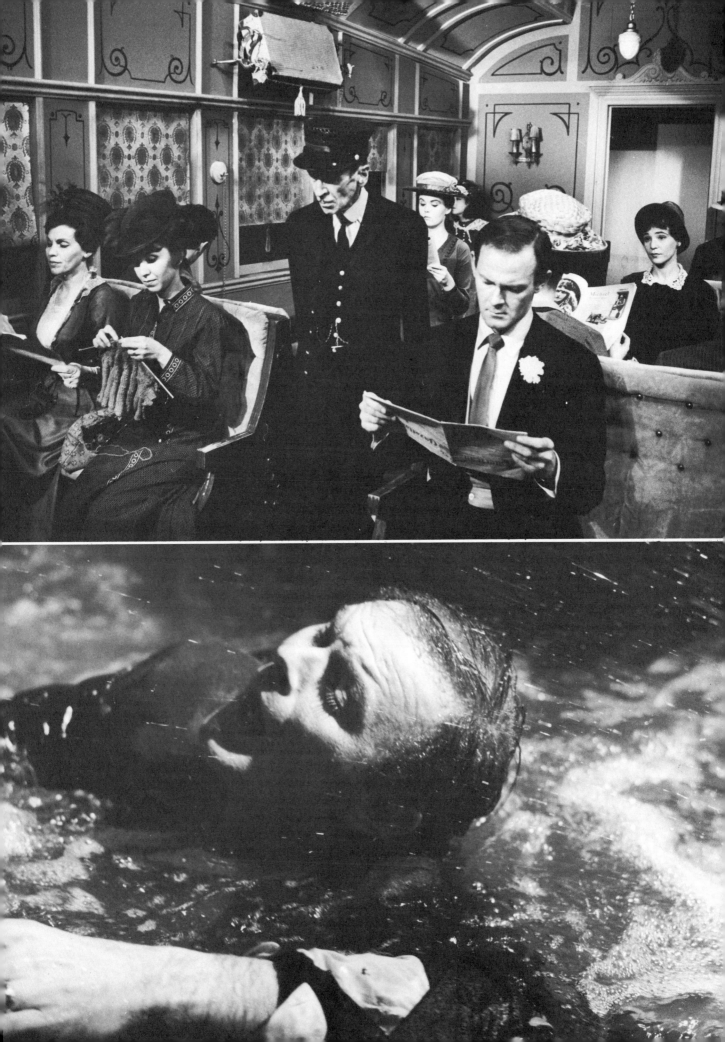

side a train compartment flooded with water. Inside, the passengers are singing a wordless ditty and blissfully bathing. As the Groom opens the door and enters he suddenly finds himself in a bathing suit as well. In the midst of the fun, one of the passengers gives a warning, and the water is quickly drained from the car leaving the passengers in normal clothes, sitting stiffly in their seats. A conductor enters and eyes the passengers suspiciously. The moment he leaves, however, the water is let back in and the passengers gaily resume their fishing and swimming.

Gradually, however, the scene darkens as a storm approaches and swiftly moving clouds appear overhead. In a flash, the Groom is being tossed in the midst of a raging sea, and when he cries out for help, the Bride appears. In her efforts to reach him, she drowns. By now the Groom is clinging to a table, but he soon loses his grip and sinks into the opaque water. As he is drawn into the vortex of the sea, a waltz is heard in the distance. As it grows louder, the Groom is seen holding a bunch of balloons and floating through an elaborately gilded ceiling wearing only a few shreds of clothing.

He lands on a ballroom floor where a number of couples are dancing, seemingly oblivious of his presence. Embarrassed by his torn clothing, he slinks by the dancers toward a door and then out into a large lobby. Behind the desk stands the sinister-looking manager, who is, of course, Death. The Groom begs for his key, and with alternating laughter, the Manager and his lackey tell the Groom they have his room: "In this hotel there is a room for everyone." They make the Groom lie down on a low bench and quickly pull from behind their desk a stack of wooden boards. With incredible swiftness they construct a coffin about the Groom, nailing down the lid with ferocious hammer strokes.

Then, with ceremonial mien, they lift the coffin to their shoulders and vanish with it. The coffin, however, has no bottom, and the Groom is left lying on the bench. Without moving, he waits until the receding footsteps of the Manager and the Lackey have gone, and then opens his hand as the camera pans in for a closeup. In his palm, the Groom holds the long-sought key.

Menotti with fellow composers Samuel Barber, Aaron Copland (standing), Virgil Thomson and William Schuman at Thomson's apartment in the Hotel Chelsea, early 1950s.

Chapter Seven

THE CHURCH STAGE

Martin's Lie

Opera da chiesa in one act,
libretto in English by the composer

Martin	Boy-soprano
Naninga	Mezzo-soprano
Father Cornelius	Tenor
The Stranger	Baritone
The Sheriff	Baritone
Timothy	Boy-soprano
Christopher	Boy-soprano
Orphans	Chorus

World premiere in Bristol Cathedral, Bath, England, June 3, 1964. Commissioned by CBS Television (television premiere on CBS, May 30, 1965). Unpublished. Scored for flute, oboe, clarinet, bassoon, trumpet, two horns, trombone, timpani, percussion, harp, viola, cello, bass.

Like *Maria Golovin,* which was also a commission for television and aired by NBC following its stage premiere in Brussels, *Martin's Lie* might have also been grouped with Menotti's television operas. But as both began life on a stage rather than on a screen, they are considered elsewhere. The television connection, however, forms a direct link between *Martin's Lie* and *Amahl and the Night Visitors,* and there are other ties as well. Both are one-act chamber works, and both are products of the special relationship Menotti has always had with children. But where *Amahl* was expressly conceived for children (or for the child in each of us), *Martin's Lie* was conceived for adults.

Martin's Lie was Menotti's first attempt at church opera, a contemporary form of liturgical music theater that has its roots in the Middle Ages or before, when Bible stories were enacted to reach an illiterate public. Though *Martin's Lie* has no biblical basis, nor is it liturgical in any

sense beyond the prayers sung by Martin and his fellow orphans, it is a reminder of a too-often forgotten biblical precept—"Love thy neighbor as thyself." In remembering this, and in sacrificing his life for that of another, Martin makes of love a greater virtue, Menotti believes, "than either truth or justice."

Martin's Lie is one of Menotti's tautest pieces of theater. It is set in northern Europe in the sixteenth century when, in Menotti's words, "tolerance was considered weakness and cruelty a necessity." Its single scene takes place in the kitchen of an old convent that has been converted into a home for orphan boys. Its lean score is of the greatest simplicity and opens with a prelude *(lento)* intoned first by the brass and then winds, establishing a sense of period through the starkness of the phrases and the intervals used.

As the curtain rises, Naninga—a good-hearted woman who is housekeeper at the orphanage—

Martin (Michael Wennink), who has died for his beliefs, is borne to his final rest by fellow orphans, Bristol Cathedral, 1964.

has gathered the boys around her and is finishing a fairy tale about a prince who opens forbidden doors with the touch of a magic, golden rose. Her song—*legato* and sustained—is sung at first to an unadorned accompaniment by the harp. At a crucial point, she breaks off, telling the boys the tale will be completed the next day. Despite their pleas, she remains adamant, for it is time for prayers and bed. *A cappella* and in chant style, Naninga and Father Cornelius begin the prayers, which are echoed by the boys: "Merciful God, you who forsake neither deer nor robin, watch over us." When they are finished,

As he opens the door, a stranger staggers in; he has been wounded and is obviously desperate. Martin explains he is an orphan and offers to wake Father Cornelius. "No," answers the Stranger, "let me think." Against a series of rising chords that continually expand in range and density, the Stranger informs Martin that his (the Stranger's) life is in danger; he is being pursued and will be tortured and burned because "I choose to pray to God in my own way." "Are you a heretic, then?" Martin asks. "Must we not fight for whatever truth God has revealed to us?" the Stranger counters. This taut exchange is typical

Naninga tells Martin it is his time to sleep in the kitchen, where each night a boy is posted to guard the food from huge rats.

Wishing Martin good night, all slowly exit, singing as they go *"Dominus firmamentum meum."* A dozen bars of interlude follow, whose quick, scampering rhythmic figures suggest Martin's fears at being left alone and the presence of the rats. Before he has time to dwell on either, there is a violent knocking at the door, and a voice cries out "Open! Open!" As the voice repeats the plea seconded by sharp chords in the orchestra, Martin is at first undecided as to what he should do, and then finally answers the call.

of the intense declamation and recitative throughout *Martin's Lie,* which has no arias as such other than Naninga's opening song.

"I know you are wicked," Martin cries, moving away from the Stranger. "Father Cornelius warned us about your evil ways." "How can a soldier who fights for God be wicked?" the Stranger asks. "God has appointed you to be my savior." "But," rejoins Martin, "it was not you I was waiting for. It was my father. . . . My mother died when I was born, but no one knows who my father is. Surely he will appear one day to take me home." After a slight pause, the Stranger asks, "Could I not be your father?" "Oh, no,"

Menotti rehearsing Wennink and Donald McIntyre for the dramatic exchanges between Martin and the Stranger.

Design by Lila de Nobili for *Martin's Lie*.

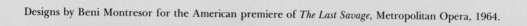
Designs by Beni Montresor for the American premiere of *The Last Savage*, Metropolitan Opera, 1964.

Act I: the courtyard of the Maharajah's palace.

Act I: the Hunt.

Act I, Scene 2: Kitty's triumphant capture of Abdul.

Poster art by Jamie Wyeth for the premiere of *The Boy Who Grew Too Fast*, 1982.

Drawing by Pasquale Grossi for *Chip and His Dog*, 1980.

replies Martin, "you would have known my name . . . you would never have asked me where my father was." "Why couldn't I be your father?" the Stranger demands. "Why would God have sent me to you of all the children in the world if you were not my son?"

There is a sudden and strident knocking at the door, and the Stranger realizes his pursuers have caught up with him. Desperately he begs Martin, "Let me be your father. . . . Why wait for a father who does not need a son? No one has ever needed a son more than I do now. Martin, in the name of God, be my son!" Deeply moved,

iously asking what has happened. The Sheriff tells the cleric that a heretic is being hidden in the orphanage: "The Count of Nevers . . . the King has ordered him arrested, tortured and beheaded on the spot." When Father Cornelius denies any knowledge of the heretic, the Sheriff accuses him of lying: Two neighbors saw him knocking at the convent door less than a half an hour ago, and it being opened to him. "It is he who let him in," the Sheriff declares pointing to Martin. When Martin denies this, the other boys beg him not to lie. Father Cornelius attempts to defend Martin and finally the Sheriff says he will

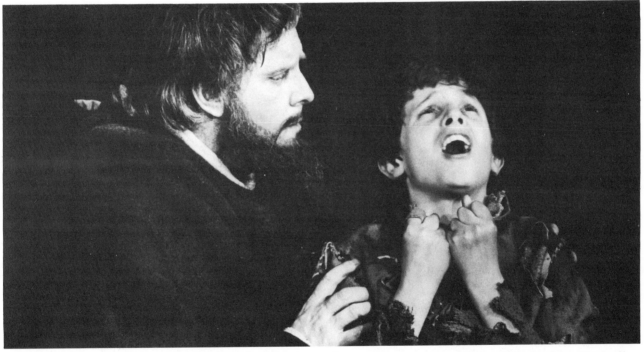

Martin quietly answers, "Yes, father," and as the knocking becomes more persistent and the orchestra more agitated, Martin hides the Stranger in a secret place only he and his friend Christopher know of.

Once the Stranger is safely secluded, Martin runs to the door and opens it. The first person to enter is the Sheriff, who gives orders to his men to search the orphanage. Musically, the Sheriff is drawn in very strong colors that equate him as much with cruelty as the Stranger is equated with compassion. On being questioned, Martin denies having seen anyone. A moment later, Father Cornelius and Naninga enter anx-

leave the two together so that Father Cornelius can get at the truth. Otherwise, he threatens to burn down the convent.

To cradling figures played by strings and harp, Father Cornelius reminds Martin that lying is a sin and by lying harm might come to him, Naninga and his little friends. "Should one keep the door closed when one is waiting?" Martin cautiously asks. "Waiting and for whom?" the priest demands. "My father!" At this point Father Cornelius loses his temper: "I have told you a thousand times you have no father." "But he came tonight," Martin replies triumphantly. "Now I understand," says Father Cornelius. "The

Father Cornelius (William McAlpine) questions Martin (Wennink) while the Sheriff and his men search the orphanage in quest of a heretic.

scoundrel made you believe he was your father. . . . Even if your father were still alive he could never know you exist. . . . Your mother, bless her soul, saw him once and never asked his name."

"But he knows I am here," Martin counters. "I called him many times . . . with my magic call. He could have heard me across the world." The priest tries to argue rationally with Martin without realizing how little power reason has in the face of faith. Frustrated, Father Cornelius tries a different tack: "Haven't I been a father to you?" "No," Martin replies quietly. "You don't always kiss me good night, you don't always ask why I am sad, and it was not me you saved first when the fire broke out last summer. You're more afraid for yourself than me." At this juncture, Naninga bursts into the room; the soldiers are tearing the orphanage apart looking for the Stranger. Naninga pushes Christopher forward saying, "You're his best friend. Put some sense in his head." Left alone, the two boys talk about everything but the Stranger—from a friend's new sling to their ongoing rat count (Christopher leads with 266 sighted to Martin's 105).

"I've had enough of this," the Sheriff says as he returns to the room to a brisk, military strain in the instruments. "Martin, beware! Do you see that man there? Not only does he have an axe with him, but also all sorts of instruments of torture. If you still refuse to reveal all you know, I shall put you in his hands." As the children crowd about Martin, begging him to confess, the Sheriff draws Father Cornelius to one side: "All I want to do is frighten the child, for I am sure only fear can loosen his tongue . . . he has too much imagination to be courageous" (an echo of *The Consul*, where the Secret Police Agent reminded Magda: "Courage is often the lack of imagination").

When Martin still refuses to speak, the Sheriff signals one of his henchmen to advance toward the boy, at the same time putting the same question to Martin over and over: "Did you hide a man here?" As the henchman comes nearer, the boys and Father Cornelius beg Martin to tell. Their voices and pleas grow in strength and volume and against their cries and swelling chorus the Sheriff commands, "Answer, Martin, or you will die!" Just as the henchman is face to face with Martin, he collapses on the floor. Father Cornelius drops to the ground and takes Martin in his arms. Though it is evident the boy is dead, the priest whispers in his ear, "Listen, whoever he was, he *was* your father."

"Why do you lie to him, monk?" the Sheriff asks. "A lie is a little thing, my Lord," Father Cornelius responds. "I have learned that love is stronger than any sin." To a somber chant in the orchestra, he rises with Martin's body in his arms, and all onstage sing, "Heavenly father, you taught us to love both friend and enemy . . . bestow your mercy on all defeated pilgrims whose love is greater than their mortal breath." To repeated and ecstatic "Amen" 's, and to tolling bells, Martin's body is carried from the room to the nearby graveyard to be laid to rest.

The Sheriff (Otakar Kraus), as one of his henchmen threatens Martin with a blade, demands that the boy tell where the Stranger has hidden.

The Egg

An operatic riddle in one act,
libretto in English by the composer

Manuel	Baritone
Saint Simeon	Tenor
The Basilissa, Empress of Byzantium (Pride)	Soprano
Areobindus (Lust)	Baritone
Gourmantus (Gluttony)	Baritone
The Basilissa's Sister (Envy)	Mezzo-soprano
Eunuch (Sloth)	Baritone
Pachomius (Avarice)	Tenor
Julian, a soldier (Anger)	Non-singing
Beggar Woman	Soprano
Priscus	Boy-alto

World premiere in Washington Cathedral, Washington, D.C., June 17, 1976. Unpublished. Scored for flute, oboe, clarinet, bassoon, trumpet, horn, percussion, harp, organ, violin, viola, cello, and bass.

The Egg, Menotti's second church opera, is of even greater economy and simplicity than *Martin's Lie*. It is an engaging tale told almost entirely in dramatic recitative amid patches of *arietta*s. Together, these are stretched between four choral sections that form the pillars supporting the work. The writing is attractive throughout and of the utmost transparency. In particular, Menotti achieves arresting harmonic colorations by the sudden juxtaposition of distant and normally alien tonalities. The prologue, for example, contains this progression: F major, D-flat major, A major, C minor, E-flat minor, A-flat minor, G major.

The allegorical story recounted here has been drawn from church history and centers on the first and most famous of a group of "pillar" hermits known as stylites. This was Saint Simeon (A.D. 395–459), who lived atop a pillar sixty feet high for thirty years. The opera, which is set in the Byzantine Empire during the fifth century, opens with a choral processional from the rear of the sanctuary to the front altar with the chorus chanting:

Now my friends I shall begin to tell,
The happy tale of unhappy Manuel.
Who found in what he lost outside a door,
The answer he was looking for.
Men plead for love, preach against greed,
But then claim more than they need.
To these unchartered pilgrims who wander astray,
My simple riddle will, perhaps, show the way.

In a desert in Syria, Saint Simeon is seen perched atop his pillar as a parched, exhausted figure staggers across the sand. At first Simeon does not realize it is his nephew Manuel and believes it to be the Devil in a new guise coming to tempt him off his pillar. When he at last recognizes Manuel, he says resignedly, "If I remember well, my nephew was a dreadful child, far worse than the Devil. If you are Manuel, you're not a temptation; you're a punishment for my sins, and as such I have to welcome you."

Manuel addresses his uncle as "Saint Simeon," and Simeon reacts strongly, echoing Annina in *The Saint of Bleecker Street:* "Whoever said I was a saint? I am a poor sinner hoping for forgiveness by praying and fasting and mortification of the flesh." Besides, he adds, he is not the only one doing penance: "Haven't you heard of Brother Sabinos, who only feeds on grass? Haven't you heard of the Siderophores, who weigh their bodies with heavy chains?" Impatient to get on with his prayers, Simeon asks why Manuel has crossed the desert. The boy replies he has been "laughed at by the rich, despised by the poor, mistrusted by my friends, fired from every job, neglected by the church, avoided by the wise. . . . What is wrong with me? What is my life about? If at least I knew the meaning of it, perhaps I wouldn't feel so useless."

To a peppy, almost irritated strain, Simeon replies he has no such answers, for he has abandoned life and waits only for God to free his soul. But, he continues, he understands the turbulence Manuel feels, for he once felt it himself when an angel visited him, arriving in a flurry of blazing wings. It was Easter, and the angel gave Simeon an egg, saying, "In that egg is the answer to your prayers. Break it, open it if you can, then you'll learn the secret of life." Simeon tried to open it but was unsuccessful and finally threw it away. "I admit it was a rash thing to do, but it kept me from praying; angel or no angel, praying comes first." When Manuel asks where the egg is, Simeon replies it is buried in the sand near him; if Manuel can find it, he can have it. With a cry of joy that his fortune is made, Manuel begins digging violently in the sand, directed by Simeon from atop his pillar. The music becomes more and more agitated until it finally bubbles forth in D-flat major as Manuel unearths the egg. This section concludes with a rising then falling scale pattern that forms one of the work's basic structural units.

Simeon tells Manuel to let him know what is inside should he open the egg. Then, against contrasting and expanding bell-like octaves in the instruments, Simeon sings a lovely laud to God—the closest thing to an aria during *The Egg*. A trumpet blast breaks into Simeon's song and leads to the next choral block as the scene shifts to the Byzantine court of the Basilissa. The Empress, like the courtiers we meet shortly, is symbolic of one of the seven deadly sins; in the Basilissa's case, it is pride.

In stately style (*lento e maestoso*) the Empress's court assembles praising the Basilissa's wisdom, beauty, piety and mercy. Areobindus (Lust) calls for silence and tells the Basilissa a man named Manuel has been arrested as a blasphemer; he claims to have been given a holy-egg from Saint Simeon containing the meaning of life. The Basilissa orders Manuel brought before her, and the boy recounts the tale of the egg and how his uncle was unable to open it. "God must find it unworthy," says the Basilissa proudly, after trying in vain to crack the egg, "of an Empress to open her own eggs. Call my cook Gourmantus (Glut-

tony). I'm too lofty for such menial tasks." The cook enters and is delighted to hear about the egg. He has just devised a new and heavenly dish, and an angel's egg is exactly what he needs to complete it. In an amusing *arietta* (which rocks between *allegro* and *andante moderato*), Gourmantus details his recipe, which, in part, calls for Indian pepper, parsley, salt, the heart of a dove, the eyes of a lark, the tongue of a squirrel, ground pearls, lamb's blood, porcupine oil and white raisins.

The Basilissa is impressed and orders Gourmantus to begin by breaking the egg. After repeated tries, he is forced to give up. "Your recipe," comments the Basilissa, "is a failure, dear Gourmantus, and I'm sad that I must lose such a wonderful cook, for I'm sure you'll want to hang yourself after your nose is cut off!" The

Menotti's 1978 production at Spoleto's Festival dei due Mondi, with Matthew Murray as Manuel and Anastasios Vrenios as Saint Simeon . . .

Empress then calls her chief eunuch (Sloth) to try his luck with the egg. "Tomorrow," he replies lazily. "I'll have to think about it. In a week, I'm sure I'll have the answer." The Basilissa demands he find the answer at once, and the Eunuch suggests he be allowed to sit on it and hatch it. This infuriates the Empress, who has the Eunuch thrown into the dungeon, as the orchestra (which has thus far done little more than provide underpinning for the dialogue) suddenly boils over angrily.

While the orchestra sulks in silence, the Empress in free, unaccompanied recitative calls next

on Pachomius (Avarice), who advises her not to worry about opening the egg, but instead to dip it in gold and keep it as a relic. He offers to negotiate the acquisition of the egg from Manuel; in an aside to the boy, Pachomius says he will get a fantastic price for the egg if Manuel will split it in half with him. "Is this the meaning of the egg?" Manuel wonders aloud—"Money?" Pachomius tells the Empress the price is twice the egg's weight in rubies. The Empress agrees to pay it, but only if the egg is opened before her eyes. Manuel tries anew to crack the egg, but has no more success than before. The Empress dismisses Pachomius and orders that he hand over the treasury keys to her lover Areobindus.

"I'm no chemist or theologian," Areobindus comments. "What else can the egg be except a new source of pleasure? . . . Grind it into a fine powder to be sniffed or licked in the secret of our chamber." As the Basilissa orders this done, her sister (Envy) urges Manuel not to let the Basilissa have the egg: "Under that coat of paint she's nothing but a lascivious old hag. If it weren't for her, it is I who would be sitting on the throne." Manuel, however, is helpless to act, and the Empress orders Julian (Anger) to crush the egg under his shield. To a freewheeling cadenza for clarinet, the soldier tries to split the egg open, but the more he strikes the egg, the more it resists. The frustration drives him to the brink of frenzy; before he loses his reason, the Empress orders him to stop. Turning to Manuel, she orders him out: "You've made fools of my court with your tales of angels and the egg of stone. Throw him out of the palace and have him banished from the city."

As the command is executed, the third choral section intervenes. Again, it is in praise of the Basilissa and leads us to the opera's final scene, set outside the palace. As Manuel laments his bad luck, a beggar woman approaches asking for help for her starving child. "If I were rich," Manuel answers, "your poor child would not be starving. I don't have money, but take this egg. It is worth two handfuls of rubies." Thanking him, the woman takes the egg and cracks it open with no difficulty and feeds it to her child. Amazed, Manuel asks what it contained. Only the white and a yolk, she answers. "At last I understand," he cries exaltedly. "The egg will open only if given away." At this, the Empress enters with her entourage on the way to the church; Manuel tells her the secret of the egg was to give it away.

"The man is making fun of us," she retorts angrily. "Have him whipped to death." Her order is stayed by the arrival of Saint Simeon, sent by an angel to save Manuel, "who in his innocence deciphered God's somber warning, and revealed to me the error of my life." He reveals to the audience the work's moral: "It is not by sitting on a column or chastising the flesh that we shall earn eternal bliss. Among people we must walk to share what God has given." As Simeon and Manuel enter the cathedral to place the shell of the egg on its altar, the chorus sings out majestically, "Glory to God, Amen."

. . . and his world premiere mounting at Washington Cathedral two years earlier, with Esther Hinds as the Basilissa.

Chapter Eight

THE CHILDREN'S STAGE

Help, Help, the Globolinks!

An opera in one act for children and people
who like children,
libretto in English by the composer

Emily (a student)	Soprano
Madame Euterpova (the music teacher)	Soprano
Dr. Stone (Dean of St. Paul's School)	Baritone
Tony (the bus driver)	Baritone
Timothy (the janitor)	Tenor
Miss Penelope Newkirk (the mathematics teacher)	Mezzo-soprano
Mr. Lavender-Gas (the literature professor)	Baritone
Dr. Turtlespit (the science professor)	Bass
School children	Chorus
Globolinks	Dancers

World premiere Hamburg, Germany, December 21, 1968. Commissioned by the Hamburg Opera. Published by G. Schirmer with a German translation by Kurt Honolka. Dedicated to Francis Phelan. Scored for flute (piccolo), oboe, clarinet (bass clarinet), trumpet, horn, tuba, percussion, piano, harp, strings.

This stage of Menotti's career is probably a more proper place for *Amahl and the Night Visitors,* for it was with *Amahl* that Menotti launched a special brand of music theater for children. "If art should be a wholly abstract activity and not concern itself with the problem of communication," Menotti has observed, "then there is little sense in writing an opera for children. But if, as Jean-Paul Sartre has said, and as I believe, art not only lives in the eye of the beholder, but actually cannot exist without his co-operation, then an opera for children is an exciting challenge and an exhilarating experience. Of all audiences, children are the most enthu-

siastic—but also the most delicate and the easiest to lose. Children are quickly amused—and quickly bored. They forgive no sin less readily, fear no ghost more than boredom.

"Like Madame Euterpova in my *Globolinks,* they believe that beauty *cannot* be boring. Prolixity, therefore, is the first pitfall of which to beware; arias are to be frowned upon (a child will accept only the kind of short, simple melody he can sing himself) and lengthy, psychological explanations avoided (a child brings his own explanations). Once a character is damned, for example, no ingenious denouement or beautiful melody is going to save him.

The schoolbus meets some unexpected traffic, creatures from outer space, forcing the driver, Tony (Raymond Gibbs), the violin-wielding Emily (Judith Blegen) and other children to flee on foot—New York City Center production, 1969.

"If a child's ability to detect a naked emperor is debatable, one thing, however, is certain: If he *does* detect one, he's going to tell you about it. Although a child will favor make-believe in his own games, he still has a fierce eye for realistic detail on the stage and will denounce ferociously any compromise. A sword must be a sword, and blood must be blood. Nor does a child acknowledge the presence of other people in the audience; the show is for him and him alone. If he has anything to ask, he will ask it in a loud voice with brutal disregard for his neighbor—or for anyone onstage or in the orchestra pit. 'Mood' music, too, is an irrelevancy; no amount of beautifully evocative music will keep a child from announcing that he must go pipi if he feels the time has come.

"Why then do I enjoy writing for such a tyrannical public? First of all because it is the only really candid audience left—an audience which comes to the theater without aesthetic preconceptions, which cares little who the composer is and asks him no questions. Second, because I'm an overgrown child myself and have always felt at home with children.

"*Amahl* was written for the child I was and belongs to the children of my generation. It is sentimental, full of feeling for the magical and love for home. *The Globolinks*, instead is written for the new generation; there is no mention of time, magic is confined to the realm of realistic possibility and emotions are reviewed with cool sophistication."

The inspiration for *Help, Help, the Globolinks!* was not only children, but Menotti's fascination with the contemporary dance theater of Alwin Nikolais and its strong use of color, its particular brand of humor (which to Menotti seemed especially suited to children), its fantasy and originality of movement and its creative use of electronic music. To Menotti, Nikolais was as symbolic of the avant-garde as he (Menotti) was of traditional means. When the request came from the Hamburg Opera for a companion piece to *Amahl and the Night Visitors*, the idea began to take shape in Menotti's head for a confrontation between the new and the old, between technology and established musical order, between mechanization and emotion.

He took the idea to Nikolais and said he would undertake the commission if the choreographer would join him to create the Globolinks and their movements. "What is the opera about?" Nikolais asked. "It's about us," Menotti replied. Intrigued, Nikolais agreed, and the first work done on the opera was the creation of the Globolink music in Nikolais's New York studio.

"Although I agree with Madame Euterpova," Menotti said at the time of the American premiere of *Globolinks* in Santa Fe, "that this kind of music is for the Globolinks and not for us, I wrote the electronic music quite seriously and not to make fun of it. Actually, I make more fun of myself in this opera than the avant-garde. I am, you see, symbolized by the character of Madame Euterpova. That is the reason the character is so sentimental, melodramatic and even a bit ludicrous. She is also a collage of all my music teachers, and I retain a great affection for her even while realizing how anachronistic her position is in the world of music. But ultimately I am convinced she will win in the end—not the Globolinks."

Still, it is obvious Menotti also has affection for his outer-space creations, for in the score there is this note: "Although the Globolinks are indeed sinister creatures, it is hoped that the choreographer and designer will treat them not only with awe but with a touch of humor as well." That touch of humor seems to have been extended not only to the whole idea of science fiction, but to a once much-touted Swedish science fiction opera, Karl-Birger Blomdahl's *Aniara*.

Cast in a prologue and four scenes, *The Globolinks'* overture begins with three sustained trumpet blasts answered by three string *pizzicati*, Menotti launches a rollicking, rocketing fugue subject that is cut off just after the exposition by a booming announcement over a loudspeaker: "Attention! An important police bulletin . . . Unknown flying objects from another planet and strange, dangerous creatures identified so far only as Globolinks have landed on Earth . . . Be on your guard and report all incidents to your local police station. THE GLOBOLINKS ARE HERE!"

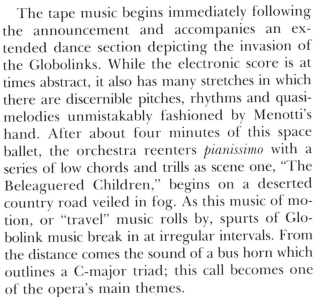

The tape music begins immediately following the announcement and accompanies an extended dance section depicting the invasion of the Globolinks. While the electronic score is at times abstract, it also has many stretches in which there are discernible pitches, rhythms and quasi-melodies unmistakably fashioned by Menotti's hand. After about four minutes of this space ballet, the orchestra reenters *pianissimo* with a series of low chords and trills as scene one, "The Beleaguered Children," begins on a deserted country road veiled in fog. As this music of motion, or "travel" music rolls by, spurts of Globolink music break in at irregular intervals. From the distance comes the sound of a bus horn which outlines a C-major triad; this call becomes one of the opera's main themes.

The horn blast provokes a violent Globolink reaction through the power of tonality, and what is more potent than C major? The headlights of an approaching schoolbus are seen shining dimly through the fog. As the bus enters the stage, a blinding ray from a Globolink stops it dead. Alighting from the bus filled with sleeping children, Tony the driver opens the hood to inspect the motor. He finds nothing wrong; as he ponders the matter, eerie light shapes float in the air accompanied by bits of electronic music.

Frightened, Tony calls out. His voice wakes Emily, who leans out the window of the bus asking, "What are those sounds?" Just then, a very bright shape flashes across the sky, and Emily jumps off the bus and runs to Tony, as the Globolinks suddenly show themselves. At the sight of them, the other children, now awake, cry out in alarm. Emily and Tony jump back on the bus, and Tony sounds the bus's horn for help. At the horn blast, the Globolinks retreat in utter confusion. Tony switches on the radio hoping for news and hears that "groups of dangerous Globolinks have invaded various parts of the country. No weapon so far has proven effective against them except the sound of music, to which they seem to be extremely allergic. Therefore if you are lucky enough to be able to play an instrument, we advise you. . . ." The radio crackles and goes dead.

Knowing the school cannot be too far away,

Menotti with one of his Globolinks at the time of the world premiere, Hamburg State Opera, 1968.

Tony herds the children off the bus, and they begin to slowly advance up the road. But a short distance away, the Globolinks appear again, and the children scramble back to the safety of the broken-down bus. It is decided that someone with a musical instrument for protection must go alone to the school and bring back help. But Mickey has forgotten his clarinet, Teddy did not bring his piccolo and Sally has left her cello at

power of music. "Let music clear your path," Tony sings, "and point to the way. Converse with sweet melody and let it be your guide." The children repeat this luxurious melody, answered in canon by Tony as Emily asks, "Shall I go now? Will I get there?"

Then, moving up a fourth to G-flat major, Emily sings the melody herself as she sets forth to find help. The children wave her on, and

school. Only Emily brought her violin. The children cheer her, crying "We're saved," but Emily is apprehensive about going off in the night alone: "But who will defend me? And how shall I find the way?"

Menotti then begins the first concentrated stretch of music in the score, as he has previously confined the vocal writing to dramatic recitatives without a clear-cut key base. Now he turns to the comfortable key of D-flat major, and its warmth suffuses the orchestra and the stage. Tony puts his arm protectively around Emily and begins a flowing ensemble based on a folklike tune that is rapturous in its affirmation of the

Tony toots the horn one last time as Emily tucks her violin under her chin and begins to play a pastoral melody derived from the bus's horn call. As the girl disappears, her music develops into a short interlude that is eventually blotted out by a return of the Globolink sounds. These lead us into the second scene of the opera, "The Teachers." It is set in Dr. Stone's office at St. Paul's School. As the curtain rises, he is peering out the window, anxious about the children: "The school bus left this morning at nine; the train should have arrived at ten; it is now five. Where can the children be?"

Dully, Timothy the janitor parrots Dr. Stone's

At the schoolhouse, Dr. Stone (Gene Boucher), who becomes a Globolink, confers with his staff—Miss Newkirk (Jean Kraft), Mr. Lavender-Gas (Clyde P. Walker), Dr. Turtlespit (Richard Best), Madame Euterpova (Ellen Faull) and Timothy (Douglas Perry)—New York City Center staging.

170

worry. "What a terrible day," Dr. Stone moans. "And your troubles aren't over yet," Timothy adds. "The music teacher is in the waiting room." To a decisive, *fortissimo* figure in the orchestra, reminiscent of the Magician's entry music in *The Consul*, Madame Euterpova sweeps in carrying a basket of musical instruments and launches into a tirade. With great exaggeration and pomposity (like an angry Valkyrie), she tells Dr. Stone she is resigning. "I have an artist's soul," she continues in the vein of Nika Magadoff. "You haven't the slightest notion of what an artist's suffering can be. Therefore my money, please," she demands with a highly theatrical gesture.

When Dr. Stone asks for an explanation, she explodes scornfully. "Those dreadful, wretched children. As they left for their spring vacation they all promised . . . to take their music books with them and to practice their instruments at home. . . . Not one of them has kept his word. . . . It will be the end of the world when music dies. Why don't you teach *that* to your children?" When Dr. Stone suggests that music is not the most important subject in the school, she lunges at him declaring, "You are the culprit! What does music mean to you? Nothing. You are as deaf as a hardboiled egg." Suddenly pointing an accusing finger at him, she asks "What is 'la,' for example?"

Triumphantly, Dr. Stone replies that "la" is a note. "No," Madame Euterpova retorts, " 'la' is a sound." She strikes his desk with a tuning fork that hangs from a chain around her neck, hums an A and demands Dr. Stone sing it. "A dean doesn't sing," he replies, sitting down. With a sense of momentary defeat, Madame Euterpova laments in a tragic manner, "No one knows how to sing any longer and unlock the loud voice of the heart, except singers, of course, but they have to be paid for it. . . . Therefore, if music must be bought, my wages please, and then adieu!" "Later," Stone barks, trying to be rid of her. But to a vigorous *allegro* she attacks from a new front: "Later is too late. Music teaches you to be on time, my dear sir! The downbeat can't wait. One, two, three"—she beats the rhythm on Stone's desk.

Losing his temper, Dr. Stone advances men-

acingly toward Madame Euterpova. "I have more important things to worry about. . . . The children should have been here today . . . Something dreadful must have happened." Finally cowed, Madame Euterpova picks up her basket and retreats toward the door, pausing to throw a coquettish glance at Dr. Stone. "I love you," she declares theatrically as she slips out the door. Taken by surprise, Dr. Stone stares after her in disgust. He then goes to the sofa to lie down and turns on the radio nearby. Its voice warns, "The Globolink invasion is continuing and the situation is becoming alarming. . . . They seem indestructible and are able to penetrate walls and doors without any effort. . . . Once you are touched by a Globolink, you lose all power of speech, and you yourself are turned into a Globolink within twenty-four hours. Musical instruments seem to be the only effective counter-weapon, and. . . ."

Dr. Stone reaches over and turns the radio off, scoffing at the announcement. He covers his eyes with a handkerchief and leans back as if to go to sleep. The light in the room immediately changes, and out of nowhere, three Globolinks appear to ripples of electronic sound. After looking around, they approach the reclining figure of Dr. Stone and with curiosity bend over to touch him. At this contact, he tears the handkerchief from his eyes, stares for a moment incredulously at the monsters, then rushes terror-striken to the desk to ring the school bell. Greatly alarmed by the sound of the bell, the Globolinks disappear.

Timothy rushes in, and when Dr. Stone opens his mouth to speak, he is able, to his horror, to produce only electronic noise. Frightened, Timothy calls for help, and the other teachers rush in. Looking at each other in bewilderment, they launch into a comic trio: "How sinister, how strange," which is interrupted by the melodramatic reentry of Madame Euterpova.

She has come to warn the others of the Globolinks and to tell them with self-satisfied solemnity that music is their only hope. She then commands everyone to fetch their instruments to rescue the beleagured children. When Mme. Euterpova hears Dr. Stone's pathetic attempt at speech, she grasps the situation at once: "Dear Dr. Stone has been touched by a Globolink. . . ." Approaching him she says, almost with disgust, "And I wanted to marry you! I always told you it was more important to blow a trumpet than to speak on the telephone. . . ." When he begins crying, she melts and offers to try to save him. Striking her tuning fork, she commands Dr. Stone to sing the note. At first only electronic noises come out of his mouth, and then, with a superhuman effort, he manages to produce a recognizable human sound. With Madame Euterpova's prompting, he gradually produces an A, which he sings on the syllable "la." Aware that as long as he holds on to this note he will remain human, he begins to repeat it over and over.

While Dr. Stone sings, Timothy enters with a huge tuba and enthusiastically begins to play an elephantine accompaniment to the repeated "la" 's. Leaving Timothy to guard Dr. Stone, Madame Euterpova goes to pack the children's

instruments. Pausing at the door for one final word of encouragement, she repeats the "la" 's and sings the first phrase of the duet "Là ci darem la mano" from Mozart's Don Giovanni as she throws a kiss to Dr. Stone and exits. Stone continues repeating "la," and soon bored, Timothy settles down on the sofa and dozes off. Soon the light in the room dies, and a Globolink appears and approaches Timothy. Dr. Stone tries to warn the janitor but can only dully sing "la." Timothy, however, awakens just as the Globolink is about to touch him and blows a fortissimo note on his tuba. The Globolink gives out with a

fearful electronic cry, shudders and collapses on the floor dead.

The noise brings the teachers back, led by Madame Euterpova who exclaims, "Marvelous. . . . We now have a melodic cannon." Solemnly she knights Timothy with her tuning fork and proclaims him her artillery commander. This is too much for Mr. Lavender-Gas, who demands to know from Madame Euterpova, "Who asked you to be our leader?" Terming him a pompous ass, the music teacher calls for an election and browbeats the others into designating her the general. Against the motive heard at her first entrance, she commands her troops to line up for inspection and reviews them in a mock-Napoleonic manner. Then, standing on a chair, she addresses her army: "Let the trumpet blaze and the cello plead and the oboe meditate. . . . Wake the cat with drum, catch the butterfly with flute. . . . If you either sing or play, keep the Globolinks away."

The others take up the strain, and led by Madame Euterpova, who holds her tuning fork proudly before her, they head off to a rousing march in B-flat major in search of the children. Dr. Stone runs after them still chanting "la, la, la. . . ." The scene shifts back to the country road for scene three, "The Rescue." Clustered around the bus, the children look haggard and worried. To take their minds off the danger, Tony suggests they all sing one of the school's songs. As if enraged by the song, the Globolinks, more emboldened and belligerent than before, advance on the children. Even the sound of the horn seems to have lost its effect on them. Just as all seems lost, a trumpet fanfare is heard announcing the brigade of teachers. The Globolinks freeze for a moment and then are seized by uncontrollable panic and vanish. Into view come Madame Euterpova and her troops, followed by Dr. Stone pulling a cart filled with the children's instruments. Subtle changes in Dr. Stone's face suggest that all is not well.

With shouts of joy, the children run to welcome their teachers. Miss Newkirk notices that Emily is missing, and Tony tells her that Emily has gone for help. An ensemble follows in which the teachers speculate on Emily's fate; it is cut

In the steel forest, Emily (Blegen), saved from the Globolinks, is reunited with classmates and teachers.

short by an imperious clap of Madame Euterpova's hands. "We must leave immediately," she orders, but Dr. Turtlespit suggests that Dr. Stone might be of help, as he has a touch of the Globolink in him. "Can you really help us?" Madame Euterpova asks Dr. Stone. Nodding his head and repeating his "la," he rises off the ground and flies away. As he disappears, Madame Euterpova tells the children to take up their instruments and follow her. To another march, this one in C major, the music teacher valiantly leads her expanded army off in the direction taken by Dr. Stone.

The final scene, "The Forest of Steel," is set in a strange landscape of large, intricate, abstract forms that look like metal trees, as though the Globolinks had frozen nature into dead forms. From the distance comes the sound of Emily's violin. She soon enters and begins to wander among the strange shapes looking for the road to the school. A Globolink appears, and she chases it away with an elaborate cadenza on her violin. Exhausted by this effort and her long walk, she lies down on the ground with her violin next to her and dozes off.

As soon as she falls asleep, another Globolink approaches her, picks up the violin with great curiosity and plucks one of its strings. At the sound, the Globolink drops the violin as if stung by a bee and runs away. Emily awakes to find her instrument has been smashed in the fall. Globolink lights begin to flicker all about her as the orchestra churns nervously and quickens its pace. As Emily cries out for help, the orchestra breaks off abruptly and the voice of Dr. Stone is heard intoning "la, la, la." He then flies in looking more and more like a Globolink.

Emily rushes to him, but he stops her with a gesture before she can touch him. As Dr. Stone desperately tries to make himself understood to Emily, he turns into a full-fledged Globolink. At this change, Emily faints, and Dr. Stone flies away; it is the fate, Menotti seems to be saying, of all who do not love music. As Dr. Stone vanishes in the sky, the band of children and teachers is heard, and the steel forest melts away. By the time the band enters, the scene has been transformed into a vast, empty plain lit by sun-

light, or in a recent production by Menotti, a lush, shimmering forest of real trees. Seeing Emily, the children break off their playing and rush to her side.

Thrilled to see her schoolmates, Emily thanks them all and then relates the tragic fate of Dr. Stone. "Well, well," Madame Euterpova muses philosophically, "I must look for a husband elsewhere." As the male faculty members nervously step aside and seek protection behind Miss Newkirk, Madame Euterpova assembles the children about her, and with an inspired look and in a broad, imposing theme tells them, "Children, I hope this has been a lesson to you. Unless we keep music in our souls, a hand of steel will clasp our hearts, and we will live by clocks and dials instead of air and sun and sea." This, then, is the moral of *The Globolinks*, but before we can take it or Madame Euterpova too seriously, Miss Newkirk interrupts admonishing Madame Euterpova not to be a bore just because she is a music teacher.

"Right you are," Madame Euterpova replies brightly, "beauty cannot be boring." With a sharp voice she calls everyone to order, and once again in command of the situation, she leads the little army away, all happily playing their instruments in a blare of C major. As the stage empties, a baby Globolink appears and waves to the audience. He then chirps an electronic bit that unmistakably contains the bus-horn motif. Are the Globolinks becoming immune to music and learning to sing? Menotti leaves us with this disquieting thought as the little Globolink helps close the curtain.

Madame Euterpova (Faull) tells her students that they must always keep music in their souls.

The Trial of the Gypsy

Dramatic cantata in one scene,
libretto in English by the composer

The Gypsy	Boy-soprano
Three Judges	Boy-altos
Chorus	Boys' Choir

World premiere at Alice Tully Hall, New York, May 24, 1978. Commissioned by the Newark Boys' Chorus. Unpublished. Scored for piano with drums ad lib.

This twenty-two-minute scene is the first of two works written not only for children, but to be performed solely by them. It is also unusual in the composer's catalog in that it may be staged or performed in concert. *The Trial of the Gypsy* is an extremely simple and attractive piece that begins with a prologue accompanied by drumrolls. In it, the boys' choir summons the townspeople to assemble in the main square for the trial of a gypsy. Three Judges enter to a crisp march followed by the Gypsy, handcuffed and escorted by two guards. The first judge swears the Gypsy in, and the other two tell him he is accused on four counts—vagrancy, theft, sacrilege and sorcery. "How do you plead?" the Judges demand. "I'm no vagrant," the Gypsy answers, "but a wanderer."

As to the second charge, the boy tells the Judges, "A gypsy takes but never steals." As for the seven ducklings that are missing, they "saw I was hungry. As they were kind-hearted . . . they began to follow me and to cry 'Gypsy boy! Eat us please!' " Against this narrative, Menotti instructs the choir to imitate the sound of quacking on a series of indefinite pitches. As for the third count of entering the church "like a vandal" and causing "havoc and scandal," the boy answers that he only followed the church bells, and, as it was cold and stormy, he entered the church to join in the singing.

A soft hymn suddenly turns to outrage (in the form of a canon) when it becomes the voice of the churchgoers crying out, "How do you dare to come into a church without shoes, without socks, dressed like a gypsy?" "But I am a gypsy," the boy replies, and to prove it he begins to play his fiddle as the piano supports the pantomime with a rhapsodic, gypsylike strain.

As to the final charge, the Judges demand to know if the boy talked to ghosts in the middle of the night. The boy replies that "the wind stole my lamp. . . . 'Wind, oh wind, where have you taken my lamp?' " he asks the night air as the choir freely imitates the sound of wind over scampering scales in the piano. The Gypsy tells the Judges the wind answered he had taken the lamp to the moon: "Can't you see how pale she is? I must light her ashen face, I must rouge her yellow cheeks or the sea will not sigh, the witch will not dance, and the fiddle will not cry."

"But," interrupts the first judge, "we are told you charged money for predicting people's future." But the Gypsy pleads, "I can't help it if my Tarots never blunder, never lie. . . . Cut this pack, and let me tell you what the future holds for you." To the first judge, the Gypsy foresees a house on fire. "In such tricks I don't believe," the judge says, "but I think I'd better leave." To the second, the Gypsy sees the judge's wife falling into a well; he also departs quickly. And to the third, he sees thieves ransacking his house. He, too, runs off followed by the choir. Left alone, the Gypsy asks the audience: "Anyone else would like his fortune told? No? Goodbye then," and he runs off as the scene comes to a bright, rapid end.

Chip and His Dog

Opera for children in one act,
libretto in English by the composer

Chip (a very poor boy)	Boy-soprano
Chip's Dog (Gregory Alexander Lafayette)	Non-singing
A Royal Messenger (very self-important)	Boy-alto
A Page (a red-nosed comic character)	Boy-alto
The Princess (beautiful and haughty)	Boy-soprano
A Doctor (bespectacled and pompous)	Boy-soprano
A Courtier (very old with a nasal voice and a silly, fatuous expression)	Boy-alto
A Gardener	Non-singing
Clowns	Non-singing
Courtiers	Boys' Choir

World premiere in Guelph, Canada, May 6, 1979. Commissioned by the Canadian Children's Opera Chorus. Published by G. Schirmer. Scored for piano and drums.

Like *The Trial of the Gypsy, Chip and His Dog* features a cast of only children. It has, however, a more elaborate plot, a more developed and through-composed though slim score, and runs some fifteen minutes longer. Cast in two scenes, it also relies on a piano-and-drums accompaniment, as the fragile qualities of solo treble voices could be easily overshadowed by orchestral instruments alone or in combination. Though the story of *Chip* is exceedingly simple and the text unassuming and naïve, the vocal parts contain intervallic and rhythmic demands that, for children, are sophisticated.

In two parts—the first in the workshop where Chip makes musical instruments and the second in the throne room of a mythical kingdom—the opera begins with a mock-tragic prelude of only eight bars. When the curtain rises, Chip and his dog (played by a child in a shaggy-dog costume) are lying on a straw pallet looking very dejected. To the dog, Chip sings a charming melody in F major that is one of the principal musical ideas of the opera and that returns several times during its course. He tells the animal there is no money left and if a customer doesn't show up soon, they will surely die.

Just then, there is a knock on the door, and when Chip opens it he sees a royal messenger followed by a page who echoes everything the Messenger says. The Princess, it seems, has heard that Chip's dog can perform wonders and has

The Royal Messenger and his Page tell Chip that the Princess wants to buy his marvelous dog, in the Spoleto U.S.A. mounting designed by Pasquale Grossi, 1980.

sent her messenger to audition him. Jubilantly embracing the dog, Chip cries, "We're saved . . . for my dog's a genius." In a sprightly aria, Chip explains to the Messenger that he is down on his luck because the things he decided to build, the public was not interested in: "I made a flute, everyone played the lute. I made a violin, everyone played the mandolin."

"But I'm told your dog is unique," the Messenger comments. "What does he do?" "Anything but speak," Chip replies proudly, and puts Gregory Alexander Lafayette through his paces. First he commands him to stand and give a military salute (accomplished to a phrase of "The Star-Spangled Banner"), then the dog plays a trumpet fanfare and a drum flourish. He next dances a minuet and a waltz, solves a math problem, traces Chip's name on the floor with his paw, and finally kisses his master as the piano jokingly quotes the opening theme from Wagner's *Tristan und Isolde*. Overwhelmed by the dog, the Messenger demands to buy him for the Princess, a bored and unhappy girl who requires new diversions daily.

Chip at first refuses, but when he is reminded that Gregory Alexander Lafayette will dine on beef and milk out of a bowl of gold, he realizes he must think of what is best for the dog. As Chip makes the deal with the Messenger, the dog begins to howl. Chip puts him on a leash and then, kneeling beside him, attempts to console him in an aria of farewell (D major, *andante calmo*). As Chip begs the dog not to forget him, the Messenger leads Gregory Alexander away leaving Chip alone, weeping.

A rather elaborate interlude connects the two scenes. It is the weightiest bit of music in the opera—chordal and highly chromatic. The flowing, transparent accompaniments that characterized the music of the first scene return, however, when the curtain rises on scene two in the palace. The Princess sits surrounded by courtiers. An air of gloom dominates the scene. The attendants attempt to amuse the Princess with first a joke, a gift and then a clown performing somersaults. She disdainfully rejects each in turn, finally demanding the clever dog her messenger promised to bring to court.

To measured, ceremonial music, Gregory Alexander is led into the room by the Messenger followed by the Page. Seeing the dog—thin, old, crossed-eyed, straggly—the Princess is aghast. The Messenger asks her not to judge him until she has seen the marvels he can perform. She agrees, and decides to rename the animal "Fifi," which produces an indignant response from Gregory Alexander. The messenger then commands the dog to perform his tricks, but Gregory Alexander mixes them up.

At first with suppressed giggles, then with increasing abandon, the Princess breaks into peals of laughter, echoed by the court. When the laughter dies down, the Princess commands the dog to curtsy to her. When he does not, she becomes angry. "The dog must be sick," the Messenger suggests. The Princess summons her doctor to examine him. After looking at the dog's tongue and taking his pulse, the Doctor pronounces Gregory Alexander "fit as a fiddle." At this, the Princess turns threateningly to the dog saying, "If you don't obey, I shall . . . lock you in jail and starve you to death."

Chip, who has been hiding in the crowd of courtiers, now runs forward, in tears, to embrace his dog and plead for mercy. When the Princess learns that Chip is the dog's former owner, she asks why Gregory Alexander will not obey her. "First of all," Chip replies, "a dog doesn't like to have his name changed. . . . You must not forget dogs, too, have a heart, and no heart is for sale. A heart must be won by patience and love. . . . Be a loving host and offer him what he likes most . . . the freedom to go back home with his master."

Dejectedly, the Princess asks what will she be left with. "Something to treasure," Chip answers, "gratitude boundless and love without measure. . . . That's quite a lot, for none of these things can ever be bought." "But if you go," the Princess says sadly, "I'm left alone, and I would like to have both of you sit on my throne." Chip offers her a choice: "He, as *your* dog, and I as your foe, or he, as *my* dog and I as your beau." The Princess chooses the latter, calls for a crown for Chip and to the cheers of the chorus, Chip and his dog join her on the throne.

A Bride from Pluto

A chamber opera for children
in one act,
libretto in English by the composer

Billy	Baritone
His Father, a tailor	Bass-baritone
His Mother	Mezzo-soprano
His Girlfriend, Rosie	Soprano
The Queen of Pluto	Coloratura Soprano

World premiere at the Kennedy Center for the Performing Arts, Washington, D.C., April 12, 1982. Commissioned by Kennedy Center's Arts Education Program under a grant from the Joseph Kennedy family. Unpublished. Scored for flute (piccolo), clarinet, bassoon, two trumpets, horn, piano, synthesizer, timpani, percussion, strings.

"For a child," Menotti reflected on the eve of the premiere of *A Bride from Pluto,* "something is either good or bad. You can't have a character who is both at once, as human beings really are. That, a child would not accept. He wants to know from the beginning who is bad and who is good, and he wants the bad ones to be punished and the good rewarded. You can't escape from a child's fundamental principles."

This, to Menotti, was the basic tenet at the roots of his most ambitious children's opera since *Help, Help, the Globolinks! A Bride from Pluto* is, in effect, a modern version of a classic European folktale, the best-known version of which is Hans Christian Andersen's *The Snow Queen.* Its characters are drawn in black and white. Billy is the spoiled, ungrateful son of model, self-sacrificing parents, while the Queen of Pluto is a selfish, evil figure who is, in the end, duped and paid in like coin for her heartlessness. In the course of this short one-act piece, Billy learns what it means to have a loving family and fiancée, and what the true values of life are.

Because of the recent appeal to a child's sensibilities through science-fiction films and space-video games, Menotti felt that his opera had to keep pace with the advanced imagination of the children of the 1980s. "My new opera reflects the changes in a child's imagination today," he has commented. "Fairy tales have become a bit unfashionable. The new folklore for children is

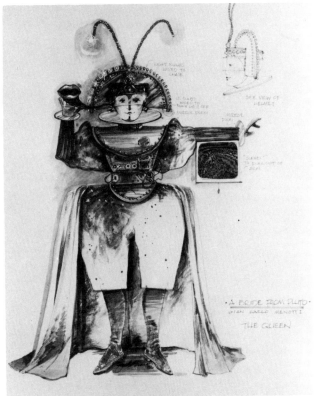

Costume sketch for the Queen of Pluto designed by Zack Brown for the Kennedy Center world premiere.

extraterrestrial. It's not quite my realm, despite *The Globolinks*, but I decided to go along with what a child really wants to hear about. That is why I have the Queen of Pluto arriving in a spaceship, wearing a costume of flashing lights and surrounded by all manner of electronic gadgetry.

"Still, I am trying to make children understand that the human heart is more important than all this fascinating machinery. I want them to enjoy the Queen and her trappings, but ultimately I want them to side with Billy, when he refuses to have his heart and soul replaced with electronic equipment and become, like the Queen, immortal. If this thought is what they take home with them, then, for me, *A Bride from Pluto* will have justified itself."

The tiny overture for the opera (actually more an introduction for the opening family scene, as it segues immediately into the stage action) is a microcosm of the opening gambit Menotti has long used to begin works as diverse as his Piano Concerto and such operas as *The Medium* and *The Saint of Bleecker Street*. Four measures built on a stark, descending melodic idea (*lento maestoso*) give way to a bustling *allegro*—a *scherzo*-like theme that in many guises has threaded its way through Menotti's writing from *Amelia al ballo* forward.

It is painfully clear from the outset that Billy is a spoiled, dislikable lad. He is convinced that he is exceedingly handsome and far too good to live in the meager home that is the best his parents can provide. And he makes no secret of his dissatisfaction. As he works beside his father, a tailor, Billy complains about his lot, his life—in short, everything. The Father, then the Mother and his girlfriend Rosie attempt to reason with him, but nothing they say seems to make a dent. The complaints continue through dinner: "I must eat off golden dishes and have butlers, cooks and maids to take care of all my wishes," Billy declares.

The Father's patience soon wears thin, and he orders Billy from the room. Left alone, the Mother laments in the first *arietta* of the opera that it was her great love for Billy that spoiled him and made him so impossible. As she finishes, Billy rushes back into the room exclaim-

ing that a strange object has landed in their yard, leaving a trail of fire behind it. Like Amahl, Billy is not believed by his mother, who fears her son has become ill.

Shortly, however, the back wall of the house becomes transparent, revealing a huge spaceship, whose door slowly opens. In an extended and lively ballet sequence, making striking use of a synthesizer in the orchestra, the Queen of Pluto and her attendants slowly descend and enter the room. With a burst of laughter from the Queen, the wall becomes opaque once again and the spaceship and the Queen's attendants disappear from sight.

Imploring the earthlings not to fear her, the Queen introduces herself in a rousing *arietta* that echoes the bravura writing for Kitty in *The Last Savage*.

> *I am the Queen of Pluto,*
> *The brightest, the nicest,*
> *Of all the twinkling stars,*
> *More beautiful than Venus,*
> *More comfortable than Mars.*

She has come to the Earth in search of a husband, and having seen Billy on a television monitor in her spaceship, she has decided that he is the ideal mate. ("I don't like Plutonian boys, they look like toys. They're strong, big and active, but not so very attractive.")

Billy, at first, is overjoyed: "I'm going to be a king," he crows. "Oh Billy, don't be a fool," the family pleads; "she's not the girl for you." "To me, she looks like a pinball machine," Rosie adds. But Billy will not listen, and eagerly cooperates with the Queen as she reads from a checklist to make certain that Billy has "all the requirements of a man who lives on Earth: Two eyes, two ears, one chin, two lips, one nose, two arms, two legs and one stomach with a belly button."

"But what is it," the Queen questions, "that makes your heart go bum, bum, bum bum?" "My soul," Billy answers. "It isn't on my list," the Queen says suspiciously. "Where is it? What is it?" She decides to consult her computer, and begins pressing buttons on her chest that set her headgear flashing with multicolored lights. All she can come up with, however, is "filet of sole" and "the bottom of a shoe." "You have a hole in your sole?" she asks in disbelief.

When Billy tells the Queen that she is wrong, she hits her electronic panel in anger and tears off some of the wires, causing a short circuit. Billy tries to explain to her that his soul cannot be seen, and that without it, he would be dead. "Disgusting," she rejoins. "We do not die on Pluto. . . . Our hearts are electronic. And after we get married, I'll have your heart extracted and

comes up with a plan. But she demands a price: "If I save you, will you give me your heart and your soul, that very soul she despised?" Billy agrees to marry Rosie the next day.

Rosie has Billy exchange his clothes for that of the mannequin in the Father's shop. When the Queen returns, she studies the mannequin with puzzlement, until Rosie tells her that "to please your Majesty, we bore in him a hole and took

replaced with solid plastic."

Billy is terrified at this prospect and begs his parents to help him out of the situation. The parents and Rosie plead with the Queen for Billy's sake. But she remains adamant. In a show of strength she aims a ray gun at some crockery on a shelf, and blasts it to bits. Delighted with the effect this has on the stunned family, she begins to dance about, mouthing "Plutonian" phrases.

In the midst of her vigorous dance, she breaks off abruptly when one of her legs seems to give way. Helped by two attendants, she hobbles outside to the spaceship to have her batteries recharged. In her absence, Billy again pleads with his parents to save him. It is Rosie, however, who

his soul apart. So now there is plenty of space . . . to install a supersonic heart." Delighted, the Queen takes the mannequin in her arms as the walls become once again transparent, revealing the luminous, phosphorescent spaceship ready to take off. Holding the mannequin, the Queen walks slowly toward the ship, while the Father, Mother and Rosie wave good-bye. In the most lyrical and extended section of the score, the four humans then exchange thanks, and Billy begs for forgiveness.

Rosie reminds him that "there may be kingdoms in the sky and treasures buried in the sea, [but] nowhere in the whole world you'll find a house as dear as home," a sentiment echoed by the others as the curtain falls.

The Father (Robert Keefe), the Mother (Dana Krueger), Rosie (Camille Rosso) and Billy (Nicholas Karousatos) cower before the otherworldly power of Billy's dream bride, the Queen of Pluto (Pamela Hinchman), Kennedy Center production, 1982.

The Boy Who Grew Too Fast

An opera for young people
in one act,
libretto in English by the composer

Miss Hope (the teacher)	Soprano
Lizzie Spender	Child
Mrs. Skosvodmonit	Mezzo-soprano
Poponel (her son)	Tenor
Dr. Shrink	Tenor
Miss Proctor	Mezzo-soprano
Little Poponel	Boy soprano
Mad Dog (a terrorist)	Bass-baritone
Policeman	Non-singing role
Students (Arthur, Jim, Ricky, Annabelle, et al.)	Children's chorus

World premiere Wilmington, Delaware, September 24, 1982. Commissioned by the Du Pont Company and OperaDelaware. Unpublished. Scored for flute (piccolo), oboe, clarinet, bassoon, horn, trumpet, trombone, timpani, percussion, synthesizer, strings.

Menotti has described *The Boy Who Grew Too Fast* as his final piece for children. But so successful has he been with this particular genre of music theater, it would probably be best to take this declaration with more than a pinch of salt. In terms of its performing forces, this work follows naturally on the heels of *A Bride from Pluto*. Menotti's structuring of the piece, however, is quite different in form.

Where *A Bride from Pluto* is in effect a miniaturized opera (with a tiny overture, arias, duets, etc.), *The Boy Who Grew Too Fast* is freer and more open in design. There is no instrumental prelude; the work begins with a hymn of thanks sung by schoolchildren. The majority of the plot is acted out through recitative or sparsely accompanied conversational lines. Every now and then an aria or a duet seems to be emerging from

Miss Hope (Denise Coffey) and Poponel (Phillip Peterson) in the schoolroom. Miss Proctor (Joy Vandever), Poponel and Dr. Shrink (Frank Reynolds) with the reducing machine . . .

the fragmentary fabric of the whole, but its flow is always breached before the moment can develop further.

The message of *The Boy Who Grew Too Fast* is very close, however, to that of *A Bride from Pluto*. It urges children not to be conformists and to remember that "Whatever name you bear, whatever face, don't be too proud of it, but neither be ashamed. Be glad that in His wisdom God decided that you should be you."

This facile work centers on a very shy boy named Poponel Skosvodmonit. Because of his unusual height, he is teased and laughed at by the other children in his class at school. He begs his teacher, Miss Hope, to do something to help him, and she takes him to Dr. Shrink, who claims he can reduce Poponel's size.

(To treat the boy, the doctor is pulled out of a performance of a "mad opera by that dotty man Menotti." This is not Menotti's only joke during the course of *The Boy Who Grew Too Fast*. In the opening scene, as roll is being taken in the classroom, Miss Hope welcomes the children back from vacation—"All except, of course, Andrew Porter, who flunked again." Porter, the music critic of *The New Yorker* magazine, has been less than an enthusiastic supporter of Menotti's music.)

In bringing Poponel down to normal size, Dr. Shrink cautions the boy that if he doesn't conform to everyone about him and agree with everything said to him ("If everyone hates op-era, pretend to hate it too"), he will start to grow again. Poponel agrees and climbs into the Doctor's miraculous reducing machine. After a series of loud electronic noises, Poponel emerges from the machine the size of the other children.

The next day at school he is accepted as the equal of his classmates, who promise to be his friend. At that moment, an escaped terrorist—Mad Dog—bursts into the classroom and takes the children prisoners. Miss Hope begs him to spare her students, and Mad Dog agrees to keep only one as a hostage. However, each of the children in turn refuses to act as the hostage. When Miss Hope asks Poponel if he will say "Yes," the voice of Dr. Shrink is heard warning Poponel not to go against the crowd. Disregarding the Doctor, he agrees. Because he has taken a different path from the others, Poponel begins to grow again. Soon, he is Mad Dog's size. Poponel attacks the terrorist, knocks him out and saves the other children. Proudly he tells his classmates, "I shall stay the way I am, and if you punch me ever again, you'll wind up like him" (pointing to Mad Dog, sprawled on the floor). Miss Hope then pronounces the moral:

Be glad of what you are,   *Be glad to be yourself.*
Whether fat or thin,   *Don't try to be another,*
Short or tall,   *For what you are,*
Black or white.   *Nobody else can be.*

. . . Miss Proctor, Little Poponel (Peter Lugar) and Dr. Shrink after the treatment; and Miss Hope with her pupils and Poponel, who has captured Mad Dog, a terrorist (Alan Wagner).

29 Janvier 1952

Milly
S & O *

Mon cher Gian-Carlo Menotti

vous avez fait la plus belle œuvre qui se puisse voir au théâtre. Elle se déroule comme une plante. Elle s'ouvre à la lumière et se ferme la nuit. Je pleurais en face d'une perfection qui s'impose chaque seconde et qui bouleverse le cœur.

Hélas je ne vous ai pas trouvé dans les coulisses

Je vous aime et je vous embrasse

Jean Cocteau
*

Chapter Nine

THE SPOKEN STAGE

A Copy of Madame Aupic
Play in three acts,
in English

Steve Martin (an art critic)
Albert (a butler)
George Norris (a painter)
Gogo (his mistress)
Madame Renée Aupic
Martha

World premiere at the Theater-in-the-Dale, New Milford, Connecticut, August 27, 1947. Unpublished.

Throughout his life, Menotti has responded as much to the pull of words as he has to that of notes. In addition to librettos for himself and others, he has written plays, theatrical sketches (produced at Spoleto under the pseudonym of Mario Felder), screenplays, short stories and poetry. "My passion," he admitted, while the Green Chair Honors Professor at Texas Christian University in Fort Worth in the spring of 1976, "is really literature. . . . I'm a composer simply because I can't get away from music. It is a torture. I would rather be a writer or study philosophy. I have a superstition that the one night I would fall asleep without reading, I would die."

It was during the run of *The Medium* on Broadway that Menotti's career veered for a brief while from musician to writer. He received offers from both MGM and David O. Selznick to create film scripts with or without music. He decided in favor of MGM, and in 1947 went West (the cross-country drive that later produced the poem for the fourth movement of *Landscapes and Remembrances*). Menotti's three-month Hollywood stay resulted in two scripts—*The Bridge* and

A Happy Ending. The first dealt with a band of refugees who left Austria during World War II and settled in Hungary. When the hostilities were over, they decided to return to Austria. To do so meant crossing a bridge at the frontier between the two countries. Because they did not have passports, the Austrians rejected them. Crossing back to the Hungarian side, they were refused reentry because they lacked the necessary papers. For a week, the group lived on the bridge because neither country would accept them as citizens. Though MGM thought the subject matter was "too depressing" for the postwar generation saturated with war films, the hopelessness of the refugees' cause would shortly be reflected in the score of *The Consul.*

A Happy Ending (later reworked and retitled *The Beautiful Snowfall* to avoid confusion with Kurt Weill's musical *Happy End*) was better received, and the studio even began casting the screenplay. But eventually, it too was rejected. While *A Happy Ending* might not have been right for the Hollywood fantasies of the late 1940s, it remains a fascinating screenplay with an unusual twist at its end. It is, in a certain sense, a

Letter to Menotti from poet Jean Cocteau, which opens with the words,
"You have created the most beautiful work that can be seen in the theater."

suspense story except that the action at times takes place in the minds of the characters rather than in real life. Each commits the same murder mentally in different ways, yet none of the "murderers" would dare admit to themselves what they had imagined.

The plot is set in a forsaken small village in the northern part of Lombardy. In a dilapidated old villa lives the Carezzi family, who barely eke out a living through their meager income. At the center of the family is the mother, a paralyzed woman in her fifties whose complete immobility has frozen any kind of life, any hope in those around her—her scatterbrained husband, her young son Rico, and his older sister Liana. All realize that as long as the mother lives, none of them can escape the monotonous depressing routine of waiting on her and caring for her.

It is, of course, her death that is fantasized by each of them. The tension in the house is heightened by the arrival of a young boarder, Lalo Morandi. He is a painter who is at work on a set of designs for a production of Bellini's *Norma* at La Scala, and has come to the countryside to work quietly. He falls in love with Liana, however, and later he, too, mentally dreams of Mrs. Carezzi's death, as she is the barrier to his marrying Liana.

The only note of happiness in the house is provided by a group of children who live in the neighborhood and who come each day to play at the Carezzi villa. They use Mrs. Carezzi as part of their games. Her role is that of a prop. She becomes an altar when they play at church; she becomes the kitchen when the children cook a meal for their dolls; they spread doll clothes on her arms to dry when the game is "laundry"; they hide things in her clothes when they have treasure hunts; and she becomes a throne when they play king and queen.

Finally, it is the children in their innocence who commit, involuntarily, the murder everyone has dreamed of. Mrs. Carezzi has been left alone with the children on Christmas evening. They decide to play "Christmas" and make her their tree. They wheel her into the garden and adorn her with tinsel, greenery and other decorations. From neighboring houses, the voices of parents are heard calling the children. They run home forgetting Mrs. Carezzi outdoors. When her family returns later that evening, they find her, in her wheelchair, frozen to death in the snow.

Later, there would be one further flirtation between Menotti and the screen, when, in 1961, he wrote a television script entitled *A Chance for Aleko*. Never produced, it was written as a vehicle for Menotti's surrogate son, the Greek actor Nikiforos Naneris, just as his major play, *The Leper*, was written for his adopted son, Francis Phelan. Though Menotti's means were very different in these two dramatic works, basically their themes were the same—a need to accept one's self and then be useful to one's fellow man.

In many ways *Aleko* is autobiographical and, in terms of Naneris, biographical. It deals with the arrival in New York of a young boy from a

Playwrights Menotti and Eugène Ionesco during a meeting at the Festival dei due Mondi, Spoleto.

small village in Greece, Aleko Andreakopoulos. His dream is to be an actor, and he is in search of someone who will give him the chance to fulfill this ambition. Ironically, the person he least expected to be of help—his uncle Victor—is the one who ultimately gives Aleko his chance—the chance not for fame and wealth, but the chance to fulfill himself as a human being.

The principal legacy, however, of Menotti-minus-music rests with his two plays. *A Copy of Madame Aupic* was written in his mid-thirties. After an unsuccessful premiere in summer stock, Menotti put it away for a dozen years until French playwright Albert Husson translated it and produced it in Paris in 1959 with Madeleine Robinson. It is a somewhat stiff, highly stylized comedy (with more than a nod toward Noël Coward) which grew out of Menotti's attraction to a line from Yeats that he quotes during Act II: "I love the sorrows in your changing face."

There is only one set for the play's three acts—the living room of George Norris's country home somewhere in New York state. It is furnished with great elegance and refinement with many paintings of apparently excellent quality and great worth. Steve Martin, an important art critic and a middle-aged man of monarchial plumpness, is waiting for George and Gogo to return from a walk. He has been invited to their home for the weekend. The visit marks a reunion between Steve and George after a seven-year breach brought about by Steve's discovery that George supported himself as a painter by faking old masters and selling them as originals.

Unknown to George, Steve has recently heard from his friend's former love, Renée Aupic, and has invited her as his weekend companion to surprise George. The surprise turns to comic opera when Steve meets Gogo. She is an exact copy of Madame Aupic. "My masterpiece," George tells Steve with bravura. "When Renée suddenly broke off the affair," he explains, "I was desperate. Then this crazy idea came into my head. . . . Why couldn't I create Madame Aupic just as I could create a Tintoretto?"

To confuse matters, when Renée arrives she is, though still a handsome woman, in total contrast to Gogo, and does not recognize herself as

she was in the younger woman. She is first amused and touched when she learns what George has done, and then put out and intrigued. In the second act a few days later, Steve finds he is falling in love with the copy of Madame Aupic, while George finds the contemporary Renée even more desirable than ever before. Meanwhile, Madame Aupic's fascination with her double is turning to annoyance.

She is disarmed, however, when George confesses he has fallen in love with her anew. "I suddenly realized," he tells Renée, "that it is not only you, but the changing in you that I loved, and that I could never recapture that in anyone else." Gogo, however, has grown jealous of George's attention to Madame Aupic, and her jealousy bursts into flames when she is told Renée is George's former mistress. The play heats up from simmer to boil in Act III, when Renée appears dressed exactly as Gogo, or rather as herself when George first fell in love with her.

Little by little Gogo realizes the role in which George has cast her—she is simply another of his fakes. In a fit of anger, she cries out that she will not be discarded like a poor imitation, for she *is* now Madame Aupic. With this she tears at Renée's gown and hair, demanding George choose between them. His choice is for the original rather than the copy. Gogo packs her bags, and as she leaves with Steve, she extends her hand to Renée saying "Goodbye, Mrs. Norris." Wistfully, Renée takes her hand answering, "Goodbye, Madame Aupic," not unlike Vanessa would bid Erika farewell a decade later.

Menotti, who in 1967 directed an Italian production of Jean Anouilh's *Médée*, plays a tape of his incidental music for Osvaldo Ruggeri and Anna Magnani, his stars, and designer Rouben Ter-Arutunian.

The Leper

Drama in two acts,
in English

The Queen
Alexios (her eldest son)
Nikitas (her younger son)
Zoe (her daughter)
The Old Man
Palladius (son of the Byzantine Emperor)
Kosmas (the innkeeper)
Irene (his wife)
Michail (the goldsmith)
Dimitrios (the tailor)
Kirillos (the tailor's apprentice)
Amphissia (the melon vender)
Bardas (the architect)
Anatellon (a Saracen slave)
Aglaia (his sister, also a slave)
Manuel (a leper)
Nilus (a leper)
Accryda (the nurse)
A Potter
Two Children (apprentices to the Smith and the Potter)
Baker's errand boy (non-speaking)
Ariadne (a dancer—non-speaking)
Bakur (the queen's bodyguard—non-speaking)
Musicians, lepers, people of the town

World premiere at the Fine Arts Theater of Florida State University's Department of Theater, Tallahassee, April 24, 1970. Unpublished.

"When I write operas," Menotti reflected on the eve of the premiere of *The Leper*, his most ambitious non-musical work to date, "unsympathetic critics are apt to say that they are not operas but plays with music. Now that I have written a play, I won't be surprised if some of them say that it is not a play but an opera without music. Evidently, many people don't know what an opera is (or perhaps I do not know what a play is). I must recognize, however, that there is a grain of truth in both criticisms, for in operas of other contemporary composers, I often miss the tension of drama, and in most modern plays, I miss the emotional grandeur and sweep of music. It is not an easy task to combine these elements. By injecting lifelike, dramatic tension in an opera, one runs the risk of becoming prosaic, and in looking for emotional grandeur in a play, one can easily become pompous and lethargic.

"In the operatic field, of course, I can find my way around with a more instinctive step. I am hardly at home in the world of dramatic prose, and God only knows whether or not in trying to

Francis (Phelan) Menotti as Alexios, the central dramatic figure in *The Leper.*

reach the attic, I have fallen into the cellar. But one thing I know, *The Leper* is the kind of play I have always wanted to write—quite out of fashion in style from what is being written today, but very much in keeping with my anachronistic heart. Even the subject of the play is somewhat out of style. To remind the minority that they all must finally become a constructive element of society and not only challengers and destroyers is hardly a fashionable point of view today. There are no villains, however, in my play, for I believe that every evil deserves our pity, and that we are all responsible for it."

Where *Madame Aupic* is a comedy of manners, *The Leper* is a play of morals, symbols and ideas. To be sure, there is a symbolic layer to *Madame Aupic* as well, but it is far less telling and secondary to a clever plot. Also the language of *The Leper* is richer in imagery than the stilted banter of *Madame Aupic* (it came, after all, over twenty years later). *The Leper,* as Menotti has outlined, deals with the effect a minority out of control wreaks within the established framework of society, however compassionate the rulers and lawmakers of that society may be.

Menotti has chosen to make this point in a period setting that allowed him a greater range of poetic expression than would be possible in a contemporary setting. Menotti's exploration of the role of society in regard to its misfits, and the responsibilities of both in an ordered structuring of life, is self-revealing. John Gruen found the play to be another reflection of Menotti's obsession of being useful to society, and he believed the leper to be symbolic of the homosexual. Certainly this is one approach to the play, but it is a highly restrictive one. The text of *The Leper* indicates, as does the entire body of Menotti's writing, that his theme is not nearly so self-serving or parochial. The concern here is the relation of a minority to the majority, and how within given social parameters both can work together with tolerance while balancing their needs and accomplishments. Menotti makes quite clear the denouement that is inevitable when the majority rule with too heavy a hand and the minority play a corruptive rather than constructive part within the ordering of society.

As Gruen correctly points out, the crux of the play rests in an extended and emotional speech for the Queen, the leper's mother, when her only daughter, Zoe, chooses to live with her brother rather than in the safe, accepted confines of the Palace. Hardly containing her sorrow and contempt for her people, the Queen rebukes them with this speech:

It is not enough that Christ died for you. Now and again and forever you will send His martyrs to their torture to atone for your own cowardice and your greed and your envy and your hate. Yes, I would have stopped her, for I know my son and do not fear him. I would have made him stop her, for he's not a lycanthrope who must be fed with healthy blood, but a lost human being like us all, listening for warnings in the darkness. If you all long ago had walked toward him—if you had all kissed him with brotherly love—there would be no need today for sacrifice and tears. But no . . . not only did you have the leper exiled as is the custom, but you have trained your dogs to snarl at him, and you have spat at him, and let your children aim their stones at him. No word is filthy enough to point out a leper, no scorn too pitiless, no laughter too indecent. And so you have turned a poor, thwarted boy into a spiteful, vengeful being. You have turned the corrupted into a dangerous corruptor; and you, who feed his hunger for revenge, will be his first victims. . . . You who first cursed him, then laughed at the misshapening of his body . . . how quickly you changed your tune at the sound of his money. And now that you realize that he is not only rich but also generous, clever, and amusing, you no longer laugh *at* him but *with* him and pretend not to see that his laughter hides a hideous grin. Before I could guide him you all rushed to feed his spiteful vanity with all the precious poisons he could buy. Refusing to make him useful, you made him dangerous. For it is he, the leper, that now rules over your tastes; it is he you all began to imitate without realizing that he is destroying in you what he envies most. You denied him both love and understanding, and now he's making you into brittle, loveless creatures. You have exchanged your hearts for his wit, your honesty for his glitter. And while this city starves, while your children grow cruel and callow, you go on revering these monstrous idols and applauding their indecorous jests—and excuse yourselves by filling your hearts with their barren irony."

The drama is set in the main square of a city-state in twelfth-century Byzantium. In the midst of the morning's activities, a group of four lepers appears led by Alexios, the Queen's elder son, who was exiled when he contracted leprosy (the part was written for and created by Menotti's adopted son, Francis Phelan). The crowd calls for the death of the lepers, but the Queen holds them in check. Alexios demands the gold that is his rightful inheritance left him by his father, the former king. Despite his mother's plea that the land suffers from weeks of drought, and the money in the treasury—Alexios's gold—must be used to buy wheat so that the city can survive, the boy continues to demand what is his by law.

At last, the Queen, in the name of justice, has no choice but to order the gold transferred to her son, but warns him that he must live by the laws set down for lepers; if he breaks these laws, she will not raise a finger to help him. The second scene of the act is set a week later. Alexios returns to the city and begins to spend his gold in a profligate manner, ordering rich cloth, great feasts, rare wines and beautiful slaves. Hungry for his money, the merchants and townspeople who formerly cursed him now vie with each other to serve him.

By the second act, Alexios's splurging and debauchery have reached new heights, to the disgust of his mother. She has resolved to have him arrested and condemned to death unless he curbs his behavior. Zoe, Alexios's sister, pleads with her brother to be reasonable and offers to share his life in the leprosarium if he will obey their mother. With this, she kisses him and leads him away. When the Queen discovers what has happened, her sorrow and indignation overflow in her great speech to the people.

In the final scene of *The Leper,* the Queen confronts Palladius, who had hoped to marry Zoe. To placate his anger, she tells the young man there are two alternatives—to go outside the city walls and raze the leper colony to the ground, or to go with her into the cathedral and pray—not for Zoe—but against the famine that grips the land. Finally persuading Palladius against violence, the Queen strikes a Menottian *Leitmotiv* saying, "Nothing heals the heart quicker than

its constant use."

Presently, Nikitas, Alexios's brother, runs out of the palace to play in the square. He is shortly approached by Alexios wearing a gold mask and a jeweled gown. He entices his brother to come and live in the palace he has built in the leprosarium, which is more beautiful than that of their mother. As if hypnotized, the boy begins walking toward Alexios's outstretched arms. At this moment, the Queen reenters the square in time to watch, horror-struck, what is happening. She cries out wildly to her bodyguard Bakur to slay Alexios, as Nikitas's nurse rushes forward to rescue the boy. Kneeling by Alexios's broken body, the Queen takes his head in her arms and murmurs with infinite tenderness, "It was *you* I loved best, my most gifted, most beautiful, most beloved son."

The Queen (Beverly Evans) cradles the body of Alexios, her "most beloved son," Spoleto U.S.A. production designed by Rouben Ter-Arutunian, 1982.

Chapter Ten

THE LATE STAGE

L'ultimo selvaggio

(The Last Savage)
Opera in three acts,
libretto in Italian by the composer

The Maharajah of Rajaputana	Bass
Mr. Scattergood (an American millionaire)	Bass-baritone
Kodanda (the Maharajah's son)	Tenor
Kitty (Mr. Scattergood's daughter)	Soprano
The Maharani of Rajaputana	Contralto
Sardula (a servant girl)	Soprano
Abdul (a peasant)	Baritone
Two Indian Scientists	Tenor and baritone
Two American Tailors	Tenor and baritone
An English Tailor	Tenor
A Catholic Priest	Bass
A Black Protestant Minister	Baritone
A Rabbi	Tenor
An Orthodox Priest	Tenor
A Philosopher	Baritone
A Physician	Baritone
A Painter	Tenor
A Poet	Tenor
A Composer	Baritone
A Concert Singer	Soprano
A Scientist	Tenor
A Society Woman	Contralto
A Business Woman	Soprano
Major Domo	Non-singing

IN INDIA: Hunters, princes, ladies-in-waiting, palace attendants.

IN CHICAGO: Journalists, military and civil authorities, politicians, society women, debutantes, various guests.

World premiere in French at L'opéra-comique, Paris, as Le dernier sauvage, *October 22, 1963. American premiere in English at the Metropolitan Opera, New York, as* The Last Savage, *January 23, 1964. Italian premiere with original libretto as* L'ultimo selvaggio *at the Teatro la Fenice, Venice, May 15, 1964. Commissioned by the Paris Opéra. Published by Belwin-Mills with an English translation by George Mead. Scored for three flutes (piccolo), two oboes, three clarinets (bass clarinet), three bassoons (contrabassoon), four trumpets, three horns, three trombones, tuba, timpani, percussion, piano, two harps, strings.*

The American premiere at the Metropolitan Opera, 1964: Sardula (Teresa Stratas), Maharajah (Ezio Flagello), Abdul (George London), Maharani (Lili Chookasian), Kitty (Roberta Peters), Kodanda (Nicolai Gedda) and Mr. Scattergood (Morley Meredith).

The Last Savage, as this opera is best known in America, occupied Menotti for well over a decade, and when it was finally finished, he described it as being in the shape of a funnel. "The first act is huge, the second smaller, and the third is smaller yet. If Satie can write music in the shape of a pear, why can't I write music in the shape of a funnel?"

In reality, however, the shape of *The Last Savage* was a matter dictated more by fate and the vagaries of the French national theaters than by any premeditated choice on Menotti's part. Originally the piece was a commission from the

Paris Opéra. George Hirsch, then the director, asked Menotti for a big work—"a huge spectacle." As often happens, Menotti fell behind in meeting his deadline, and only one act was completed when the management of the Opéra changed. "Don't make your work such a spectacular," said the new director, A. M. Julien. He also objected to the first title, *Le dernier super-*

homme, on the grounds that it was "too intellectual." Instead he suggested *L'homme sauvage.* In the meanwhile, Rudolf Bing of the Metropolitan Opera agreed to take the American premiere of the work, but he too had trouble with the title and did not like the idea of producing an opera called *The Wild Man.* Finally, Menotti effected a compromise, and *The Last Savage—Le dernier sauvage*—settled the matter, though for a while longer the Italian title was *L'ultimo superuomo.* But soon, it, too, was brought into line.

This is Menotti's first *opera buffa* since *The Old Maid and the Thief,* and significantly enough his only other work (other than the discarded *Island God*) to have its libretto cast first in the composer's native tongue. The translations used in France and America were free and often had little to do with the original, which is full of charming word plays and rhymes, and which fits the musical lines far more snugly. As Menotti has pointed out, the translating of an opera is frequently a thankless task, more difficult than that of a poem or a play, for in addition to maintaining the overall meaning of the text, the translator must fit each syllable to each note while preserving the rhythm of the music and the spirit of the text and the musical phrase. In this instance, Menotti made the assignment even more difficult for his translator George Mead by insisting he keep as well the rhyming scheme of the original Italian. (Presumably, the problems were the same for Jean-Pierre Marty, who provided the French translation.) The inevitable result was moments in which the translation seems forced and contrived. Still, given the problems involved, a good deal of the spirit of the original was retained.

For *The Last Savage,* Menotti had confessed that he took as a model Mozart's *Le nozze di Figaro*—not so much its music and formal plan as its dramatic makeup. *Figaro* has no one central character, but a series of dramatic peers who share one fate in common: All are trapped by love, though each in a different way. Beyond this dramatic parallel, however, Menotti views his characters in *The Last Savage* as "stock figures straight out of the *commedia dell'arte.* My Maharajah is a cousin to a Mozart pasha, my Sardula

Poster for the world premiere of *L'ultimo selvaggio,* performed in French at the Opéra-Comique of Paris, 1963 . . .

is a sister to Despina, and my Vassar girl is another Norina. To me all successful comedies—operas or plays—must be based on fundamental human characteristics. . . . Lyric comedy must spring from basic classical sources. It should aim further than just a few seasons on Broadway, which is the most a comic play usually gets, because most comedies today are based only on jokes.

"I must say that I do not feel any special leaning toward comedy; as a matter of fact, I am rather afraid of it. I think most artists are. Where we know why people cry, we do not ever really know why people laugh. Laughter has an elusive quality which defies analysis. In real life if someone smashes a bottle on a man's head it is a pretty horrifying sight. But when it happens on the screen it makes us roar with laughter. Why?

"When you write a comedy you can never be sure when or where the audience is going to laugh, and you also run the danger of being labeled superficial. Most people don't take laughter seriously, where often some of the most profound things in art have been said with a careless smile. I find, too, that frequently gloom is mistaken for profundity, and that audiences and critics think that what sounds very light, fluffy and spontaneous is to be taken at face value. They do not realize how very difficult it is to make things sound so easy and amusing."

Abdul, the "savage" of the opera's title, has been described by Menotti as representing a duality within himself. "In this slightly schizophrenic nature of mine, one half yearns for solitude and the cave—solitude for work and contemplation, the cave for simplicity and peace, freedom from the complexity and pace of modern life. But the other half is driven by a guilt complex, a fear of not being useful to humanity and of being trapped by love. In *The Last Savage*, Abdul is trapped and brought back by Kitty, not by the cage and the hunters she uses, but by love. Abdul becomes involved with her, therefore with what she represents, and this spells his doom.

"Of course, he could not really escape. None of us can escape the 'civilizing' influences. To some extent, my earlier operas treat this same theme—*Amelia Goes to the Ball, The Old Maid and the Thief*. It's always love, in the form of a woman, which ends up by trapping the man and subduing him. However, I do feel that whether we like it or not, we shall all be forced back to nature. Why then have I chosen to cast this rather baleful theme in the form of an *opera buffa?* Because I feel that contemporary music has failed to give us the real comic spirit. Today's music can be sardonic, but it has no real joy. . . . The secret of *opera buffa* is that the music itself is joy. The audience may become infected by it, but if

the audience laughs, it is because the music is laughing. . . .

"Composers who distort their music into grotesque sounds to elicit laughter from an audience (and how often we still hear the old tricks of a 'wrong' bass to a completely harmless melody, or an obvious onomatopoeic groaning and squeeking of instruments?) defile their craft. The

. . . and Act II, Scene 1, of that production, with Kitty (Mady Mesplé) in Chicago with her "savage" (Gabriel Bacquier).

great masters of *opera buffa*—Mozart, Donizetti, Rossini—never lower themselves to such tricks. No matter how grotesque the situation onstage, the music maintains its coolly dignified laughter."

Beyond its poise and an ability to make us smile, *The Last Savage* preserves other elements indigenous to a classic *opera buffa*. For the first time in a long while, Menotti has returned to set pieces, or closed forms. These include recitatives of almost a *secco* variety as opposed to the more dramatic *parlar cantando*, arias as opposed to narratives or soliloquies, and duets, sextets and other traditional ensemble numbers. All are housed within a lightness of texture that is best described as Rossinian, even though the orchestration is unusually large. *The Last Savage* also boasts the first full-dress overture for a Menotti opera since his previous two early comedies.

Dramatically there is a parallel to *opera buffa* as well. As Menotti points out in the opening page of a book he created from *The Last Savage*—a free retelling of the story accompanied by drawings of Beni Montresor, who created the sets and costumes for the American premiere—this is "an opera without a villain. With no one to reward or punish, you will therefore find little or no suspense in the unfolding of the plot. To make matters worse, there *is* a plot, contrary to all canons of good taste in contemporary theater; and there is nothing Brechtian about the scenery, which is made of solid *papier-mâché* and is as full of realistic details as a wedding cake."

The overture, or *"Preludio"* as Menotti labels it in the score, is a brilliant, rollicking affair, basically in C minor *(allegro con brio)* but which teases throughout with an interplay of major-minor tonalities built on the same root note. It recalls the spirit and often the rhythms of the Piano Concerto. There are three contrasting themes: the first breezy and busy, the second mocking and the third tender and affectionate. Only one recurs in the opera itself (which offers some idea of the extraordinary and spendthrift way melodies pour forth in this work), and the three are more tossed about and contrasted than actually developed. But the result is one of delight, and the overture thrusts us, without a

chance for breath, immediately into the plot. For this reason it has no formal ending, but simply melts into the stage action as the curtain rises.

The first scene of Act I takes place in a room in the palace of the Maharajah of Rajaputana, somewhere near the Himalayas. The Maharajah and Mr. Scattergood, comfortably seated in front of a small table, both armed with bank statements and other documents, are examining the prospect of an eventual marriage between their offspring. The Maharajah checks his figures with a pencil, Mr. Scattergood with an adding machine. In the background stands an ever-ready major domo.

Having compared automobiles, airplanes and wives, Mr. Scattergood in a quick *arietta* enumerates his property—three chalets in Austria, two châteaus in France, three villas in Italy, a *finca* in Peru, and two skyscrapers in New York—much like a modern Leporello. To this, the Maharajah adds one hundred and twenty villages and six cities. The two men decide that a union might be possible. The difficulty is that both children are so headstrong. Scattergood suggests they consult the Maharani, but the Maharajah says that it would do no good. "She is an ignoramus. . . . The only reason I can stand her is because she is the mother of my only son." Scattergood is amazed. "You have only one son from twenty-seven wives?" The Maharajah tells him confidentially that twenty-six of his wives are sterile. "People were suggesting that I was not quite virile. They were all quite mistaken. The wedding was hardly done when she gave birth to a son. . . . Fair-haired, blue-eyed, I could not have done better if I tried."

At this moment, the Maharani, so fat that she can hardly walk, enters slowly supported by Sardula. She falls onto a heap of cushions and remains motionless like a sphinx. The Maharajah turns to Scattergood and elaborates on his wife. Originally this was a bouncing aria, but Menotti trimmed it by half when he prepared the opera for publication. This cut joins others already made between the premieres in Paris and New York—a *duettino* between Abdul and Sardula at the end of Act I (later restored in the printed score), and an aria for Abdul at the opening of Act III.

"Well," the Maharajah concludes, "if you think she can help, put the question to her." Timidly, Scattergood asks for the Maharani's advice. Over a quasi-comic oriental motif piped by the oboe, the Maharani responds mysteriously, like an oracle, "You take care of your daughter! We'll find a way to make our son obey." Both men marvel at her sound common sense. The Maharajah orders his major domo to find Kitty and Prince Kodanda and summon them to him. As he departs, a group of Indian masons enter carrying large blocks of stone, and with extraordinary speed and to a brilliant *allegro* driven by percussion, they construct (over a *passacaglia* bass) a wall that separates Scattergood and the Maharajah, his wife and Sardula. When Kitty and Kodanda join them, the stage has been divided into equal halves with the Americans on the right and the Indians on the left. Their conversations are independent dramatically, yet musically they gradually mount to a full-scale ensemble.

The music and the action at first seesaw from group to group as the Maharajah and his wife attempt to persuade Kodanda to consider Kitty, and Scattergood makes his case for a marriage with the Prince. In the midst of this sextet (the

first of several), Menotti adds a light, breezy solo section for Kitty, which, like the majority of her music, is written high and brilliantly, with rapid coloratura passages. She tells her father there is no way she will consider marriage until she has fulfilled the mission that brought her to India— to find the last primitive cave man. He will be the basis for her Ph.D. thesis in anthropology, which she is completing at Vassar.

Meanwhile, Prince Kodanda also resists the idea of a union, especially with anyone but an Indian girl. He, too, originally had a brief solo moment, which Menotti eliminated from the printed score.

The Maharajah turns to Sardula for support, and in rolling, *Così*-esque triplet rhythms, she seconds the Maharajah, adding to Kodanda, "You need a girl with plenty of money, one who has oil wells flowing like honey." The arguments on both sides of the wall grow more heated until Kitty finally agrees to the marriage, but only after she has captured her savage. As to Kodanda, he says he will obey his parents if Kitty will give up anthropology. With this settled, all launch into another sextet; *The Last Savage,* more than any work that preceded it, displays Menotti's deft flair for creating ensembles in which several musical and dramatic thoughts are juggled simultaneously.

In this sextet, which begins *pianissimo* and *staccato* much like "*Fredda ed immobile*" from the end of Act I of *The Barber of Seville,* Kitty and Kodanda weave long, sustained lines over and through the pinpoints of sound that the others are singing. In it, each character contemplates Kitty's savage and the problem he presents. At its conclusion, the Maharajah claps his hands and the masons appear to tear down the wall as quickly as they had put it up. This is done to the same music in reverse (but not in strict retrograde) to which the wall was built.

With the wall removed, the Maharajah and Scattergood compare notes on the situation. Having reached an impasse, Scattergood once more suggests consulting the Maharani. To the earlier Oriental tune, she says, after a moment's thought, "If we cannot find an honest-to-goodness wild man, then, of course, we must in-

Thomas Schippers, conductor for the world premieres of *Amahl and the Night Visitors* and *The Saint of Bleecker Street,* rehearsing at the Metropolitan Opera for the U.S. premiere of *The Last Savage.*

vent one." "What a woman, what a genius," the two fathers chime. Sardula interrupts and shows her true Despina colors by manipulating the drama toward her own ends. "I know a man who could do it," she suggests, and recommends her boyfriend Abdul. Scattergood asks Kitty to bring him in. As she runs to fetch Abdul, the Maharani, who has been staring pointedly at Scattergood, pulls him aside. "I have the impression you and I have met before. . . . Were you ever in Hong Kong?" "No," Scattergood answers, and the Maharani, unconvinced, mutters in an aside: "This is getting sillier and sillier, but his face is so familiar."

The busy music to which Sardula exited returns as she leads Abdul in. To very pompous, ceremonial chords in the orchestra, the Maharajah begins questioning the young man. This leads to a witty quintet, as deft and *staccato* as the preceding sextet but not as extended. The Maharajah offers Abdul money to pose as a wild man for Kitty to capture, Abdul expresses doubt about the plan, and Sardula begs him to think of their future and accept the money.

In a bouncing *allegretto*, the Maharajah delivers a short patter aria in which he reassures Abdul that there is nothing to pretending to be a savage. "You never learned to speak, your intelligence is weak. At first you are ferocious, then be timid and surprised." He lets out a Tarzan-like cry, and Abdul gets the point: "As they do in Hollywood?" Scattergood, the Maharajah promises, will pay you a fee. "What about a thousand dollars?" Scattergood offers. When Abdul hesitates in amazement, Scattergood thinks he is holding out for more money, and soon the figure is up to $100,000.

"What would I do with all that money?" says Abdul in a frightened voice. But Sardula is not at a loss for ideas or words. In a graceful *duettino*, Sardula convinces Abdul to accept the farce and with it the money. But when it comes to signing the contract with Scattergood, Abdul backs off once again. At this point Sardula bursts into tears, and the distressed Abdul quickly signs. This leads to yet another quintet, in which the first of a number of what might be called mini-morals is aired (in this respect, *The Last Savage*

recalls *The Old Maid and the Thief*): "When a problem must be solved, a woman's tears can show us how." The quintet builds to an ecstatic pitch against triumphant chords in the orchestra as the curtain falls on the first scene.

Between scenes one and two there is an extended orchestral interlude entitled *"Caccia,"* or "The Hunt." It depicts Kitty's safari into the surrounding jungle to look for her savage, with Scattergood and the Maharajah along, ostensibly to do some tiger hunting. It begins with a trumpet fanfare that sets a martial tone for the combat to follow. The interlude is brilliant and restless, driving the music forward to a *fortissimo* climax of highly rhythmic, heavy chords. As these die away in the lower reaches of the orchestra, a solo trumpet sounds once more, this time behind the scene.

When the curtain rises for scene two, we are in the great court of the palace of the Maharajah in late afternoon. To a rocking figure in the orchestra, an offstage chorus chants, "O my hunter, far away, at the fading of the light, lest you wander far astray, I'll be waiting through the night." Sardula sits at a ticker-tape machine reading the day's stock market quotations to the dozing Maharani. When she is certain the Maharani is sound asleep, she begins to tiptoe away, but is suddenly stopped by the appearance of Prince Kodanda, who attempts to embrace her.

He declares his love for Sardula, and a lively duet ensues. Kodanda presses his suit ardently, while Sardula tries to dampen his passion. Finally, the only recourse left to her is a slap. At this moment horn calls are heard in the distance announcing the returning hunters. The Maharani awakens and calls for the court to be assembled. As the music in the orchestra becomes more feverish, servants enter with torches and little by little the stage is filled with guards and men and women of the court.

To a brisk and jaunty march in E-flat major, the band of hunters very slowly begins to make its appearance, preceded by a troop of soldiers in glittering uniforms. Porters, gamekeepers and attendants are followed by a group of invited princes with their retinues, who are greeted by the Maharani. The march peaks on a C-major

The highborn Kodanda (Gedda) woos the servant Sardula (Stratas) in Beni Montresor's fanciful décor at the Metropolitan Opera.

chord as the chorus cheers "the mighty hunters, triumphantly returning." Finally, the Maharajah enters with Kitty and Scattergood, all looking very self-satisfied as they display a huge cage containing Abdul dressed savagely in leopard skins. In a great outcry, the chorus registers its amazement, and then Kitty, in a bravura aria, invites everyone to take a better look at her catch.

After a brief recitative with two volleys of coloratura fireworks, Kitty immodestly recounts the derring-do of her capturing of Abdul, in a marchlike figure that oscillates between G-sharp minor and B major. "The nails on his fingers could tear you asunder; his voice is like thunder! Whatever features his beard may be hiding, oh see how soft his eyes, how sweet and confiding." And to a further coloratura volley mounting to top D, she speculates his looks "may well be hiding a noble heart." Returning to the opening figure she tells the crowd, "I will reach him, I will teach him. . . . I'll gain the admiration of the whole world of science. Everyone will call me the greatest of them all!"

The Maharajah invites the court scholars to give their opinion, warning them *sotto voce* that

one false word and he will cut their heads off. They examine him in three languages and conclude that he is indeed unique. Scattergood presses Kitty to set a date for her marriage to Kodanda, but Kitty reminds her father that first her discovery must be investigated and certified, and she must take her savage back to be seen in the United States. During the nervous ensemble that follows, in which each of the principals expresses reaction to this unexpected turn of events, the Maharani manages to whisper in her husband's ear some advice on how to handle the situation.

Calling for silence, the Maharajah suggests that a formal engagement between Kitty and Kodanda be agreed upon, and they consent. To a lighthearted march tune, everyone goes inside the palace for a banquet celebrating Kitty's find. As they exit, the Maharani gives Scattergood her arm, asking, "Were you ever in Singapore?" Confused, Scattergood replies "No," and the Maharani intones a second time, "This is getting sillier and sillier, but his face is so familiar."

Left alone onstage in his cage, Abdul soliloquizes on all that has happened to him in so short

Menotti directing Act II, Scene 2, at the Metropolitan Opera, with cast and chorus at work onstage beneath a huge mobile . . .

a period of time and all that is in store for him in the months ahead. Concluding that "a man who lets a girl make up his mind has no right to complain," he begins a gentle, reflective aria (*adagio ma non troppo,* E-flat major) in which he resigns himself to the role he has agreed to play. "Only for you, lovely Sardula, I have renounced my freedom and peace. Hunting and plowing, reaping and sowing, all that gave me repose and release." As he bids farewell to his "mountains and quiet meadows," certain that "money and riches can give me no more," the curtain falls.

Whereas the first act of *The Last Savage* was given entirely to exposition, with a disarming denouement slated for the third act, the second is devoted to satire. The core of the opera, its aim is to prove Menotti's contention that our so-called civilization is more savage than the jungles in which Abdul was tracked and captured. In three scenes that juxtapose Chicago and India, the middle act opens in Kitty's boudoir in Chicago a few months after the capture of Abdul. At one side of the room Kitty is sprawled on a huge couch, chattering (à la Lucy) on the telephone. On the other side of the room Ab-

dul, still in his leopard skins, and with his hands chained together, is having his measurements taken by a trio of tailors—two American, one British.

As the tailors measure and feud among themselves as to how best to dress Abdul (with the British tailor generally in disagreement with the others), Kitty fills in a friend on Abdul's history ("Since the day we caught him, he applies everything I've taught him"). This antiphonal din is abruptly broken off when Abdul pushes the tailors aside declaring he has had enough. Quickly Kitty hangs up and grabs her whip. Keeping Abdul at bay with the whip, she tries to reassure the tailors that there is nothing to fear, but they gather up their bolts of cloth, tape measures and pincushions, and frightened, make their way to the door as Abdul cries, "Get out!"

As the last tailor rushes through the door, Kitty tries to calm Abdul by removing the chains from his wrists. She tells him that there is something further she must teach him—the art of love. This is sung in a vaulting phrase that rises to high D, and then drops nearly two octaves. This flourish leads directly into a *duettino* as Kitty tells Ab-

. . . and his staging of the scene for Spoleto U.S.A. in Charleston, with Abdul (William Stone) contending with debutantes.

dul in short, nervous phrases that "it's a complicated subject with a complicated object." When Abdul says he doesn't wish to learn, Kitty grabs her whip and pops Abdul with it until, on his knees, he agrees to be an obedient student.

"First," says Kitty (*adagio, ma non troppo*) "we learn the art of kissing." Kitty's amorous, *legato* phrases are paired in most instances with clipped, disquieted phrases for Abdul as he begins to tremble at the thought of what lies ahead. When Abdul resists again, Kitty puts his arm around her waist and moves her lips close to his. When they finally make contact, from the lower reaches of the orchestra slowly emerges a highly chromatic passage that sounds suspiciously like a reference to the first kiss between Tristan and Isolde in Wagner's opera. Surprised and a bit dazed, it is Kitty who now pulls away. Catching her breath, she comments that "for a prehistoric savage, you're not too bad. . . . But civilized love's another matter. It is poetry." Abdul, she continues, was indulging in a bit of prose.

To demonstrate civilized love, Kitty pulls Abdul over to the sofa, and begins his instruction: "First we have a little bit of music, then we turn the lights down low, then some whiskey. . . . Whiskey is the surest way, that's the best technique of love in America today." Then to the mounting *Tristan*-esque figure, Kitty tells Abdul a couple must move closer and closer, place their hands one on the other, say they adore one another, and then pour more whiskey. This leads once again into the catch phrase "Whiskey is the surest way in America today," which punctuates the entire seduction scene. As the music builds and Abdul moves closer, Kitty repeats the formula: "Kisses on kisses, whiskey on whiskey." Against a high tremolo E in the strings, with cascading chromatic scales underneath, a blackout follows—just in the nick of time. The orchestra bursts out into *fortissimo*, darting motives that are reminiscent of, but do not quite resemble, ideas from the overture. Gradually, the passion of the interlude is spent, and Kodanda enters in front of a drop that pictures the gardens of his father's palace. This second scene consists entirely of a recitative and aria for the Prince, in which he reflects on his love for Sardula, who

he hopes is beginning to love him.

The aria is rhapsodic (*lento, molto espressivo*), and to graceful, rounded neoclassic figures in the orchestra, Kodanda muses, "As long as my heart is hoping and wondering, to suffer and doubt is almost a pleasure." This lovely aria was extended by Menotti in the printed score, greatly improving its shape. It accomplishes more than drawing us into Kodanda's mind; it forms an island of quietude between the two hectic outer scenes of the act.

When the scene shifts back to the Scattergood apartment, it is to the living room where a reception is to be held to display Abdul to the press, society and the curious. Abdul is alone in the room as the curtain goes up, but is soon joined by Scattergood. He tells Abdul his work is finished once the reception is over, and a car will whisk him to the airport. Abdul confides to Scattergood that his battered heart is torn between obedience, pride and passion. In a bubbling patter aria, Scattergood replies the sooner Abdul is out of Chicago the better off he will be. "I'm the slave of a thousand masters," Scattergood moans, "a thousand aggravations, defeats, disasters. The telephone, the dictaphone, the office, the auditor, the refrigerator, the elevator, the creditors, the debtors, the telegrams and letters, the tax bills, the repair bills, liquor bills and sleeping pills. Save yourself dear fellow. Get out while yet you may. Appointments, officials, and all those damn initials—the PTA, the UN and NATO, the contribution to Spoleto!"

The aria ends in a final outburst of bravura as Kitty enters. She gives the word to open the doors, and above an orchestral tremolo, a jagged theme is stated that will later become the subject of an elaborate double fugue as the reception-lecture-cocktail party builds to a deafening crescendo. As the guests pour in, they rush to the platform to inspect Abdul, who stands there motionless. When the seats in the room are filled, the angular rising theme is broken into by sharp chords that eventually turn into a sort of progressive jazz stretch. Kitty bangs a gavel repeatedly to quieten the room, and when at last there is silence, she addresses the throng in an extended *scena*.

Typically for Kitty, her aria opens with a showy cadenza. This is followed by a mixture of dramatic recitative ("You must remember that when he arrived here, he was a wild man from the jungle"), *arioso* ("He understands everything he ought to, he holds a fork as he was taught to") and finally a full-scale ensemble in which Abdul expresses his embarrassment, the chorus its skepticism and Kitty her triumph. This ensemble is an outsized waltz, resplendent with pyrotechnics for Kitty that climax on a held top E-flat in *alt*.

After enthusiastic applause, Scattergood calls on the assemblage ("You, the most enlightened class of society") to step forward and present themselves one by one to Abdul, beginning with the clergy. It is at this point Menotti launches his double fugue; this time the motto is sounded a fourth higher than originally and *allegro con brio*:

A quartet of ministers (Catholic, Protestant, Jewish and Orthodox) lead off, each disputing the claim of the other much like the quarrelsome Jews in Strauss's *Salome*. Soon a philosopher and a doctor join in, while a society matron ogles Abdul and invites him to dinner. The press bombard him with questions ("How do you like Chicago? What do you think of American women?") as the melee grows into a sort of contemporary *Meistersinger* riot scene.

Kitty tries in vain to keep the crowd from frightening Abdul, but it is too intent on impressing him. A trio of giddy debutantes chime in with a banal ditty, while a politician and members of the military add their two cents' worth. The mounting tension is broken off by a biting chord. A modern painter steps forward carrying a blank canvas topped by a tube to which is attached a chain. "I am the chief exponent of the new school of painting," he intones. "I paint with a chain, and my genius consists in the choosing of a fixture that brings out the true artistic texture." He then pulls the chain and a flood of multicolored paint is released onto the canvas, creating a series of gaudy streaks, to the ap-

plause of the crowd.

Another sharp chord brings forth a poet. "I am the chief exponent of the new school of poetry," he announces, and recites his latest poem:

I!	*God is me,*
I!	*And I am he,*
I am me,	*God and I and me,*
And me is I.	*Me-me-me-me,*
I!	*I!*

He, too, is greeted with an ecstatic ovation. Finally, a composer joins the others followed by a string trio and a soprano. "I am the chief exponent of the new school of music," he sings. "In the theater I'm obscure but progressive, and at last I have succeeded in avoiding the dramatic and expressive. My style is dry and drastic, when I write chamber music I am dry but sarcastic. But when I write for orchestra I erupt like a volcano" (to prove the composer's point, the orchestra gives out here with a thundering blast of percussion). This section might be labeled "Menotti's Revenge," and his barbs are aimed at "the new aleadodecaphonic style" in which the onstage composer specializes.

The string trio and soprano perform the composer's latest opus (a twelve-bar piece built on an obvious tone row). Against its hard, sparse lines, the soprano wails a single sentence (in German, of course): *"Tag ohne Schmerzen ist wie Nacht ohne Kerzen."* Overlapping the final notes of the trio is the second theme of the *"Preludio,"* which plunges us back into the other half of Menotti's figure. In this part of the "cocktail" ensemble, a mad scientist comes forward to Abdul with a small black box, telling him, "I press this little button so and blow the blasted universe to pieces."

As the "pillars" of society and the arts continue to tug at him, he cries out to Kitty, "How can you bear to live like this with madmen such as these?" At the height of the mayhem, Abdul demands that everyone stop. "Kitty my darling," he continues, "I love you, but if this is your civilization and these the people you admire, I want no part of it . . . I'll end my life among the shadows!" With this he rushes toward the door, knocking over anyone and everything in his path.

As he dashes out, a huge mobile hanging from the ceiling comes loose and falls on the guests while the orchestra explodes in rage.

Act III is set in a jungle clearing in the depths of the Indian wilderness, one month later. Following a fanfare, a chorus of Indians laden with baskets and provisions enter slowly, followed by a band of palace guards and soldiers who set up a tent for the Maharajah. To a droning chorus ("Long is the journey, slowly pass the hours. Sunlight and shadows heavy on my shoulders"), Kitty and Scattergood enter in hunting costumes. With the Maharajah's help, they have returned to find Abdul. Scattergood has told Kitty the whole thing was a trumped-up affair, but she wants to hear this from Abdul himself.

To a grandiose march strain, the royal party enters, preceded by a page with an enormous spray gun filled with insect repellent. After giving orders for the hunt to continue, the Maharajah and the Maharani enter the tent with Scattergood and Kitty. Left alone with Sardula, Kodanda tries to kiss her. She warns him to be prudent, but he declares his intention to marry her. Dismissing him, Sardula, in a soft and lyric aria *(adagio ma non troppo)*, is consumed with guilt. She wants the Prince, but feels she cannot simply abandon Abdul, not realizing her former boyfriend is now head over heels in love with Kitty. Addressing Abdul's memory, Sardula asks, "How shall my lips deny it? Shall I weep? Shall I smile? How may the words be spoken to tell you that in love a promise may be broken?" It is not only one of the opera's tenderest moments, but one of the loveliest arias Menotti has written for soprano since Amelia's "While I Waste These Precious Hours." In three parts, the return of the opening melody is exquisitely embroidered by Menotti and concludes in A major. The aria had begun in A minor, and this shift in tonality makes it clear that however sympathetic Sardula is about Abdul's plight, she is not going to miss the chance of marrying Kodanda.

As Sardula leaves, Scattergood and the Maharani emerge from the tent and sit in two camp chairs. After a moment of banter about the weather, the Maharani is suddenly gripped by the realization of where she had previously known Scattergood. Greatly agitated, she staggers to her feet: "My God . . . It was one of those little ships on the Nile. You were so young and I had no hips." Dumbfounded, Scattergood also remembers: "That little dove, so avid for love, that was you?" "Then you haven't forgotten?" sighs the Maharani. "Forgotten?" Scattergood exclaims. "How could I forget those things we did there by the pyramid!"

Leaning on Scattergood for support, the Maharani confesses to him that Kodanda is his, not the Maharajah's son, and thus Kitty is Kodanda's sister. Their marriage is, of course, impossible. The two give vent to this revelation in a brisk *duettino* and resolve that the marriage will never take place. "But I make one condition," the Maharani tells Scattergood in grave tones: "My dear Maharajah must have no suspicion." Scattergood agrees, and as they part, the Maharani eyes him coquettishly adding, "You could still be quite a lover!"

There is a sudden commotion and sound of trumpets as a band of soldiers returns with the recaptured Abdul. He begs the Maharajah to release him and leave him in peace. The Maharajah then launches into one of the most delightful and clever ensembles in the opera. Cast in two halves, these are separated by recitative-like exchanges between the principals. "Just a moment, just a moment," the Maharajah leads off followed one by one by the other principals chiming in to assure Abdul they have only come to pay him his money. Kitty confesses to all that she loves Abdul, Sardula tells Abdul her heart has undergone a change and the confused Maharajah demands, "What the devil is this?" As he rants the others philosophize that "this is nothing new or strange; love can never last forever."

Abdul, however, declares his love for Kitty is impossible, and eagerly the Maharajah seconds him. "Although I love you," Abdul tells Kitty, "I will never face again that dreadful world you say you love so well." In a loving strain Kitty, to the amazement of all, tells Abdul she will gladly live in a cave with him if that is what he wants. With yet another flight of coloratura, she tells the others, "You all may go home now, and I will stay with the man I adore." This is too much for the Maharajah, who calls on Scattergood to put an end to this nonsense. To his astonishment, Scattergood sides with his daughter. Frustrated, the Maharajah cries out, "This is what always happens when you do business with the Americans!"

To further add to his bewilderment, Kodanda comes forward and asks his father's blessing for a marriage with Sardula. When the Maharani supports her son, the others remind the Maharajah that "love is not a thing for logic." This leads to a septet, one of the opera's happiest moments. To an expansive melody in D-flat major, Abdul reflects, "Ah, how fortune waits in hiding to surprise us. See this lovely, lovely creature, once my terrifying teacher. Who'd predict that she would love me?":

Ah, how for-tune waits in hid-ing to sur-prise us

Then other of the principals in turn adds his or her feelings to the ensemble:

Kodanda: "My adorable Sardula, after all care and sorrow, I shall take you for my wife."
Sardula: "I was nothing but a servant, I had never hoped for money. . . ."
Scattergood: "I am now so well respected, never one for fun and games, yet in India I have a son . . ."
Maharajah: "Who would have thought at the beginning, that my so ingenious planning . . . would end in disaster?"
Maharani: "Who'd believe that I'd discover that young man who was my lover?"

Before the flowing set piece is brought to its rousing end, everyone together intones the opera's moral: "Wiser men from king to peasant only gamble on the present. What may happen by and by, only fools will prophesy." Calmer and now resigned, the Maharajah gives word to break camp, Abdul goes into his cave and Kitty kisses her father affectionately. Scattergood tells Kitty she is crazy to stay in the jungle, but she explains this is only a beginning: "Just leave me the money when Abdul isn't looking, and when

you're in the city send me a butler and a man to do the cooking." Scattergood warns her that "if Abdul finds out he'll kill you." "Kill me?" Kitty echoes with a peal of laughter. "A man who is a lover has no will of his own!"

She then disappears into Abdul's cave while Scattergood joins the procession about to return to the Maharajah's palace. Kitty emerges from the cave with Abdul, and all, in an eloquent final ensemble, say their farewells. As it grows darker, Abdul spreads a blanket under a tree on the opposite side of the stage from his cave and leads Kitty to it. Holding her tenderly, he reassures her with a long kiss. In a reflective, simple duet, Kitty and Abdul sing of their love and the beauty of their world. As they cuddle on the blanket, Kitty gives a signal unseen by Abdul. Against the second-act fugue subject, a line of servants led by the Major Domo enter on tiptoe bearing a refrigerator, a bathtub and a television set, which are carried into the cave. The fugue subject turns into a merry *fugato* that has the last laugh at Abdul and those in the audience who think they are smarter than a determined girl such as Kitty. But with the appliances secretly installed in the cave, Menotti wonders (in his *Last Savage* book), "Will they be happy?" He then asks wistfully, "Are we happy?"

All the conveniences: Kitty (Peters) and Abdul (London), back in the jungle, go native.

The Most Important Man

Opera in three acts,
libretto in English by the composer

Toimé Ukamba	Bass-baritone
Dr. Otto Arnek (a distinguished scientist)	Tenor
Leona (his wife)	Mezzo-soprano
Eric Rupert (Arnek's assistant)	Baritone
Cora (Arnek's daughter)	Soprano
Professor Clement	Tenor
Professor Risselberg	Tenor
Professor Bolental	Baritone
Professor Hisselman	Baritone
Professor Grippel	Baritone
Under-Secretary of State	Baritone
Mrs. Agebda Akawasi (a native leader)	Soprano
Servants, natives, soldiers	Chorus

World premiere at the New York State Theater, Lincoln Center, New York, March 7, 1971. Commissioned by the New York City Opera. Unpublished. Scored for two flutes, oboe, clarinet, bassoon, two trumpets, two horns, trombone, percussion, piano, strings.

It was inevitable that the Ford Foundation, which underwrote so many new American operas during the 1960s, and Menotti would eventually get together. The result of this union was *The Most Important Man*, a work obsessed with social and political concerns, and the opera that by Menotti's own admission gave him more trouble than any other of his stage pieces. It is his first full-length theater piece since *The Last Savage* of eight years earlier, which in its mixing of races is it a sort of comic sister to *The Most Important Man*. With it he tells a tragic tale, one laced with questions of greed, power and destructive human relationships.

At the root of these is the issue of black versus white, but it is not handled in the usual stereotype of the "bad" white man and the "good" black man. Menotti's issue is bigger. Black and white are only shades within a bigger drama. The question is what man does to man, and how age-old prejudices can surface in even the most enlightened human beings.

"We whites," Menotti has said, "with all our desire to be fair to the black man, remain hypocrites, or at least so far we have. We are open to integration until it touches our own private lives; then, there is enormous resistance. In spite of all our protestations, the thought that a black man could take one of our places in society frightens us. This is the reason many were shocked by this opera. Even a scientist cannot swallow the fact that his daughter has an affair with a black man. By the same token, his fellow scientists are shocked to think a black man could have discovered a great secret which had evaded them, and that thanks to him the black race holds the potential power to dominate the world."

There is also an autobiographical pull to this work that was previously felt in *Martin's Lie* and *The Leper*. It is the long-felt need in Menotti's life for a son, someone to be responsible for. This need led him to the adoption of Francis Phelan, a young actor he met in New York. Though the humanistic and filial strands of the opera are

excellent dramatic material, neither was fully explored. In this work, more than in any other, Menotti was defeated by time. Two months before its world premiere, the opera was only half finished in sketch form and the orchestration of Act I was barely begun. As the day of the first performance approached, parts of the last act were still unwritten and a large percentage of the orchestration still not done. Working around the

heightened role played by the orchestra as almost an uncredited character in the drama, underlining and commenting on the emotions and progress of the plot.

It leads off with a vigorous, rising theme that will come to be associated with Toimé. After fourteen brooding bars, the curtain rises over a rapid figure that never extends itself beyond *mezzo piano* and that weaves a sense of mystery

clock nonstop, somehow Menotti brought the piece together in time, but it meant the orchestra had to sight-read the last act at the premiere.

This haste, unprecedented even for Menotti, is felt in the quality of both the words and the music. Obviously he is aware of this, and for the successful Italian premiere in Trieste, much of the work was extensively revised. Yet, in America, it represents the nadir of his career. But to those aware of the place of *The Most Important Man* in the totality of Menotti's work, it is a score that signals the ongoing tightening of his music theater. Rather than writing arias, he writes extended statements for voice that are often boiled down to tense declamations. There is also the

and apprehension. The first scene is in Dr. Arnek's laboratory in a White African state. It is late at night, and in the darkness, the figure of a man can be distinguished. He is ransacking shelves as the opening orchestral *presto* gradually spins itself out. Suddenly a light in the room is switched on, and Dr. Arnek is seen at the door pointing a pistol at the prowler.

To repeated, strong chords in the orchestra, Arnek orders the man not to move. Leona, Arnek's wife, rushes into the room followed by Arnek's assistant Eric. Reassuring Leona and Eric that he is unharmed, Arnek orders the intruder to put up his hands and turn around. As he does, the orchestra repeats the ominous Toimé theme.

Two worlds: the intruder Toimé (Allan Evans) agrees to work with Arnek (Renato Cioni) in the production directed by Menotti and designed by Pasquale Grossi for the Teatro Giuseppe Verdi, Trieste, 1972.

Dr. Arnek recognizes his former student at once. Toimé's bitter, drunken responses to Arnek's questions alarm Leona, but the doctor asks her and Eric to withdraw and leave him alone with Toimé; reluctantly they do so.

Dr. Arnek gives Toimé an injection to quiet him. "Am I being anesthetized, sterilized or simply castrated?" he asks belligerently. "What is it? Morphine, dexedrine, amphetamine, Caroline, Josephine, L.S.D., D.D.T., Diddlededee? Or is it plain embalming fluid?" Toimé continues to rave as the orchestra again sounds his theme before proceeding to jazzy figurations that accompany the rantings. Slowly Toimé's stream-of-consciousness begins to take shape. In disjointed phrases he speaks of his experiences after his studies with Arnek in "sweet-rotting Europe, Negro-loving Europe. Sorry but no place for you here . . . Too many already . . . Not enough work for our own people . . . But we love you . . . Brilliant boy . . . Nice trick-performing dog!"

"Why didn't you come to me?" Dr. Arnek asks quietly. "To assist your Swiss-Swedish-Belgian-blond assistants?" Toimé responds accusingly. "No thank you! They're not smart enough for me." Worried, Leona looks into the room, but again Arnek reassures her: "He'll fall asleep soon. I'll stay here with him." As Leona leaves, Toimé continues to ramble in a surrealistic, monologue as the drug takes effect.

As Toimé loses consciousness, the stage darkens and the orchestra begins the first interlude (molto lento). It paints the passing of time in open sonorities, principally intervals of sixths and thirds. From them emerges one of those long-lined melodies that are such a Menotti specialty:

Un poco piu mosso, ma sempre molto disteso

When the curtain rises again, we are in the lab some days later. Toimé and Arnek are engaged in intense conversation. Toimé is now sober as he tells Arnek accusingly, "You are white and behave like a white; it is I who wouldn't behave like a black. . . . Did any pupil ever work as hard? I was sure it would be me that you would take.

. . . Oh! what a fool I was. It was a white man you chose, although of all your pupils I was the best." He tells Arnek he ran away "like a forsaken bride" when he was not made the doctor's assistant. "I drowned my blackness in your white gin. . . . Among bums there is no color."

Arnek begs Toimé to forgive him, remain with him and help him. "I'm tired and ill," he continues, "and time is running out for me." His experiments, he adds, are on the brink of completion, but they cannot be finished alone. "Even my assistants think me mad," he confides. "One by one they abandon me. The last one is Eric. . . . He, too, has lost faith in me. I need a fresh approach, a fresh eye." (What Arnek's experiments are or where they are leading him is never clarified by Menotti. We are only told the man who completes them will become the most important man in the world.)

Toimé turns from Arnek crying that for him it is too late: "My heart is as black now as my skin." In an impassioned plea (andante molto maestoso), Arnek, unfolding a huge anatomy chart, tells Toimé to "look at the landscape of your mind, that infinite field of dreams tended by secret monsters, invisible, untamed. . . . Look at your heart, the secret measure of your soul . . . the shameless drummer who can shatter your nights with desire or freeze your eyes with fear." He begs Toimé to consider the wonder of man, "wrought by a divine scientist far more prodigious than you or I," and to use rather than squander his gifts.

Moved, Toimé agrees to work not for Arnek, but with him. "Let me be your son, Master. I swear to you whom I love above all living men no one can work as hard as I can. But you must love me, too, above all other pupils. Only as a son, your son, I can again become a man." The doctor replies that not out of pity or guilt, but out of love he will take Toimé as a son, embrace him as a son and kiss him as a son. In this stirring moment, the orchestra underlines the intense emotions of the two as the second scene ends.

The flood of sound melts into the rapid allegro heard at the first of the opera, and when the curtain rises the scene is the living room of Ar-

During the next interlude (which like much of *The Most Important Man* was rewritten by Menotti after the premiere), the orchestra tells us long before the emotion is expressed that Toimé is deeply attracted to Cora, and that further seeds of conflict are being sown. Scene four is again in the living room. Toimé, Leona and Arnek have just finished lunch. As Toimé gets up from the table and leaves the room, Leona begins to upbraid her husband for treating Toimé as a member of the family. "Even the cook, who's black herself, threatens to leave if she is made to wait on him." Indignantly, Leona adds, "You must think of our reputation . . . or we won't have a single friend left . . . Even with my door locked at night, I have trouble going to sleep. I mean to put a stop to it."

Calmly, Arnek answers that he needs Toimé, and Toimé needs their love. This is more than Leona can stomach. "Love," she explodes. "What nonsense is this? Must we *live* with everyone we love? . . . For seven years I have humored your fancies, and I've borne all kinds of hardships so that you could build yourself this phantasmagoric 'center of research.' . . . What have you discovered? Nothing." She warns Arnek that he is on the brink of losing Eric, and if he goes, she will go too. Here Menotti plants the first hint that something intimate is going on between Leona and Eric. Frustrated by her husband's indifference to her fears, Leona reveals she tried to commit suicide by cutting her wrists. "Look at the scar," she cries. "Eric was reading in the next room. He heard me fall, broke down the door and carried me to my bed. . . . Had Eric not been nearby I might have died."

As she continues to berate Arnek, he sits quietly as though hearing nothing of what she is saying. The orchestra soon takes over Leona's anger as the curtain falls on this tableau, which is in effect the fourth of a series of isolated scenes with which Menotti tells his story.

In the final scene of the first act, Toimé is seen in his sparsely furnished laboratory later the same night. As he works intensely under a small halo of light, Cora enters noiselessly in a white gown, her hair undone. Hanging over the balustrade of the staircase, she begins reciting lines from

nek's house a few months later. Toimé searches for a book when Cora, returning from vacation, appears at the door. In a quixotic soliloquy she tells him she is only sometimes Cora, Arnek's daughter, and other times Juliet, Cleopatra, Medea or Electra. "An actress? Perhaps . . . I'm everything and nothing." Toimé is puzzled, but before Cora can elaborate, Leona enters. She asks Toimé to leave them alone, and as he exits he picks up Cora's suitcases. Once Toimé is out of the room, Leona clasps Cora in her arms hysterically. "I'm so glad you came. You don't know what I'm going through. Your father is out of his mind. This black person, Toimé . . . is living with us. None of the neighbors will set foot in this house, and Eric, poor Eric, your father hardly knows him anymore." Toimé reenters to get Cora's last bag, but Cora takes it instead and with her mother goes upstairs. Toimé stares after her.

Leona (Maria Luisa Nave) tells Cora (Joanna Bruno) that Toimé, a black man, now lives in their home.

Shakespeare's *Romeo and Juliet:* "O gentle Romeo! If thou dost love, pronounce it faithfully, or if thou thinkst I am too quickly won, I'll frown and be perverse and say . . ."

Toimé interrupts her savagely, asking to be left alone. But it is quickly apparent that Cora desires Toimé as much as he wants her. As the scene increases in tension, the music becomes more possessive and passionate. Toimé finally takes Cora in his arms. Pulling away, she says almost defiantly, "I face my fate at last."

A few heraldic measures that symbolize Arnek open Act II. They return shortly after being swept away by an *allegro moderato* and carry us into the first scene of the act. It is two years later in a conference room of the Institute of National Science in the capital. Around a large table, members of the Institute and the Under-Secretary of State are listening intently as Dr. Arnek is revealing the results of his experiments. As he finishes, the gathering breaks into applause, and the scientists begin to talk all at once in excited confusion; this forms a swift and intricate quintet. To restore order, Professor Clement strikes the table with his gavel. Arnek tells the group it is too early to measure the effect or force of his findings and they must proceed with caution. The Under-Secretary suggests an immediate meeting with the President, to which Arnek replies he has not decided whether to entrust his secret to the government.

Professor Clement replies that by "revolutionizing human society" (which suggests Arnek's

discovery is linked to genetics), the doctor has made a breakthrough that would make their nation the most powerful on earth. He suggests, however, that before the government receives the formula there should be proper guarantees. Arnek agrees, adding over his motive that they must look beyond patriotism. "This is a universal problem," he adds. Are we worthy of holding the destiny of the world in our hands?

"Now, only one man controls the secret," Arnek continues. "It might be wiser to trust one intelligent man rather than a group of despots." This provokes another storm of dissent from the scientists. When they are again calmed by Professor Clement, Arnek reveals it was Toimé who made the discovery, not himself, and that he controls it. As the orchestra strongly etches the Toimé theme, Arnek asks his assistant into the room and presents him to the gathering. The Professors and the Under-Secretary are stunned to see Toimé is black. "Although our goal was the same," Arnek comments, "it was a blind alley I was working in. The inspiration that led to the truth was Toimé's only."

Questioned closely, Toimé admits that he is no longer a citizen of the country, having renounced his citizenship when he went to Europe. "Why are you willing then," the Under-Secretary demands, "to share with us the secret of your formula?" "I never said I was," Toimé answers. "Don't you think it is a dangerous thing," Professor Risselberg asks, "that one man only be trusted with such a powerful weapon?"

Toimé (Evans) and Arnek (Cioni) disclose their discoveries to members of the Institute.

"It depends on the man," Toimé responds. When asked if he thinks he is that man, Toimé nonchalantly replies, "Why not?" while the others cry out, "Arrest him," "The man is mad."

Dr. Arnek attempts to restore sanity by assuring that Toimé will share the secret, but first science and government must deserve his trust. Professor Clement proposes the conference resume the next day, and as the room empties, Toimé turns to Arnek asking his forgiveness: "I'm still afraid of them, and they're afraid of me." The scene is broken off as the orchestra begins an interlude, a low-lying and foreboding canon. This type of interlude is more the exception than the rule in Menotti's operas from *Island God* through *Juana La Loca*. When they occur, interludes are the outgrowth of the mood and material of the preceding scene and are usually constructed on ascending passages that seem to push the music and action forward. Imitative or contemplative ones such as this are rarer, though they do exist—in *Maria Golovin*, for example.

The canon is later displaced by the more typical rising figure, which peaks with great force before leading us into the second scene—Dr. Arnek's living room the next day. Cora, Leona and Eric are meeting with Professors Clement and Hisselman and the Under-Secretary; they have come to enlist the family's support in obtaining the formula. Their fear is that Toimé will use his discovery to create a ruling race of black men who will in turn avenge themselves on their former white masters.

They suggest the discovery be announced by Arnek, Eric and Toimé. Leona agrees but knows Arnek will not. She tells the others she is certain Arnek is letting Toimé have full credit for some "perverse masochism." She says, however, she will do what she can and asks them to leave so that Arnek will not know of their visit. Once the visitors are gone, Leona begs Eric for help. He replies their only hope is Cora, but adds that "she won't do it because she loves Toimé." Cora, to Leona's dismay, admits this is true. As Leona curses her daughter, the curtain falls. After vigorous running passages in the strings, the interlude climaxes on strident chords followed by a

long silence. Softly, as from a distance, come mysterious, ritualistic sounds. They prepare for the arrival of Mrs. Agebda Akawasi, an influential native leader.

She is admitted to the living room and asks to speak to Mrs. Arnek. To a solo marimba, to which are later added lower strings, Mrs. Akawasi tells Leona her village never liked having Dr. Arnek and his laboratory in their midst, and now the area is filled with armed soldiers; the situation is intolerable. "What evil magic is your husband up to?" she demands. Leona defends Arnek by saying that her husband is no witch doctor and that his discovery will benefit the entire world. The problem is not the doctor's work, she adds, but his assistant Toime. Mrs. Akawasi asks to see Toimé alone, which leads to a violent outburst in the orchestra, setting the mood for the powerful confrontation to follow.

At first Mrs. Akawasi addresses Toimé patronizingly as "my son." He quickly rejects this: "I'm not your son—our black skin doesn't even make us cousins." "I see you are black like us," she retorts, "and I fear for you and us. . . . I warn you, young man, if you bring us trouble we will be the first to let you down." Furious, Toimé, now abandoned by his own people, orders her out of the house. With dignity, Mrs. Akawasi replies this is not his house and he cannot order her to leave. Frustrated, Toimé calls for Dr. Arnek and demands he get rid of Mrs. Akawasi. "I am afraid you must obey him," Arnek tells her. As she leaves, Leona returns and, angry at her husband's continued blind support of Toimé, warns him this action can only lead to trouble.

The interlude separating the third and fourth scenes is the shortest in the opera and suggests the quick passing of time, for the curtain rises on the same scene a short while later; Leona and Arnek are alone. When the doctor tells his wife he has never been more miserable than in this, his moment of glory, she tries to convince him that Toimé is to blame: "You laid the groundwork and helped him find the way, but he hid from you the progress he was making. . . . Do you realize what would happen to this country if he should control the government? He is a black and a foreigner. He will be killed, of course." She pleads with him to announce the discovery as his own, adding that Eric will support his claim. When Arnek refuses, Leona plays her trump card: "Has he told you that he is sleeping with your daughter?"

Arnek refuses to accept this even when Leona calls Eric in to corroborate her accusation. Arnek calls for Toimé, who readily confirms the relationship. Arnek tells Toimé sadly that it is not

his and Cora's love that disturbs him, but the fact they did not confide in him. Angered by what he considers hypocrisy, Toimé cries out, "You lie, you lie. Down with the whole world if even you must lie." Hearing angry voices, Cora rushes in. Turning on her, Toimé shouts, "Tell him about the child you carry—my child." Shaken, Arnek replies he is more shocked by Toimé's stream of hatred than he is wounded by the deception. When Toimé turns on Arnek again, calling him a fraud, the doctor asks to be left alone.

The room empties except for Arnek and Eric. Reluctantly, Arnek admits he has been wrong to trust Toimé, and gives Eric the combination to the safe holding the formula. In a pathetic closing strain, Arnek laments, "Oh God! What have I done? Is this what they call patriotism? Go Eric, go. I don't want to hear your answer."

The third act more than any other shows the pressure under which Menotti worked to finish *The Most Important Man.* The opening scene of the act in Arnek's laboratory lacks breadth and working-out. In particular, Toimé's murder of Eric on finding him removing the formula from the safe is neither well prepared nor convinc-

ing. Though Eric has a gun, he cannot bring himself to shoot Toimé. Taking advantage of this, Toimé strangles Eric and then screams for Cora. Unable to move at first after the murder, he finally responds to Cora's pleas to take the formula and run away with her. As the curtain falls, gunshots are heard in the distance as the two dash out the door, across the lawn and into the dense protectiveness of the woods.

After an extended martial interlude, the curtain rises on a clearing in the forest. Toimé has been shot as he fled, and he begs Cora to burn the formula. She, however, cannot bring herself to destroy it; she uses as an excuse the fact that a blaze would betray their hiding place. Besides, she adds, "I want the world to know what a great man you are." "I never was a man," Toimé responds bitterly. "It was your father's lie to tell me I was a man only to lead me to the slaughter like a beast. . . . For me, there's nothing left but to die like a beast with bare fangs, with flashing claws, hungry for blood."

Cora reminds Toimé it is of no consequence whether she burns the formula or not, for her father would only retrace Toimé's steps. "No," Toimé answers; "he is not the kind to betray twice. Like a pitiful Judas, he, too, is finished, for he will not survive his guilt. Burn the formula; the world does not deserve it. . . . The lights are on, the stage is set. Give me a performance, Cora. It must be your greatest as it will be your last." To a melodramatic accompaniment, Cora intones a ritualistic chant to Hymen as she lights the papers and dances about the fire. The flames attract their pursuers, and out of the black of the forest comes Dr. Arnek's voice. Cora pleads with her father to save Toimé, but Toimé rejects any offer of help. In a gesture of defiance, he pulls out Eric's revolver and is shot down by a volley of fire from the soldiers.

Arnek and the militia rush in, and the doctor cradles the dying Toimé in his arms. "A man you said," Toimé reminds Arnek. "If that was not a lie, then let me die as a man. Help me up. It is too early to forgive and soon may be too late. . . . If I must die, I want to die standing." As Toimé struggles to his feet with Arnek's help, the curtain falls slowly over a grief-laden postlude.

The fugitive Toimé (Eugene Holmes) with Cora (Bruno) in the tragic final scene, Menotti's world premiere staging, New York City Opera, 1971.

Tamu-Tamu

(The Guests)

Chamber opera in two acts,
libretto in English and Indonesian
by the composer

The Americans:
    Mr. Hudson   Baritone
    Mrs. Hudson   Soprano
    Doctor   Tenor
The Indonesians:
    Ananto   Baritone
    Radna (his pregnant wife)   Soprano
    Indra (his second and younger wife)   Soprano
    Nenek (the grandmother)   Mezzo-soprano
    Kakek (the grandfather)   Non-singing
    Djoko (the wounded son)   Non-singing
    Solema (the daughter)   Child's part
    Priests and soldiers   Chorus

World premiere at the Studebaker Theater, Chicago, September 5, 1973. Commissioned by the Ninth International Congress of Anthropological and Ethnological Sciences. Unpublished. Scored for flute, clarinet, trumpet, horn, timpani, percussion, piano, harp, three violins, three cellos, bass.

After the problems that beset *The Most Important Man,* and the structural and musical weaknesses that riddled its score, Menotti bounced back with remarkable resiliency, in *Tamu-Tamu.* It is a tightly made work (approximately as long as *The Globolinks*), and theatrically it delivers a well-aimed and sharp blow. Its impetus came from an unexpected corner—a group of anthropologists who wanted a work created that would illustrate the theme of their 1973 convention: "One Species, Many Cultures." The commission went to Menotti during the period the United States was desperately attempting to phase out its long entanglement in Southeast Asia. This unpopular and divisive war in Vietnam was a potent factor behind the libretto of *Tamu.*

But the opera's theme is larger than a simple story of war; the Vietnamese conflict was only Menotti's springboard. What concerned him more was the confrontation of cultures and the responsibilities all human beings have toward each other. It is, in effect, one further reverberation of the themes within *The Most Important Man.* "It is difficult for an artist today," Menotti has written, "not to feel that his contributions are marginal or superfluous to a social pattern which has relegated him to the field of entertainment. . . . But the many people who still believe that the artist should confine himself to esthetics seem to forget that the operas of Verdi, Beethoven and Mozart made strong political and social statements just as Goya, Picasso and Titian did in their paintings, and Dante, Voltaire and Tolstoy in

211

their books. . . .

"I do not agree with Sartre that the work of a contemporary artist must by force be politically committed. On the other hand, there's nothing more moving than an art which devotes itself to a noble human cause and nothing more challenging for an artist than to feel needed within a social structure. Perhaps it is true that more often than not an artist's political views are somewhat naïve; but at least they generally state something. How is it that the press, which is usually so ironic toward politically-minded artists, doesn't make equal fun of the politician's speeches, which can succeed within a whole hour of rhetoric in saying absolutely nothing?"

In the early stages of discussion about this commission, Menotti met with Dr. Sol Tax of the University of Chicago and Dr. Margaret Mead, among others. During these talks Menotti discovered that "we all shared at least one conclusion: that man's inhumanity to man and man's racial hatred are not only the result of ignorance, but also of a certain emotional deadness which makes man unable to share his enemy's feelings."

This conclusion would become the basis of *Tamu*, as would Dr. Mead's observation to Menotti that ours is an age when man experiences the sufferings of others mostly through the press and the television screen, that people placidly witness all manner of atrocities while eating TV dinners.

"Of course we are all sorry," Menotti adds, "indignant and even horrified by what we see, but . . . ours is only a mimicry of real feeling. Just as we have been conditioned to applaud music we don't wish to hear again, stare admiringly at paintings we would not dream of hanging in our living room and praise books we can scarcely skim through, so have we been taught to enact the ceremony of pity without actually feeling any real pain.

"If the role of the anthropologist is to explain to us why a certain sociological group or race behaves in a certain way, the only contribution an artist can make to their findings is to take us emotionally among those people so their experiences and sufferings can become our own. . . .

The message of *Tamu-Tamu* . . . is a simple one, or to use the word of an unkind critic, a 'naïve' one indeed: One must be taught to feel again. . . .

"An evil man is fundamentally a man in whom emotional atrophy is complete. It explains how a learned theologian or a devout king could send hundreds of people to the stake and watch them being burned alive without feeling that they themselves are being burned. They genuinely declared that they were sorry for their victims and deplored the necessity of burning them. . . . But is their hypocrisy that much different from our brand of pity as we watch the horrors of war being flashed before our eyes? Whether we like it or not, we must learn to identify ourselves not only with the killed but also with the killer, for, unfortunately, we are both."

The idea of an Indonesian family whose suffering and blood is brought to the doorstep of an American family was entirely Menotti's. He wanted to show two civilizations in conflict—one that we know well and one that we don't; Indonesia seemed appropriately foreign and exotic to Menotti, much as Japan did to Puccini. But *Tamu* is no more Indonesian than *Madama Butterfly* is Japanese. Nor does *Tamu* have any of the racial questions that permeated *The Most Important Man*. Race is not the issue here; compassion and involvement are.

To prepare his libretto, Menotti consulted the Indonesian consulate in New York, where he was helped with certain customs and expressions, as well as the language itself. The latter poses no problem for an audience, because so clearly is the drama's premise laid out, and so vivid is the action, that the opera is conveyed on its own dramatic momentum rather than any verbal one. In many ways the striking theatrical device on which the work is built (a photograph in the newspaper viewed casually by an American couple at breakfast suddenly comes to life in their living room) is one found in a majority of Menotti's librettos: A seemingly calm but actually potentially explosive situation is suddenly ignited by an unexpected or unanticipated outside force.

Musically, the score of *Tamu-Tamu* is clean and trim, and the instrumental writing is of an impressive economy and effectiveness. The Indonesians are characterized in the main by the percussion, chiefly through gamelanlike bell and gong sounds, which flavor the action without calling undue attention to their exoticism. The vocal lines are largely song-speech patterns; there are arias as such for each of the principals, including a haunting lullaby, but they are stitched into the overall fabric, and arise from the action, serving as commentary rather than showcases.

Both acts of the opera are set within a typical suburban American home just before Christmas. The prelude is constructed according to what is, by now, a recognizable Menottian formula: a slow declarative opening (*adagio maestoso*), in this case a motive symbolizing the Indonesians, followed by a nervous, rising figure in the strings (*allegro moderato*). As the *allegro* climaxes and begins its descent, it is broken into by a return of the opening chords, foreshadowing the conflict to come. The *allegro* makes a brief reappearance settling into the lower strings in a repetitive, turning pattern. Above it crisp chords suggest the falling of snow, and from the distance are heard three phases of "Silent Night."

As the curtain rises, Mrs. Hudson enters from the bedroom to join her husband for breakfast. They are quietly hostile to each other; both are nursing hangovers and their marriage has obviously been blunted by years of noncommunication. As she settles on the sofa, and he loses himself in the pages of the morning paper, she comments, "How shall I fill the barren hours? How shall I kill the worm of anguish? I know we love each other . . . Is that reason enough to live? . . . If only I had a child. Is it my fault?" As she goes to the kitchen and pours a cup of coffee, her husband hands her the paper saying, "Look at this and cheer up. How would you like to be in their shoes?" As the orchestra again sounds the theme of the Indonesians, a photograph is projected on a scrim showing an Indonesian family fleeing a burning village, herded by soldiers with rifles. "Who are they?" Mrs. Hudson asks. "A family from God-knows-how-to-pronounce-it," her husband replies dully.

"Don't you feel sorry for them?" she de-

The Hudsons at breakfast: Sylvia Davis and Robert J. Manzari in the world premiere production of *Tamu-Tamu*, Chicago, 1973.

mands. "Of course, I pity them," he counters . . . "but who can judge from here? Who can tell who's right, who's wrong? Perhaps they deserve their fate. . . . There is plenty near us to worry about! They are too far and foreign. Can man's true feeling reach that far? . . . They'll be forgotten in ten minutes." With this he puts on his coat, grabs his briefcase and leaves for his office. Left alone, Mrs. Hudson begins clearing away the breakfast dishes, humming softly to herself. As she gets out the carpet sweeper, the front door bell rings twice. When she opens the door, she finds the Indonesian family grouped exactly as in the newspaper photo. The orchestra plays the Indonesian theme more violently than before, and the Asian family pours into the house. One of the children has been wounded and is bleeding, and no sooner are they inside than the grandfather collapses on the floor. For a moment, time seems to be suspended, and Mrs. Hudson, confronted with a surreal situation she does not comprehend, wonders if she is going mad. What she finally understands, however, is the reality of the child's wounds, and the need to help and worry about explanations later. She springs to the phone and calls both a doctor and her husband, then rips open the boy's shirt to clean his wound.

Gradually the room calms down, and Mrs. Hudson tries to make her unexpected guests comfortable. Her husband phones her back and she begs him to come home at once, as she thinks she is going mad: "Remember the photo you showed me this morning? Well, they're here. . . ." As she hangs up, Indra begins comforting the children and trying to get them to sleep. Mrs. Hudson gives Solema a doll she had as a girl, and Radna begins a soothing lullaby (*andante molto calma*) that Mrs. Hudson later takes up. This section is one of the few islands of repose during *Tamu*, and one of the loveliest, most tranquil moments in all of Menotti:

> *Mouse is asleep, cat is asleep,*
> *And soon my baby will slowly forget to weep.*
> *Lark in the sky, shark in the deep,*
> *Seek the dark for dreaming as they fall asleep.*

The instruments take up the lullaby, elaborat-

The Indonesians: a soldier terrorizes Indra (Sumiko Murashima), Ananto (Sung Kil Kim), Radna (Sung Sook Lee) and Djoko (Horas Hutagalung).

ing on it in canon. As the curtain falls to denote a lapse of time, the lullaby continues on as an interlude, becoming increasingly complex and agitated. As its energy gradually subsides, the curtain rises on the ringing doorbell. All awaken as Mrs. Hudson admits her husband. He tries to make sense of the situation, demanding to know how the Indonesians got to his home and what they want. His anxiety, however, only aggravates the situation.

He discovers, however, that Indra speaks a tiny bit of English, and with her help Mr. Hudson is able to untangle the relationships between his unexpected and uninvited guests. A moment later, the Doctor finally arrives. He is a nervous, self-important man who shares a good deal in common with other character tenor roles, in Menotti's works—the Magician in *The Consul*, Dr. Zuckertanz in *Maria Golovin* and King Kaspar in *Amahl*. When Mr. and Mrs. Hudson cannot explain the presence of the Indonesians nor the boy's bullet wound, and when the Doctor realizes the grandfather is not asleep but has died, he refuses to become involved with the Indonesians, despite the pleas of the American couple. As soon as the Doctor has left, the Indonesians, too, realize the grandfather is dead, and as Ananto takes a burial sheet out of his sack, Radna and Indra begin moaning, soon joined by Nanek. As elaborate wailing is taken up by the instruments, the scrim wall opens and priests appear, obliterating time and space, and place Kakek on a funeral bier. The mourning turns into chanting as the priests exit with the body, and the curtain falls on the first act.

After a short declarative figure in the orchestra, the second act begins with a brief canonic passage, which is shortly displaced by the opening motif. When the curtain rises, the Indonesians and the Americans have settled down almost as one family. Mr. Hudson is at his desk, his wife is reading, Indra is hanging clothes up to dry and in the bedroom the children are watching television. "As soon as the snow storm is over," Hudson tells his wife, "and the phones are working again, I shall call the hospital and . . . they will take care of them."

A trio of arias follow as life in the room continues in a workaday rhythm. In short, jagged phrases, Mrs. Hudson questions her life and its meaning, and a few moments later her husband daydreams about Indra and the exoticism she represents: "Sun-bleached islands, languorous seas, soft winds." He asks himself if life has passed him by. Finally Ananto in a more narrative vein looks back and tries to understand how and why "a quiet night on a full moon" was suddenly shattered by gunfire that forced the family to grab what it could and flee into the night.

Mrs. Hudson and Indra emerge from the bedroom where they have exchanged their clothes as a surprise for the others. The Indonesians are amused, but Mr. Hudson is indignant and embarrassed by his wife's naked breasts. The tension in the room is broken by outcries from Radna; her labor pains have begun. Radna's agony increases while those about her attempt to comfort her. When her pain is at its most intense, there is a blackout, and the ensuing interlude plays out in music the birth.

When the lights come up again, a party is in progress celebrating the arrival of another son for Ananto. There are toasts all around, and it is obvious Mr. Hudson has had too much to drink. He grabs Indra and asks her to dance. Escaping his grasp, she replies that rather than dancing with him, she will dance for him. As the other Indonesians sing, she begins a narrative dance about working in the rice field. As the music mounts to a frenzy of excitement, there is a violent knocking at the door.

Before Mr. Hudson can reach it, the door is flung open violently, and a group of armed soldiers rush into the room. Over the protests of the Hudsons, they push the Indonesians behind the scrim. On a brutal, dissonant, sustained chord, the sound of gunfire fills the theater as the family is massacred. After a blackout the lights return and the room is exactly as it was at the opening of the opera. Mrs. Hudson is clearing away the breakfast dishes, and her husband is folding up his newspaper. "Anything interesting in the paper?" she inquires. "Nothing much," he answers. Mr. Hudson puts on his coat and leaves for work as his wife gets out the carpet-sweeper and begins her housework.

The Hero

Opera in three acts,
libretto in English by the composer

David Murphy (the hero)	Baritone
Mildred (his wife)	Mezzo-soprano
Barbara (his cousin)	Soprano
Dr. Brainkoff	Tenor
The Mayor	Bass
Jeweler	Tenor
Shopkeeper	Baritone
The Guide	Baritone
White Couple	Mezzo-soprano and baritone
Black Couple	Soprano and tenor
Townspeople	Chorus

World premiere in the Academy of Music, Philadelphia, June 1, 1976. Commissioned by the Opera Company of Philadelphia. Unpublished. Scored for two flutes, two oboes, two clarinets, two bassoons, four trumpets, three horns, percussion, harp, strings.

*T*he *Hero* was a commission for the American Bicentennial celebration of 1976, and Menotti felt that amid the rhetoric and flag-waving the country needed an affectionate Swiftian kick in the pants. He has made it clear, however, that *The Hero* is only incidentally political satire. The opera was conceived as "a humorous comment on contemporary society and on its self-satisfaction and greed. It is a spoof of those leaders who, to protect their own interest, choose the mediocre and the expedient, and glorify the innocuous—the man who sleeps, and thus cannot interfere with or bother anybody."

Menotti goes on to add that "this is an opera celebrating the American sense of humor. It is a gentle, good-natured plea for Americans to wake up to reality, to abandon all self-congratulatory illusions, to return to their former rugged individualism and to the uncompromising honesty of their ancestors. They should be aware of the danger of letting themselves be led by a sleeping man. 'Who is David Murphy?' He is the prototype of the yes-man, achieving stature by agreeing with everyone's views and by turning a blind eye to corruption. In other words, he is the perfect man for a dishonest society. It is on 'the man who sleeps' that the people around him feed their selfishness. Barbara [his cousin] stands not only for David's conscience but also for the new courage and honesty of American youth who dare to challenge the long-standing myths of 'success' as a sine qua non of respectability, and search instead for self-respect and inner peace.

Act I of Menotti's Juilliard School production, 1980, with Fredda Rakusin as Mildred and Nicholas Karousatos as her awakened husband, David (left),'and the composer with the world premiere cast, Lyric Opera of Philadelphia, 1976—David Griffin, Diane Curry, Nancy Shade, Dominic Cossa.

Being a comic opera, none of the characters are drawn with hate or contempt. Even the trio of villains—Mildred, the Doctor, the Mayor—should deserve our sympathy because, after all, they are part of our own weakness."

This tale of a modern Rip Van Winkle is thin but no more improbable than many an established *opera buffa*. Though the language of the libretto is at times more obvious ("To sleep or not to sleep, that is the question") than amusing, and at other times meant to shock (a four-letter word in its opening lines), *The Hero* is crafty, and its seams are few. The music is transparent, the lightheartedness of the score harks back to *The Last Savage* and it even recaptures some of the spontaneous heart-on-the-sleeve qualities of *Amelia*. The story is closer to *Amelia* than to *The Last Savage*, however, being less knotted and lower in profile, and *The Hero*'s waltz tunes and general gaiety make it the closest Menotti has come to writing operetta. There are a number of attractive arias (particularly Barbara's "My Sleeping Beauty" in Act I) as well as a charming quartet that caps the last act.

Following a short, peppery prelude with political overtones implied by trumpets, the curtain rises on David Murphy's bedroom. A black couple and a white couple have just paid Barbara two dollars a person for a glimpse of David, who has become a national hero by sleeping away a decade of his life. Barbara begins her lecture, part of the tour, over a rising fanfare figure used throughout the opera as a foundation motive:

After a quick description of other cases in medical history of prolonged sleep, Barbara points out a model of the monument that will commemorate David's sleep record; it is a replica in marble of his bed. The climax of the tour comes with a view of David asleep. As Barbara pulls back the curtains, a trumpet call is sounded—the first of a series in the score. Over its final note come sustained, somnolent chords from deep in the orchestra as the tourists gaze admiringly at David.

Bedroom comedy: Shade as David's cousin, Barbara, in the Philadelphia staging, 1976 . . .

"Any questions?" Barbara asks brightly. "Does he make any noise?" "Sometimes he snores, sometimes he mumbles . . . patriotic words such as 'recession,' 'strikes,' 'investigations,' 'drugs.' " "But who gets all the money?" "This is a non-profit organization. One half goes to the town and the other to his wife, of course. Don't you realize how expensive it is to look after a hero? The constant medical care, the mail, the telephone calls, publicity, parking lots, guided tours, pamphlets. . . ." "But how do you know he's been asleep all the time?" To another trumpet voluntary, Barbara reveals a tape machine with a wire from it attached to David's arm. She then turns a knob, and David's breathing can be heard amplified throughout the room. Marveling at what they have seen and heard, the tourists exit.

Moments later, Mildred, David's wife, and an outrageously comic character, bursts into the room. Barbara reports the amount of money collected that day and then announces that she will no longer act as tour guide. Before she can explain to a puzzled Mildred, there is a knock at the door, and a group of shopkeepers enter ceremoniously. In a lively waltz ensemble, they present gifts to Mildred for the unveiling the next day, marking ten years and seven days of uninterrupted sleep by David.

Mildred accepts their gifts, and as they leave, she takes up the waltz ecstatically, marveling at the presents and singing her own praise. She runs to her room to try on the dresses, hats and jewels, forgetting about Barbara, who remains behind with David. It is evident that where Mildred cares only about profits, Barbara is in love with David. She begins her aria, "My Sleeping Beauty" (F minor, *andante calmo),* in which she confesses she has adored him from childhood. Twice he has been stolen from her—first by Mildred and then by sleep. Bidding him farewell, she leans over the bed and like "a trembling thief," steals a kiss. Again the trumpet motive is sounded and David awakens, opens his eyes and sits up in bed. Barbara stares at him for a moment and then cries for Mildred.

At the sight of David awake, Mildred faints. When she is revived, David is out of bed confused and full of questions. "I think you had

. . . and Griffin with Curry as the same mounting's conniving, clandestine lovers, Brainkoff and Mildred.

better sit down," Mildred advises him, and as the orchestra plays a series of eerie chords, Mildred begins explaining to David what has happened, and the curtain falls on Act I. When it rises next, David and Mildred are in the exact same positions, with Barbara nearby. *"Voilà!"* Mildred exclaims theatrically, while David shakes his head in disbelief. "I have wasted ten years of my life," he bemoans. "On the contrary, dear," Mildred retorts, "They have been your most glorious years. They have made you a celebrity."

She is interrupted by the ringing of the doorbell. It is the Mayor and Dr. Brainkoff, who freeze in horror on seeing David awake. When the Mayor finally finds his voice, he asks if David realizes what a panic this will cause. "We have invested a fortune in your sleep. The whole town will be bankrupt. . . . You must go back to sleep for everybody's sake." Defiantly, David launches into a spirited aria (A major, *allegro*) in which he reminds the mayor that whatever the town's loss, his is greater—ten years of his life. At its conclusion, angry voices are heard outside. Barbara runs into the bedroom to warn David that he has been seen through the window and a crowd of storekeepers, creditors and even the bank manager are downstairs demanding admittance as a rumor has reached the town that David is awake.

Frightened, Brainkoff and the Mayor shove the reluctant David into bed and cover him up as the crowd breaks into the room. Reassuring them that they are mistaken, Mildred draws the bed curtain to reveal David looking as if he were peacefully asleep. She then berates them all for causing such a disturbance and forcing their way into her home. Cowed, the crowd apologizes and quickly leaves. David has obviously been shaken by the mob's anger and is willing to consider going back to sleep until the ceremony the next day is over and the new record for uninterrupted sleep is established.

Doctor Brainkoff gives David a pill and, like a first cousin to the Magician in *The Consul*, he sings "Close your eyes and surrender, leave to us pain and sorrow. In the dream world one is welcomed, life is kinder, love is tender. . . ." He is joined by Mildred and the Mayor in a *pianissimo* trio urging David to go to sleep. Left alone to take his pill, David continues to hesitate, wondering if he is doing the right thing: "Isn't an honest citizen more valuable than a sham hero? . . . Shall I satisfy my vanity or my conscience?"

Barbara comes in with a glass of water, but begs David not to take the pill. It is only greed that makes the Mayor, Brainkoff and Mildred insist he return to sleep. "They are a very crooked trio," Barbara reveals. "They have been gathering money by cheating on the revenues your sickness has brought to this town." Hearing Mildred and Brainkoff returning, Barbara helps David into bed and then hides behind a screen. Peering into the room, Mildred and Brainkoff are satisfied that David has taken the pill and is once again sound asleep. In a broad reference to Watergate, they bring the tape machine to the couch in order to cut out the portion of the tape that recorded David's awakening. As they try to doctor the tape, it becomes more and more tangled. It also becomes evident that Mildred and Doctor Brainkoff are having an affair and plan to use their share of the money to run away together.

When they leave, taking the tangle of tape with them to repair, David leaps out of bed furious. Barbara tells him that no matter what happens she will stand by him and encourages him to face courageously the reality of the situation. Part of this reality is David's awareness that little by little he has begun to fall in love with his cousin. As their duet mounts rapturously, they kiss.

The last act takes place in the city square. Tourists and dignitaries are arriving for the unveiling, and a tour guide is selling tickets to the reception that will follow the ceremony. For only ten dollars, he tells the two couples from Act I, they can meet the governor, be served Chicken à la King and hear the famous soprano of the Metropolitan Opera, Madame Vocestanca, who will sing "The Star-Spangled Banner," "Mi chiamano Mimì" and "By the Waters of Minnetonka" (in the orchestra Menotti discreetly weaves together a phrase from each of the selections). Soon the last of the officials arrive and take their place on the platform with the Mayor, Brainkoff and Mildred.

When everyone is finally quiet, the Mayor begins his welcoming speech. Menotti uses this moment to pay tribute to America while drawing a caricature of this pompous politician:

Who discovered the steamboat? We.
Who shot the first man onto the moon? We.
Who first crossed the Pacific, I mean the
*   Atlantic in a plane?*
Who invented peanut butter and the pill?
We, we, we.

After his speech, the Mayor pulls the cover from the monument revealing David in the marble bed. The crowd is shocked, then outraged. David quiets them long enough to explain his presence and deliver the opera's moral:

A lie can make life more bearable,
While truth, alas, has no mercy.
But lying has a double edge,
And with such a knife the cleverest of surgeons
Cannot cut deep without himself being wounded.

Crying, "Hate me if you like, but let me be myself," David ends his soliloquy just as the crowd becomes menacing and begins to threaten him and all of the others on the platform, who panic and begin to run in different directions, with the Mayor pursued by the largest group. Barbara enters and in a soaring aria calls David a true hero. He comes down off his monument, and, as they embrace, Mildred and Dr. Brainkoff crawl out from under the grandstand. In attempting to sort out the situation, Brainkoff asks David: "Who stays with whom? Who leaves with whom?" "It is very simple," David replies, "let love decide." That, of course, leaves Brainkoff with Mildred and David with Barbara. Each couple then sings a paean to love, forming the quartet that ends the opera more or less in the nature of an epilogue. At its conclusion, the fanfare figure is sounded one final time, and the score comes to rest resolutely in C major.

Act II as seen at Juilliard: David (Karousatos), facing his public, makes a plea for understanding.

Juana La Loca

Opera in three acts,
libretto in English by the composer

Juana (Infanta of Spain)	Soprano
Felipe (her husband)	
Ferdinand (her father)	Baritone (to be sung by the same person)
Carlos V (her son)	
Miguel de Ferrara (a knight)	Tenor
Ximenes de Cisneros (Bishop of Toledo)	Bass
Doña Manuela (a lady-in-waiting)	Mezzo-soprano
Nurse	Mezzo-soprano
Two ladies-in-waiting	Soprano and contralto
Marquis de Denia	Baritone
Catalina (Juana's daughter)	Child's part
Chaplain	Non-singing
Carlos V as a boy	Non-singing
Clerics, courtiers, grandees	Chorus

World premiere San Diego, June 3, 1979. Commissioned by the San Diego Opera. Unpublished. Scored for two flutes (piccolo), two oboes (English horn), two clarinets (bass clarinet), four horns, two trumpets, two trombones, tuba, percussion, timpani, harp, piano, strings.

*J*uana La Loca was Menotti's first large-scale period opera. Though certain of his previous works *(Sebastian* and *Amahl,* for example) were set in a historic time, locale was not an issue but a dramatic flavoring. In *Juana La Loca,* however, sixteenth-century Spain is a vital ingredient of the plot. The opera covers the life of the surviving child of Spain's Isabel and Ferdinand from her marriage in 1496 to Philip the Handsome (Felipe) to her death in 1555, imprisoned and abandoned.

Menotti has centered the action of the opera on the abuse suffered by Juana at the hands of the three men who were dearest to her—her father, her husband and her eldest son. All three attempted to wrest the Spanish throne from her control following the death of Isabel, and when they were unable to take it by legal means, Juana was declared insane and kept locked away for forty-two years. Her life was incredibly operatic as were the extraordinary political balance of the times and the fierce ambitions for power that overrode all moral considerations. But despite the theatricality of these elements, *Juana La Loca* is no simple story of power or politics. It is an extravagant love story.

From the age of sixteen when Juana was wedded to Felipe, her adoration of him knew no reason or normal bounds. It seems apparent that from the first moment they met, Juana hardly drew a breath that was not prompted by her obsessive love. She was a classic *folle d'amour,* and her marriage created a scandal in European courts because it was consummated before the official wedding ceremony. The unreasoning force of Juana's love, however, was never returned. To Felipe, she represented Spain's throne, power and little else. After Isabel's death in 1504, the Queen having named Juana her sole heir, a struggle ensued for Isabel's legacy. In this battle, Ferdinand and Felipe were of a like mind in only one regard—the discrediting of Juana so

Act I, Scenes 1 and 3, as staged by Menotti for the 1984 Spoleto Festival U.S.A.: the passionate first meeting of Felipe (Louis Otey) and Juana (Adriana Vanelli), and, ten years later, the betrayed heroine forgiving her faithless beloved on his deathbed.

that the throne could pass to one of them.

Felipe died of smallpox in 1506, and though by then Juana had recognized his greed for what it was and had stood firm against his efforts to take her crown, she never swerved in her love. With Felipe's death, this love crossed from adoration to worship. She commanded that his coffin be carried in a morbid procession throughout Spain, and she would frequently open it so that she could kiss the feet of her beloved. After such a display, Ferdinand had little difficulty in committing Juana as mad. She spent the final forty years of her life as a prisoner in the castle of Tordesillas, rejected by all she loved and written off by the world as insane.

It is surprising that so melodramatic a story has been so little exploited operatically, although Juana's son Carlos long ago achieved operatic immortality in two Verdi operas: *Ernani* and *Don Carlos.* Actually, Eugène Scribe prepared a libretto on Juana's life for Donizetti, but it was never set. Later he passed it on to Antonin Louis Clapisson, who put it to music. It also seems that Verdi's pupil Emanuele Muzio wrote a *Giovanna la pazza,* but evidently couldn't get it staged. And in contemporary opera, Juana makes only a brief appearance in Ernst Křenek's *Karl V,* so Menotti had a virtually clear field in treating the queen and her tribulations.

The opera was tailor-made for Beverly Sills, who created the title role, and Menotti regards it as entirely romantic: "Artists are always bad prophets about their art," he said at the time of *Juana La Loca*'s premiere, "but I feel that we will go back again to romanticism, just as in painting they are beginning to do this. And in music, even a man like Penderecki is trying to find a way back to a more conventional language.

"One of the reasons I have adapted this harmonic language for my theatrical pieces is because I believe firmly that theater cannot be exciting unless you have a balance of dissonance and assonance. It's the only way to produce dramatic effects. There is nothing else in the world which has the joyous impact of a major chord. Neither Schönberg nor Stravinsky could achieve what Strauss or Puccini did in a single moment with a major chord. If you use a harmonic language based mainly on dissonance, you actually kill dissonance and with it one of the major weapons of dramatic music."

Each act of *Juana La Loca* was structured by Menotti as a confrontation between Juana and one of the men in her life (cannily, Menotti requires all three men be portrayed by the same singer—a symbol of the similar part each played in Juana's life). In Act I it is Felipe; in Act II, it is Ferdinand; and in Act III it is Carlos. In the course of the work the soprano performing Juana must range from a young, excitable bride to a pathetic hag who has been crushed and left to die. It is a virtuoso part that demands intense drama one moment, high lyricism the next.

The final scene of the opera makes the drama of Juana almost painfully poignant. As she lies on a mat of straw, covered with sores and vermin, Miguel, now a priest, comes to comfort her. Suspiciously she draws back crying, "Does God, too, covet my crown?" He assures Juana that God has no need of her crown; "He will give you another crown far brighter than gold." "But, does God exist?" she cries, desperate to believe in anyone, anything.

This, of course, is the work's moral: Salvation comes not through an individual but through faith. It is the precept Menotti has preached both glibly and seriously since *Amelia al ballo.* In *Juana La Loca* the action and the music move swiftly and inexorably toward the final scene and this message. It does so through a score couched in intensely lyric and melodramatic terms, one that pours out an almost self-indulgent wealth of melodies. At the same time, however, there is with this a surprising impression of compactness and exactitude considering the work's richness. It is a score that will probably take time to assert itself fully, but to anyone willing to listen with open ears and an open heart, it represents Menotti working with a renewed sureness.

Typical of him, he hurls the audience immediately into the maelstrom of the drama without introduction or preparatory music. The curtain sweeps up on a flurry of trumpets offstage and a churning in the orchestra that mirrors the excitement onstage. In a castle in the Netherlands, Juana and her ladies-in-waiting are preparing for

the arrival of Felipe, whom Juana is to meet for the first time. As she is being dressed, a group of her ladies peering through a window describe the arrival of Felipe. At the same time a knight, Miguel de Ferrara, warns Juana that the arrival of love is something to fear rather than to welcome, but in a pitch of excitement she hardly listens to him. Miguel, who secretly loves Juana, is a symbol of fidelity. It is he as a priest who will visit Juana in her cell at the end of the opera holding out the promise of God's love.

Surrounded by her court, Juana orders the doors of her room thrown open and minutes later Felipe strides in. The two stare at each other in silence, obviously attracted and fascinated. They each then dismiss their retinue and after initial pleasantries, declare their love in a sensual duet. The principal material of this duet will return at intervals as a symbol of Juana and her love for Felipe. As the duet becomes more heated, Juana puts up little resistance to Felipe's incandescent ardor. But being of an impulsive nature, she forces herself to break out of his embrace and call for her chaplain. When he arrives, she demands to be married to Felipe at once to avoid committing a mortal sin. Bewildered, the Chaplain has the couple kneel in front of him and as he begins reciting the marriage

vows in Latin, the curtain falls, and the orchestra begins the first of four interludes heard during the course of the work.

These interludes, among the most striking music in the score, were composed for the New York premiere (September 16, 1979, at the New York State Theater). Menotti had once again been extremely late in finishing the score of *Juana La Loca,* and the final notes of the orchestration was written only a matter of hours before the dress rehearsal. At the time there was no room for niceties such as interludes. They had to wait for the second series of performances on the opposite coast. The first interlude grows out of the love duet and develops its principal theme.

It leads directly into a dramatic sequence originally planned by Menotti for the premiere but not completed in time. In her palace in Brussels, Juana awaits Felipe's return from Germany. She is surrounded by Moorish servant-maids who instruct her in the art of sorcery, in which she has childlike faith. Miguel interrupts to announce the arrival of the Bishop of Toledo. After scolding her for heretical practices, he reminds her that she is the sole heir to her mother's throne and that her first duty is to Spain. He craftily suggests that while Juana is away from Spain with Felipe, it would be best to

Act II, Scene 1, at Spoleto U.S.A.: Juana's father, Ferdinand II (Otey), comforts his bereaved daughter (Vanelli).

appoint her father regent and give him the authority to govern. When the Bishop presents a draft to this effect for Juana's signature, she asks for time to consider the matter and orders him to leave.

As Miguel warns her not to sign the document and hints that her husband is both scheming and unfaithful, Felipe enters. He demands to know what the Bishop wanted from her. She refuses to answer, and this leads to another impetuous duet for the two, this one as heated as the first. But here the heat grows out of conflict rather than love. Felipe accuses Juana of behaving outrageously during his absences, consulting gypsies and sorcerers. She challenges him about the other women in his life. Knowing that Felipe desires her throne, she asks him what he will do next: "Court the Queen so that you can cheat your wife? Woo your wife so that you can trick the Queen?" Furious, Felipe calls his guard, ordering him to allow Juana to have no visitors and to be confined to her rooms as she is mentally unbalanced. Then turning to her, Felipe says menacingly that "until you hand me as a token of love what you so freely offered to your father, you shall not sit next to my throne, or share my bed, or leave these rooms." When an impassioned plea fails to move Felipe, she collapses crying, "Ah! Felipe . . . my children or the king . . . the bastard knows how much I want him."

The next interlude provides a short, agitated link to the final scene of Act I, set in Felipe's bedroom. He is dying, and next to him is one of Juana's ladies-in-waiting, Manuela. She has been Felipe's mistress, and as he attempts to kiss her and touch her hair, Juana enters unnoticed. For a moment she listens to their erotic whispers, and then, in a fury, leaps at Manuela. Armed with a pair of scissors, she cuts off the girl's long, blond hair and stabs her in the cheek. As Manuela runs screaming from the room, Juana throws her hair on Felipe's bed. Standing over him, she reminds him she offered him love but all he wanted was her crown. Now that he is dying, what good is a crown? What he needs is love, the very love he sullied and betrayed. "Do not fear, Felipe," she adds calmly, as he begs for forgiveness, "I shall not leave you. The love I gave you was a gift

World premiere: Juana (Beverly Sills) in prison with her daughter Catalina (Nancy Coulson)—Act III, Scene 1.

forever. It cannot be reclaimed or disowned." As a priest chants *"Requiem aeternam"* and Juana whispers softly, "Sleep," Felipe dies.

Act II opens on a deserted plain near Tortoles late at night. Funereal chants in Latin mingle with the howling wind. A sinister procession slowly enters and fills the stage: Felipe's coffin carried by young knights and followed by Juana, smoky torches and clerics. Camp is made, and Juana orders her retinue to leave her alone with Felipe as trumpet volleys sound offstage. Throwing open the lid of the casket, Juana begins her mightiest and most extended aria. It is

a declamatory *scena* of great power, built of several contrasting sections beginning in E minor *(lento molto):* "At last my master lies unmasked. Is this then the face of love?" As she questions the dead Felipe on the meaning of love, the chorus of monks offstage continue to chant their *"Requiem aeternam"* 's. The aria builds with bitter intensity as Juana cries out, "And now I close this lid forever. . . . the broken toy that bares its rusty coils and sheds sawdust from its wounds must be thrown away."

Her ravings are interrupted by a messenger who announces the arrival of her father. Juana assembles her court as Ferdinand strides in fol-

lowed by his courtiers and soldiers. Ferdinand bows to his daughter as Queen of Castille, and she falls into his arms begging him for the love she has sought so desperately for so long. Their reunion leads to the next interlude, which enlarges on the strong melody to which Juana has just told her father, "Anoint me with your love and I shall reign again. I need no seal or crown. My realm is in your heart." At its conclusion, the curtain rises on a room in Ferdinand's castle. Alone with the Bishop of Toledo, he reflects on the current political situation. Yes, Juana behaves as an obedient daughter; yes, she has entrusted the government to him; but no act of succession has been signed; she is still Castille's legal ruler, and an obstacle to a united Spain.

The Bishop suggests that Juana's fiery temperament could provide a means for declaring her unfit to rule. After all, her eccentric behavior has already caused concern among the people and the court. Hasn't she been seen addressing her husband's coffin as if he were alive? Proclaim yourself supreme ruler, he urges Ferdinand, and the church will support you. At this moment, Juana enters with her young son Carlos and her newly born daughter Catalina. Ferdinand broaches the question of Juana's abdication in his favor, but she becomes suspicious and evasive. Angered, Ferdinand demands she obey him. If she refuses to abdicate, her son Carlos will be taken from her and trained as Ferdinand's successor, and Juana will be declared insane and unfit to rule. Stunned by her father's words, she still refuses to give in to his demands. Livid, he exits, and minutes later the Marquis de Denia and a squad of soldiers enter and remove Carlos by force. Left alone in the room, Juana collapses in front of the door sobbing and calling out to her father.

Act III is set in Juana's prison room within the Castle of Tordesillas. Many years have passed, and Juana (now ragged and disheveled) shares her dismal solitude with Catalina. In order to keep their spirits up, Juana teaches her daughter to dance and sings to her a sparkling, lively tune about three handsome horses trotting home. It is sung to a cantering accompaniment that has almost a flamenco feel to it.

Act III, Scene 1, at Spoleto U.S.A.: the long-awaited son, Carlos (Otey), at last comes to the cell of Juana (Vanelli) and Catalina (Iris Chrisanthis).

After a fanfare of trumpets, the door to Juana's cell is thrown open, and Carlos with his court walks in and bows to his mother. Juana is at first amazed and then wild with joy, certain that her son has come to release her. However, Carlos informs Juana of her father's death and he produces a paper that he asks Juana to sign, telling her it is the authority needed to gain her freedom. Crushed, she realizes it is just another attempt to wrest the throne from her. Sadly she tells Carlos to leave the document and she will consider it.

On leaving, he whispers to the Marquis de Denia: "Make her understand that my sister must come away with me and that her jewels belong to the crown." Having overheard her son's instruction, Juana tells Denia with all the dignity she can muster that she will never receive her son again. "Tell Carlos," she adds, "that he will make a good ruler for he is a shameless thief." She orders Denia to leave, saying she will prepare Catalina to join her brother. The supercharged and deeply moving farewell of Juana to Catalina is among the most deeply felt passages in all of the Menotti operas. Juana calls her daughter to her, and slowly decks her out with the royal jewels as the orchestra limns a tender, elongated melody in B major. "I shall be waiting for you," Juana tells Catalina softly; "you alone can free me, for who is there left to love me? Please don't forget your mother whose heart and whose crown you now take with you. Find in men's hearts the same love I give you and have never received. God bless you my angel. Don't cry, and walk out like a queen."

The singing B-major line forms the backbone of the last interlude and into it are woven several other motives that have come to be associated with Juana and her love. When the curtain rises again, we are in the same room but thirty years later. Juana crouches on the filthy floor strewn with bits of food, rags and a couple of empty bowls. Sick and racked with pain, she drags herself around like a dying animal, uttering eerie, disjointed birdlike calls and fragments of sentences in Latin.

It is an extended, largely unaccompanied mad scene that ranges up to top D-flat (it was se-

verely truncated at the San Diego premiere, and in its place Sills substituted spoken hallucinatory phrases). The orchestra breaks violently into Juana's raving as Miguel in the garb of a monk enters her cell. "Do not fear, Juana," he comforts her. "No human love I bring you, for God's love is the only love that's infinite, constant and true, the only immortal love." In these final ecstatic phrases, Miguel holds out the hope that God offers his love asking nothing in return. "Do you promise?" Juana sobs. As she falls to the ground dead, the music serenely melts away on a D-major chord in a questioning wisp of sound.

Act III, Scene 2, at Spoleto U.S.A.: Juana (Vanelli) in her final madness, comforted by the faithful Miguel (Philip Bologna).

Dialogue IV

JA: Would it be possible to adapt *The Labyrinth* for the stage?

GCM: It would be very difficult indeed, if not impossible. But with the many new technical devices in the theater, and perhaps by mixed media, a more resourceful stage director than I am might be able to achieve this improbable feat. Mind you, I'm not against the idea, but basically I would like to leave it as a television work if only it could be given more often. The unfortunate custom to present works on television once and then wait at least another year before they can be shown again makes me wish I had written *The Labyrinth* in such a way—as I did *Amahl*—that it could also be given on the stage.

JA: What led you to write *The Leper,* and what were your models for this play?

GCM: The style I adopted for *The Leper* is unusual nowadays, and Americans in particular are not familiar with this sort of drama, which found its last champions in Claudel, Giraudoux and Anouilh. It is poetic drama which does not attempt to be realistic in any way.

JA: Do you consider it as a work in progress?

GCM: Not really. It does have a few problems that I have to solve, but they are very slight ones such as small cuts to make the passage from one scene to the next more swift or graceful. I plan to publish it more or less the way it stands.

JA: You have said you consider it to be one of your major pieces. What are your reasons?

GCM: Well, it is because it expresses my feelings about an ethical problem that has bothered me for many years. It is a theme that had been gnawing at my conscience for a good

many years, even before I began writing it. I simply had to get it out of my system. Like *The Consul,* the play was an outburst of indignation and I think works born out of such deep feelings are generally valid and important works in the general appraisal of an artist. Frequently they are the most telling.

JA: Why was this theme necessary to express only in words?

GCM: It could not possibly have been an opera, for opera cannot express a syllogism or illustrate an epigram. *The Leper* is an intellectual play that deals more with abstract ideas and moral issues than emotional tensions. This takes it out of the realm of music.

JA: Discuss the effect the two Spoleto Festivals have had on your creative life.

GCM: Well, I don't think they have destroyed it, but they have certainly gotten in the way. My greatest enemies, as you have pointed out elsewhere, are time and haste, and there is always less time and more haste because of the two Spoletos. I have written many works since I inaugurated the two festivals, some of which I think are among my best, but some of them are, undeniably, still in an unfinished state. Curiously enough, I think one of the works I am particularly fond of—my mass—was written during one of the festivals and at least one act of *Juana La Loca* was conceived while staging one of the festival's productions. So, you never know. But I must admit that most of the works I have composed during the last twenty years show signs of haste and are still in need of being revised or at least polished with greater care. I am reminded so often of the words of Valéry, who said that a work of art is never finished, only abandoned. How very true! But in my case they are often aban-

The composer today, in one of the libraries at Yester House, his home in Scotland.

doned in truly shameful condition that dishonors the author.

JA: Can you comment on the elusive word "inspiration"? And how do you work? Is it always at the piano?

GCM: The piano is very important to me but not essential. I help myself at the piano, but usually I have my ideas away from the piano and then go to it to "check" them, so to say. I often am surprised by their actual sound and either discard or change them, sometimes considerably. But I love to improvise at the piano and much of my music stems from such improvisations. As far as inspiration goes, I think God gives an artist the gift to see perfect beauty as a pure essence. Then the artist tries to remember it and to get it on paper or canvas. For me, art is a form of memory. I, of course, am not the only one who has said this. James Joyce said it too, and even Picasso. The artist has a very quick glimpse of what is beautiful and he tries to convey it. As far as a composer goes, melody can only be explained as a form of memory. Nobody can analyze what constitutes a melody—a good melody. Take for example the Barcarole from *The Tales of Hoffmann;* nothing but three notes repeated over and over again. Or consider the very simple opening of Beethoven's "Moonlight" Sonata with its magic universal appeal. What makes it so? I think melody springs from a sort of collective unconsciousness; its universal value comes from an archetypal source. I don't know how else to explain it.

The torment of the artist is, of course, the realization that no matter how hard you struggle or how much craft you possess, you can only hope to capture a small particle of that glimpse of total beauty God has permitted you to behold. An artist is like a man with a divining rod. You search and search until the stick begins to shake. You know then you have come across a source. So you begin to dig in the hope of finding it. Of course some artists' sticks never shake, but let me assure you that if it does the artist is immediately aware of it;

when a composer finds a good theme, he recognizes it as such and uses it again and again. He knows he has struck water! Unfortunately most artists only *pretend* to have struck water and their music is nothing but a mimicry of the *real* discovery

JA: And yet, you tend not to repeat melodies, with the exception of the trio theme and Magda's big aria in *The Consul.*

GCM: As I told you, one of the qualities of a good composer is being able to recognize and weigh the value of his material. Perhaps I don't think my themes are good enough to bear too much repetition or I find myself incapable of developing them as I should. Wagner, of course, was a master at squeezing every melodic and harmonic possibility from his themes. I have often been accused of not fully using my material. People have said to me: "My God, why don't you stop pouring out themes and give us a chance to hear what you have already found so that we can appreciate it and remember it?" It is probably a serious fault in my technical ability or—which would be even more serious—a certain lack of imagination in handling my little treasures.

JA: You seem to have a tremendous facility for writing music.

GCM: I have a *certain* kind of facility, but believe me I have to work terribly hard on my music. I don't have any facility in a technical sense and must work very slowly in realizing on paper what I have in my head. I don't have, for example, perfect pitch; I am an abominable sight reader; my rhythmical sense lacks precision, etc., and the spontaneity you and others seem to admire in my music has come about very painfully. My music tends to be inventive melodically, but lazy harmonically. Sam Barber always used to torture me about my bass lines, saying, "For God's sake, can't you *move* that bass note and stop building everything over a pedal?" It is true! I am apt to write a lot of my thematic material on a pedal note, a terrible habit I now do my best to cure. Let me say, too, that just as the actual act of composition is very painful for me, so is expressing in words my ideas and beliefs. I am apt to express myself only emotionally, and I don't always say what I really think, but only what I feel at the moment. I read recently a fascinating article which said that there are two kinds of minds—a visual mind and an abstract mind. Mine is completely visual; that's why its horizon is limited. If you say "two apples," I see two apples. If you say "my grandmother," I "see" her, wrinkles and all, even if I have never met her. Those with more abstract minds are of course better mathematicians; I can see *two* apples but when it comes to fifty apples, it becomes very confusing and I stop counting! So it is very difficult for me to order my ideas unless I make notes, close off other possibilities and deal only with the problem at hand.

JA: There has long been a dichotomy between your acceptance by the public and your frequent lack of acceptance by the press. Can you offer some explanation?

GCM: I think some critics have been upset with me because I do not fit into their preconceived ideas of a historical musical development. They feel that composers such as Boulez and Stockhausen represent the direction where music should be going. All of a sudden they come up against a crazy Italian composer who is going a completely different way. It is as if one of the many horses pulling the cart of musical "progress" (some people still believe that music develops like an industry!) were not pulling in the direction they wish it to go, therefore they feel they have to whip the rebellious beast. I guess I am a bit of a problem for them. So many articles written about me are entitled "The Menotti Puzzle" and "The Menotti Problem," as if I were some sort of sickness that has to be cured. That perhaps explains the violence with which I am attacked. I am never surprised at the bad notices, but I am continually surprised at their vehemence. I don't think there is any other composer today who has received such in-

credible insults at the hands of the press. The New York *Times* has even written that I am a man of no talent. Well, modestly, I think I do have *some* talent. As Rossini said: "I know I'm not Bach, but I also know that I am not Offenbach."

JA: If, metaphorically, you could stand at *Amelia Goes to the Ball* and look down the line of your operas to *Juana La Loca*, what would you see?

GCM: I have to say first that I do not believe that art is ever a development or a progress. I think art is expression, and what you write at seventy is not necessarily better than what you write at seventeen. The work at seventeen has the advantage of youth, and the one at seventy has the advantage of more experience. An artist very often writes his best work in his twenties and can never recapture what he accomplished in his youth. I think my works changed as I changed. *Amelia* was certainly a very academic work; there was the obvious influence of Verdi's *Falstaff*, of Mozart, and its format is that of a conventional *opera buffa*. The same could be said of *The Old Maid and the Thief;* I was still searching for my own real voice. But both works have the freshness of youth and I do not disown them. (Sam Barber, to make me angry, insisted all of his life that *Amelia* remained my best opera!) With *The Medium* I finally began speaking with more assurance and individuality. However, even in the later *Consul* and *The Saint of Bleecker Street* there is much that is still tentative; a certain shyness in my lyrical impulse, a fear of letting it go its own natural course lest it become obvious rather than inevitable. (How wonderfully courageous was Verdi when it came to that and how much his youthful courage paid off in his later works!). I became more daring in *The Last Savage* and even more in *Juana La Loca* where I let my lyrical impetus go absolutely free, not bound by any fear of stylistic anachronisms or melodic influences. While my early works have the merit of freshness, I feel that my best works came when I found freedom and serenity, no longer worried about finding a personal style and let my natural personality give it its imprint.

JA: What recordings of your music do you like?

GCM: As you know, I have a horror of "frozen" music so it is very difficult for me to judge recordings of my work. When I first hear them, I often say, "That's very good; that's just the way it should be," but then I hear them years later and say to myself, "How could I have approved of that? It could be so much better." The interpretation of music is necessarily fluid according to temperament and mood and changes as people change in an ever-changing world. What seems "right" now is not necessarily going to be right in the future. It is also silly to think that a given tempo is *the* tempo, and recordings tend to create this idea. A wonderful interpreter may take a work at a slower tempo than one would logically take and still make the music even more convincing and expressive, but a lesser-talented musician, taking the piece at the same tempo, would ruin it. I don't think a definitive recording of my music exists. And if I am honest with you, I must confess that I never replay recordings of my music. I rarely hear them more than once, just enough to say, "Well, I like that, or I don't like that." I know it is important to have things recorded, but I am terrified that people may take them as the *only* way to perform a particular piece. So many people (critics and musicologists included) get to know music from records, and when they go to a concert, if what they hear doesn't match their recording, they think the music has been misinterpreted. This is very damaging for music.

JA: What about future commissions? What do you still wish to accomplish?

GCM: All of the works I have ahead of me—a new organ piece, the opera *Goya* for Placido Domingo and a work for the Westminster Choir—I hope to finish quickly. The opera, in fact, is already quite far along. But if I'm still alive when this current batch of commissions is finished, I would like to stop composing. I know it will not be easy, for composition is a sort of sweet torture that I try to avoid but at the same time I can't live without. But I really must take two or three years off to edit what I have written and put it into decent shape.

JA: You have said Italy gave you life, America raised you and Scotland will bury you. Do you still hope to end your life in Scotland?

GCM: I do feel I shall die in Scotland because I plan to retire there, but if my estate will leave enough money, I would like to have my body sent to Westchester to be buried next to Sam Barber. A plot awaits me there, and in Sam's will he instructed that, if I am buried elsewhere, a marker should be put on that empty plot that reads "To the memory of a great friendship." But I fully expect to be with him.

Yester House, an hour's drive from Edinburgh.

Chronology

Compiled and annotated by Joel Honig

This listing comprises all known or acknowledged works completed by Menotti, from his enrollment at the Curtis Institute of Music in 1928 to the present. All texts are by Menotti himself, unless otherwise indicated or unless—as in the *Missa "O Pulchritudo,"* for example—he is obviously not the author. Similarly, Menotti directed the premieres of all his stage works, unless other details are given.

Dates are of the first paid public performance; if no premiere can be ascertained, works are listed by date of publication. Where alternate casts or personnel were used, as in *Maria Golovin,* the artists listed are those who appeared on opening night.

For her help in compiling this chronology I wish to acknowledge, with thanks, the unbounded patience and cheerful cooperation of Lisa Archuletta of G. Schirmer. Elizabeth Walker, librarian of the Curtis Institute of Music, unearthed a long-ignored student work and provided help and encouragement. Jeanne Behrend Mac-Manus, Orlando Cole, John Bitter, Dorothy Livingston, and Rohini Coomara were kind enough to share their unfailing memories of Menotti's early career.

VARIATIONS ON A THEME OF SCHUMANN 1930

For piano solo

World premiere:	May 5, 1930 Curtis Institute of Music, Philadelphia
Pianist:	Jeanne Behrend

A student work, composed while Menotti was attending Curtis. A set of eleven variations based on Schumann's setting of Rückert's "Zum Schluss," Opus 25, no. 26, it was awarded the 1931 Carl F. Lauber Composition Prize.

VARIATIONS AND FUGUE FOR STRING QUARTET 1932

World premiere:	May 12, 1932 Curtis Institute of Music, Philadelphia
Violin:	James Bloom
Violin:	Frances Wiener
Viola:	Arthur Granick
Cello:	Samuel Geschichter

Based on an unpublished theme of Antonio Caldara, this student work was performed on the same program with Samuel Barber's *Dover Beach.*

PASTORALE AND DANCE FOR STRINGS AND PIANO 1934

This is Menotti's first completed work after graduation from Curtis in 1933. It was composed in Vienna and first performed there, privately, at a chamber music concert in Menotti and Barber's studio on January 4, 1934. Edith Evans Braun was the pianist, and Barber conducted. A public premiere was given soon afterward in Vienna, with Carl Bamberger conducting.

The U.S. premiere was given on March 20, 1935, by the Philadelphia Chamber String Simfonietta, comprising eighteen members of the Philadelphia Orchestra, Fabien Sevitzky, conductor. Menotti himself was the soloist, in his only public appearance as a pianist.

SIX COMPOSITIONS FOR CARILLON 1934

Preludio
Arabesque
Dialogue
Pastorale
Canzone
Étude

Composed in 1930 and 1931 at Mountain Lake, Florida, while Menotti was studying the carillon with Anton Brees, bellmaster of the Mountain Lake Singing Tower.

ITALIAN DANCE 1935

For string quartet

First known performance:	June 30, 1935 BBC radio concert, London, England
Violin:	Jascha Brodsky
Violin:	Charles Jaffe
Viola:	Max Aronoff
Cello:	Orlando Cole

A *tarantella,* given its premiere by the Curtis Quartet

TRIO FOR A HOUSEWARMING PARTY   1936

For piano, cello, and flute

An occasional piece, written to celebrate Eric Gugler's renovation of the New York City house of Mrs. John Bitter.

The work was first played in the spring of 1936 by Gian Carlo Menotti, piano; Rohini Coomara, cello; and John Bitter, flute.

AMELIA AL BALLO   1937
(AMELIA GOES TO THE BALL)

Opera buffa in one act

World premiere: April 1, 1937
                    Philadelphia Academy of Music
Orchestra: Curtis Institute Orchestra
Conductor: Fritz Reiner
Sets: Donald Oenslager
Staged by: Ernst Lert

English version by George Mead

CAST

Amelia . . . . Margaret Daum
Her Friend . . . . Edwina Eustis
Husband . . . . Conrad Mayo
Lover . . . . William Martin
Police Chief. . . . . . . Leonard Treash
Cook . . . . Wilburta Horn
Maid . . . . Charlotte Daniels

Presented on a double bill with Milhaud's *Le pauvre matelot*

POEMETTI   1937

For piano solo

Giga
Ninna-Nanna (Lullaby)
Bells at Dawn
The Spinner
The Bagpipers
The Brook
The Shepherd
Nocturne
The Stranger's Dance
Winter Wind
The Manger
War Song

A group of children's pieces dedicated to the memory of Maria Rosa Menotti, Gian Carlo's youngest sister

THE OLD MAID AND THE THIEF   1939

Radio *opera buffa* in fourteen scenes

World premiere: April 22, 1939
                    Broadcast on the National
                    Broadcasting Company Blue Network
                    (WJZ, Radio City, New York City)
Orchestra: NBC Symphony
Conductor: Alberto Erede

CAST

Narrator . . . . Joseph Curtin
Miss Todd . . . . Mary Hopple
Bob. . . . . Robert Weede
Laetitia . . . . Margaret Daum
Miss Pinkerton. . . . . Dorothy Sarnoff

First staged by the Philadelphia Opera Company, February 11, 1941.

THE ISLAND GOD   1942

Tragic opera in one act

World premiere: February 20, 1942
                    Metropolitan Opera House, New York City

Conductor: Ettore Panizza
Stage director: Lothar Wallerstein
Sets and
  costumes: Richard Rychtarik

Originally written in Italian and entitled *Ilo e Zeus*. English version by Fleming Macliesh.

CAST

Ilo . . . . Leonard Warren
Telea . . . . Astrid Varnay
Luca. . . . . Raoul Jobin
A Greek God . . . . Norman Cordon
Voice of a Fisherman . . . . John Carter

Followed by *Pagliacci* at the premiere.

This work was withdrawn by Menotti. Two interludes from the opera were first performed on October 19, 1945, by the Boston Symphony Orchestra, under Serge Koussevitzky.

THE CATALOGUE   1943

Terzetto with libretto from "a well-known publication"

World premiere: December 1943
                    Curtis Institute of Music, Philadelphia

A humorous musical rendition of the 1943–44 Curtis catalogue, the work was written in honor of Mary Curtis Bok and was first performed at a Curtis Christmas party. It is scored for three singers and piano, with bassoon obbligato evoking a Donizetti cadenza. The piece has been revived several times at Curtis.

SEBASTIAN 1944

Ballet in one act and three scenes

World premiere:	October 31, 1944
	International Theatre, New York City
Scenario:	Gian Carlo Menotti
Choreography:	Edward Caton
Settings:	Oliver Smith
Costumes:	Milena (executed by Eaves)
Conductor:	Alexander Smallens

CAST

Courtesan		Viola Essen
Prince		Kari Karnakoski
Fiora	His Sisters	Lisa Maslova
Maddalena		Yvonne Patterson
Sebastian		Francisco Moncion
Fortune Teller		Nina Golovina
Countess		Jacquelyn Cezanne

Pages, Courtiers, Passersby, Peasants, etc.

A suite from the ballet, comprising five sections—*Introduzione, Barcarola, Baruffa, Cortège,* and *Pavane*—was first presented on August 8, 1945, by the New York Philharmonic, Alexander Smallens, conductor, at Lewisohn Stadium.

CONCERTO IN F FOR PIANO AND ORCHESTRA 1945

In three movements

World premiere:	November 2, 1945
Orchestra:	Boston Symphony
Conductor:	Richard Burgin
Soloist:	Rudolf Firkusny

THE MEDIUM 1946

Tragic opera in two acts

World premiere:	May 8, 1946
	Brander Matthews Theater, Columbia University, New York City
	Produced by Columbia Theater Associates in cooperation with the Columbia University Department of Music
Broadway premiere:	May 1, 1947
	Ethel Barrymore Theatre, New York City
	Produced by Chandler Cowles and Efrem Zimbalist, Jr., in association with Edith Lutyens, together with *The Telephone*

Settings:	Oliver Smith	Horace Armistead
Costumes:	Fabio Rieti	Horace Armistead
Conductor:	Otto Luening	Emanuel Balaban

CAST

Monica	Evelyn Keller	Evelyn Keller
Toby	Leo Coleman	Leo Coleman
Flora	Claramae Turner	Marie Powers
Mrs. Gobineau	Beverly Dame	Beverly Dame
Mr. Gobineau	Jacques La Rochelle	Frank Rogier
Mrs. Nolan	Virginia Beeler	Virginia Beeler

Originally commissioned by the Alice M. Ditson Fund of Columbia University. The Broadway production closed on November 1, 1947, after 212 performances.

THE TELEPHONE, OR L'AMOUR À TROIS 1947

Comic opera in one act

World premiere:	February 18, 1947
	Heckscher Theater, New York City
Settings and costumes:	Saul Steinberg
Conductor:	Leon Barzin
Broadway premiere:	May 1, 1947
	Ethel Barrymore Theatre

CAST

Lucy	Marilyn Cotlow
Ben	Frank Rogier

Written as a curtain raiser to *The Medium (q.v.).*

ERRAND INTO THE MAZE 1947

Modern dance

World premiere:	February 28, 1947
	Ziegfeld Theatre, New York City
Choreography:	Martha Graham
Settings:	Isamu Noguchi
Lighting:	Jean Rosenthal
Conductor:	Louis Horst

CAST

The Woman (Ariadne)	Martha Graham
The Man (Theseus-Minotaur)	Mark Ryder

THE BRIDGE 1947

A HAPPY ENDING (later reworked and retitled The Beautiful Snowfall)

Film scripts

Menotti signed a contract with MGM in the summer of 1947 to write a screenplay. Neither was produced.

A COPY OF MADAME AUPIC   1947

Comedy drama in three acts

World premiere: August 27, 1947
                     Theatre-in-the-Dale,
                         New Milford, Connecticut
Producer: Louis Townsend
Settings: J. D. Fitz-Hugh

CAST

Steve	Sam Wren
Albert	Walter Armitage
George Norris	Thomas Beck
Gogo	Marguerite Lewis
Madame Renée Aupic	Olga Baclanova
Martha	Cele McLaughlin

Written in 1943, the play was revived on March 25, 1959, at the Théâtre Fontaine in Paris, in a two-act translation by Albert Husson, starring Madeleine Robinson.

À L'OMBRE DES JEUNES FILLES EN FLEURS   1947

Ballet

Based on *Within a Budding Grove,* the second novel of Marcel Proust's *Remembrance of Things Past,* this unproduced work was to have been choreographed by Antony Tudor for the Ballet Theatre.

THE CONSUL   1950

Opera in three acts

World premiere: March 1, 1950
                     Shubert Theatre, Philadelphia

Producer: Chandler Cowles and Efrem Zimbalist, Jr.
Conductor: Lehman Engel
Settings: Horace Armistead
Costumes: Grace Houston
Lighting: Jean Rosenthal
Choreography   John Butler
  (dream
  sequence):

Broadway   March 15, 1950
  premiere: Ethel Barrymore Theatre, New York

CAST

John Sorel	Cornell MacNeil
Magda Sorel	Patricia Neway
The Mother	Marie Powers
Chief Police Agent	Leon Lishner
First Police Agent	Chester Watson
Second Police Agent	Donald Blackey
The Secretary	Gloria Lane
Mr. Kofner	George Jongeyans
The Foreign Woman	Maria Marlo
Anna Gomez	Maria Andreassi
Vera Boronel	Lydia Summers
Nika Magadoff	Andrew McKinley
Assan	Francis Monachino
Voice on the Record	Mabel Mercer

Closed November 4, 1950, after 269 performances.

A LITTLE CANCRIZAN FOR MARY   1951

For three singers

A humorous setting of "Happy Birthday to You," with one of the parts "to be sung standing on one's head." Twenty-four other composers contributed to this volume of musical greetings, which was conceived and compiled by Samuel Barber as a present for Mary Louise Zimbalist on her seventy-fifth birthday.

THE MEDIUM   1951

Film

World premiere: September 5, 1951
                     Sutton Theater, New York City

Producer: Walter Lowendahl, released by Transfilm
Orchestra: Symphony Orchestra of Rome
Conductor: Thomas Schippers

CAST

Flora	Marie Powers
Monica	Anna Maria Alberghetti
Toby	Leo Coleman
Mrs. Nolan	Belva Kibler
Mrs. Gobineau	Beverly Dame
Mr. Gobineau	Donald Morgan

An eighty-four-minute movie, filmed in Rome

APOCALISSE   1951

Symphonic poem

World premiere   October 19, 1951
  (first two   Syria Mosque, Oakland Civic Center,
  movements):   Pittsburgh
Orchestra: Pittsburgh Symphony
Conductor: Victor de Sabata

World premiere   January 18, 1952
  (complete   Academy of Music, Philadelphia
  work):
Orchestra: Philadelphia Orchestra
Conductor: Victor de Sabata

  I: *Improperia (adagio, solenne)*
 II: The Celestial City *(andante sereno)*
III: The Militant Angels *(allegro ma non troppo),* added after the 1951 premiere

RICERCARE AND TOCCATA ON A THEME FROM   1951
THE OLD MAID AND THE THIEF

For piano solo

First known   November 1, 1951
  performance: Town Hall, New York City
Pianist: Ania Dorfmann

AMAHL AND THE NIGHT VISITORS
1951

Television opera in one act

World premiere:	December 24, 1951, over 35 stations of the NBC-TV network
Conductor:	Thomas Schippers
Settings and costumes:	Eugene Berman
Choreography:	John Butler
TV director:	Kirk Browning

CAST

Amahl	Chet Allen
Mother	Rosemary Kuhlmann
First King	David Aiken
Second King	Leon Lishner
Third King	Andrew McKinley
Servant	Francis Monachino
Peasants	Melissa Hayden
	Glen Tetley
	Nicholas Magallanes

The first professional production was given on April 9, 1952, by the New York City Opera.

THE HERO
1952

For voice and piano

Dedicated to Marie Powers, with text by Robert Horan, this is the first setting by Menotti of someone else's words.

CONCERTO FOR VIOLIN AND ORCHESTRA
1952

In three movements

World premiere:	December 5, 1952 Academy of Music, Philadelphia
Orchestra:	Philadelphia Orchestra
Conductor:	Eugene Ormandy
Soloist:	Efrem Zimbalist

THE SAINT OF BLEECKER STREET
1954

Music drama in three acts

World premiere:	December 27, 1954 Broadway Theatre, New York City
Producer:	Chandler Cowles
Production supervised by:	Lincoln Kirstein
Settings and costumes:	Robert Randolph
Lighting:	Jean Rosenthal
Conductor:	Thomas Schippers

CAST

Assunta	Catherine Akos
Carmela	Maria Di Gerlando
Maria Corona	Maria Marlo
Her Dumb Son	Ernesto Gonzales
Don Marco	Leon Lishner
Annina	Virginia Copeland
Michele	David Poleri
Desideria	Gloria Lane
Salvatore	David Aiken
Concettina	Lucy Becque

Closed April 2, 1955, after 92 performances.

RICERCARE SU NOVE TONI
1956

For piano

Written for mezzo-soprano Marya Freund for her eightieth birthday.

THE UNICORN, THE GORGON AND THE MANTICORE (THE THREE SUNDAYS OF A POET)
1956

Madrigal fable for chorus of twenty-four, ten dancers, and nine instruments

World premiere:	October 21, 1956 Coolidge Auditorium, Library of Congress, Washington, D.C.
Scenario:	Gian Carlo Menotti
Choreography:	John Butler
New York premiere:	January 15, 1957 New York City Ballet, City Center, New York Produced by the Ballet Society

Settings:	Jean Rosenthal	Jean Rosenthal
Costumes:	Robert Fletcher	Robert Fletcher
Conductor:	Paul Callaway	Thomas Schippers

CAST

	Washington	New York
Unicorn	Talley Beatty	Arthur Mitchell
Gorgon	John Renn	Eugene Tanner
Manticore	Dorothy Ethridge	Richard Thomas
Poet	Swen Swenson	Nicholas Magallenes
Count	Loren Hightower	Roy Tobias
Countess	Gemze de Lappe	Janet Reed
Doctor	John Foster	Jonathan Watts
Doctor's Wife	Ethel Martin	Lee Becker
Mayor	Jack Leigh	John Mandia
Mayor's Wife	Lee Becker	Wilma Curley

VANESSA
1958

Opera in four acts by Samuel Barber; libretto by Menotti

World premiere: January 15, 1958
                    Metropolitan Opera House, New York City

Conductor: Dimitri Mitropoulos
Designer: Cecil Beaton
Choreographer: Zachary Solov

CAST

Erika	Rosalind Elias
Major Domo	George Cehanovsky
Vanessa	Eleanor Steber
Anatol	Nicolai Gedda
Baroness	Regina Resnik
Doctor	Giorgio Tozzi
Footman	Robert Nagy

MARIA GOLOVIN
1958

Opera in three acts

World premiere: August 20, 1958
                    American Theater, U.S. Pavilion,
                    Brussels World Exposition

Presented by the NBC Opera Theater

Producer: Samuel Chotzinoff
Settings: Rouben Ter-Arutunian
Costumes: Supervised by Helene Pons
Lighting: Charles Elson
Conductor: Herbert Grossman

U.S. premiere: November 5, 1958
                    Martin Beck Theatre, New York City

Produced by David Merrick and the National Broadcasting Company, in association with Byron Goldman

CAST

	Brussels	New York
Donato	Richard Cross	Richard Cross
Agata	Ruth Kobart	Ruth Kobart
The Mother	Patricia Neway	Patricia Neway
Dr. Zuckertanz	Herbert Handt	Norman Kelley
Maria Golovin	Franca Duval	Franca Duval
Trottolò	Lorenzo Muti	Lorenzo Muti
The Prisoner	William Chapman	William Chapman
Servant	John Wheeler	John Kuhn

Closed November 8, 1958, after 5 performances. Produced on television, March 8, 1959.

INCIDENTAL MUSIC FOR COCTEAU'S LE POÈTE ET SA MUSE
1959

For strings, piano, and percussion

World premiere: June 12, 1959
                    Teatro Caio Melisso, Spoleto, Italy

Costumes: Marcel Escoffier
Director: Franco Zeffirelli
Conductor: Carlo Franci
Soloist: William Lewis, tenor

CAST

The Poet	Tomas Milian
The Muse	Relda Ridoni
The Young People	Raimonda Orselli
	Leo Coleman
	Roberto Pistone

A "mimodrame," with sets and scenario by Cocteau, based on "James Deanism" and dealing with posthumous fame.

A HAND OF BRIDGE
1959

Opera in one act by Samuel Barber; libretto by Menotti

World premiere: June 17, 1959
                    Teatro Caio Melisso, Spoleto, Italy

Settings and
costumes: Jac Venza
Conductor: Robert Feist

CAST

David	René Miville
Geraldine	Patricia Neway
Bill	William Lewis
Sally	Ellen Miville

ALBUM LEAVES
1959–62

Sketches

Menotti contributed several pseudonymous works to the Festival of Two Worlds (Spoleto) during its early years. Although a complete list of these ephemera is beyond the scope of this chronology, one may cite from the 1961 season, for example, *Il pegno, Le amiche, Il ventriloquo,* and *I deportati* by "Mario Felder," and *Posta, Camping,* and *Arrivo a Roma* by "Howard Chadwick" the following year.

INTRODUCTIONS AND GOOD-BYES
1960

Miniature opera

World premiere: May 6, 1960
                    Carnegie Hall, New York City

Orchestra: New York Philharmonic, Choral Arts Society
Conductor: Leonard Bernstein

SOLOISTS

Baritone: John Reardon
Xylophone: Walter Rosenberger

A nine-minute opera, with prologue and epilogue, by Lukas Foss, for which Menotti wrote the libretto. Originally composed for the Festival of Two Worlds in Spoleto, Italy, the work was scheduled for the 1959 season but was never staged there. One singer ("Mr. McC.") portrays the host at a cocktail party; the guests are represented by the chorus.

A CHANCE FOR ALEKO   1961

Play for television

Originally entitled *The Chance*, this unproduced work was written early in 1961 for the *"Robert Herridge Theatre"* on CBS.

THE LABYRINTH   1963

Television opera

World premiere: March 3, 1963, over the NBC-TV network

Settings: Warren Clymer
Costumes: Noel Taylor
TV director: Kirk Browning
Conductor: Herbert Grossman

CAST

The Bride . . . . Judith Raskin
The Groom . . . . John Reardon
The Spy . . . . Elaine Bonazzi
The Old Man . . . . Robert White
The Executive Director . . . . Beverly Wolff
The Desk Clerk . . . . Leon Lishner
The Bellboy . . . . Nikiforos Naneris
The Astronaut . . . . Frank Porretta
Death . . . . Leon Lishner
Death's Assistant . . . . John West
Italian Opera Singer . . . . Eugene Green
Executive Director's Secretary . . . Bob Rickner

THE DEATH OF THE BISHOP OF BRINDISI   1963

Cantata for chorus, children's chorus, mezzo-soprano, and bass solo, and orchestra

World premiere: May 18, 1963
                     Music Hall, Cincinnati

Conductor: Max Rudolf

SOLOISTS

The Nun . . . . Rosalind Elias
The Bishop . . . . Richard Cross

First staged at the University of New Mexico, Albuquerque, January 11, 1968.

L'ULTIMO SELVAGGIO   1963
(THE LAST SAVAGE)

Comic opera in three acts

Written in Italian and originally entitled *L'ultimo superuomo* (The Last Superman). French version by Jean-Pierre Marty; English version by George Mead.

World premiere: October 22, 1963
                     Opéra-Comique, Paris

U.S. premiere: January 23, 1964
                     Metropolitan Opera, New York City

Settings and
  costumes: André Beaurepaire   Beni Montresor
Conductor: Serge Baudo   Thomas Schippers

CAST

	Paris	New York
Maharajah	Charles Clavensy	Ezio Flagello
Maharani	Solange Michel	Lili Chookasian
Kodanda	Michele Molese	Nicolai Gedda
Mr. Scattergood	Xavier Depraz	Morley Meredith
Kitty	Mady Mesplé	Roberta Peters
Abdul	Gabriel Bacquier	George London
Sardula	Adriana Maliponte	Teresa Stratas

MARTIN'S LIE   1964

Church opera

World premiere: June 3, 1964
                     Bristol Cathedral

Produced by the Bath Festival Society in association with the Labyrinth Corporation of America and the Columbia Broadcasting System

Settings and costumes: Anthony Powell
Conductor: Lawrence Leonard

The English Chamber Orchestra and chorus of St. Mary Redcliffe Secondary School

CAST

Father Cornelius . . . . William McAlpine
Naninga . . . . Noreen Berry
The Stranger . . . . Donald McIntyre
Sheriff . . . . Otakar Kraus
Martin . . . . Michael Wennink
Christopher . . . . Keith Collins
Timothy . . . . Roger Nicholas

The American premiere, scheduled for January 24, 1965, was canceled by CBS-TV owing to the death the same day of Winston Churchill. It was seen on May 30, 1965, with the above cast, in the Bristol production.

LEWISOHN STADIUM FANFARE   1965

For brass, timpani, and percussion

World premiere: June 21, 1965
                   Lewisohn Stadium, New York City

Orchestra: Metropolitan Opera Orchestra
Conductor: Fausto Cleva

Written for the Metropolitan Opera's inaugural summer concert.

INCIDENTAL MUSIC FOR ANOUILH'S MÉDÉE   1966

World premiere: December 20, 1966
                   Teatro Quirinale, Rome

Menotti made his debut as a director of prose drama with this production, which starred Anna Magnani.

CANTI DELLA LONTANANZA   1967

Song cycle for voice and piano (in Italian)

World premiere: March 18, 1967
                   Hunter College Assembly Hall, New York City

Soprano: Elisabeth Schwarzkopf
Piano: Martin Isepp

Gli amanti impossibili (Impossible Lovers)
Mattinata di neve (Snowy Morning)
Il settimo bicchiere di vino (The Seventh Glass of Wine)
Lo spettro (The Specter)
Dorme Pegaso (Pegasus Asleep)
La lettera (The Letter)
Rassegnazione (Resignation)

INCIDENTAL MUSIC FOR ROMEO AND JULIET   1968

World premiere: April 19, 1968
                   Grande Salle, Palais de Chaillot, Paris

Composed for Michael Cacoyannis' production, staged by the Théâtre National Populaire.

HELP, HELP, THE GLOBOLINKS!   1968

Opera in one act for children "and those who like children"

World premiere: December 21, 1968
                   Hamburg State Opera with *Amahl and the Night Visitors*

U.S. premiere: August 1, 1969
                   Santa Fe Opera with *Le Rossignol*

	Hamburg	Santa Fe
Settings:	———	Willa Kim
Costumes:	Lieselotte Erler	Willa Kim
	Alwin Nikolais	Alwin Nikolais
Lighting:	Nicolas Schöffer	Georg Schreiber
Choreography:	Alwin Nikolais	Alwin Nikolais
Conductor:	Matthias Kuntzsch	Gustav Meier

CAST

Tony	William Workman	William Workman
Emily	Edith Mathis	Judith Blegen
Dr. Stone	Raymond Wolansky	John Reardon
Timothy	Kurt Marschner	Douglas Perry
Madame Euterpova	Arlene Saunders	Marguerite Willauer
Mr. Lavender-Gas	Franz Grundheber	Clyde Phillip Walker
Dr. Turtlespit	Noël Mangin	Richard Best
Penelope Newkirk	Ursula Boese	Jean Kraft

THE LEPER   1970

Play in two acts

World premiere: April 24, 1970
                   Fine Arts Theater,
                     Florida State University, Tallahassee

Produced by Chandler Cowles in conjunction with the Florida State University Department of Theater

Settings and costumes:	Holmes Easley
Lighting:	Larry Riddle
Jewelry:	Kenneth J. Lane

CAST

The Queen	Patricia Neway
Alexios	Francis Phelan
Nikitas	Bruce Pfeffer
Zoe	Sharon Crowe
The Old Man	Jack Sydow
Palladius	Dalton Cathey
Kosmas	Bill Shipley
Irene	Pamela Bailey
Michail	James Wrynn
Dimitrios	Chuck Rubin
Kirillos	Bud Ritch
Amphissia	Barbara Manford
The Potter	Ron Fayad
Bardas	Paul Stoakes
Anatellon	Rick Alley
Aglaia	Jennifer Meyer
Manuel	Jerry O'Donnell
Nilus	Charles Bessant
Serphius	Terry McFall
The Nurse	Carolyn Werner
The Smith's Apprentice	Chris Meyer
Woman of the town	Elaine Smith
Baker's errand boy	Tony Tartaglia
Ariadne, a dancer	Dusty Truran
Bakur, the Queen's bodyguard	Tony Afejusu

Musicians, townspeople, children

TRIPLO CONCERTO A TRE   1970

Triple concerto for three concertato groups of solo instruments, and orchestra, in three movements

World premiere: October 6, 1970
                       Carnegie Hall, New York City

Orchestra: American Symphony Orchestra
Conductor: Leopold Stokowski

For three groups of soloists:

Oboe: Arthur Krilov
Clarinet: Joseph Rabbai
Bassoon: William Scribner

Violin: Mary Blankstein
Viola: Maxine Johnson
Cello: Jascha Silberstein

Piano: Rex Cooper
Harp: Lise Nadeau
Percussion: Lawrence Jacobs
                       Alan Silverman

THE MOST IMPORTANT MAN   1971

Opera in three acts

World premiere: March 7, 1971
                       New York State Theater, Lincoln Center,
                       New York City

Produced by: New York City Opera Company
Settings: Oliver Smith
Costumes: Frank Thompson
Lighting: Hans Sondheimer
Conductor: Christopher Keene

CAST

Toimé Ukamba . . . . Eugene Holmes
Dr. Otto Arnek . . . . , . . . Harry Theyard
Leona Arnek . . . . Beverly Wolff
Eric Rupert . . . . Richard Stilwell
Cora Arnek . . . . Joanna Bruno
Professor Clement . . . . John Lankston
Professor Risselberg . . . . Joaquin Romaguera
Professor Bolental . . . . Thomas Jamerson
Professor Hisselman . . . . William Ledbetter
Professor Grippel . . . . Don Yule
Under Secretary of State . . . . Jack Bittner
Mrs. Agebda Akawasi . . . . Delores Jones

SUITE FOR TWO CELLOS AND PIANO   1973

World premiere: May 20, 1973
                       Alice Tully Hall, Lincoln Center,
                       New York City

SOLOISTS
Cello: Gregor Piatigorsky
Cello: Leslie Parnas
Piano: Charles Wadsworth

TAMU-TAMU (THE GUESTS)   1973

Chamber opera in two acts

World premiere: September 5, 1973
                       Studebaker Theater, Chicago
Settings and
  costumes: Sandro La Ferla
Lighting: F. Mitchell Dana
Producer: Ken Myers
Conductor: Christopher Keene

CAST
Husband . . . . Robert J. Manzari
Wife . . . . Sylvia Davis
Radna . . . . Sung Sook Lee
Nenek . . . . Theresa Teng Chen
Anonto . . . . Sung Kil Kim
Indra . . . . Sumiko Murashima
Solema . . . . Ferlina Newyanti Darmodihardjo
Kakek . . . . Joseph Hutagalung
Djoko . . . . Horas Hutagalung
Doctor . . . . Douglas Perry
Priest . . . . Samuel Terry
Soldiers . . . . Michael Takada
                                           Damon Ho
Soldiers and
  Assistant Priests . . . . Glenn Asato
                                      Jiro Shimotak

THE DAYS OF THE SHEPHERD   1974

Ballet in four seasons

Winter: Courtship and Games
Spring: Promises and Farewells
Summer: Solitude and Encounters
Fall: Homecoming and Reunions

A pastoral work in the Spanish idiom, commissioned in 1973 by the Harkness Ballet and as yet (1985) unproduced.

FANTASIA FOR CELLO AND ORCHESTRA   1976

World premiere: January 16, 1976
                       Turin, Italy

Orchestra: RAI Orchestra
Soloist: Laurence Lesser, cello

A one-movement work originally—and incorrectly—entitled *Capriccio.*

LANDSCAPES AND REMEMBRANCES   1976

Cantata in nine movements

World premiere: May 14, 1976
                     Uihlein Hall, Performing Arts Center,
                         Milwaukee

Orchestra: Milwaukee Symphony and Bel Canto
                         Chorus
Conductor: James A. Keeley

SOLOISTS
Soprano: Judith Blegen
Mezzo-soprano: Ani Yervanian
Tenor: Vahan Khanzadian
Bass: Gary Kendall

THE HERO   1976

Comic opera in three acts

World premiere: June 1, 1976
                     Philadelphia Academy of Music

Orchestra: Opera Company of Philadelphia
Settings: Eugene Barth
Costumes: Carol Luiken
Lighting: Lee Watson
Conductor: Christopher Keene

CAST
Barbara . . . . Nancy Shade
David Murphy . . . . Dominic Cossa
Mildred Murphy . . . . Diane Curry
Dr. Brainkoff . . . . David Griffin
Mayor . . . . Gary Kendall
Guide . . . . Richard Shapp

THE EGG (AN OPERATIC RIDDLE)   1976

Church opera in one act

World premiere: June 17, 1976
                     Washington Cathedral, Washington, D.C.

Conductor: Paul Callaway
Costumes: Constance Mellen

Musicians and volunteer members of the Cathedral
Festival '76 Chorale.

CAST
Manuel . . . . Matthew Murray
St. Simeon Stylites . . . . Anastasios Vrenios
The Basilissa, Empress of Byzantium (Pride). Esther Hinds
Areobindus, favorite of the Basilissa (Lust) . . Sigmund Cowan
Gourmantus, the cook (Gluttony) . . . . Gimi Beni
Priscus, the cook's boy . . . . Peter Fish
Eunuch of the Sacred Cubicle (Sloth) . . . . . . Gene Tucker
Pachomius, the treasurer (Avarice) . . . . Richard S. Dirksen
Sister of the Basilissa (Envy) . . . . Dana Krueger
Julian, Captain of the Guard (Anger) . . . . . . Frank Phelan
Beggar Woman . . . . Regina McConnell
                Members of the Court

SYMPHONY NO. 1 IN A MINOR   1976
("THE HALCYON")

World premiere: August 4, 1976
                     Saratoga Performing Arts Center,
                         Saratoga, New York

Orchestra: Philadelphia Orchestra
Conductor: Eugene Ormandy

CANTILENA E SCHERZO   1977

For harp and string quartet

World premiere: March 15, 1977
                     Alice Tully Hall, Lincoln Center,
                         New York City

SOLOISTS
Harp: Osian Ellis
Violin: James Buswell
Violin: Ani Kavafian
Viola: Walter Trampler
Cello: Leslie Parnas

Choreographed by Martha Graham as *Shadows* and first
presented at the Lunt-Fontanne Theatre, New York City,
May 24, 1977.

THE TRIAL OF THE GYPSY   1978

Dramatic cantata in one act for four boy soloists, boys' chorus, and
piano

World premiere: May 24, 1978
                     Alice Tully Hall, Lincoln Center,
                         New York City

Conductor: Terence Shook, Newark Boys' Chorus
Pianist: Barbara Chernichowski

CAST
The Gypsy . . . . Andre Hardmon
The Judges . . . . Ivan Bonilla
                         James Byrd
                         Sean Sirmans

LULLABY FOR ALEXANDER   1978

For piano

World premiere: July 29, 1978
                     Lennoxlove, Haddington, Scotland

Written for, and performed at, the christening of Menotti's
godson, Alexander, marquess of Douglas and Clydesdale

MIRACLES

1979

Eight musical miniatures based on poetry written by children

World premiere: April 22, 1979
Tarrant County Convention Center Theater, Fort Worth, Texas

Orchestra: Fort Worth Symphony and Texas Boys' Choir

Conductor: John Giordano

From a published anthology of 200 poems written by English-speaking children around the world, all between the ages of five and thirteen, Menotti chose the following to set his musical version:

"My Poem" (Ethel Hewell, 11, Philippines)
"My Uncle Jack" (David Amey, 10, England)
"I Love Animals and Dogs" (Hilary-Anne Farley, 5, Canada)
"A Strange Place" (Peter Rake, 12, England)
"I Am a Nice Boy" (Martin O'Conner, 10, New Zealand)
"A Thundery Day" (Susan Meader, 10, England)
"Two Million Two Hundred Thousand Fishes" (Danny Marcus, 8, United States)
"The Night" (Amy Goodman, 11, United States)

Twelve songs were originally planned.

CHIP AND HIS DOG

1979

Opera for children in one act, to be performed by children

World premiere: May 6, 1979
War Memorial Hall, University of Guelph Guelph, Ontario

Settings: Antonin Dimitrov
Costumes: Olga Dimitrov
Lighting: David Wallett
Musical director: Derek Holman
Pianist: Bruce Ubukata
Percussion: David Kent, William Winant

CAST

Chip . . . . David Coulter
Dog . . . . Andrea Kuzmich
Messenger . . . . Priscilla Heffernan
Page . . . . John Kuzmich
Princess . . . . Laura Zarins
Courtier . . . . Heidi Hobday
Doctor . . . . Valarie Williams
Gardener . . . . Avril Helbig
Scribe . . . . Breffni O'Reilly
Clowns, Guards, Ladies-in-Waiting,
Court Ladies, Noblemen, Merchants, Cooks

Premiered at the Guelph Spring Festival, celebrating the Year of the Child (1979), on a double bill with Richard Rodney Bennett's *All the King's Men.*

MISSA "O PULCHRITUDO"

1979

World premiere: May 11, 1979
Uihlein Hall, Performing Arts Center, Milwaukee

Orchestra: Milwaukee Symphony and Bel Canto Chorus

Conductor: James A. Keeley

SOLOISTS

Soprano: Brenda Quilling
Mezzo-soprano: Cynthia Munzer
Tenor: David Bender
Baritone: David Berger

JUANA LA LOCA

1979

Opera in three acts

World premiere: June 3, 1979
Civic Theater, San Diego

Director: Tito Capobianco
Settings and costumes: Mario Vanarelli
Lighting: Don Abrams
Conductor: Calvin Simmons

CAST

Doña Manuela . . . . Susanne Marsee
Juana La Loca . . . . Beverly Sills
Nurse . . . . Jane Westbrook
Miguel de Ferrara . . . . Joseph Evans
Felipe, husband of Juana . . . . John Bröcheler
Chaplain . . . . Vincent Russo
Ximenes de Cisneros, bishop of
     Toledo . . . . Robert Hale
Fernando, king of Spain . . . . John Bröcheler
Carlos V as a boy . . . . Wade Gregg
Marqués de Denia . . . . Carlos Chausson
Emperor Carlos V . . . . John Bröcheler
Ladies-in-Waiting . . . . Marcia Cope
                               Martha Jane Howe
Catalina . . . . Nancy Coulson

A SONG OF HOPE
(AN OLD MAN'S SOLILOQUY)

1980

For baritone, chorus, and orchestra

World premiere: April 25, 1980
Hill Auditorium, Ann Arbor, Michigan

Orchestra: Philadelphia Orchestra and University of Michigan Choral Union

Conductor: Stanislaw Skrowaczewski
Baritone: Leslie Guinn

MOANS, GROANS, CRIES, SIGHS (A COMPOSER AT WORK)

1981

Madrigal for six voices, a capella

World premiere:
The King's Singers:

August 31, 1981
Usher Hall, Edinburgh

Jeremy Jackman, countertenor
Alastair Hume, countertenor
Bill Ives, tenor
Anthony Holt, baritone
Simon Carrington, baritone
Brian Kay, bass

FIVE SONGS

1981

For tenor and piano

World premiere:

October 21, 1981
Merkin Concert Hall,
    Abraham Goodman House, New York
    City

Tenor: Joseph Porrello
Piano: Kenneth Merrill

The Idle Gift
The Longest Wait
The Eternal Prisoner
The Swing
The Ghost

The fifth song, not written at the time of the premiere, was first performed on December 12, 1983, at the Flagler Museum in Palm Beach, Florida, by Porrello and Merrill.

A BRIDE FROM PLUTO

1982

Chamber opera for children in one act

World premiere:

April 12, 1982
Terrace Theater, Kennedy Center,
    Washington, D.C.

Settings and
    costumes: Zack Brown
Lighting: Zack Zanolli
Choreography: Helen Anne Barcay
Conductor: Lorenzo Ricci Muti

CAST

Billy . . . . Nicholas Karousatos
His Father, a tailor . . . . Robert Keefe
His Mother . . . . Dana Krueger
His Girlfriend, Rosie . . . . Camille Rosso
The Queen of Pluto . . . . Pamela Hinchman
    Her Retinue, Dancers

THE BOY WHO GREW TOO FAST

1982

Opera for children in one act

World premiere:

September 24, 1982
Opera Delaware
    Grand Opera House, Wilmington

Settings: Cynthia du Pont Tobias
Costumes: Joseph Brumskill
Lighting: Patricia A. Connors
Conductor: Evelyn Swensson

CAST

Miss Hope . . . . Denise Coffey
Lizzie Spender . . . . Miriam Bennett
Mrs. Skosvodmonit . . . . Sara Hagopian
Poponel . . . . Phillip Peterson
Dr. Shrink . . . . Frank Reynolds
Miss Proctor . . . . Joy Vandever
Little Poponel . . . . Peter Lugar
Mad Dog . . . . Alan Wagner
Policeman . . . . Thomas Littel
    Schoolchildren

MUERO PORQUÉ NO MUERO

1982

Cantata for soprano, chorus, and orchestra

World premiere:

October 15, 1982
Cathedral of St. Matthew the Apostle,
    Washington, D.C.

Orchestra: Orchestra and chorus of the Catholic
                University of America
Conductor: Robert Ricks
Soprano: Marvis Martin

Based on a poem of St. Teresa of Avila, *"Vivo sin vivir en me,"* written after the ecstasy of Salamanca in 1571.

NOCTURNE

1982

For soprano, string quartet, and harp

World premiere:

October 24, 1982
Alice Tully Hall, Lincoln Center,
    New York City

SOLOISTS

Soprano: Marvis Martin
Harp: Karen Lindquist
Violin: James Buswell
Violin: Lynn Chang
Viola: Walter Trampler
Cello: Leslie Parnas

CONCERTO FOR DOUBLE BASS AND   1983
ORCHESTRA

World premiere:	October 20, 1983
	Avery Fisher Hall, New York City
Orchestra:	New York Philharmonic
Conductor:	Zubin Mehta
Soloist:	James VanDemark

MARY'S MASS   1984

For choir and congregation according to the new English liturgy

World premiere:	June 10, 1984
	Basilica of the Assumption of the Blessed
	Virgin Mary, Baltimore
Choral director:	Larry Vote
Organ:	Chapman Gonzalez
Choir:	Members of the Church of the Archdiocese
	of Baltimore

Commissioned by the Maryland Catholic Conference in celebration of the 350th anniversary of the founding of Maryland

RICERCARE   1984

For organ

World premiere:	June 28, 1984
	Grace Cathedral, San Francisco
Soloist:	John Weaver

Commissioned for the 1984 annual convention of the American Guild of Organists

Discography

Compiled by Mark Tiedtke

The Early Stage

Amelia al ballo

Complete (Angel 35140). Margherita Carosio (Amelia), Rolando Panerai (The Husband), Giacinto Prandelli (The Lover), Maria Amadini (The Friend), Enrico Campi (The Chief of Police), Silvana Zanolli (First Maid), Elena Mazzoni (Second Maid). Orchestra and Chorus of La Scala, Nino Sanzogno conducting.

Overture (RCA Victor 15377). The Philadelphia Orchestra, Eugene Ormandy conducting.

"Amelia cara" (Parlophone AT 0275). Gianpiero Malaspina, baritone.

"While I Waste These Precious Hours" (RCA Victor LM 2529). Leontyne Price, soprano.

The Old Maid and the Thief

Complete (Mercury 90521). Margaret Baker (Miss Pinkerton), Judith Blegen (Laetitia), Anna Reynolds (Miss Todd), John Reardon (Bob). Orchestra of the Teatro Verdi di Trieste, Jorge Mester conducting.

Overture (P.CB 20502). Turin Radio Orchestra, Alfredo Simonetti conducting.

Ricercare and Toccata on a Theme from *The Old Maid and the Thief*. Ania Dorfmann (RCA Victor LM 1758); Raymond Lewenthal (Westminster 18362).

The Broadway Stage

The Medium

Complete (Odyssey Y2 35239). Evelyn Keller (Monica), Marie Powers (Madame Flora), Beverly Dame (Mrs. Gobineau), Frank Rogier (Mr. Gobineau), Catherine Mastice (Mrs. Nolan). Emanuel Balaban conducting.

Complete (Columbia 7387). Judith Blegen (Monica), Regina Resnik (Madame Flora), Emily Derr (Mrs. Gobineau), Julian Patrick (Mr. Gobineau), Claudine Carlson (Mrs. Nolan). Opera Society of Washington, Jorge Mester conducting.

Complete in French (RCA France 640.006/7). Eliane Lublin (Monica), Denise Scharley (Madame Flora), Nicole Menut (Mrs. Gobineau), Claude Genty (Mr. Gobineau), Solange Michel (Mrs. Nolan). Richard Blareau conducting.

Complete film soundtrack (Mercury MGL 7). Anna Maria Alberghetti (Monica), Marie Powers (Madame Flora), Beverly Dame (Mrs. Gobineau), Donald Morgan (Mr. Gobineau), Belva Kibler (Mrs. Nolan). Rome Radio Orchestra, Thomas Schippers conducting.

The Telephone

*Complete (Odyssey Y2 35239). Marilyn Cotlow (Lucy), Frank Rogier (Ben). Emanuel Balaban conducting.

Complete (Louisville LS 767). Paula Seibel (Lucy), Robert Orth (Ben). Jorge Mester conducting.

Complete in French (RCA France 640.006/7). Liliane Berton (Lucy), Jean-Christophe Benoit (Ben). Richard Blareau conducting.

The Consul

*Abridged (Decca DX 101). Marie Powers (The Mother), Patricia Neway (Magda Sorel), Gloria Lane (The Secretary), Cornell MacNeil (John Sorel), George Jongeyans (Mr. Kofner), Leon Lishner (Chief Police Agent), Maria Marlo (The Foreign Woman), Andrew McKinley (Nika Magadoff), Lydia Summers (Vera Boronel), Maria Andreassi (Anna Gomez), Francis Monachino (Assan), Mabel Mercer (Voice on the Record). Lehman Engel conducting.

Act II Sc.2 excerpt in Swedish (Swedish EMI C153-35350/8). Includes Arne Hendriksen, Benna Lemon-Brundin, Isa Quensel, Bette Björling, Brita Hertzberg, Eva Prytz, Leon Bjorker. Sixten Ehrling conducting.

"To this we've come." Inge Borkh (G.DB 11537), Eileen Farrell (Angel 35350), Patricia Neway (New World Records 241).

The Saint of Bleecker Street

*Complete (RCA Victor LM-6032). Catherine Akos (Assunta), Maria di Gerlando (Carmela), Maria Marlo (Maria Corona), Leon Lishner (Don Marco), Gabrielle Ruggiero (Annina), David Poleri (Michele), Gloria Lane (Desideria), David Aiken (Salvatore). Thomas Schippers conducting.

Maria Golovin

*Complete (RCA Victor LM-6142). Franca Duval (Maria Golovin), Richard Cross (Donato), Patricia Neway (The Mother), Genia Las (Agata), William Chapman (The Prisoner), Herbert Handt (Dr. Zuckertanz), Lorenzo Muti (Trottolò). Peter Herman Adler conducting.

The Dance Stage

Sebastian
   Abridged (Desto 6432). London Symphony Orchestra, Jose Serebrier conducting.
   Suite (Columbia ML 2053). Robin Hood Dell Orchestra, Dimitri Mitropoulos conducting.
   (RCA Victor ARL1-2715). NBC Symphony, Leopold Stokowski conducting.
   Barcarole (RCA LM 1726). Boston Pops Orchestra, Arthur Fiedler conducting.

The Unicorn, the Gorgon and the Manticore
   Complete (Angel 35437). Thomas Schippers conducting. (Golden Crest CRS 4180). The Paul Hill Chorale. (University of Michigan 0012). University of Michigan Orchestra and Chorus.

The Concert Stage

Concerto in F for Piano and Orchestra
   (G.QALP 176). Yuri Boukoff, pianist, with the Paris Conservatoire Orchestra, Andre Cluytens conducting. (Vanguard VRS 1070). Earl Wild, pianist, with the Symphony of the Air, Jorge Mester conducting.

Concerto for Violin and Orchestra
   (RCA Victor LM-1868). Tossy Spivakovsky, violinist, with the Boston Symphony, Charles Munch conducting.

The Death of the Bishop of Brindisi
   (RCA Victor LSC-2785). George London (The Bishop), Lili Chookasian (The Nun). The Boston Symphony, Erich Leinsdorf conducting.

Missa O Pulchritudo
   (Fonit Cetra SDN 001). Spoleto Festival, Christian Badea conducting.
   (Westminster Choir WC-5). Westminster Choir, Joseph Flummerfelt conducting.

The Television Stage

Amahl and the Night Visitors
   *Complete (RCA Victor LM 1701). Chet Allen (Amahl), Rosemary Kuhlmann (His Mother), Andrew McKinley (Kaspar), David Aiken (Melchior), Leon Lishner (Balthazar), Francis Monachino (The Page). Thomas Schippers conducting. (Original 1951 television cast.)
   Complete (RCA Victor LM 2762, LSC 2862). Martha King (His Mother), Kurt Yaghjian (Amahl), John McCollum (Kaspar), Willis Patterson (Balthazar), Richard Cross (Melchior). Herbert Grossman conducting. (1963 television cast.)

The Children's Stage

Chip and His Dog
   *Complete (Aquitaine-CBS Records Canada MS 90567). David Coulter (Chip), Andrea Kuzmich (Dog), Laura Zarins (Princess), Priscilla Heffernan (Messenger), John Kuzmich (Page), Valarie Williams (Doctor), Heidi Hobday (Courtier), Erica Giesl (Cook). Canadian Children's Opera Chorus, Derek Holman conducting.

*Asterisk indicates original cast recording.

Bibliography

Books about and by Menotti

Grieb, Lyndal. *The Operas of Gian Carlo Menotti*. Metuchen, N.J.: Scarecrow Press, 1974.

Gruen, John. *Menotti*. New York: Macmillan. 1978.

Menotti, Gian Carlo. *Amahl and the Night Visitors*. Narrative adaptation by F. M. Frost. New York: McGraw-Hill Book Co., 1952.

———. *The Last Savage*. With drawings by Beni Montresor. Greenwich, Conn.: New York Graphic Society, 1964.

———. *Help, Help, the Globolinks!* Adapted by Leigh Dean, illustrated by Milton Glaser. New York: McGraw-Hill Book Co., 1970.

Tricoire, Robert. *Gian Carlo Menotti: L'homme et son oeuvre*. Paris: Seghers, 1966.

Other Books, Periodicals, and Newspapers

Ardoin, John. "The Frantic, Nonstop Preparations for a New Menotti Opera." New York *Times*, September 16, 1979.

———. "A Welcome Gift." *Opera News*, June 1981.

Barber, Samuel. "On Waiting for a Libretto." *Opera News*, January 27, 1958.

Briggs, John. "Menotti—Opera Magician." *International Musician*, November 1961.

Butler, Henry. "A Measure of Menotti." *Opera News*, February 8, 1964.

Chotzinoff, Samuel. "The Guilt of Gian Carlo Menotti." *Holiday*, June 1963.

"Composer on Broadway." *Time*, May 1, 1950.

Diamonstein, Barbaralee. "Menotti's Worlds." *Art News*, May 1974.

Eaton, Quaintance. *Opera Production: A Handbook*. Minneapolis: University of Minnesota Press, 1961.

———. *Opera Production II: A Handbook*. Minneapolis: University of Minnesota Press, 1974.

Ewen, David. *The World of Twentieth-Century Music*. Englewood Cliffs, N.J.: Prentice-Hall, 1968.

———. *Composers Since 1900: A Biographical and Critical Guide*. New York: The H. W. Wilson Company, 1969.

Fryer, Judith A. "Realism: A Major Factor for Menotti's Operatic Style." *The Opera Journal*, 1974.

Gelb, Arthur. "Theatrical Suspense in a Composer's World." New York *Times*, November 2, 1958.

Groth, Howard. "Gian Carlo Menotti and the American Lyric Theatre." *NATS Bulletin*, December 1958.

Gruen, John. "When the New York Critics Damn You . . ." New York *Times*, April 14, 1974.

Klein, Howard. "Menotti at War with Menotti." New York *Times*, May 29, 1966.

Kolodin, Irving. " 'The Cloak' Uncovers Menotti." *Saturday Review*, March 1, 1952.

———. "From 'Amelia' to 'The Saint.' " *Saturday Review*, January 29, 1955.

———. "Farewell to Capricorn." *Saturday Review/World*, June 1, 1974.

Lillich, Meredith. "Menotti's Music Dramas." *Educational Theatre Journal*, December 1959.

Menotti, Gian Carlo. " 'The Medium' in Four Mediums." *Saturday Review*, February 28, 1948.

———. "Opera Isn't Dead." *Étude*, February 1950.

———. "My Conception of Hell." *Saturday Review*, April 22, 1950.

———. "Credo." New York *Times*, "From the Mail Pouch," April 30, 1950.

———. "A Plea for the Creative Artist." New York *Times Magazine*, June 29, 1952.

———. "Notes on Opera as 'Basic Theatre.' " New York *Times Magazine*, June 2, 1955.

———. "A Proposal for an International Arts Festival." *National Music Council Bulletin*, January 1957.

———. "From a Librettist's Notebook." New York *Times*, November 2, 1958.

———. "Reflections on Opera Buffa." *National Music Council Bulletin*, Winter 1963–64.

———. "I Am the Savage." *Opera News*, February 8, 1964.

———. "If the Emperor's Naked, a Child Will Know." New York *Times*, December 21, 1969.

———. "A Point of Contact." *Opera News*, December 27, 1969, and January 3, 1970.

———. "And Where Do You Run at 60?" New York *Times*, July 18, 1971.

Prideaux, Tom. "Renaissance Man of American Music." In *Life International*, New York: E. P. Dutton & Co., 1959.

Rizzo, Francis. "Diary of Two Deadlines." *Opera News*, March 13, 1971.

Rothe, Anna, ed. *Current Biography, 1947*. New York: The H. W. Wilson Company, 1947.

Salzman, Eric. "Menotti." New York *Herald Tribune*, January 19, 1961.

Sargeant, Winthrop. "Wizard of the Opera." *Life*, May 1, 1950.

———. "Imperishable Menotti." *The New Yorker*, February 27, 1960.

———. "Orlando in Mt. Kisco." *The New Yorker*, May 4, 1963.

———. "Gian Carlo Menotti." In *The International Cyclopedia of Music and Musicians*, edited by Oscar Thompson. New York: Dodd, Mead & Co., 1975.

Taubman, Howard. "Proving Opera Can Be Modern." New York *Times Magazine*, March 19, 1950.

———. "Gian-Carlo Menotti," *Theatre Arts*, September 1951.

———. "Operatic Fusion: Drama, Music Joined Skillfully by Menotti." New York *Times*, August 31, 1958.

Wolz, Larry. "Gian Carlo Menotti: Words Without Music." *Opera Journal*, September 1977.

Index

(Page numbers in italics refer to photographs)

Picture Credits